HJ793 .B7
013410
Bryce, Ro
Broughto
Canada ar
World Wa
c200

2006 02 21

CANADA AND THE COST OF WORLD WAR II

CARLETON LIBRARY SERIES

The Carleton Library Series, funded by Carleton University under the general editorship of the dean of the School of Graduate Studies and Research, publishes books about Canadian economics, geography, history, politics, society, and related subjects. It includes important new works as well as reprints of classics in the fields. The editorial committee welcomes manuscripts and suggestions, which should be sent to the dean of the School of Graduate Studies and Research, Carleton University.

192 The Blacks in Canada:
A History
(second edition)
Robin Winks

193 A Disciplined Intelligence:
Critical Inquiry and Canadian
Thought in the Victorian Era
A.B. McKillop

194 Land, Power, and Economics on
the Frontier of Upper Canada
John Clarke

195 The Children of Aataentsic:
A History of the Huron People
to 1660
Bruce G. Trigger

196 Silent Surrender:
The Multinational Corporation
in Canada
Kari Levitt

197 Cree Narrative:
Expressing the Personal Meanings
of Events
Richard J. Preston

198 The Dream of Nation:
A Social and Intellectual
History of Quebec
Susan Mann

199 A Great Duty: Canadian
Responses to Modern Life and
Mass Culture, 1939–1967
L.B. Kuffert

200 The Politics of Development:
Forests, Mines, and
Hydro-Electric Power in Ontario,
1849–1941
H.V. Nelles

201 Watching Quebec:
Selected Essays
Ramsay Cook

202 Land of the Midnight Sun:
A History of the Yukon
*Ken S. Coates and
William R. Morrison*

203 The Canadian Quandary
Harry Johnson

204 Canada and the
Cost of World War II:
The International Operations
of Canada's Department of
Finance, 1939–1947
*Robert B. Bryce
Edited by Matthew J. Bellamy*

Canada and the Cost of World War II

The International Operations
of Canada's Department of Finance
1939–1947

Robert B. Bryce

Edited by Matthew J. Bellamy

Foreword by Gordon Robertson
Afterword by J.L. Granatstein

Carleton Library Series 204
McGill-Queen's University Press
Montreal & Kingston • London • Ithaca

© 2005 McGill-Queen's University Press
The Tribute to Robert Bryce by Gordon Robertson is published
by permission of the Canada School of Public Service, copyright 2001.

ISBN 0-7735-2938-1

Legal deposit second quarter 2005
Bibliothèque nationale du Québec
Printed in Canada on acid-free paper that is 100% ancient forest free
(100% post-consumer recycled), processed chlorine free

This book has been published with the assistance of the Department of
Finance Canada through a contribution under the Research and Policy
Initiatives Assistance program.

McGill-Queen's University Press acknowledges the support of the
Canada Council for the Arts for our publishing program. We also
acknowledge the financial support of the Government of Canada
through the Book Publishing Industry Development Program (BPIDP)
for our publishing activities.

Library and Archives Canada Cataloguing in Publication

Bryce, Robert B. (Robert Broughton), 1910–1997.
    Canada and the cost of World War II : the international operations of
Canada's Department of Finance, 1939–1947 / Robert B. Bryce ; edited by
Matthew J. Bellamy ; with a foreword by Gordon Robertson ; and an
afterword by J.L Granatstein.
(Carleton Library ; 204)

Sequel to Maturing in hard times.
Originally an unpublished document, written 1990, and sent to C. Scott
    Clark, Deputy Minister of Finance, on Sept. 3, 1999.
Includes bibliographical references and index.
ISBN 0-7735-2938-1

    1. Canada. Dept. of Finance—History. 2. Finance, Public—Canada—
History—20th century. 3. Canada—Economic policy—1930–1939.
4. Canada—Economic policy—1939–1945. I. Bellamy, Matthew J., 1967–
II. Title.

HJ793.B79 2005   352.4'0971   C2005-901398-2

Interior design and typesetting in 10/12 Baskerville
by Daniel Crack, Kinetics Design

Contents

Foreword vii
Gordon Robertson

Preface xiii
Kevin G. Lynch

Introduction 1

1 The Unprepared Beginnings 11
2 The EAC and Trade Problems 30
3 The Air Training Plan Negotiations 41
4 Financing Britain 52
5 Scarce US Dollars and the Hyde Park Declaration 85
6 US Economic Arrangements and Dollars Galore 117
7 Mutual Aid to Allies 146
8 Financing Britain Further and Keynes's Visits 189
9 Working up to Bretton Woods 225
10 International Institutions 254
11 The 1946 British Loan and Settlement 283

Afterword 323
J.L. Granatstein

Notes 333

Bibliography 377

Index 385

Foreword

Robert Bryce's contributions during the forty years that he spent as a public servant, from 1938 to 1978, were profoundly important during his times and continue to be so in our present century. No one thought more deeply than he did about the role of the public service as a neutral, permanent, and professional body committed to working with whatever government the democratic process returned. Bryce saw the parliamentary system as an effective reconciliation of the democratic assertion of the preference of the voter, on the one hand, and the continuity of the values and interests of the state as symbolized by the constitutional monarchy, on the other. The role of the public service was to provide the collective memory of policies and laws, as well as to exercise the capacity to assess the consequences of changes whose implications might not have been understood fully in the fury of an election. And always this had to be achieved with professional neutrality and without partisan favour.

In Canada, this British parliamentary system was given an additional dimension in the British North America Act of 1867: a federal system with the distribution of the major fields of governing and law-making between a federal parliament and government in Ottawa and provincial legislatures and governments in their respective capitals.

In an address at Carleton College on 10 October 1956, Bryce led off a series of lectures on "Financing Government in Canada" with his presentation, "The Constitutional Basis of Canadian Government." This provided a superb sketch of the essential elements of change, from the conference in London in 1866 to Confederation and its growth from four provinces to ten to the weaknesses in the system so harshly revealed by the Great Depression of the 1930s.

A Royal Commission on Dominion–Provincial Relations in the late 1930s recommended an extensive revision of the financial basis of

Confederation and some changes in the allocation of legislative responsibilities, but the Dominion–Provincial Conference of 1941 failed to agree. A post-war "Green Book" proposed tax rental agreements to finance expenditures for social services, but it, too, failed to reach agreement. As Bryce put it in 1956: "The problem was then approached step by step and a good deal was accomplished along the lines that had been sketched out as a comprehensive programme ... It was emphasized that these agreements were merely temporary expedients and involved no change in the rights of the provinces, but merely an ad hoc financial arrangement of mutual advantage." Renewals of tax rental agreements for five-year terms, requiring no constitutional change, and specific provision for an old age pension plan for persons over seventy that did, contributed to the establishment of a method – at which Bryce became so skilled – whereby change and flexibility were achieved gradually.

Bryce's greatest challenge in the problem of reconciling the political verdict of the moment with the need for neutral permanence occurred in June 1957 with the election of the Diefenbaker government, the first Conservative government in twenty-two years. A change of government and party at this point, after so long a reign by the Liberals under King and Louis St Laurent, would have been stressful in the best of circumstances, but the incoming prime minister's suspicions made the transfer even more difficult. Diefenbaker had never been in office, federally or provincially. He had spent years on the Opposition benches, during which time he developed a profound distrust of the public service – made up of the "Pearsonalities" who were so obviously comfortable under the outgoing Liberal government. How could they possibly be trusted?

Bryce had been secretary to cabinet (a title then better known and more used than clerk of the Privy Council) since 1954. One of his most engaging qualities was a complete openness combined with a sense of humour that made it impossible to believe that he could harbour ill will toward anyone. He quickly won Diefenbaker's complete and unwavering confidence. It is difficult to overestimate the importance of that accomplishment for the preservation of the tradition of a professional, non-partisan public service. It would not have been difficult for a suspicious prime minister to have insisted on a friendly secretary to sit with his cabinet. It was only in 1945 that King had finally let Arnold Heeney enter, even though technically he had been secretary since 1941. The implications for professional neutrality in general may have been serious if that key position had been lost.

Bryce joined the Department of Finance in 1938 on his return to

Canada after three years at Cambridge University working with the legendary J.M. Keynes and then two years at Harvard University. He brought to North America Keynes's revolutionary proposals for regular interventions by government to counter economic cycles, including deficit spending to deal with the problems of the economically depressed world of that day. The theories of Keynes and the mind of Bryce were the source of many of Canada's post-war economic policies by which reconstruction was achieved without the unemployment that had followed World War I.

In a 1976 panel discussion as part of the Study of Parliament Group entitled "New Parliament; New Government; Old Public Service," Bryce challenged the "old public service" part. He stated that "the Public Service renews itself and has been renewing itself." He extrapolated on his assertion with these thoughts:

On quality ... let me say something. I knew a lot of the top public servants thirty years ago because I was made, rather against my will, the secretary of the Treasury Board, back in 1947. I put in seven years in that job. I got to know all the various DMs in that rather unpleasant capacity. How do they compare with the quality of the people that now are there? On intellectual quality it is hard to make a sweeping judgement ... But they are in the same league, if I can put it that way ...

On professional capacity, there is now no doubt that the top servants are more highly qualified professionally, both in their specialties such as economics or the environmental sciences, and in management, than those of thirty years ago. There is much more professional competence before you get the job. Whether that was offset by any enthusiasm or flair in the old days before people were so highly educated in their specialties, I do not know, but on the question of professional standing – there is no doubt about it.

The 1960s and 1970s were years of concern about financial management, stimulated in part by the great increase in the expenditures of all governments in Canada. The auditor general had expressed concern, and the Glassco Commission had been established. It reported in 1962: "Let the managers manage." Fifteen years later, it was apparent that reform had not improved things. In the period of 1962 to 1975, spending by all governments in Canada, in relation to Gross Domestic Product, rose from 29.4 per cent to 40.9 per cent. In 1979, nine years after he had retired from the Department of Finance, Bryce was invited to give his views to a new Royal Commission on Financial Management and Accountability. Bryce stated that he was skeptical about the commission's endorsement "of elaborate systems of goal-setting and the evaluation of efficiency and effectiveness in many fields where these defy measurement." He went on to say:

I have gone through enough government decisions to believe that there is no easy generalization possible about how to form sensible judgements about the major issues, particularly in the case of new programs or major changes in old ones. However, I agree with the Commission that the Board of Management (as a possible new title for the Treasury Board) and the various departments and agencies owe it as their clear duty to the Canadian people to use the best systems of accounting, of cost analysis, of measuring benefits and efficiency, if that can be done, and of managing, as the report says, with a sense of frugality.

The onerous job of deputy minister of finance and the problems of federal–provincial relations, for which Bryce was economic adviser to the prime minister from 1970, when he retired from the Department of Finance, to 1971, left him little time to pursue his great interest in international finance. In October 1971, however, he was elected by Canada, Ireland, and Jamaica to represent them on the executive board of the International Monetary Fund. His work in Washington with the Fund, until 1974, gave him greater opportunity to bring international perspectives to the domestic Canadian scene that he knew so well.

Bryce was never really at rest. But the recreational activities into which he threw his energy and zest were very different – or could be very different – from those that engaged him when he was "at work."

Relaxation at the Five Lakes Fishing Club included everything but fishing – perhaps Bob had got too much of fish or fishing as a mining engineer during university summers. But canoeing with Bob was not for repose or contemplation. He was enormously strong and skilled on the worst portages. He was equally strong in the water but thought a swim should have an intellectual and social quality as well as a physical one. The breaststroke is best for talking as you go, and we covered countless miles in this way as Bob explored and commented on the tax and budgetary problems of the moment, the paradox of having federal assistance for post-secondary education but no federal role in education except the cash register, and any number of other issues. He had one of the most comprehensive and innovative minds I have ever encountered.

Bob wasn't all intellect and serious purpose, however. No one enjoyed a good poker game more than he did. He could bring his mathematical skills to bear on the odds as he calculated whether he was up against a bluff or something that would beat his full house. Bob's laugh if he won – and as great a laugh if he lost – was uproarious: his lungs were as strong as his legs, and his joy in life was abounding.

Bob's wife, Frances, was the right partner for someone whose mind was constantly active with problems of the nation or the world. To say that she was not interested in them would not be entirely right – it's just that she knew they were there and that Bob would deal with them. For her the really interesting things, apart from her family, were artistic – painting, illustration, writing, innovations of all kinds – which she performed or commented on with a touch of wry humour that seemed to say that these things, unlike Bob's preoccupations, were not all that serious. As a Scrabble contestant at Five Lakes, Frances was handicapped by her conviction that the patterns she could make on the board with her little squares were more interesting than the scores they might yield: scores were for small minds incapable of lateral thinking.

The Bryces got along perfectly. One could not imagine a better-suited couple. Their family – two sons, Robert (Rocky) and Sandy, and a daughter, Marjorie, and five grandchildren – completed a warm circle of love, mutual interest, and support.

When Bryce finally retired in 1978, both his family and his friends knew that he would have to do something: so powerful an intellectual motor could not operate properly without a load to stabilize it. He decided to write a history of the Department of Finance. The resulting book, *Maturing in Hard Times*, is full of information and comment of substantial interest to today's public servants.

Even those of us who know how much things have changed are jolted by learning from his book that the department, created in July 1867 by a transfer of officers, clerks, and messengers from the former United Province of Canada, totalled precisely twenty-eight persons, all of them lacking knowledge of economics or finance. The lack of professional capacity continued through the ups and downs of the economy, World War I, and the Great Depression. This last crisis was what finally led to change and to the appointment in 1932 of the first really qualified deputy minister of finance, W.C. Clark. Bryce's history is a knowledgeable account of the problems and policies of Canada that undergird today's structures.

Robert Bryce left his mark on the public service of Canada and on Canada itself, invariably for the better. This is beyond dispute.

Gordon Robertson

Preface

This book – detailing the international activities of Canada's Department of Finance during World War II – is the concluding contribution to understanding public policy by one of our country's most distinguished federal officials, Robert Bryce. Beyond being a work of focused scholarship, it is also a testament to a remarkable quality and style of public servant – and policy making – that delivered outstanding achievement for Canada and the Allied cause, and became a vital part in shaping global institutions, such as the International Monetary Fund, that continue to play a central and sustaining role in the world economy.

Despite an undergraduate degree in mining engineering, Bob Bryce's chosen field became economics. He studied under John Maynard Keynes at Cambridge, and then helped articulate and advance Lord Keynes's demanding new macroeconomic approach during a fellowship at Harvard. Returning to Canada, he put in a brief stint at the Sun Life Insurance Company but in 1938 was convinced to join the Department of Finance (after a demanding competitive examination) by the deputy minister, W.C. Clark. It was the beginning of a career that, as historians H. Graham Rawlinson and Jack Granatstein write in their book *The Canadian 100*, would see his hand "in virtually every important decision of government for almost forty years."

He began as one of really only a handful of Finance officers and would handle a wide range of issues from international trade to financing war production, currency and exchange controls, and Canada's role in planning for global reconstruction. By 1947, he was assistant deputy minister of Finance and secretary of the Treasury Board. In 1954, Prime Minister Louis St Laurent named him secretary of cabinet (a position also known as clerk of the Privy Council). In 1963, after a decade of service as the senior bureaucrat in government,

Bryce switched back to Finance as deputy minister, overseeing seven years of expanding federal budgets to serve ambitious social legislation.

Final retirement – after chairing a Royal Commission on Corporate Concentration – did not end Bryce's dedication to public service and especially to the Department of Finance. With the encouragement and support of deputy ministers T.K.(Tommy) Shoyama and Grant Reuber, he set to work researching and writing a history of the department, from Confederation through the Great Depression of the 1930s. That book, *Maturing in Hard Times*, was published in 1986 through McGill-Queen's University Press.

With the support of subsequent deputy ministers, Bryce also turned his attention to Finance's vital work in managing major fiscal, currency, and economic issues at home and in the international arena during World War II. Age and failing health, however, made it impossible for him to complete such a sweeping story by himself. He was joined by David Slater, who had just retired as chair of the Economic Council of Canada (and had also served as a senior officer at Finance); his focus in the book was on the department's involvement in the domestic side of economic policy during the war. The result, in 1995, was the privately published work, *War Finance and Reconstruction*, authored by Slater, but with two chapters (on wages and prices and on reconstruction policy) contributed by Bryce.

Bryce, meanwhile, continued to research and write his own companion volume on the department's international policy challenges and actions over the war period, including foreign exchange controls, our role in the Lend-Lease arrangements between the United States and the beleaguered United Kingdom, Canada's billion-dollar gift to England, the Bretton Woods conference, and the framing of Canada's approach to post-war internationalism and aid. A first draft was completed by 1990, but it remained in his private papers at the time of his death in 1997.

It was this manuscript – *Canada and the Cost of World War II: The International Operations of Canada's Department of Finance, 1939–1947* – that the Bryce family shared with Finance in 1999. While mostly factual narrative, conscientiously researched, it also contains moments of personal memoir, including brief anecdotes and insights into the character and role of government leaders and officials in Ottawa, London, and Washington. On both counts – as formal history and human revelation – it was clear that this work deserved to be preserved and promoted.

To realize this goal, the department enlisted the participation of McGill-Queen's University Press. It also became clear, however, that the Bryce manuscript – on its own – had limitations that were natural to a first draft but that would constrain its value to an interested audience. That is why Matthew Bellamy, an instructor of economics and history at Carleton University, joined the project. Not only did he edit the manuscript itself, he has provided chapter introductions and photo captions that establish the broader economic and historical context surrounding the Finance story.

Two other prominent Canadians have also contributed to this volume, reinforcing the scope of Bob Bryce's history of the Department of Finance, and his own stature. The book begins with a tribute to Robert Bryce by Gordon Robertson, himself a former clerk of the Privy Council, based on a speech he delivered at the 2001 opening of the Robert Bryce Room of the Canadian School of Public Service (the government's management development "university"). The book ends with an afterword by Jack Granatstein, the distinguished Canadian historian. His comments further confirm crucial aspects of the department's wartime role (sometimes understated by Bryce) and remind us that Finance in these same years was also waging – and winning – a fiscal and logistic war on the home front.

The result is a book that, while of specific interest to economists and historians of the period, has broad resonance for all public servants and, I am sure Bob Bryce would agree, especially for the Department of Finance. Throughout the book there echoes a deep and abiding national pride that sought proper respect for our country's role and interests without sacrificing a spirit of co-operation and commitment to the shared challenge of war. And this strong sense of the nation found expression in a broader global perspective, inspired by a concern to build international institutions necessary for a successful peace, and a world that worked better for all.

At the root of this book, therefore, is Bryce's firm conviction that public service *matters* – and that institutions *matter* – to the life of a country. The Department of Finance is one of those institutions, where the work of public policy can and does play a vital role in building and enhancing the well-being of Canadians. It is a role, as this volume attests, that can reach well beyond our borders, helping to shape a better global community for generations to come.

Publication of this work would not have been possible without the active, enthusiastic, and highly professional involvement of colleagues and experts inside and outside the Department of Finance. I would like to recognize the role played by John Sargent, most recently senior adviser to the deputy minister, who was the initial champion and *animateur* in ensuring that this work be made available to a wider audience. I also want to share my deep appreciation for the contribution made by the department's chief librarian, Eileen Bays-Coutts – the current *animatrice* responsible for the planning and supervision needed to bring this book to publication – and her associate, Bonnie Fraser. I also wish to acknowledge David Chenoweth of the Department of Finance for his insightful assistance in the final stages of this project.

From Carleton University, Dr. Duncan McDowall, professor of history, provided an initial appreciation and analysis of the Bryce manuscript that was a model of thoughtful, positive criticism. His suggestions are reflected throughout this work. From McGill-Queen's University Press, the support and guidance of Philip Cercone, executive director, has made itself felt, and this book is a result of that partnership.

I also want to recognize the fundamental role of the Bryce family itself – the late Alexander (Sandy) Bryce, and his brother Robert and sister Marjorie. By sharing their father's work with us, they have helped ensure that it achieves the goal he set: to make "younger officers of the Department of Finance aware of the challenges of their predecessors" – and much more.

Finally, let me acknowledge the senior champions who supported Bob Bryce's histories of Finance. These were the series of outstanding deputy ministers who consistently understood that sustaining a department so that it can manage the challenges of tomorrow successfully demands a vibrant appreciation of the past. I am honoured to have been the final caretaker in this vital process.

Kevin G. Lynch
Deputy Minister
Department of Finance
2000–2006

Robert B. Bryce upon graduation from Cambridge University, England, in 1934.

Bryce shortly before joining the Department of Finance in 1938.

Prime Minister William Lyon Mackenzie King signing a loan agreement with the United Kingdom in 1946. With him, on the left, are Clifford Clark and Robert Bryce of the Department of Finance.
National Archives of Canada PA112258

Members of the Wartime Prices and Trade Board: Yves Lamontagne (left), Hector McKinnon, R.C. Berkinshaw, K.W. Taylor, Donald Gordon, Dr. Bouchard, W.A. Mackintosh, Dean Shaw, and F.A. McGregor.
National Archives of Canada PA213459

Prime Minister King (left) and O.D. Skelton at the signing of the British Commonwealth Air Training Plan agreement. The Canadian government paid out more than $1.6 billion, three-quarters of the total cost of the plan, between 17 December 1939 and 31 March 1945.
National Archives of Canada PA200350

Finance Minister J.L. Ralston announces Canada's billion-dollar wartime budget in Parliament, 24 June 1940. *National Archives of Canada PA195346*

The Bank of Canada's Graham F. Towers (left) and the Bank of England's Montagne Norman, in London, 1941. *National Archives of Canada PA123225*

Prime Minister King (right) on a visit to the residence of President and Mrs. Franklin D. Roosevelt, Hyde Park, New York.
National Archives of Canada C47567

An Alaska Highway US army engineer on reconnaissance, 1942. Fearful of a Japanese invasion, the US pushed for the construction of a highway from Dawson Creek, British Columbia, to Big Delta, Alaska. The highway was rammed through forest wilderness and five mountain ranges in only eight months.
National Archives of Canada C25738

November 1943 test run of the first X-Dominion locomotive built in Montreal and destined for India under the Mutual Aid Board agreement.
National Archives of Canada PA116138

A crowd gathers to witness the launching of the SS *Toronga Park*, the first Mutual Aid ship to Australia. *National Archives of Canada C000762714*

Bryce at his desk in the Department of Finance, Ottawa.

Two mandarins at a Montreal meeting of the United Nations Relief and Rehabilitation Administration, September 1944: Norman Leon Gold (left), chief of allocations coordination, Bureau of Supply, and Henry F. Angus, special assistant to the undersecretary of state for external affairs.
National Archives of Canada PA114628

Lester B. Pearson, Canadian ambassador to the United States, signs the Bretton Woods Pacts, 28 December 1945.
National Archives of Canada C20129

Malcolm MacDonald, British high commissioner to Canada, signs the 1946 financial agreement between Britain and Canada. Behind him are Clifford Clark (left), Gordon Munro, J.L. Ilsley, and W.L.M. King.
National Archives of Canada PA112297

At the signing of the United Kingdom Loan Agreement providing a fifty-year credit by Canada to Britain are Clifford Clark (left), Robert Bryce, Wilfrid Eady, Norman Robertson, Malcolm MacDonald, Gordon Munro, J.L Ilsley, and Prime Minister King.
National Archives of Canada PA150450

Canadian delegation, United Nations Conference on International Organization, May 1945: C.S. Richie (left), P.E. Renaud, Elizabeth MacCullum, Lucien Moraud, Escott Reid, W.F. Chipman, Lester Pearson, J.H. King, Louis St Laurent, W.L.M. King, Gordon Graydon, M.J. Coldwell, Cora Casselman, Jean Desy, Hume Wrong, Louis Rasminsky, L.D. Wilgress, M.A. Pope, and R. Chaput.
National Archives of Canada C47570

CANADA AND THE COST OF WORLD WAR II

Introduction

This book is a history of the international problems and activities of Canada's Department of Finance during World War II, from 1939 to 1947. These include a variety of arrangements for financing Britain's requirements for Canadian munitions and food and the division of costs of the British Commonwealth Air Training Plan. They also include the arrangements for conserving and supplementing Canada's supply of us dollars, including exchange controls and the Hyde Park Declaration with the United States. It covers the financing of relief to the liberated population of Allied nations through both military and civilian channels, and also the department's role in the establishment of the International Monetary Fund and the World Bank.

I participated in many of these activities as a young officer of the department; this book, therefore, is written from the viewpoint of an observer and a participant. It is not a *mémoire* – I have neither the detailed memory nor the aid of a diary to cover the many activities and discussions of these years. It is based mainly on records in the archives, supplemented by secondary sources and some personal recollections. I had entered the department in October 1938 as an economist familiar with monetary and international economics. My field of work had not yet crystallized, so I was available to take on a wide variety of tasks, including many in the fields covered by this book.

This introduction is intended to acquaint the reader with some salient facts about the department and those who worked in it. It includes a brief account of the leading figures with whom the department dealt in other departments and the Bank of Canada, plus a brief reference to some of the leading British and American officials with whom we had to reach and carry out agreements.

To describe the department, we must begin with its remarkable deputy minister, William Clifford Clark, whom everybody called

"Dr Clark" in recognition of an honorary degree he received in 1935 after his first few years in the department. Clark had been a brilliant and industrious student at Queen's and Harvard, set up the Commerce course at Queen's, then in 1923 went to Chicago and later New York to work as one of the earliest business economists in the US, for Straus and Company, a major real estate finance company.[1] This was a very vulnerable type of business in New York in 1930, and when it failed, Clark returned to Queen's. Prime Minister Richard Bennett attracted him from there, first, in 1932, to be an adviser to the Imperial Economic Conference and shortly after that to be deputy minister of finance, a position that had been vacant for two-and-a-half years. Almost from the beginning, Clark was an outstanding success in advising on budget policies, persuading Bennett to establish the Bank of Canada and devising some legislation to deal with western farm debt and other legislation to initiate a major housing policy. He was an entrepreneur as a senior civil servant, throwing himself into problems and potential solutions. Clark's shortcoming, however, was in organization. He disliked administration and was slow in taking on able people to assist him in meeting the serious problems of the Depression. As a result, he was grossly overworked.

When the war began, the department (apart from the comptroller of the Treasury's offices, noted below) included about 330 people. Most of these were engaged in specialized or routine operations: 125 at the Mint, 50 in the Housing Branch, 60 in the Accounts Branch, and 35 in auditing and custodial units. Of the remaining 60, most were clerical and support staff. Only about 15 officers or versatile senior clerks were available for working out policies for war finance. These were in three groups. The largest group was the Treasury Board staff under the direction of Cliff Ronson, assistant deputy minister, who was the de facto secretary of the board and a tough administrator. It included Bill Smellie, clerk of estimates, an old-timer used to following the rules; Charlie Mackenzie, who dealt with civilian personnel matters; Elgin Armstrong, who specialized in defence questions; and several other senior clerks. They had to carry on through the war the scrutiny and presentation to the Treasury Board itself of the details of war expenditures and were available only occasionally for work on other assignments. The second group of potential policy advisers were Hector McKinnon, the commissioner of tariffs, and his two assistants. McKinnon was almost immediately appointed chairman of the Wartime Prices and Trade Board, which took up most of his time.

The third and main group of personnel working on war measures included those working directly under Clark himself. I numbered among this group, which also included Kenneth Eaton, our tax expert, who had been five years in the department; Harvey Perry, a more junior but versatile tax expert; David Johnson, the solicitor to the Treasury; and George Lowe, an administrative troubleshooter. To these five, several others were to be added later from time to time. Clark and the minister devised and applied their main financial war measures with this small nucleus of men.

In the work I did on inter-Allied financial problems, I had much to do with the comptroller of the Treasury Board, B.G. McIntyre, and several of his officers. Their offices made the actual disbursement of war expenditures and kept detailed records of financial commitments. They were excellent sources of information that we could use in our short-term forecasts of our payments to and receipts from the British government as well as our disbursements and receipts of US dollars. The two men chiefly involved were Orrie Hodgkins, assistant comptroller of the Treasury, who spent much of the war in London, and A.V. Franklin, the chief Treasury officer of the Department of Munitions and Supply, one of the very few people who understood the intricacies of the convoluted accounts arising out of the British war contracts and our own.

The department worked more closely with the Bank of Canada during the war than it had needed to do before. In particular, the governor of the bank, Graham Towers, a man of acute intelligence and cool judgment, was a source of advice to the finance minister, the prime minister, and occasionally to cabinet as a whole. He was nearly always available to Clark when the latter wished to get a second opinion on important matters. Towers's main task early in the war was to be chairman of the Foreign Exchange Control Board when it was working out its policies and processes. Later he became chairman of the War Finance Committee, which supervised the issue of the huge Victory Loans and the less spectacular but equally important savings bonds. Also consulted by the department was Donald Gordon, the remarkable deputy governor of the bank, who complemented Towers's abilities perfectly. He was later to become the very powerful chairman of the Wartime Prices and Trade Board when its regulations were greatly strengthened. Others at the bank included David Mansur, diverted from the short-lived Central Mortgage Bank to be Towers's troubleshooter;[2] James Coyne, the bank's internal legal officer and draftsman early in the war; Louis Rasminsky, whom Clark succeeded in luring away from the League of Nations Economic Secretariat early in 1940 to become the first research director of the Foreign Exchange Control Board and ultimately its chairman (alternate);[3] and J.R. Beattie, the deputy director of the Research Division, who helped us with budgets, tax measures, and other ideas.

From the beginning of the war until the end, the department had close working arrangements with External Affairs. Clark, and only Clark, dealt at the highest levels of External Affairs with O.D. Skelton, the undersecretary of state for external affairs (and chief adviser of the prime minister) until he died early in 1941. But Mackintosh and I, and others later, saw Norman Robertson frequently, both before and after he became undersecretary, for he was particularly concerned with economic affairs, including both domestic and external matters. Later I had much to do with Hume Wrong, whom I greatly admired, on Mutual Aid and other relations with both Britain and the US. We had less occasion to deal with Hugh Keenleyside or Lester Pearson, but more with Henry Angus and John Deutsch, who were working on economic subjects.

As J.L. Granatstein points out in *The Ottawa Men*, and others elsewhere, the officials working on war measures in Ottawa during World War II were as a whole a relatively small group who knew one another well, frequently lunched together at the cafeteria of the Chateau Laurier, and occasionally visited one another's homes on the weekends. This intermingling cut across departmental lines and seniority. We were all very busy, we believed in what we were doing, and we had few jealousies or quarrels. We were not as close to the businessmen who had come to Ottawa to work on the war effort, who lunched at the Rideau Club and tried, reasonably, to get home for their weekends. There was no coolness between the two categories, however, and we had very few arguments over jurisdiction and differences of approach.

The department was fortunate in its two wartime ministers of finance. J.L. Ralston was the first and gave us a strong, serious leadership.[4] He was conscientious to a fault. In fact he was too fussy about detail, to an extent that prevented him from getting as much as possible out of himself and those who worked for him. In July 1940, he left Finance to become minister of national defence after the tragic death of Norman Rogers, who had been killed in an airplane accident. James Lorimer Ilsley, member of Parliament for Digby-Annapolis-Kings in Nova Scotia since 1926 and minister of national revenue since 1935, was appointed minister of finance to succeed Ralston.[5] We already knew and liked him. He had been our acting minister frequently during Finance Minister Charles Dunning's long illness in the late 1930s. A modest man of austere habits, Ilsley was intelligent, industrious, and well-read. In private he had a delightful, ironic sense of humour often expressed in mimicry, but he would not display his irony in public because it was politically dangerous to do so. He understood problems and arguments very quickly – so well that he saw both sides of most of the issues that came before him, finding it difficult to reach decisions. He used to debate both sides with us in his office. Ilsley was a fitting minister to match wits with Clark, Towers, and Donald Gordon, who in 1938 became deputy governor of the Bank of Canada and when war broke was assigned to the Foreign Exchange Control Board. At several critical times in the late years of the war, Ilsley worried himself sick and had to get away to relax.

In working out our relations with Britain and the United States, we saw a good deal of two other strong ministers. One was C.D. Howe, as minister of munitions and supply.[6] He, too, was a very intelligent man, but he experienced none of Ilsley's difficulty in making decisions. He was a good judge of character and delegated to those he trusted the power to act on his behalf. He got on well with the other minister with whom we dealt frequently in connection with our financing of Britain. This was Louis St Laurent, a man as judicious as Ilsley but as businesslike as Howe, and very careful in the role that the prime minister had assigned him. This was, in cabinet's development of its decisions, to understand, take into account, and express the views of French Canada, as well as to exercise leadership in the Quebec caucus when these decisions had to be defended.[7]

Of Prime Minister Mackenzie King so much has been written that it is not necessary to say much in general, except that before the war began, Clark already had developed a close relationship with him that was strengthened by the events of the war. Oddly enough, it culminated in settling a most unwarlike subject on which Clark expressed most unorthodox views. Clark had become convinced by the labour unrest of 1943, and by his study of social problems and policies both current and in post-war planning, that the government should introduce a system of family allowances. He persuaded a reluctant Ilsley to propose this for inclusion in the 1944 legislative program. Meanwhile, the prime minister had come to like the proposal very much, despite a serious division of opinion in cabinet and Howe's scathing opposition to it in principle. When the appointed day for deciding on it in cabinet arrived, Ilsley had to leave early and asked if Clark could take his place in explaining the plan. King immediately approved. Clark sold it to the ministers (all but Howe) in a most un–civil servant like manner. This delighted King, who recorded in his diary for the day that the last thing he did before going to bed was to phone Clark to express his gratitude.[8] (I may add, in a personal vein, that I was immediately told by Clark to get to work and draft the plan.)

Others in the department, such as W.A. ("Bill") Mackintosh or I, rarely saw or spoke to the prime minister, although on a few occasions I accompanied Clark to meetings of the War Committee or cabinet. Our views, either personal or as part of a committee report, sometimes would reach him by way of Robertson or Arnold Heeney, the secretary to the War Committee. More privately, we enjoyed close access to Jack Pickersgill, who prepared statements and speeches for the prime minister and frequently passed on news, views, and ideas to him.

The department grew during the war, but not much. Its first and greatest acquisition was Bill Mackintosh, head of the department of economics at Queen's, a trusted friend and former colleague of Clark's who had a very comprehensive and keen knowledge of the Canadian economy. He was also a most effective civil servant and member of committees. His instinctive ability to identify the central point in a problem and bring it out with his tactful, dry wit saved us many hours of time and frayed tempers. Everyone got along well with him. A more dynamic and temporary addition to the department was Walter Gordon, at that time a successful young chartered accountant in Toronto. He came to the department to work on the tax rental agreements, the price ceiling, and other important projects. He had to leave early in 1942 because of a recurrence of gout, which had incapacitated him before.[9] About the same time that Gordon left, Mitchell Sharp arrived from Winnipeg, where he had been working as an economist in the grain trade; he stayed on for the duration and beyond. He assisted the minister with many matters relating to price control, especially those on farm products, and quickly became a member of the department's inner circle, which met at Ilsley's request on many evenings to debate at length difficult decisions that were going to confront him in cabinet.

In early 1941, Clark arranged that James Coyne, from the Bank of Canada, would move temporarily to Washington to represent the department in dealing with the US Treasury and other departments, and the Canadian procurement agencies there, and in working out the Hyde Park Declaration of 21 April 1941, which was to overcome the Canadian shortage of US dollars required for war purposes. After seven months, Coyne returned to Ottawa and was replaced in Washington by A.F.W. Plumptre, a leading monetary economist who was to represent both Finance and the Wartime Prices and Trade Board from early 1942 until the end of the war.[10] In the fall of 1941, David Johnson, solicitor to the Treasury, went overseas on leave, first with External Affairs and later with the army. He was replaced on an acting basis by Ross Tolmie from Income Tax, a more articulate and active legal officer. At about the same time, J.B. Taylor, a Canadian working in a financial business in New York, came into the department to assist Eaton on tax and related matters. In the following year, when we were having serious problems in forecasting our short-term balance of payments with the US, Clark brought in Frank Knox, a monetary economist from Queen's, to assist us on a part-time basis, and Alec McLeod, his graduate student, on a full-time basis.

When time and circumstances permitted Mackintosh to turn his attention to post-war problems and plans in 1943, he began to bring in some economists for that purpose. The first was M.C. Urquhart from Queen's, who had been a distinguished student under Mackintosh some years earlier. Later came T.L. Avison, an experienced financial analyst from the foreign investment section of Sun Life, and several more junior officers. Most of this post-war planning related to domestic issues, including the transfer of industrial capacity and manpower to peacetime purposes. Those working on post-war measures moved, along with Mackintosh, to the Department of Reconstruction, when it was organized in December 1944. Mackintosh himself was brought back to Finance in late May 1945 to serve as acting deputy minister when Clark collapsed, shortly after the end of the war in Europe, from a serious illness that kept him away from work until the end of December 1945. A large part of Mackintosh's time had to be devoted to Dominion–Provincial proposals and meetings.

It should be noted, even though it is not part of this history of the international activities of the department, that the Housing Branch of the department continued some of its pre-war duties throughout the war and was also used to assist in the building of houses where they were needed for war purposes. By 1944, as the demobilization and relocation of ex-servicemen was beginning, a crisis developed in regard to the supply of houses, and the activities and personnel of the branch were rapidly expanded under new legislation. This led by the end of 1945 to the transfer of the administration of the Housing Acts to the newly established Central Mortgage and Housing Corporation.

Something should be added about the British and Americans with whom we worked. On the British side, Clark's first contacts were with J.A.C. Osborne of the Bank of England, who was sent to Canada twice during 1939 to represent the Treasury. He had been in Canada from 1934 to 1938 as the first deputy governor of the Bank of Canada. He knew Clark and Towers well and was trusted by them and others at the Bank of Canada. Osborne reported to Sir Frederick Phillips, the second secretary of the Treasury in charge of Overseas Finance.[11] When Towers went to London representing the minister of finance in December 1939, he met first with Phillips and reached an understanding with him on the scale and nature of our financial assistance to Britain for the next six months that was approved by the chancellor of the exchequer the next day. Phillips had several meetings in Ottawa with Clark and others in 1940 before he took up his position in Washington as head of Treasury Mission, a position he held until his sudden death in 1943. During that period, Clark and Towers met with him several times and developed a considerable measure of respect and trust. Meanwhile, Sir Wilfrid Eady became the joint second secretary of the Treasury in London (a position similar to an associate deputy minister in Ottawa);[12] we dealt with him at second remove through the senior Treasury representative in Ottawa, Gordon Munro. Munro had been a banker in London after a distinguished military career in World War I, during which he was seriously wounded. He was at the British High Commission in Ottawa and usually had as his assistant a civil servant from the Treasury who dealt with us in the department on a day-to-day basis. When the financial situation between Canada and Britain became critically difficult in 1944 (as is explained in chapters 8 and 9), the British government sent out Lord Keynes to represent the Treasury, along with Eady and several others. Keynes, of course, was John Maynard Keynes, the renowned economist of Cambridge, who first made his mark working in the Treasury between 1915 and 1919 and through his widely published polemical book, *The Economic Consequences of the Peace*, in which he scathingly described the Peace Conference at Versailles in 1919. I had been a student of Keynes at Cambridge and found myself, by sheer coincidence, serving as secretary of the meetings we had with him in Ottawa in 1944. (I was also chief critic behind the scenes of certain of his ideas.)

Our financial contacts with the US government were nearly all with Henry Morgenthau, Jr, and his Treasury Department.[13] President Franklin Roosevelt had selected Morgenthau to deal with the British and French and their allies during 1939 and 1940 because he was the senior member of his administration most in support of the Allied cause. King had made the acquaintance and won the respect of Morgenthau in 1940 when the latter was on holiday in Canada. As a result, Morgenthau communicated a number of times with King on rather delicate issues, and the two met in Washington in April 1941 in preparation for the meeting between King and Roosevelt that produced the Hyde Park Declaration. Clark had to take up some serious matters with the US Treasury at the end of 1940 when Lend-Lease was being worked out and the British were "broke." Morgenthau took an immediate liking to Clark, despite the difficult situation that Clark was putting before the Treasury. As a result, the main financial discussions between Canada and the US over the next three-and-a-half years were carried on between the two of them. Clark used Coyne and later Plumptre to follow up these matters with other US Treasury officials, including notably Harry Dexter White, the director of monetary research in the Treasury Department. He was later to become famous as one of the chief architects of the International Monetary Fund. As time went on, after the US had entered the war, Clark met more frequently with White to settle issues arising out of the Hyde Park Declaration, although the difficult meetings on the final settlements in 1944 were with Morgenthau; Ilsley was present at some of these 1944 meetings, as well.

Clark, Gordon, and later Plumptre had some discussions with a considerable number of other American officials, notably in connection with the working out of Hyde Park. These included such senior persons as Harry Hopkins, the president's general assistant, who lived right in the White House. They will be noted in the text as relevant.

CHAPTER ONE

The Unprepared Beginnings

Only twenty years after the end of World War I, Europe was plunged back into the nightmare of total war. The attempts at collective security in the 1920s all proved futile in face of the birth of Nazi Germany and its deliberate scrapping of the post-war settlements. Still weary from the last war, France and Great Britain refused to accept the possibility of another. The Soviet Union, meanwhile, had turned in on itself, and the United States had withdrawn into its traditional isolationism. The power vacuum in the heart of Europe encouraged a revived and militarized Germany to seize the "living space" that Adolf Hitler claimed Germany required for its rightful place in the world.

Having already annexed Austria and Czechoslovakia, Hitler's forces invaded Poland on 1 September 1939. The attack sparked a critical response from Britain and France, who until then had embraced a policy of appeasement. The two countries no longer could sit idly by in the face of German aggrandizement. Thus, on 3 September 1939, just two days after the German invasion of Poland, both France and Great Britain declared war on Germany. Europe was once more at war. It would be the most devastating war in human history.

When World War I broke out, Canada's prime minister, Robert Borden, immediately pledged Canada's support to the Mother Country, Great Britain. This time, however, things were different. Canada's prime minister, William Lyon Mackenzie King, was profoundly aware of the long-term consequences of Borden's actions. King knew that by toeing the imperial line – that is, by automatically following Britain's lead in war – Borden had alienated Quebec. King, whose paramount concern always was to maintain national unity, was unwilling to do anything that might cause disaffection in any of the provinces, especially Quebec. Thus when asked – shortly after the outbreak of the war in Europe – if Canada would go to war alongside the British, King answered that he would "let Parliament decide." A week later, Parliament did decide. On 10 September 1939, Canada declared war on Germany.

The nation, however, was ill prepared for war. A decade of depression had taken its toll on the Canadian economy. In a vain attempt to balance the books, King's Liberal government had cut military expenditures drastically. In 1933, the defence budget had fallen to $13 million. By 1939, as a result of a decade of neglect of its military, the country could not defend its own coasts, let alone dispatch fully equipped and trained forces to help Britain. If Canada was to wage an effective military campaign in Europe, this deficiency would have to be overcome. It fell to the Department of Finance to come up with innovative methods of paying for the cost of the war, including the financing of British requirements in Canada.

This chapter chronicles the extent of Canada's unreadiness for war as well as early obstacles confronting the Department of Finance in a time of war.

Canada was not ready for the war that came in 1939 except in the one most essential political requisite, that her government, her Parliament, and her people were prepared, without serious division or objection, to accept the decision to participate. This was Prime Minister Mackenzie King's triumph, but he obtained it at the cost of a "no commitments" policy that prevented many of the lesser but important and tangible preparations from being made. Canada did not enter the war for constitutional reasons, as some experts feared it would; rather, as J.L. Granatstein reasonably concludes, "the fundamental reason for this Canadian decision was sentiment. The ties of blood and culture that bound Canada to Britain proved strong enough to compel the government willingly to follow the course it did."[1]

THE DIPLOMATIC BACKGROUND

In understanding the events of the first ten months of the war as they affected the work of the Department of Finance, one must recall some diplomatic background. Under the leadership of Borden and then of King and Bennett, the government of Canada had spent much effort to attain the objective of equality within the British Commonwealth and the possibility of independence in foreign affairs and policy. In principle, this had been achieved by the early 1930s, as far as peacetime matters were concerned. Neither the foreign service of External Affairs nor the military services of National Defence, however, were organized or staffed to act without relying on the British services for information and contacts and, in defence matters, for leadership and equipment. In External Affairs, under King's direct control, there was a revulsion against this dependence and a highly critical attitude toward British policy and actions during the second half of the decade.

The apparently inexorable march to war began during this period, after Hitler had gained full power in Germany. The period began with the setting up in 1934 of a new German air force, contrary to the Treaty of Versailles. This rearmament in the air proceeded so rapidly that by 1936 the British felt that they could not risk coming to the aid of France, as they were obliged by treaty to do, if France repulsed the German troops when they were ordered by Hitler to reoccupy the demilitarized Rhineland in March 1936. The reoccupation was contrary both to Versailles and the 1925 Treaty of Locarno, into which Germany had entered voluntarily. This action of Hitler was probably a bluff, and his troops were ordered to retreat if they were opposed. The fact that France, which had a large army if it was mobilized, did not oppose the German action greatly strengthened Hitler's hand vis-à-vis his generals and encouraged him to continue his rearmament. It led to the annexation of Austria in March 1938 and, after the crisis of Munich in September, to the German occupation of part of Czechoslovakia, and then in March 1939 to the takeover of that country as a whole.

Despite his strong stand on Canada's independent role in foreign policy and the country's lack of military power and independent diplomatic information, King encouraged the British government time after time to follow this policy of appeasement. King began this course in March 1936, ten days after the occupation of the Rhineland, having left time to gauge Canadian opinion. He informed the British government that Canada was not in sympathy with those in France who wished to resist the German action. If the UK should take action to resist the Germans, he said, she could not expect to be joined by Canada.[2] At the Imperial Conference in June 1937, King again spoke in favour of appeasement and worked hard to get the communiqué to reflect this, despite the opposition of New Zealand. During the crises leading up to the decision at Munich that Germany should be permitted to occupy part of Czechoslovakia, King repeatedly supported and encouraged Prime Minister Neville Chamberlain's efforts for "peace in our time."[3]

When Hitler occupied all of Czechoslovakia in March of 1939, contrary to the Munich agreement, it was evident that this policy had failed (including the secret indications conveyed by Lord Halifax in 1937 that Britain would not oppose German movements to the east if there were no "far reaching disturbance").[4] This failure led to a revulsion of feeling in England itself and a consequent change in British government policy, which led to a futile guarantee to come to Poland's aid were she attacked.

The efforts of the British government in 1939 to find some alternative to appeasement led to a series of memorandums to King from

O.D. Skelton, the Canadian undersecretary of state for external affairs. These memorandums were highly critical of British policy and actions and foresaw the danger of war.[5] By this time, it was too late for effective diplomatic action, but even in Ottawa little was done to prepare for the dangers ahead.

The two senior officers of External Affairs most concerned with these high policy issues were Skelton, the undersecretary, and Loring Christie, the counsellor who advised him on European and defence matters.[6] Both were very able men, dedicated to Canadian independence and opposed to what they saw as British efforts to involve Canada in imperial policies of great danger, contrary to the country's own interests. For those reasons they favoured the policy of no commitments that King followed for reasons of national unity. This reinforced King's tendency to make no commitments, even ones that would have led to greater preparedness to do things in Canada's interest if war did come, such as the training of aircrews and the production of arms and munitions. In particular, a review of the discussions from 1936 to 1939 on air training, in which King at times clearly seemed to see a major Canadian opportunity and interest, suggests a breakdown in diplomacy on the part of both the British and the Canadians, due in some considerable degree to allowing doctrinaire views on both sides to stand in the way of finding a timely practical solution to a problem of great importance and urgency.[7] Part of the trouble on the Canadian side was also financial. Despite the increase in defence expenditures in the late 1930s, their scale was still far too little to prepare adequately for an air training program large enough to make a difference in dealing with the dangers of 1940.

CANADIAN DEFENCE PROGRAMS 1935-39

In Canada in May 1935, Major General A.G.L. McNaughton, retiring as chief of the general staff to become chairman of the National Research Council, had warned the Bennett government of the very weak state of Canada's defences, the result of an obsolete British policy that assumed that "the Empire," including Canada, would not be involved in a large-scale war for at least ten years.[8] King's government came to power that same year and shortly after, in 1936, it reviewed this situation and decided to do something about it. A little had been done to increase defence expenditure in the fiscal year 1936–37, after the new minister of national defence, Ian Mackenzie, had informed his colleagues of the parlous condition of Canada's home defences. In August 1936, cabinet established a Canadian Defence Committee, consisting of the prime minister, the minister of national defence, the minister of finance, and also the minister of justice (in order to have a strong Quebec member, Ernest Lapointe).[9] The chiefs of the three services met in August 1936 with the ministers on this committee to discuss the situation. Skelton and Christie from External Affairs were also present. King recorded in his diary the favourable impressions he formed of the three service chiefs.[10] They had submitted a detailed paper to the committee with their appraisal of defence problems and policies, together with proposals to meet the situation.[11] Unfortunately, the estimated cost of the program was roughly $200 million, starting with $65 million in the first year. The cost of this program was beyond what the government felt it could afford, although, as the historian C.P. Stacey notes: "In the light of hindsight, these recommendations appear very modest."[12]

It should be observed in hindsight, as well, that in economic terms such a program would have been both feasible and beneficial in 1936–39. After considerable revision and the reconciliation of strongly divergent views in cabinet, agreement was finally reached on defence estimates for 1937–38 of about $36 million, a level that was maintained for the following year, as well.[13] (This compares with actual expenditures of about $17 million in 1935–36.) In the cabinet discussion, King had emphasized priority for the air force, which was reflected in the more rapid growth in its expenditures. This enabled that force to expand rapidly from its very low level in the depth of the Depression, but not nearly rapidly enough to meet the urgent needs of 1939 and 1940. The navy was enabled to attain its main objectives, in part because the British were prepared to sell it some of their reasonably modern destroyers at low prices. The militia spent more than either of the other services but was held on a tight rein, so that even by the outbreak of war in 1939 it was still largely armed with the weapons of 1918.[14] James Eayrs has described its treatment as "ruthless, arbitrary and inadequate."[15]

The dramatic Munich crisis of late September 1938, when Hitler secured British and French acquiescence in his seizure of the Sudetenland areas of Czechoslovakia, was the first serious shock to Canadians arising from Hitler's actions. The reaction to Munich brought a far greater, but of course belated, recognition of the very dangerous situation in Europe. In response, cabinet nearly doubled the defence estimates for 1938–39, although even then authorization for the militia was restricted, due in part to suspicion that their programs included preparations for an expeditionary force. These increased estimates of $60 million (plus $3 million for "capital" expenditures – a cosmetic device to limit the apparent deficit) got through Parliament much more easily in 1939 than the $36 million in 1937, which had met much opposition in the House of Commons and in the

Liberal caucus.[16] One-half of the $60 million was for the air force, including a special addition of $6 million for the "training of pilots."

Surveying the pre-war defence programs as a whole, Stacey sums them up as follows:

The Canadian defence program of 1936–39 was effective as far as it went. It was, of course, utterly inadequate to the scale of the coming emergency. In 1939 the country was better prepared for war, on balance, than it had been in 1914; though that is not saying a great deal. Its domestic defences, while not strong, were in better condition than they had been, and a better basis existed for expansion of its forces. But it was in no condition to intervene abroad with any effect; and many months would pass before forces adequate to such intervention could be raised, trained and equipped. Such delay could have been obviated only by the expenditure before the war of sums far greater than the government and parliament of Canada were prepared to lay out, and by a defence program undertaken long before 1937.

At the same time, it is evident that the political conditions of the time militated against a completely effective and practical program. The emphasis on home defence rather than on expeditionary action; the emphasis on the defence of the Pacific rather than the Atlantic coast; the fact that ... there was virtually no consultation or joint planning with those countries – notably the United Kingdom – with which Canada would be cooperating from the outbreak of war: all these were aspects or products of the no-commitments policy. Canadian service officers, as many of them have told the present writer, recognized these policies as unrealistic; it cannot be doubted that many politicians were privately of the same opinion. But strictly military interests were inevitably, and perhaps properly, subordinated to the political necessity for avoiding measures that might divide the country ...[17]

INDUSTRIAL PREPAREDNESS

When rearmament began in 1936, Canada had virtually no munitions industry. There was an old, largely inactive government arsenal and several small civilian aircraft manufacturers able to supply a few training aircraft to the Royal Canadian Air Force. The arms used or to be used by the slowly expanding Canadian services were of British types and design and were bought from Britain. Initially, the RCAF bought some used, obsolescent planes from the Royal Air Force, and the navy did well by purchasing good destroyers at very modest prices. Almost everything acquired from 1936 to 1939 had to be imported from Britain.[18]

When serious rearmament began in Britain in 1936, the British authorities gave some thought to the potential value of Canada as a supplementary source of arms and munitions, and aircraft. If Canada was to serve this purpose without a serious delay in wartime, factories would have to be built and equipped ahead of time and skilled workers trained. The needs of the Canadian forces, as then foreseen, would not nearly be enough to support this capital investment. It could be achieved if the British were prepared to place modest orders in Canada for some of their anticipated requirements, which would supplement Canadian orders. Britain already had the industrial plant and the skilled labour to handle its rearmament program, however, and could produce its arms at substantially less cost than it would have to pay in Canada. Moreover, the British Treasury was already conscious of its potential shortage of dollars (and gold reserves), a rather compelling obstacle to a large joint program in Canada.

As a result of this fundamental problem, very few British orders were placed in Canada during 1936–39 and very little new defence industry was established. A contract of significant size was placed with an existing factory in Hamilton to produce anti-aircraft shells, a high-priority item in Britain at the time. Other Canadian manufacturers who sought defence business in Britain were unsuccessful, and King did not wish the Canadian government to act as an intermediary.

The general subject was discussed at the Imperial Conference in London in May and June of 1937. The desirability of creating a war potential in Canada, and to a lesser degree in Australia, was recognized, but no means of achieving this were agreed on, and the Canadian government wished, in general, not to be an intermediary in the placing of British contracts in Canada.

There was one exception to this Canadian policy. The Canadian militia wanted to place a large order for seven thousand Bren guns – then a modern light machine gun – not quite a big enough order to justify building and equipping a factory. The British were intending to use the same gun on a large scale and needed a second, secure source of supply. Agreement was reached on a British order for five thousand of these guns. Two contracts for their production were placed with the John Inglis Company of Toronto, which was prepared (and qualified) to build a plant to produce them. This was done and the contracts were carried out and were succeeded during the war by many others. Because no other potential producer was invited to compete for the contracts, this joint transaction was the subject of severe controversy in Canada, as described below. There were other gun contracts made just after the war started and a small earlier contract for TNT explosives that led to production in wartime, but nothing else of consequence – except airplanes, or rather "airframes," since Canada did not make airplane engines even during the war.

The British Air Ministry sent a mission to North America in May

1938; one of its duties was to explore the possibilities of creating a war potential for the production of British-type aircraft in Canada. The prime minister sent the mission to see the airplane producers, outside Ottawa. The producers were prepared to band together and establish a central company, Canadian Associated Aircraft, with which the Air Ministry contracted to produce eighty bomber airframes of the Hampton type, with an order for larger bombers to follow. In addition, a contract for forty Hurricane fighter planes was let to another company. The latter were produced in time to be used before the Battle of Britain but apparently were replaced by a later model. The bomber program was not a success, and new arrangements for producing bomber airframes were worked out during the war.

The RCAF, meanwhile, were buying aircraft in Canada, especially training aircraft. When the British Commonwealth Air Training Plan was established late in 1939, the need for training aircraft was very great. It had to be met by drawing on all possible North American sources because in 1940 the British aircraft industry was under severe pressure and had to be dedicated entirely to meeting Britain's own air defence needs.

NON-MILITARY PREPAREDNESS

Apart from the Defence Services, there had been very little preparation for war. On 14 March 1938, cabinet set up an interdepartmental committee on emergency legislation, along with a number of other specialized supporting committees on censorship, on the treatment of Aliens and Alien property, on the treatment of ships and aircraft, and on air raid precautions. These committees reported in July 1939.[19]

The report itself was brief; appended to it, however, was a draft of proposed "Defence of Canada Regulations," which, it was suggested, should be included in the "Provisional Government War Book" if the government approved the proposed regulations in principle. Very little in these regulations concerned the Department of Finance. The committee in its report stated that "legislation of a financial nature will be needed"; it was understood that the Department of Finance was "examining this aspect of the question."

This was not strictly true. What was happening was that the Bank of Canada, with the approval of the minister and deputy minister of finance, secretly was preparing a detailed program of control over all Canadian foreign exchange transactions. The governor of the Bank had been informed, confidentially, that the Bank of England was preparing a plan to be brought into effect if war broke out, for the control of British and indeed the whole "sterling area" foreign exchange transactions. Such British control would create great problems for Canada, which relied on favourable trade balances with the sterling area to meet its deficits in trade and payments with the United States. The British controls would disrupt and restrict such transfers. Moreover, the capital and exchange markets would anticipate great troubles for Canadian international payments if controls were imposed on sterling, so turbulence in the market and withdrawals of likely capital would have to be expected if Canada did not also, in self-defence, impose controls. Secrecy in planning was vital because capital likely would flow out if markets expected the imposition of controls. In fact, secrecy was maintained; a very efficient plan of control was prepared and was ready when war did break out.[20]

No other preparations for war were made by the department. It would have been sensible for the department to have prepared a plan for a workable excess profits tax, for example; in fact, the pre-war debates in Parliament on prices for arms and the dangers of excess profits foreshadowed clearly the need for some such legislation if and when war broke out. There is no evidence, however, that any such plan was prepared, and one had to be hastily contrived once the war did start. All the evidence points to the fact that the department never made any preparatory study of war financing, other than producing a very brief memorandum on how Germany had organized and financed its rearmament.[21] There was no preparation for making considered financial decisions on the scale and nature of military programs. It must be recalled that Charles Dunning, the minister of finance, was a sick man who had submitted his resignation (although it had not been accepted) on 21 July 1938, after months of difficult debate on domestic economic issues.[22] As usual, the deputy minister was busy and tired from trying to do too much himself to find solutions to what were still pressing economic problems in a Canada not yet recovered from its Great Depression. It was uncertain, right up to the end of August, whether or not Hitler would attack Poland and whether the British would go to war if he did.

THE WAR BEGINS

Everything changed on Friday, 1 September 1939. Without warning, German troops invaded Poland at dawn. Within hours, German attack planes had bombed Warsaw and destroyed much of the Polish air force on the ground. Poland called on her allies, France and Britain, for help; both governments hesitated and took precautionary measures that day and the next. They knew, but the public did not, that they could do nothing to save Poland. It was widely felt that Britain's honour was now at stake. On Saturday the British cabinet and parliament were forcing the hands of Chamberlain and Lord Halifax, the foreign secretary. As a result, Britain declared war on Sunday morning, 3 September, and France reluctantly followed. Churchill was to say years later: "Here was decision at last, taken at the worst possible moment and on the least satisfactory ground, which must surely lead to the slaughter of tens of millions of people."[23]

The Canadian cabinet met on the morning of 1 September. It had decided unanimously on 24 August that in the event of Britain's being drawn into war as a result of an attack on Poland, Canada would have to participate, but that Parliament should decide on the basis of the government's recommendation. In that early September meeting, cabinet decided to call Parliament to meet one week hence. In announcing this decision, King added: "In the event of the United Kingdom becoming engaged in war in the effort to resist aggression, the Government of Canada have unanimously decided, as soon as Parliament meets, to seek its authority for effective co-operation by Canada at the side of Britain."[24] In the meantime, he announced, the government would take measures necessary for the defence of Canada. Canada could afford this deliberate delay without danger, and King was most concerned to make clear that Canada would decide to go to war itself, separately from Britain in a formal sense, in spite of how much Canadian action really would depend on that of Britain.

INITIAL WORK IN THE DEPARTMENT: THE SEPTEMBER BUDGET

Serious work on war issues in the Department of Finance began on 1 September, although some preparation had begun about 24 August, when Defence Services began to formulate its plans.[25] In the archives is a memorandum that I prepared, initialled, and dated 1 September 1939, entitled "Considerations Relating to War Financial Policy." In it I suggested a number of policies that found expression in the budget of 12 September, as well as others that certainly did not.[26] Preparations for an initial war budget were urgent and went forward rapidly even though it was known that Dunning was leaving and Ilsley was only temporarily in charge. I remember that we worked through that weekend when Britain declared war. Clark had his first memorandum of advice on the substance of the budget ready for Ilsley on Tuesday, 5 September 1939, the day before J.L. Ralston was sworn in as minister. It should be noted here that Ilsley's role as acting minister had been substantial during 1939 because of Dunning's persistent illness. I can remember being sent over by Clark earlier in 1939 to explain and discuss with Ilsley the proposals of Jimmy Gardiner for a form of crop insurance in the Prairie provinces, even though it was a subject on which Dunning would have known more and had stronger views.

Ilsley was going to present the budget on 12 September because Ralston had no seat in Parliament. Both ministers worked on it. However, they were busy on other things as well as on the substance of various possible tax measures. It fell my lot to do most of the drafting of the budget speech, based on general instructions from Clark and the ministers. Fortunately, we were able to get the ministers' approval of a general approach that adopted and extended the Keynesian type of analysis, and policies based on it, that Dunning had used in the April 1939 budget.

The main emphasis in the analytical part of the speech was that no matter how the war was financed, Canadians could not escape its real costs. We could lighten the burden of these costs, however, by expanding total production, employment, and incomes. The effect of borrowing was analysed, as were the advantages and disadvantages of using taxation. The implications of financing by inflationary measures were explored. Such an approach was judged the most unfair of all the ways of diverting resources to the war. However, a small and carefully regulated amount of credit expansion in the early months of war, when we had unemployed resources, would serve as an impetus to their prompt utilization. The statement went on to distinguish two periods: the initial one of expansion and preparation, and the main period of full war effort. During the initial period, real national income and revenues would increase but less rapidly than the war expenditures. The gap would be financed initially by short-term bank borrowing, with borrowing by public subscription to follow as incomes and savings increased. This borrowing would be at interest rates approximately equal to those in peacetime. Some tax increases would be desirable immediately, because the government was starting out with a budget still heavily in deficit under peacetime conditions. These tax changes were to include "an excess profits tax of general application," a war surtax of twenty per cent on personal income tax, a corresponding increase in the general rates of corporate taxes, and a variety of "increased levies on articles that are commonly regarded as being in the category of luxuries."[27]

DECIDING ON WAR EXPENDITURES

The pre-war policy of "no commitments" meant that the government began the war with no agreed on military programs and no concept of the costs likely to be involved by participation. The Defence Committee of cabinet met on 5 September with the chiefs of staff present: Vice

Admiral Nelles for the navy, Major-General Anderson for the army, and Air Vice Marshal Croil for the air force. Skelton from External Affairs was also present, and Arnold Heeney acted as secretary. The meeting discussed a long memorandum, dated 29 August and prepared by the chiefs, on "Canada's National Effort (Armed Forces) in the Early Stages of a Major War,"[28] which the prime minister had read aloud to cabinet on 1 September. In it the chiefs had suggested the possibility of raising an army corps of two divisions for overseas. This had alarmed the prime minister and cabinet. They had thought that the programs should be primarily for the defence of Canada. This attitude was expressed clearly to the chiefs in the Defence Committee. Heeney's account of the meeting indicates that no clear conclusions were reached, other than a statement of the ministers' view that the only measures to be planned now were those intended for the defence of Canada.

On the basis of this discussion, the minister of national defence, Ian Mackenzie, directed the chiefs to revise their proposals and to bring them forward again with estimates of cost for the first year of war and for the period up to 31 January 1940, presumably to use in getting spending authority from Parliament. The government, and of course the minister and chiefs, also received on 6 September the detailed views of the British authorities on what actions would be most helpful. These had been sent in response to King's inquiry of 3 September about British needs.[29]

The chiefs came up with revised proposals whose estimated costs for the first twelve months added up to about $492 million, which may be compared with the total Dominion expenditure of $532 million for all purposes in the preceding peacetime fiscal year. Of this total, $63 million was for the navy, $136 million for the air force, and $293 million for the army, which included one division overseas and a corps of two divisions in Canada (but which omitted provision for some key ancillary groups to be sent abroad in January as Britain had requested). These proposals were discussed first in a special subcommittee of cabinet, with Ralston as chairman. Ralston had consulted both Clark and Towers about them. The subcommittee concluded that the chiefs' proposals involved "an expenditure the country could not begin to afford."[30] The subject was discussed in the full cabinet most of the afternoon and evening of 18 September. Towers and Clark had been summoned to the evening session, and apparently Towers was the main critic. King writes in his diary:

Towers made an excellent statement ... making clear that what was being asked for by the Defence forces would take about a third of the national income, representing a point today which Germany has only geared up to after 7 years' intensive effort. He doubted if without materially affecting the credit of the country, we could contemplate an expenditure of over 250 millions of dollars. We might possibly go to 300 millions.

King also records the cabinet's conclusion:

Cabinet agreed that we would tell the Chiefs of Staff that they could work out between themselves the division of their needs in terms of a total of 250 millions. It was clear that Anderson's idea of 3 divisions being raised at once was out of the question. One might be arranged for despatch overseas when required and trained in Canada meanwhile. A second in Canada to be kept available for home use or despatch later if required. Recruiting has already gone too far. It was decided to stop recruitment meanwhile, also to allow men to volunteer for overseas but not to make this compulsory. Those who had already enlisted to be re-attested ...[31]

The day following this decision, which so drastically reduced the financial proposals of the chiefs of staff, Ian Mackenzie, the outgoing minister of national defence, managed to issue a public announcement of the government's defence programs looking remarkably like those that had been put before cabinet. They included the intention to organize and train a division to be available as an expeditionary force and a second division at home. For the navy, many anti-submarine and mine-sweeping craft would be built in Canada. As for the air force, there was to be a plan of intensified air training to produce pilots and airmen for active service. The list also included the intention to facilitate the purchase by the UK of essential supplies in Canada. To this was soon to be added a much larger air training plan than what was envisaged on 19 September. The minister and Department of Finance were to have much more to do with it than they did with the initial programs.

DEFENCE PURCHASING

In the early weeks of the war, the minister of finance and the department's solicitor to the Treasury had their own special responsibilities arising out of one of the controversies of the previous year. For some years before the war, there had been in Canada, as in other English-speaking countries, although less intensely than in the United States, a popular revulsion against excessive profits being made in the arms trade and a desire to "take the profit out of war." This reached a climax in Canada in 1938 following the award in late March of that year of a contract to the John Inglis Company for the production of the Bren light machine gun. The contract was made by negotiations without calling for tenders, and the company receiving it had to undertake substantial capital expenditures for the purpose. The fact that no other company was given an opportunity to compete for the business came under serious criticism. Colonel George Drew, a prominent Conservative in Toronto, led the attack. The government appointed Judge Henry H. Davis of the Supreme Court (who had been appointed to the Court by the earlier Conservative government) as a royal commissioner to look into the matter.[32] While the commissioner found no evidence of corruption or incompetence on the part of the contractor, he did criticize the lack of safeguards in awarding defence contracts and proposed that such contracts should be made only with the approval of an advisory group of qualified businessmen.

The government not only took this advice and set up a Defence Purchasing Board but it also added an impractical but popular feature to the statute. Competitive tenders were to be called and the contract awarded on this basis wherever feasible; where competitive tenders could not be obtained, there was to be a statutory limit of five per cent (before income tax) to the profits earned on the capital used in fulfilling the contract.[33] The Defence Purchasing Board was appointed in mid-July 1939, staffed largely by employees of the Canadian National Railway and Canadian Pacific Railway with industrial purchasing experience. In its short existence, from mid-July until the end of October, it placed orders – mostly after the war had started – amounting to about $44 million. More than half of these orders were for rolling stock for the two main railway companies; in smaller amounts, there were orders for motor vehicles, airplanes, construction, and machine tools, but almost no orders in Canada for weapons or munitions.

Notably, from the point of view of Finance, the statute required that all these contracts, despite their normal civilian character, had to go through the hands of the minister of finance and be recommended by him to cabinet. Although the board was part of the Defence Department, it really reported to the minister of finance. Since for most of the time, and certainly for most of the contracts, the minister was the ultra-careful – indeed, finicky – Ralston, this involved a great deal of detailed work for him and for David Johnson, the department's solicitor, whom Ralston relied on in this work. The pressure under which this extra work was done is illustrated in a story told by Johnson. He was working one night well past midnight when his buzzer from the minister rang. (In those days we were summoned like servants in this good old-fashioned way.) Rather incredulously, Johnson went down to see whether Ralston really was summoning him. The minister, in his shirt sleeves, was poring over one of those defence contracts and a memorandum Johnson had given him on it. Without even looking up, or taking any note of the hour, he addressed several questions to Johnson, handed the text back containing some detailed revisions, and picked up the next on top of the pile, leaving Johnson to return to his own pile that was needed for consideration in the morning.

The impracticability of the Defence Purchasing Board legislation was recognized as soon as the war began. A far-reaching alternative was put before Parliament and passed on 12 September (the same day that the budget was brought in and passed). This bill provided for the establishment of a minister and Department of Munitions and Supply with very broad and strong powers over procurement, production, essential commodities, and other supplies. It was modelled on British legislation in the Great War and also on legislation enacted in Britain some months earlier, in 1939. The prime minister announced that the government did not intend to bring this new act into effect until the situation required it but would commence with a War Supply Board established by order-in-council under the War Measures Act. The board would be under the direction of Ralston as minister of finance. The necessary order was passed three days later, and a prominent industrialist, Wallace Campbell, the president of the Ford Motor Company of Canada, was appointed chairman. It took time, however, to assemble a staff, and the board did not begin operations until 1 November 1939. Meanwhile, the Defence Purchasing Board carried on, and most of the purchases were of the nature described above.

When the Munitions and Supply Bill was before Parliament in Committee of the Whole, C.D. Howe dealt with the question of whether the limitation of profits clause under the Defence Purchasing Board legislation would be carried over to apply to the War Supply Board. Howe, who before entering politics in 1935 had made a fortune building grain elevator terminals, made it quite clear that what had been desirable in peacetime would not be practicable in wartime. On some occasions, time would not permit the calling of tenders; he cited one case that had already arisen: the urgent need to obtain an anti-submarine net for one of the harbours. Furthermore, many materials in time of war would have to come from outside the country, and prices in other countries were fluctuating so quickly that one could not get firm tenders based on these supplies. The minister stated that his considerable business experience over a good many years indicated the impossibility of laying down a uniform standard for profits applicable to a wide variety of purchases. He said that the Defence Purchasing Board had done its best to place contracts on the basis of a five per cent limit on profits and had used such pressure as it could bring to bear in terms of patriotism and urgency. To date, however, it had not succeeded in placing a single contract on that basis. In his opinion, that portion of the act had been proven unworkable. He concluded: "I believe that the greatest safeguard this country can have, particularly at the present time, is to have adequate machinery of control such as the set-up under the present bill, and to have the measure administered by men of experience and wisdom in the particular service, men of absolute integrity."[34]

That ended the debate. The War Supply Board was not subject to any arbitrary profit ceiling, and on Ralston's recommendation this limitation on profits on Defence Purchasing Board contracts was removed by an order-in-council under the War Measures Act on 15 September.

Ralston continued to be responsible for the Defence Purchasing Board contracts until the War Supply Board superseded it on 1 November 1939. When the latter began to function, he asked the prime minister to relieve him of this onerous duty, and the two agreed that it should go to C.D. Howe, the minister of transport.[35] This turned out to have been an inspired choice. "C.D." became the powerful minister of munitions and supply when that departmental act was brought into force on 9 April 1940, and not a moment too soon: that was the day Hitler invaded Norway and Denmark, beginning his conquest of Western Europe and ending the period of the "phony war."

We should note here, in connection with the department's brief period of responsibility for defence purchasing, that the main issue of policy at the time was whether the government should place orders for weapons and other specialized war equipment for the Canadian forces if the British were not willing to place concurrent orders – for placing such orders would greatly reduce the cost per unit. The British during this period – indeed, until the crises of May and June 1940 – were very reluctant to place important defence equipment orders in Canada, probably for financial reasons. Ralston was opposed to Canada's placement of orders for its own forces alone, especially for the army. General McNaughton, just before leaving to go to England with the First Division in early December, expressed concern to King that more was not being done to mobilize industry.[36] King promised to look into the matter and did, but it appears that he met opposition, from both Ralston and Howe, to unilateral action by Canada.[37] C.P. Stacey concludes his review of this policy with the sentence: "Few aspects of Canadian war policy are likely to surprise posterity more than the fact that measures to provide Canadian-made arms for the Canadian Army were not taken until June and July of 1940, some nine months after the outbreak of war." There is no doubt that Ralston was largely responsible for this, together perhaps with those who set the limits on war expenditure, but we in the department under Clark were not much aware of the issue.

FOREIGN EXCHANGE CONTROL

The effective preparations already described enabled the government to bring foreign exchange control into effect very smoothly, over the weekend of Saturday, 16 September. Cabinet approved the order-in-council late on 15 September, imposing the control and establishing the Foreign Exchange Control Board of five members – Towers, Clark, Hugh Scully, Dana Wilgress, and Robertson – as the controlling authority.[38] Towers was made chairman and Donald Gordon his deputy chairman in charge of operations and management. Many able men were obtained quickly to operate the control, and the chartered banks with their thousands of branches were made authorized dealers operating under the terms of the order and the directions of the board. The board was authorized to make regulations to give effect to the control (and make necessary exemptions from certain of its provisions). Enforcement of the order and regulations was carried out by the customs officers and the banks as authorized dealers. The board was authorized to set rates of exchange for various transactions. The initial rate selected, ninety cents US for the Canadian dollar, was approximately the level prevailing in the market when the control began. Buying and selling rates had to be established, of course, along with rates for sterling and other currencies as well as US dollars.

Clark (and occasionally the minister) was the only officer of the department much involved in exchange control. He attended the meetings of the board himself, taking no one with him and appointing no alternate, except when Mackintosh took on that role after he arrived. Clark was an active member, occasionally differing with Towers and Gordon on policy issues and convincing them that he was right despite their experience and expert staff.[39] Some of us in the department did have to learn enough about the board and its problems and policies to write letters and speeches for the minister and Clark. Later, of course, Clark and others in the department were much involved in measures to conserve and augment our foreign exchange resources. (These are described in chapter 4.)

THE WARTIME PRICES AND TRADE BOARD

The first of the wartime economic organizations established by the government was created on 3 September 1939, on the formal recommendation of the minister of labour. The Wartime Prices and Trade

Board's role was "to provide safeguards under war conditions against any undue enhancement in the prices of food, fuel and other necessaries of life, and to ensure an adequate supply and equitable distribution of such commodities." The chairman of the board was taken from Finance: Hector McKinnon, the commissioner of tariffs, who had a first-rate knowledge of Canadian industry and trade, the gift of common sense, a feel as to what was politically feasible, and the confidence of King over a long period of years. In addition, on 3 September, David Sim, commissioner of excise, and F.A. McGregor, commissioner of the Combines Investigation Act under (at that time) the minister of labour, were appointed to the board. Both of these men were very knowledgeable of Canadian business practices as visible from Ottawa. Within a few days, they were joined on the board by Dean A.M. Shaw, director of the marketing service in the Department of Agriculture, in whose field serious problems were to be expected, and Charles Hebert, a member of the Tariff Board, who would leave a few months later to go on active service. McKinnon quickly brought in Kenneth Taylor, a distinguished academic economist, who had worked for McKinnon in the past on tariff matters, to be the board's secretary and chief operating officer.[40]

In contrast to the Foreign Exchange Control Board with its long period of preparation and very complete set of controls, the WPTB used its broad powers very selectively and carefully during its first two years. The board saw its role at this time as controlling prices by controlling supply and demand. As Taylor described it in early 1941: "The control of the price structure as distinct from the price level is the problem of organizing supply and preventing the occurrence of avoidable shortages."[41] The board was alert and skilful in dealing with shortages arising from causes outside Canada, notably the sudden shortage of wool, the panic buying and external control of sugar supplies, and the virtual disappearance of the normal sources of supply of cod liver oil. In other cases, organized efforts were necessary to deal with potentially dangerous domestic shortages, as in the case of coal and mill feeds. By supply arrangements, price changes were kept to the necessary minimum. The board did impose maximum prices in a number of cases where shortages were inevitable, notably crossbred wool and rents for housing in certain areas of local shortage due to causes arising from the war. In some cases, temporary maximum prices were imposed to head off unnecessary price increases that were arising out of temporary shortages.

FINANCING BRITAIN

It became clear some months before the war that Britain would require some financing in Canada or by Canada in the event of war, and J.A.C. Osborne of the Bank of England, who for several years had been deputy governor of the Bank of Canada, visited Ottawa for some preliminary soundings.[42] Possibilities of British borrowing in the Canadian market and Canadian borrowing in New York were ruled out. The possibility of "repatriation" of British holdings of Canadian securities, however, seemed more promising. Nothing definite was decided; when the war began, no plan or understanding was in place regarding method or scale of financing.

During the early weeks of the war, the problem of financing arose in regard to several British purchases of Canadian supplies, and the British Treasury's concern to restrict Canadian dollar expenditure was very evident, both in regard to purchases of particular traditional imports and in its reluctance to place orders for munitions in Canada. It was agreed that financing arrangements should be made of general scope and not in regard to specific transactions.[43] The costs involved in the British Commonwealth Air Training Plan already were emerging in negotiations, and it was clear that the government of Canada was going to have a difficult time with its total commitments for war purposes, including the financing of British (and other sterling area) requirements in Canada in addition to Canada's expenditures on its own programs. Settlement of the limits on financing was going to have to wait for some weeks, but it was agreed in October that a beginning would be made in repatriation by redeeming before maturity the 3.5 per cent sterling Government of Canada Loan maturing in 1950.[44] This would be paid off with sterling obtained by the Bank of Canada in exchange for Canadian dollars supplied to the UK in Ottawa. In addition, further sterling would be accepted temporarily in this way, pending the working out of some other financial arrangements. (The further development of this problem and the means of meeting it are covered in chapter 3.)

CHAPTER TWO

The EAC and Trade Problems

Canada had always been a trading nation. The trade in cod – "the beef of the sea" – had initially brought Europeans to Canada's shores in the sixteenth century. Thereafter, Canada exported fur, timber, and wheat to European markets in return for much-needed capital and technology. In the twentieth century, a new generation of export products emerged. As a result, Canada's total trade in value terms by 1939 was $1.68 billion.

The war, however, was threatening to destabilize international trade and, thereby, Canadian prosperity. The prospect of military blockades, trade restrictions, and currency controls worried nations like Canada that relied on imports of capital and technology and exports of natural products and other goods.

By 1939, the Department of Finance had become a "key player," as the jargon of bureaucracy would put it, in modern decision making. It fell to that department, therefore, as well as to the newly created Economic Advisory Committee, to solve the trade problems that accompanied the war.

The establishment of the advisory committee was one in a series of government actions designed to meet the exigencies of war. As Hitler's armies made their triumphant way across northern Europe in the first few years of the war, the challenge of the EAC was threefold: (1) to preserve Canada's export-based industries in the face of lost and disrupted markets; (2) to limit imports while not doing damage to the Allied cause; and (3) to conserve and generate foreign exchange, particularly US dollars. This chapter examines how effectively these challenges were met.

On 14 September 1939, by order-in-council, the government established an Advisory Committee on Economic Policy, broadly mandating its duty to be, "of its own motion or upon request of any Minister of the Crown, to investigate, report and advise upon questions of economic and financial policy and organization arising out of Canada's participation in the war, and to report to the cabinet Committee on

General Policy, on Supply or on Financial Questions as the case may be."[1] Normally this committee reported to cabinet's War Committee, which became the name of the Committee on General Policy referred to in the order, but on numerous occasions it reported directly to Council, i.e., cabinet, indeed sometimes by the chairman of the advisory committee's oral report.

This committee was set up on the formal recommendation of the prime minister, probably with the advice of O. D. Skelton and Arnold Heeney, who was at that time the prime minister's principal secretary. They probably consulted Clark, as it seems to have been understood from the beginning that he would be chairman of the new committee.[2]

This Economic Advisory Committee, as it was normally called, included ten of the leading senior officials from the departments concerned with economic affairs. W.C. Clark was chairman. G.F. Towers, the governor of the Bank of Canada, was an active member who brought his keen and skeptical mind to bear on a variety of problems quite outside his normal field of responsibility. Charles Camsell, the highly respected deputy minister of mines and resources, was a less active but important member, as was R.H. Coats, the long-time dominion statistician. Coats was one of the earliest of the intellectual leaders of the public service and a close friend of King. Norman Robertson, the chief economic officer of the Department of External Affairs and later undersecretary, was one of the most useful members. Dr. G.S.H. Barton, the scholarly deputy minister of agriculture, was a member who had many troublesome problems to bring before the committee, frequently assisted in this by Dean A.M. Shaw, his director of marketing. Scully, the commissioner of customs, was on the committee for his knowledge of trade practices and Canadian industry; Dana Wilgress was there for his great knowledge of the Canadian export trade and foreign markets. Hector McKinnon was a member in his capacity as chairman of the Wartime Prices and Trade Board and for his encyclopedic knowledge of Canadian trade and industry. Lt-Col Henri Desrosiers, associate deputy minister of national defence, was a member chiefly because he was one of the few senior French-Canadian officials, though he was also valuable as a channel into Defence. Although there was no member from the Labour Department at the beginning, there was a series of them later. The committee had difficulty getting a member to represent the economic side of the War Supply Board and later of the Department of Munitions and Supply, but representatives were obtained as needed, and for a while R.A.C. Henry, a former deputy minister of marine, represented these interests (as did C.D. Howe) when the subject warranted it.[3]

Clark appointed me to be secretary of the committee as soon as it was established. I helped him with the preparation of his reports in the early months before Professor W.A. Mackintosh arrived from Queen's in mid-December to be his special assistant. Mackintosh attended the meetings and took over the drafting of most of the reports. I made surprisingly detailed minutes of the discussion at the meetings, mainly for Clark's own use (and Mackintosh's). These were never circulated or approved by the committee but were available on loan to any member wishing to consult them. For me, as a junior officer, the committee was an opportunity to attain insight into how my elders and betters thought, argued, and came to agreements. It was also an incomparable source of contacts and information.

The EAC almost certainly was the first general-purpose interdepartmental committee of top-level officials established in Ottawa. Inevitably, it had to innovate in methods, as well as deal with unfamiliar and unforeseen problems. It was composed of very busy senior officials whose collective personal knowledge and judgment were sought by the prime minister. Most of its meetings were held in the evening, with relatively short notice regarding subject matter and usually without advance circulation of papers. Occasionally, the subjects referred to it had already been before cabinet, where divisions of opinion had arisen leading the prime minister to seek the advice of this committee of officials to help resolve the issues. In other cases, and increasingly as time went on, individual ministers would refer matters to the committee before taking them to cabinet, or a member of the committee would get the chairman's agreement to consider the subject before advice was given to ministers. There were often differences of view between members of the committee even after lengthy discussion. The committee had to deal with this problem by recording the divergent views and arguments, pro and con, but with the chairman's assessment of where the consensus lay. The minutes, which were working papers, were not the operative documents of the committee. The reports were. Initially these were prepared by the chairman, with varying degrees of assistance from the secretary, and occasionally they took the form of draft telegrams to London prepared by Robertson. After Mackintosh arrived, he became, in effect, a member of the committee. He was occasionally the acting chairman and more commonly the main author of the reports. His sense of humour as well as good judgment did much to hold the committee together and make its informal procedures effective.

The committee functioned very actively and effectively in its informal way in dealing with economic policies and wartime organization until August 1941. It was then relatively inactive until it was asked to consider the organization of responsibility for work on post-war reconstruction and related measures. This it did in late 1942 and early 1943. Later in 1943, the committee held several meetings on its own volition to review the working of the wage control measures, which were also being reviewed by the newly constituted National War Labour Board. In September, the government asked it for advice in dealing with the conflicting majority and minority reports of that board. These were the last important reports of the committee. By early 1944, the focus of the government's attention had shifted to the program of post-war legislation enacted that year, which was considered in more ad hoc meetings of senior officials.[4]

The present chapter is concerned with the work of the committee in regard to trade and other external arrangements, including the tourist trade and export controls in the early years of the war.

NEW EXPORT ARRANGEMENTS

The first group of subjects needing attention covered the policies to be followed and measures to be taken in dealing with the traditional exports of Canada to Britain, particularly agricultural exports. The British government had set up very quickly some centralized buying arrangements, shipping controls and priorities, as well as various measures to deny supplies to Germany and to ensure that neutrals in Europe did not pass on imports to that country. Moreover, the British authorities were very conscious of their prospective shortage of US and Canadian dollars and the consequent need to economize in purchases.

As a result of these actions and considerations, the peacetime commercial marketing arrangements no longer applied, giving rise to a need for central bargaining over prices and terms, to consider what new marketing arrangements were needed and how to deal with those agricultural products normally exported but of which the British felt it necessary to reduce their imports substantially. Prices had to be settled for selling bacon, cheese, and canned salmon. Arrangements were made to sell greatly reduced shipments of apples. Much thought had to be given to how to sustain the apple producers when the important British market was practically eliminated. The international marketing and processing arrangements for silver fox furs were greatly disturbed by the war; new arrangements had to be worked out to preserve that little industry, which was important in the constituency of Prince Edward Island, where Ralston, the new minister of finance, was soon to stand for Parliament. The committee was persuaded by ministers to meet delegations from the Nova Scotian apple growers and the PEI fox farmers in working out these rescue efforts.[5]

WHEAT

Wheat was by far the largest agricultural export and gave rise to the greatest troubles in making arrangements and contracts with London. The wheat issue was of great political importance and very difficult to resolve. The subject came before the committee as a matter of urgency in the second week of its existence. The Canadian government had been trying, unsuccessfully, to reduce its involvement in wheat marketing during 1938 and 1939. Now it had to back up the Wheat Board, which was offering to buy wheat from the 1939 crop at a floor price of seventy cents, down from eighty for the 1938 crop. The grain exchange was functioning. It had been the government's policy to keep it open and rely on it for export sales. The British, on the other hand, had centralized grain purchasing at the outbreak of war, as they had told the Canadian authorities in 1938 they would do.[6] They wanted Canada to close the grain exchange and make bulk bilateral contracts for wheat at negotiated prices. The Canadian ministers, however, decided not to do so. The British purchasing authorities had bought ten million bushels in wheat futures at market prices from the Canadian Wheat Board late in August as a precaution just before the outbreak of war. They then made no moves to buy more from Canada in September, when the market prices were higher. After consulting cabinet, the minister of trade and commerce referred the matter to the Economic Advisory Committee, on 29 September. The committee reported back quickly, stressing the seriousness of the impasse that had developed, urging that efforts be made to arrange a sale of "at least 50 or 60 million bushels," and suggesting that a high-level approach be made by a cable from prime minister to prime minister. This was done immediately, but to no avail. In his reply to King, Chamberlain cited the need to settle the financing that Britain could expect to get in Canada, as well as the need to make new coordinated arrangements for purchasing. The EAC again considered possible marketing arrangements and suggested partial matching of British purchases on the Grain Exchange by sales by the Wheat Board, with an overriding assurance that the British could get the agreed on quantity for not more than an agreed "fair and reasonable" price. Agreement on such arrangements could not be reached despite continued efforts, and the British bought only a small amount on the market before navigation closed. So great was the shortage of shipping, however, that none of the grain bought in late August or afterwards was shipped before the close of navigation. As a result, the Canadian ports were badly congested and the impasse in policy continued.[7]

Further efforts were made to arrange large wheat sales, by the mines and resources minister, T.A. Crerar, the senior member of cabinet from the West, who went to London with a strong group of officials to come to some understanding with the British on a wide range of issues (of which more is said in later chapters). When he made two radical proposals to the British and to his colleagues in Ottawa for large wheat sales, neither side would agree to them.[8] Wheat was so important politically, and its price so potentially volatile, that the Canadian ministers could not agree to accept the risk of a long-term contract at prices acceptable to the British ministers. Arrangements were worked out whereby the British purchased their current requirements through the Winnipeg Grain Exchange in January and April. (By this time the British experts saw the advantage of keeping the Exchange open.) Before any further purchase was made, Hitler's armies overran Norway, Denmark, Holland, and Belgium, and then France fell. The wheat market collapsed in mid-May as the principal customers, other than Britain, disappeared behind the blockade. On Saturday, 18 May, the government asked the Grain Exchange to "peg" the price of wheat at the closing price of the preceding date, i.e., about seventy cents a bushel for the May future.

Over the next few very disastrous months, a bulk sale of one hundred million bushels in futures was made. By this time it was evident that Canada was to have a very large crop (finally determined at 514 million bushels, second only to the record crop of 1928). The country and the government were confronted with a huge surplus of wheat, for which additional storage facilities and large-scale financing were needed. New legislation introduced delivery quotas for wheat producers in order to share the market equitably, made allowances in pricing later deliveries to compensate farmers for farm storage, and brought in a levy on the use of wheat for consumption in Canada to bring the domestic price up to about ninety cents a bushel.

At the end of 1940, the government asked the Economic Advisory Committee to review the wheat situation again and suggest policies for dealing with the 1941 crop. The committee made a long and very serious report in January, emphasizing the magnitude of the economic and financial effects of the wheat surplus ("second only to the war itself"). It assessed the future markets to be expected during the war and recommended severe limitations on deliveries of wheat and various measures to reduce the production of wheat and yet maintain a tolerable level of farm income in the prairies.[9]

OTHER TRADE ISSUES

Other trade questions came before the committee in addition to those we have noted concerning export contracts. The first relating to imports was to decide if Canada should participate in the Empire Sugar Agreement under which Britain bought the sugar output of the West Indies and other Empire producers. The committee advised initially that Canada should enter it for the first year of the war, even though there was some question that we might do better outside it. The subject was complicated by the tariff preferences accorded by Canada to the West Indies and other Empire producers. After further discussions had taken place with the British sugar controller, the committee advised that Canada should undertake to participate for the duration of the war and a short period thereafter, subject to Canada's agreement to the basic price to be fixed and its relations to the tariff preference. It also recommended that the trade agreement with the British West Indies simply should be renewed, rather than renegotiated, as had been planned. A second minor import question was whether imports of cured pork from the US should be restricted in the spring of 1940, as they were threatening to interfere seriously with the management of the bacon supplies and market. On this the committee was divided but the majority approved the restrictions proposed by the minister of agriculture. It was a minor example of the concern of those dealing with trade policy that the minister of agriculture and his agencies were unduly and unnecessarily protectionist.[10]

A much more unusual and war-oriented problem was the policy to be followed in export controls of minerals and chemicals of strategic importance. The issue was raised in October 1939 by Camsell, after preliminary consultation between his Department of Mines and Resources and the Department of National Defence. It was decided that a detailed study of all the individual items on the list of potentially important materials should be made. R.H. Coats, the Dominion statistician, was asked to call together a group of officials from five departments to study the various items and make recommendations to the committee concerning each.[11] The first review indicated that enough information was available to determine if a scarcity was likely in Canada. It was decided to set up a continuing subcommittee from which panels could be drawn to examine the supply situation in each case. It was noted at this point that Canadian export controls could be used in co-operation with the British contraband control (i.e., those enforcing the blockade on Germany) so that Canadian licences would be sufficient to clear exports to neutrals. The EAC considered the general subject of export control again in April 1941. It then approved a proposal from its standing subcommittee on this subject to centralize, essentially for administrative reasons, the issuing of such permits in a special branch to be set up in the Department of Trade and Commerce, with delegation to others in a few cases. The committee also noted the important role of export controls in "economic warfare" and the need to coordinate policy in this field not only with the United Kingdom but also, at that time, April 1941, with the United States. It set up a special subcommittee to act for it on these questions relating to economic warfare.

Another export problem – a foretaste of problems to be faced for many years during and after the war – involved restrictions placed by Commonwealth countries and colonies on imports from Canada because they would add to the dollar shortage of the sterling area as a whole. The problem first arose from a purely British action in which a purchase of trucks for the Indian Army (for which the British government was to pay) was diverted from the Ford Motor Company in Canada to Ford in the United Kingdom. Ford Canada felt that it had had a commitment on this order, for which it had already incurred expenditures. They got the minister of finance to protest to London, but the British demonstrated that there had not been a commitment and argued that it was justified in deciding to produce the trucks in the United Kingdom.[12] (The British auto industry was seriously underutilized early in 1940 because of the decline in domestic sales.)

This incident, however, led both the Ford Motor Company and the departments concerned in Ottawa to study the export of cars from Canada to various Empire countries and colonies. It became clear that restrictions had been imposed and were being tightened on their imports from Canada; in some cases, the restrictions discriminated in favour of imports from Britain. Studies of the regulations on trade showed that the problem extended beyond cars to other manufactured products. In March, the prime minister received a strongly worded letter from the president of the Ford Motor Company of Canada (who was also the chairman of the government's War Supply Board) protesting this widespread discrimination.[13] The prime minister asked the cabinet Committee on War Finance and Supply (which rarely met) to consider the situation after preliminary study by the Economic Advisory Committee. The committee discussed the matter on 1 April 1940.[14] There was a long and complicated argument about the various implications of the restrictions on imports from Canada, and Clark laid some emphasis on the danger that Canada's favourable trade balance with Empire countries as a whole other than the UK might be wiped out. The committee was divided over how strong a position Canada should take on this matter, with Clark being more of a hawk than the others.

Clark did not report immediately on the committee's view, partly because of the pressure of other business and partly because he wanted to study the matter further. He finally managed to find time to write a lengthy report in May, while sick at home. By the time he completed it, the war situation had changed beyond recognition. Churchill had taken over from Chamberlain as the British prime minister and faced a situation of utmost gravity. On 14 May, Clark, ever dutiful, sent his report, primarily written by him, to his minister and to the secretary of the cabinet.[15] It included a long draft telegram for the prime minister to send to the British prime minister. Clark noted in the file that he had discussed the matter with Towers, who thought that it was not the time for dispatching such a message to London. On 26 June, after six more dreadful weeks of war, Heeney returned the report to Clark, referring to their telephone conversation that afternoon and noting that "in view of developments since May 15th you have decided that the Report should not be submitted to the Government at this time."[16]

TOURIST TRADE

The tourist trade had become an important source of American dollars to Canada, and officials of the Foreign Exchange Control Board felt that the Transport Department, which had the responsibility for promoting the trade, was not doing enough to meet the difficulties arising out of the war. A public relations officer of the board had visited various parts of the United States half a dozen times in the previous six months. He had found little news there about Canada, little knowledge of its attractions for tourists, and very little advertising to promote travel in Canada. Bankers whom he had seen on board business, part of which concerned currency arrangements for tourists, told him that Canada would have to advertise to tell the American people that exchange control and other wartime conditions would not interfere in any way with tourists. The committee discussed the situation at some length and decided to send a short report to cabinet urging more effort and expenditures in this field; if cabinet agreed with that, the committee would meet again with those carrying out the work, because quick action would be required to affect that year's trade. Four days later, the committee had a long meeting with the deputy minister of transport and the chief of the Travel Bureau to discuss the situation and what could be done promptly to improve it. Eleven days later, the committee discussed the issue in detail and recommended a substantial additional expenditure on advertising, including a special program to be carried out by the American Express Company. This was proposed in a long, detailed report written largely by Clark himself, a real selling job in his best tradition. When, six weeks later, the chief of the Travel Bureau reported on the favourable co-operation that they were then getting in the US and thanked Clark for the help the committee had given him, Clark replied: "Our little group is only too glad to be of assistance in any good cause." He took time to write this at the most critical period of the war, just before the evacuation of the British army at Dunkirk.[17]

MEASURES TO CONSERVE EXCHANGE

The most detailed discussions on trade matters undertaken by the committee were "measures to conserve exchange." These discussions began after the budget of 24 June 1940, in which Ralston had stated that in addition to the War Exchange Tax and the excise tax on automobiles, the government "may from time to time, in respect of certain classes of civilian imports, take other measures of a non-fiscal character for the purpose of meeting this vital need as circumstances seem to require." In a report to cabinet of 21 August 1940, the committee itself recommended a procedure for the initiation and consideration of such measures in which several departments and agencies likely would be involved and in respect of which the exchange conservation effects would have to be balanced against other effects and considerations.[18] For this purpose, the committee set up a special subcommittee to consider detailed proposals, particularly those involving restrictions on imports. One case involved control over the imports of aluminum, but this was done essentially to conserve aluminum itself, urgently needed for aircraft production in Britain. Another was to terminate the trade agreements with France and Poland because, although Canadian trade with those countries had ceased by the autumn of 1940, the termination of the agreements would indirectly increase the tariff rates on a number of less essential imports from other non-Empire sources.

There was a long list of items dealt with by the subcommittee, a copy of which is in file19 bearing my handwritten comments, but a diligent search of many files has not brought to light reports of the Special Committee or any reports of the Economic Advisory Committee itself on this subject. The result of the work, however, shows up in the schedule of imports subject to restriction under the War Exchange Conservation Act passed in December 1940. Arthur Annis has informed me that he and Mackintosh effectively drew up the schedules to the act for approval by cabinet after consultation with officials of other departments following the subcommittee discussions described above.

The key to the EAC's effectiveness, and the crucial role of Finance officials in its deliberations, is reflected in this example. After due consideration of a complicated subject, effective action was taken. As a senior committee of top public servants, it could draw on an impressive range of experience and knowledge and deal directly with problems that transcended the usual departmental responsibilities. Between them, Clark and Mackintosh produced many of the committee's reports and played a dynamic role in its discussions.

CHAPTER THREE

The Air Training Plan Negotiations

After the blitzkrieg attack on Poland in September 1939, seemingly nothing of military significance took place for several months. In fact, so little occurred that many of the children who had been evacuated from British cities at the start of the war were returned to their homes. Prime Minister Neville Chamberlain had declared war, but nothing had actually happened. This "phoney war," as it has been termed, lasted until April 1940.

The fact that there was little military action during these months meant that the Canadian government could postpone making difficult decisions. This was certainly the case with the contentious issue of conscription. Yet it was during this period that a critical part of Canada's contribution to the war got under way: the British Commonwealth Air Training Plan. Undertaken, and principally paid for, by Canadians, the BCATP eventually trained 130,000 aviators – nearly half of the Commonwealth aircrews. It was with good reason, therefore, that President Franklin Roosevelt later termed it the "aerodrome of democracy."

The Department of Finance was a dynamic force in the establishment of the BCATP. It participated in each phase of the negotiations. Prime Minister Mackenzie King's position was that Canada should not exceed its resources. The task of Finance was to make sure that this did not happen – to draw a financial line in the sand that would not be crossed. King did not want to repeat the experience of World War I when the government ran up huge deficits to cover the cost of the war, leading to post-war economic instability and dislocation. This time around, Canada would pay for more than half of the cost of the war out of current revenues.

This chapter describes the negotiations with Britain to establish the terms of Canadian involvement in the BCATP. At times, as Bryce notes in splendid detail, the negotiations proved arduous, even rancorous.

The British Commonwealth Air Training Plan was the largest military task undertaken by Canada in the early years of the war. It began on

26 September 1939, only a week after the announcement regarding the Canadian defence programs. The prime minister received a very persuasive personal telegram from the prime minister of Britain, urging Canada to be the centre of a very large advanced air training program, which would train men from Canada, Australia, New Zealand, and Britain.[1] The Canadian high commissioner in London, Vincent Massey, and the Australian high commissioner, Stanley Bruce, had initiated work on this proposal with the British Air Ministry. Massey also assisted in drafting the telegraphed appeal to King, but he kept his role on this whole matter secret from Ottawa.[2]

Despite the long pre-war history of frustrating discussions on air training plans, this new proposal attracted King, who took it to a meeting with his colleagues on 28 September. He noted his regret that it had arrived just after the government's announcement of its defence programs, some of which might have been held back to make room for the new air training plan.[3]

The British proposal was subjected to a lengthy discussion in a meeting of the Emergency Council of cabinet on 28 September, which was attended by the chiefs of staff, as well; this was followed by consultations with the chairman and vice chairman of the War Supply Board.[4] The chief of the air staff did feel able to undertake a program of this kind, provided that additional training personnel and additional aircraft of the type needed for advanced training could be obtained. The minister of finance recognized that the British emphasis on the air force had increased greatly but felt that the expenditures required to meet this demand might affect other aspects of the Canadian war program adversely. The chief of the general staff ventured the opinion that the Canadian public would not be satisfied with Canadian participation in the war if it was confined to air activity, even on a much enlarged scale; the public thought in terms of ground troops. Quebec ministers felt that where Canadian supplies and services were concerned, public opinion would be swayed by the needs and desires of the UK. King clearly was in favour of proceeding with the air training program. The proposed scheme was accepted, subject to three conditions: first, that the British could provide the necessary additional planes; second, that they could provide the necessary additional training personnel; and third, that satisfactory financing arrangements could be worked out. King sent Chamberlain a lengthy telegram to this effect, concluding with an agreement to hold joint discussions in Canada with an expert mission from Britain and similar missions from other members of the Commonwealth.[5]

These discussions turned out to be lengthy and difficult. A special cabinet committee charged with these negotiations was struck.

J.L. Ralston, the minister of finance, was probably the most active Canadian representative, sometimes substituting for the minister of national defence as well as discharging his own duties – and Ralston was very conscious of his duties. King himself played a dominant but not altogether constructive role in the process. The committee's other ministers were Norman Rogers, minister of national defence, and C.D. Howe, the minister of transport, who was also in charge of war supply and construction. Also on the committee was Ian Mackenzie, former defence minister, who in the absence of an official secretary at this early stage of the war made notes which, although not entirely clear or fully reliable, are the best Canadian source of information on all but the first meeting of these negotiations.[6]

Britain sent a large and senior delegation headed by Lord Riverdale, a leading Sheffield industrialist with some experience in public affairs, who was perhaps selected because part of the mission's mandate was to make contracts with the aircraft industry.[7] The senior British politician in the group was Captain Harold Balfour, parliamentary undersecretary of state for air; Balfour was in a junior position compared with Riverdale but was able to speak on policy issues. The senior military figure, who did not arrive until later, was Air Chief Marshal Sir Robert Brooke-Popham; he did not suffer colonials gladly – except at hockey games, which he enjoyed immensely. The British delegation also included service officials representing the Air Ministry and the Treasury. The Australian and New Zealand delegations were small, and because they travelled by sea, they arrived late and had to leave early. During their stay, they amended the plan by modestly reducing their proposed inputs and deciding to do most of their training in Australia.

The Department of Finance was active in the negotiations, as was its minister, Ralston. Clark became involved immediately after the Emergency Council meeting of 28 September. On 30 September he met with the deputy minister for air, K.S. Maclachlan; the chief of the air staff, Air Vice Marshal Croil; and Air Commodore Stedman, the air member for engineering and supply. This group examined the air force's initial estimate of the costs involved in building and operating the number and kind of training schools that the British were proposing. Shortly after this meeting, Clark requested that I assist him and the minister in analysing the British proposal and the associated cost estimates. This turned out to be my chief occupation during October and November of that year and marked my first sustained contact with the military. I was much impressed with Stedman's ability and with his willingness to suffer the questions and comments of a young whippersnapper.

When Riverdale arrived with his mission in mid-October, he submitted to King his own outline for the Dominion Training Scheme. This outline included details of the numbers to be recruited and the number of schools required to train them.[8] It proposed that 1,200 men be recruited every four weeks to train as pilots, plus about half that number to train as air observers (navigators) and about one thousand to train as air gunners – for a total of about 2,620, allowing for those failing to qualify as pilots and diverted to other categories. Forty-eight per cent of the recruits were expected to come from Canada, with forty per cent from Australia and twelve per cent from New Zealand. It was proposed that elementary flight training of pilots be done in their country of origin and that advanced training in "service" flying, as well as all training for other aircrew, be done in Canada. To this end, Riverdale proposed that Canada should establish twelve elementary flight-training schools, twenty-five service-flying training schools, one wireless school, fifteen observer schools, fifteen bombing and gunnery schools, three air navigation schools, and one armament school for instructors and maintenance personnel. The outline for the Dominion Training Scheme also included detailed information as to the content of the training courses and estimates of required aircraft and personnel. It did not, however, include cost estimates, which were to be worked out with the help of RCAF officers.

After Riverdale and his staff met with Croil, Stedman, and their assistants – including me, on some occasions – to reach agreement on technical details and cost estimates, negotiations began in earnest, on 31 October 1939. Riverdale presented his proposals to a meeting of the Emergency Council. Prior to this presentation, cabinet ministers held a brief discussion, during which King reminded the others of the proposal's origin and its acceptance in principle. Ralston expressed concern over the magnitude of the financing that would be involved. It would be necessary for the government to fit this plan into the totality of the demands that the war in general, and the British in particular, would make on us. The discussion then moved briefly to how financing this training plan related to the question of who was to pay for the cost of equipping and maintaining the squadrons to be formed from the Canadians trained under the plan.

Riverdale presented cabinet with two documents setting forth the details of the plan and its estimated costs. The total estimated cost for the forty months leading up to March 1943 was $888.5 million. Riverdale proposed that Britain would supply the initial needed equipment – mainly aircraft and engines, estimated to cost about $140 million – as a "free contribution." As for the balance, Riverdale proposed that Canada bear one half of this cost, and Australia and

New Zealand bear the other half. This implied a Canadian share of approximately $374 million. Captain Balfour gave some figures on the scale of the Royal Air Force program in Britain and its enormous expected costs.

In his response to Riverdale, King took umbrage at the suggestion that the Dominion Training Scheme was a Canadian proposal to which Britain should make a free contribution. He said that all Canadian contributions to the war effort were free contributions to a common cause. (King went so far as to state that "it is not our war," which shocked the British, as the high commissioner later told O.D. Skelton, undersecretary of state for external affairs. They did not realize that he meant by this that "it is not our war only," as was evident from the context of the discussion.) King went on to say that Canada could not go beyond her resources and would proceed subject to the advice of the minister of finance, with whom, along with the minister of national defence, the proposals would have to be discussed in detail. King noted finally that the scheme made no mention of the maintenance of Canadian squadrons in the field. National feeling, he thought, would require that certain distinctly Canadian forces be maintained overseas. As if ignoring King's comments, Riverdale responded, according to Mackenzie's notes, that the UK would take the newly trained pilots and aircrew into the RAF and be responsible for their maintenance on the fighting fronts. (He forecast the cost of one hundred fighting squadrons at $1.5 billion per annum.)

Ralston then launched into a lengthy and detailed statement. He asserted that Canada's fiscal capacity would not enable her to come "within shooting distance" of the figures suggested by the British mission. Ralston assessed Canada's fiscal capacity with reference to the country's national income, which he forecast to be $4.11 billion for the first twelve months of the war. He set the limit that could be diverted to governmental and war purposes, either spending or lending, at forty-two per cent. Apart from war expenditures, total governmental expenditures – Dominion, provincial, and municipal – were $1.13 billion, plus loans of $40 million. Defence programs that the country had already committed to were estimated to cost $320 million. The sum of these expenditures totalled $1.49 billion. Deducting this figure from forty-two per cent of the national income left $237 million available for the Dominion Training Scheme and other requirements, notably financing British expenditures in Canada, of which $93 million had already been arranged.[9]

Ralston's presentation was apparently based on the figures in a memorandum he had received that day from Graham Towers, governor of the Bank of Canada, though no doubt Ralston had discussed the subject with Towers and Clark in advance.[10] It was the same basic argument and figures that Thomas Crerar and Towers used later in conversations in London in November 1939. (See chapter 4.) These figures referred to the first twelve months of war. Mackenzie quotes me as saying during a subsequent meeting that the estimated Canadian share of the Dominion Training Scheme's costs in that year would be between $30 million and $32 million, which was not a large part of $237 million. Ralston was putting too much emphasis on the total figures for a period of forty months. In Ralston's defence, the plan was accelerated in 1940, and given their emergencies at home, the British were unable to deliver the initial complement of aircraft and equipment required under the scheme. The total cost and the Canadian share turned out to be more than was forecast, but by 1940, Canadian war expenditures were regarded as signs of national success in overcoming political obstacles.

Following the somewhat tense meeting of 31 October, negotiations over the Dominion Training Scheme proceeded for another ten meetings, culminating in a series of sessions on Sunday, 26 November 1939, preparatory to a meeting the next day with the prime minister and other ministers in advance of the departure of the delegates from Australia and New Zealand. Over the course of these meetings, the cost estimates were reviewed and amended, and various alternative cost-sharing arrangements were considered. The only substantive changes to the plan resulted from the desire of Australia and New Zealand to decrease their input of trainees to numbers proportional to their population in comparison with Canada. These changes reduced the scale of the training plan in Canada, although the Canadian ministers agreed that Canada would provide pupils to fill one service-flying training school left vacant by Australia's reduced number of trainees.

The details of the program and the estimated costs had to be revised twice to accommodate the reduced input of Australian and New Zealand trainees. In addition to these changes, the contribution of the UK in planes and other equipment was increased. As a result, the total cost of the training was estimated on 26 November 1939 at $607 million (instead of the original $888 million); of this the elementary training of Canadians would be done separately by the RCAF at an estimated cost of $68 million. The British contribution in kind was then estimated at $185 million; this left $354 million to be shared among Canada, Australia, and New Zealand. Agreement on these shares was reached that day.[11]

The Canadian share of the joint training was set at $285 million (80.64 per cent of the total cost), which together with the $68 million for elementary training involved a total expected cost for Canada of

$353 million. This figure was only $21 million less than what Riverdale originally proposed. Britain's willingness to supply more aircraft largely was offset by the cost to Canada of picking up the slack from the reduced Australian input in the program. These figures exclude the costs of training in Australia and New Zealand, to which the UK, but not Canada, would contribute.

While Britain, Australia, and New Zealand were prepared to initial an agreement reflecting these terms that day, the Canadian ministers were not, because King had stipulated two conditions that had to be met before Canada would commit to participate. These were discussed at a meeting of the Emergency Council the following day.[12] One of King's conditions for participation, that the general financial discussions between Canada and Britain then taking place in London should lead to a mutually and reasonably satisfying agreement, had been adequately met thanks to an assurance from Chamberlain in a telegram that day.[13] Not met, however, was the other condition, "that the Canadian government should receive an assurance, which they would be at liberty to announce if they so wished, that in the opinion of the UK War Cabinet the British Commonwealth Air Training Plan had preference over any other commitments in Canada's war effort, other than those already entered into." Chamberlain's reply on this point was not satisfactory to King or the Emergency Council. The leading members of the three overseas missions then joined the meeting and were informed of this conclusion. It was recognized that under the circumstances, the Canadian government could not initial the agreement. It was agreed that an announcement would be made, stating simply that the representatives of the four governments had worked out a basis of agreement that was being referred to their respective governments for decision. The request for assurance of the British Commonwealth Air Training Plan's priority over other new commitments was settled by an exchange of telegrams with Chamberlain during the next ten days.

THE QUESTION OF RCAF SQUADRONS

From its inception, the British Commonwealth Air Training Plan primarily was an arrangement to attract and train Royal Air Force recruits from Canada, Australia, and New Zealand. Britain not only lacked Canada's uncluttered and invulnerable skies, but it was about to be short of manpower as well.[14] Article 14 of the agreement stipulates that a small fraction of the schools' output was to be made available to fill vacancies in Home Defence Squadrons of the RCAF but then goes on to state: "All the other pupils on completion of their training, will be placed at the disposal of the government of the United Kingdom, subject to that government making the arrangements indicated in Article 15 and bearing liability as provided for in Articles 16 and 17 of this agreement."[15] Articles 16 and 17 together required the UK to provide, at the rates laid down in RAF regulations, pay, allowances, pensions and other non-effective benefits, and maintenance and other expenses for the pilots and aircrews who had been trained in Canada. If the government of the Dominion from which the recruit had come wished to supplement these rates, it could do so.

A controversy arose quickly between the Canadian ministers, led by King and the Riverdale mission, which was being instructed by the British War Cabinet, over the proper interpretation of Article 15, which read as follows: "The United Kingdom Government undertakes that pupils of Canada, Australia and New Zealand shall, after training is completed, be identified with their respective Dominions, either by the method of organizing Dominion units and formations or in some other way, such methods to be agreed on with the respective Dominions concerned. The United Kingdom Government will initiate intergovernmental discussions to this end."

King, Rogers, and other ministers had stated on several occasions during the negotiations that Canada would wish to form some RCAF squadrons overseas with pilots and aircrew trained in the British Commonwealth Air Training Plan.[16] This matter had not been discussed in any detail, however, and reliance was being placed on this article. Once the wording of the article had been settled, Rogers discussed the matter with Riverdale. On 8 December 1939, Rogers wrote to Riverdale asking him to confirm his understanding "that Canadian personnel from the training plan will, on request from the Canadian government, be organized into Royal Canadian Air Force units and formations in the field." Riverdale sent him an immediate reply saying that Article 15 of the agreement implied that Canadian government requests to incorporate Canadian pupils trained in Canada under the British Commonwealth Air Training Scheme into RCAF units in the field would, "in all circumstances in which it is feasible," be readily accepted by the government of the United Kingdom.[17]

The qualification was immediately deemed unsatisfactory, first by Rogers, then by King and Ralston. Ralston discussed this with Riverdale and then with Sir Gerald Campbell, the British high commissioner, who strongly urged the Canadians to sign the agreement and leave the interpretation of the offending article to the good judgment of the two governments. King was most emphatic that this was an important matter of principle, and that similar issues had given rise to trouble in the previous war. The matter would have to be taken up with London.

The reply from London, which was received through the high commissioner and the Riverdale mission, and was considered rather sympathetically by the chief of air staff and deputy minister for air, proposed that RCAF squadrons might be organized overseas at such time as sufficient Canadian aircrews and ground crews were available. This, however, was quite unacceptable to cabinet as it would limit the number of RCAF squadrons in the field and would not satisfy public sentiment in Canada.

There was another wrangle between the Canadian ministers and the British mission on 14 December 1939.[18] Canadian ministers argued that never in any of the past discussions had there been any suggestion that Canada would supply ground crews for these new overseas squadrons. Riverdale countered that if the UK were to provide the ground crews four-fifths of the personnel in the squadrons would be RAF, not RCAF. Some suggested that the Canadian ground crews working in the British Commonwealth Air Training Plan might be replaced by British crews so that Canadians could go over to RCAF squadrons, but this was dismissed by Ottawa as "offending common sense and inefficient."

THE LAST STAGES

King met with Riverdale and worked out a compromise. The UK government would, at the request of the Canadian government, arrange that Canadian personnel from the training plan would be organized as Royal Canadian Air Force units in the field, with the methods by which this would be done to be arranged by an intergovernmental committee. While Riverdale was waiting to sign this letter, he received another message from London directing him to add the following paragraph setting a financial limit on the RCAF units to be formed: "It would be a condition that the factor governing the numbers of such pupils to be so incorporated at any one time should be the financial contribution which the Canadian Government have already declared themselves ready to make toward the cost of the training scheme." [19] This was badly expressed and not supported by any reasoned argument. It reflected a general principle to which the British Treasury adhered: that the Dominions should be expected to support their military units financially in the field. It had not been possible to work this into the British Commonwealth Air Training Plan as the latter was essentially an operation in support of the British Royal Air Force. When the Canadians pressed for the formation of a substantial number of recognizable RCAF squadrons, the Treasury thought it reasonable to count toward the cost of paying and supporting such squadrons the amount that Canada was spending in support of training for the RAF. The Treasury officials explained and discussed this idea on 13 December 1939 in London with Graham Towers and Lester B. Pearson (from the Canadian High Commission there) in attendance.[20]

Unfortunately, Pearson sent the account of their discussion to Ottawa by mail rather than by cable so we did not receive the rationale of their proposal before the British Commonwealth Air Training Plan Agreement was signed.

King would not accede to financial limitation on the formation of RCAF units out of pupils trained in the BCATP, although Skelton had drawn his attention a number of times to the huge potential cost of equipping and maintaining RCAF squadrons in the field, warning that "if we call the tune we should pay the Piper."[21] King drafted a lengthy cable to Chamberlain, including in it the various drafts of the letters about Article 15, although he appears to have known that Chamberlain was in France and would not see the cable in time. The next day, King managed to bully Riverdale into signing the draft letter he had agreed to before hearing from the Air Ministry.

After a series of personal conversations with Riverdale and Sir Robert Brooke-Popham on 16 December, during which King insisted on getting the Governor General, who was in his sick bed, to lecture Brooke-Popham on his duty, he managed to get Riverdale to sign the Air Training Agreement along with him, a few minutes after midnight on 17 December 1939, King's birthday.[22]

King had gained all his objectives, and without impairing the substance of the BCATP. The Air Ministry in the UK felt that everything had turned out well. However, as J.L. Granatstein reports, "the Chancellor of the Exchequer was gloomy, pointing out to the War Cabinet that he had sent no congratulatory telegrams after the signing of the agreement. He had not agreed that Canada could insist on unlimited units of the RCAF being provided at the expense of the United Kingdom taxpayer."[23]

The chancellor did not have to foot much of a bill. For administrative and operational reasons, the new RCAF squadrons were slow in forming; in the meantime, Canada was financing the purchase of equipment for the training plan that Britain was unable to supply because their production skills and materials were needed at home. Britain and Canada agreed that twenty-five RCAF squadrons would be formed as the trained Canadian pilots and aircrew became ready and available. In January 1943, the Canadian Cabinet War Committee agreed in principle that Canada would, as of 1 April 1943, assume full financial responsibility for equipping "the 35 RCAF squadrons now forming or to be formed in the United Kingdom." Canada also would provide the full pay and allowances, clothing, and other necessities of Canadian pilots and aircrew serving in the RAF.[24] This was part of a broad revision of Canadian financing of British requirements in Canada (described in chapters 4 and 8 below).

The formation of RCAF units did not absorb as much as half of the Canadian aircrew trained in the British Commonwealth Air Training Plan. In August 1944 there were 17,111 RCAF aircrew in Royal Air Force units as compared with 993 in overseas RCAF units and formations. At the end of 1944, there were forty-six RCAF squadrons overseas, including fourteen in No. 6 Bomber Group, seventeen in North-West Europe, one in Italy, and two in Burma. Aircrew casualties at times were heavy, particularly among the bombers groups.[25]

In 1942, the original British Commonwealth Air Training Plan was revised and extended to 31 March 1945, without the bickering and hard bargaining that was so conspicuous in the 1939 discussions.[26] The plan concluded on schedule, having achieved its purpose, producing 131,553 trained aircrew for the air forces of Canada, Britain, Australia, and New Zealand. At war's end, the amounts of Britain's share still outstanding would be dealt with in comprehensive financial settlements between Britain and Canada.[27]

CHAPTER FOUR

Financing Britain

On 9 April 1940, Hitler resumed the war with an invasion of Denmark and Norway. The "phoney war" was over. One month later, on 10 May 1940, he launched a blitzkrieg on the Netherlands, Belgium, and France. The attack coincided with a change of government in Great Britain, with Winston Churchill replacing the apostle of appeasement, Neville Chamberlain, as prime minister. The main thrust of the German attack on France was through Luxembourg and the Ardennes forest. It caught the French and British forces completely off guard. The German Panzer Divisions broke through the feeble French defences and raced across northern France, splitting the Allied armies and trapping nearly the entire British army on the beaches of Dunkirk. Only by heroic efforts did the British succeed in achieving a massive evacuation of 330,000 troops. Overwhelmed by the speed and audacity of the German attack, the French capitulated, on 22 June. Germany was now in control of western and central Europe, but Britain had not been defeated.

While Britain was hanging on militarily, the war was putting an increasingly heavy strain on its finances. Without the help of its friends and allies – particularly Canada and the United States – Britain would not be able to procure the munitions and supplies necessary to defend itself.

Within this environment, the task for officials at the Department of Finance was to determine "a logical economic limit" to Canada's financial capacity to help its ally during wartime. Coming up with a sensible and practical package of measures would require political courage and economic acumen. Finance officials demonstrated both. Consequently, Canada gave its ally "munitions of war" worth $1 billion, in an act of unprecedented generosity.

There was, however, an element of national self-interest in all of this. Canada's wartime prosperity and industrial prowess relied on British orders for equipment and supplies. The grant, which was announced in January 1942 and accompanied by an interest-free loan of $700 million and other assistance, was expected to last approximately fifteen months. Instead, it was depleted before *the year ended and ultimately was succeeded in May 1943 by Mutual Aid (the subject of chapter 7). Nonetheless, Canada's gift dramatically illustrated the importance of her material contribution to the Allied cause.*

This chapter chronicles the department's efforts in procuring the billion-dollar gift.

Canada's financing of British wartime requirements was one of the few subjects that the appropriate authorities in Britain and Canada had discussed in the months before the war broke out. It was evident that financing Britain would present a problem because in peacetime Britain had a trade deficit with Canada (even in the 1930s it had carried a deficit on its balance of payments with Canada). These deficits usually were financed by Britain through payments of US dollars to Canada, in amounts within the current account surplus that the sterling area had with the United States. Canada used these US dollars to meet its deficits with the United States.[1] This payment pattern was likely to be affected and unbalanced by war in numerous respects, the most significant being a probable increase of British purchases in Canada and the United States.

The British Treasury took the initiative in proposing exploratory discussion of the subject with Canadian officials. The chancellor of the exchequer wrote to the Canadian minister of finance, Charles Dunning, on 12 April 1939, a few weeks after Hitler's takeover of Czechoslovakia. The chancellor proposed that J.A.C. Osborne of the Bank of England, who had been deputy governor of the Bank of Canada until seven months before this, visit Ottawa to discuss the question of financing Britain in case of war. Dunning agreed, and Osborne arrived later that April. Dunning, who was ill, asked Clark and Towers to discuss the matter with Osborne and report to him on their conversations.

British authorities estimated that their total requirements from Canada in the first year of a major war (including items imported as a matter of course during peacetime) would total £126 million. Taking other, normal sources of payments into account, the British would need to "fund from somewhere" at least $100 million Canadian to finance their needs.[2] The British authorities wished to know the attitude the Canadian government would take if Britain wished to borrow a sum of about that amount in the Canadian market. In the discussions, Clark favoured the UK's issuing of such a loan in Canada before the war; Dunning confirmed this at a meeting on 13 May. Dunning also said that Canada would help the UK to finance its needs in Canada during a war. Some details were discussed at the meeting, but the British representatives did not indicate whether their government would issue a pre-war loan.

The idea of a UK bond issue in Canada was a non-starter for reasons that are not clear, apart from the fact that a good alternative was available in the "repatriation" of Canadian government securities held by British investors that, by arrangement between the governments, could be brought back before maturity by the Canadian government. Sayers also mentions the possibility of the Canadian government's borrowing of US dollars in New York as a means of helping to finance such "repatriation." The Bank of Canada archives contain a copy of a cable from Towers to Catterns, deputy governor of the Bank of England, stating that "Morgan Stanley have advised us not to issue a loan in New York at present time, partly because of market conditions and partly because they fear that refunding of a sterling issue would cause too much public comment at a time when the European situation is so dangerously unsettled."[3]

The exploratory discussions with Osborne seem to have satisfied both sides that a means to finance Britain's wartime requirements in Canada could and would be found. Such an arrangement probably would start with repatriation of Canada's sterling bonds, but no decision as to dollar amounts was made. According to the official historian of British financial policy, Richard Sayers, the British were advised that Canada's need for US dollars likely would increase in wartime and that at least some of these dollars would have to come from Britain as partial payment for its purchases in Canada.[4]

Notwithstanding this pre-war consultation, and Canada's willingness to help with financing,[5] there was considerable reluctance on the part of the British to place munitions orders in Canada during 1939 and also some lack of coordination and consistency in making purchases of traditional British imports from Canada in the early weeks of the war.[6] Both of these situations implied concern in London about financing and a shortage of dollars. Osborne was sent to Ottawa again in October, this time to be joined by Sir James Rae, head of the UK Purchasing Mission. Osborne and Rae met with Clark, Towers, and, from External Affairs, N.A. Robertson. These officials quickly agreed that all credit facilities should be provided by the Canadian government, not by suppliers, as the UK purchasers had suggested in the case of base metal contracts. They also discussed total UK requirements in the first year of war and possible security issues. Towers stated clearly that it would not be feasible for Canada to finance the whole of the UK's net adverse balance in payments to and from Canada; Canada would need payment in gold or US dollars to meet the cost of increased imports of defence supplies into the country from the United States. Moreover, where Canada's ability to help finance the UK war effort was concerned, timing was important, since Canadian production and incomes had to be expanded before savings were available to borrow.⁷

Osborne reported to Phillips in London, and the Treasury replied with an initial estimate setting the balance of payments in favour of Canada in the first year of a war at $325 to $400 million Canadian. The Treasury agreed that Canadian suppliers of war materials should be paid in Canadian dollars. All credit arrangements should be centralized and cleared between the two governments, but the same should not apply to all individual remittances. The Treasury suggested that the Bank of Canada provide the UK government with Canadian dollars in Ottawa in exchange for sterling, which would be credited to the Bank of Canada in London. Repatriation of Canadian government securities should be used to reduce the balance of sterling in the Bank of Canada account. Phillips suggested that "if arrangements could be made by which we could in effect borrow whole or large part of remaining balance accruing to Canada arising out of United Kingdom–Canada transactions we should be prepared to guarantee a fixed rate of exchange for it."⁸ Phillips agreed with Osborne that Britain should not pressure Canada for unknown amounts of dollars over unlimited periods, and that there should be a ceiling placed on the amounts Britain could request from Canada. Phillips added: "In view of the large figures involved it is important for us to have some idea of what this maximum may be. Without this it is not possible for us to make any useful estimate of what our dollar position may be in say six months and then year's time." He wanted to strike an arrangement for a year, with fresh negotiations to occur toward the end of that period.⁹

The immediate result of these negotiations was an arrangement to repatriate the outstanding UK holdings of the government of Canada's 3.5 per cent loan, which was due in 1950. This involved about $91 million (after allowing for the sinking fund). The discussion of a maximum amount, such as Phillips wanted, became enmeshed in the discussions about the British Commonwealth Air Training Plan (described in chapter 3 above). Canada insisted that its share of the BCATP costs over the first year of war be deducted in determining how much was available for financing British requirements during a war. The implications of this concerned the British: not only did it limit the amount of financing that they could expect to receive, it also seemed to abrogate the results of the lengthy negotiation regarding appropriate cost sharing within the BCATP itself.

CALCULATING CANADA'S CAPACITY TO FINANCE

The placing of some limitations on the aggregate of Canada's financing – or planned financing – of its own war expenditures and of UK requirements was in keeping with normal peacetime budgeting practices. Such limitations also followed from the development of a logical basis for determining the maximum economic effort that Canada could put into the war. Officials at the Bank of Canada and Clark in the Department of Finance felt that this could be determined best as a proportion of the national income. Estimates of national income had just come into vogue, and the basic concepts of national accounts, in economic terms, were still being developed. The statistical methods of estimating national income were not yet reliable. Hailing largely from the Bank of Canada, the staff of the Royal Commission on Dominion–Provincial Relations worked out estimates that they believed were better than the higher estimates coming out of the Dominion Bureau of Statistics. Clark felt that the commission's estimates were the best available.

There were two major difficulties involved in using estimates of national income as the basis of making decisions about the maximum economic effort Canada could put into a war. The first was the trickiness of forecasting the national income in any given year – which was made still more difficult since in this case the year in question covered the first twelve months of a war. This posed problems because it involved a radical expansion of the workforce in an economy that was operating well below capacity. After years of depression, the employability of the unemployed was not known – nor was the suitability of available industrial capacity to meeting new types of demand. A very rough guess was made that the national income for the first year of war could be expected to be at most fifteen per cent higher (in current prices) than the estimate of national income for the relatively depressed year of 1938. The 1938 estimate was $3.575 billion, so the outside figure for the first war year was estimated at $4.111 billion. (Estimates published by the Bank of Canada after the war, in 1946, showed $3.9 billion for 1938, $4.2 billion for 1939, and $5.1 billion for 1940.)[10]

The second difficulty was judging the feasible percentage of national income to devote to governmental purposes, including war expenditures and financing Britain. Towers sent a memorandum from the Bank of Canada, entitled "Notes on Canada's War Potential" and dated 31 October 1939, to Clark.[11] The memorandum, which appears to have been written by Alex Skelton, states: "Even a totalitarian country such as Germany, which has been arming at top speed for three years, has not found it possible to push the ratio much beyond

50%." The memo argued that it could be assumed that Great Britain would make the maximum effort possible to finance its wartime requirements, but even with two years of intensive preparation, her ratio was unlikely to exceed forty-seven per cent during the first year of war. The Canadian upper limit (beyond which it could not go without risking a serious degree of disorganization) was likely to be much lower than the forty-seven per cent British ratio, for three reasons. First, the UK was a unitary state with full control of public expenditure, whereas Canada had a "loose federal structure." Second, the Canadian people did not experience "daily reminders that they were fighting for their lives and were therefore unlikely, at first, to be willing to sacrifice their freedom and standard of living to the same extent as the U.K." Third, UK preparations for the economic shift to war had been more extensive in both time and scale than Canada's. The memorandum concludes that "it will undoubtedly be possible for Canada to go farther in the second year of war than it can in the first. Even in the first year, if, having aimed at a ratio of 40%, we find that the shift in our economy is taking place relatively smoothly we can step up the objective. But it seems likely that to aim substantially higher than 40% in the first instance and to take unnecessary chances of disorganization would be of service neither to ourselves nor to our allies."

In his covering letter, Towers suggested committing a bit more than the $154 million that his staff's figures indicated (after deducting non-war expenditures of the municipalities, provinces, and the Dominion, as well as the $320 million of Dominion defence expenditures "already accounted for." After Clark, and presumably the minister, had gone over this analysis, they cabled T.A. Crerar in London. (Crerar, who re-entered the Liberal cabinet in 1935 as the minister of mines and resources, had gone to England in the fall of 1939 to discuss the level of Canada's contribution for financing British wartime expenditures.) The cable, dated 8 November 1939, advised Crerar to revise the figures in "the secret financial memorandum" given to him for the purposes of discussion with the British.[12] The telegram told him to use the figure of $3.575 billion to represent Canada's national income in 1938, and allow "as much as a 15% increase" for the first year of war, that is, to $4.111 billion. The total public expenditures (including loans other than those to the provinces) of the Dominion, provinces, and municipalities, including war expenditures already committed, was $1.490 billion.

The message goes on to state that if it was assumed that the Canadian government could appropriate as much as forty-three per cent of the estimated national income, this would mean $1.727 billion, which would leave a margin of only $237 million to cover financial assistance for British purchases in Canada and for the British Commonwealth Air Training Plan.

The message admitted that it was "obviously optimistic" to assume that Canadian governments could divert so large a percentage of national income during the first year of war. It admitted further that the "margin" of $237 million could "only be made available on the assumption of prompt and substantial British purchases in Canada and on the further assumption of drastic economies in our peacetime expenditures and probable early imposition of rationing programs." The message went on to discuss comparative figures for the United Kingdom based on the estimates of a British statistician, Colin Clark, and concluded that Britain was taking "under 47%" of its national income out of current production.[13]

This was the analysis used by Finance, essentially Clark, to try to establish a logical economic limit to Canada's financial capacity for war expenditures, including financing Britain. The analysis was crude, based on unreliable statistics and rough comparisons. In hindsight it is clear that the documents contained some analytical weaknesses: no effort was made, for example, to allow for Canadian war expenditures in Britain. Indeed, the Canadian figures were later, in 1940, criticized by British Treasury Officers.[14] Sayers, in his official British history of financial policy, written in the mid-1950s, sums up this Canadian venture into the realm of statistics as follows:

The probable error in the calculations could be several times as great as the residual figure of possible assistance to the United Kingdom. There was, however, no point in shooting all the possible criticisms at the Canadians, for nothing constructive could come out of it – there were not in existence the figures to support an agreement, even if the experts could agree on precise interpretation of the figures. The Canadian approach could be – and was – accepted as an attempt in good faith to settle on a scientific basis the distribution of a common burden between two single-minded nations. It gave a foretaste of the international discussions that were to be prompted by another defence need more than a decade later.[15]

On a personal note, I might interject here that I participated in some of the department's work on these calculations. The departmental records contain a calculation, made in early October 1939, of the ratio of public expenditures to national income, using the Bureau of Statistics figures, which were higher than those used by the Bank but closer to the figures now accepted for that period. I also found a carbon copy of an unfinished, unsigned memorandum, almost certainly written by me, titled "What Proportion of the National Income

Can Be Taken for Defence and Other Governmental Expenditures," in which I conclude that the maximum amount was probably between forty per cent and forty-five per cent.[16] The analysis is not very detailed; for example, it does not take into account the nature of the expenditures as compared with the nature of the available capacity, which was of great importance at that time. In that paper, which J.L. Granatstein attributes to me, I explain why Canadians could not be expected to devote as much of their national income to the war as the British.[17] I have not been able to find the original of the memorandum or discover whether it ever reached Clark or the minister. I believed at that time that we could and should increase our national income more rapidly than the Bank was estimating. This view is expressed to some degree in a 1 September 1939 memorandum I wrote on war financial policy and is reflected in the budget speech of 12 September. In a memorandum dated 15 December 1940, I state: "My own conclusion is that the percentage of national income guide is too rough and unreliable for the purposes of the Minister of Finance. In fact I think experience indicates we gravely underestimated our ability, and apparently Britain did so as well – though probably not using this method."[18]

THE CRERAR MISSION TO LONDON

T.A. Crerar of Manitoba, the minister of mines and resources, and the most senior of the western ministers, was charged with going to London to present the views about the scale of possible Canadian contributions to financing British expenditures in Canada. He was mostly concerned about the lack of any British purchases of wheat since the war had begun, and tried repeatedly and unsuccessfully while in London to make a substantial contract for wheat. All of his efforts foundered, however, on the inability of British and Canadian cabinets to agree on a price. (See chapter 2.) Crerar had several officials with him in London, as well as the resident diplomats and officers, but no one from Finance. He was expected, therefore, to address Britain's central financial question based solely on the papers he had been provided. He asked repeatedly for a man from Finance or the Bank of Canada to join him, and later specifically requested either Clark or Towers. Ralston got the prime minister to prevail upon Towers to go. Towers consented, travelling via the Clipper Flying Boat from New York to Lisbon.

Towers got to the heart of the financial issues, meeting alone with Sir Frederick Phillips in London the day before Crerar's group formally met with the chancellor of the exchequer and others at the Treasury. Towers's own written account of this high-level negotiation is so good that it should be quoted in full. It is contained in a letter of 23 January 1940 written from the Bank of Canada upon his return after a long and gloomy delay in the Azores.

Conversation with Sir Frederick Phillips
Sir Frederick Phillips asked me to see him the day before the meeting at the Treasury. He referred first to the comparisons which had been made between the war efforts of Canada and Great Britain based on figures of national income, and to a memorandum which he had written commenting on our latest presentation. He indicated that his memorandum was a rather hasty effort. I said that we could argue forever about details of such estimates, but that it was unnecessary to do so if one regarded them simply as a general approach to the problem. On that basis, I felt that the figures indicated that Canada's programs for the first year of the war represented a very substantial and serious effort. We agreed that it was unnecessary to pursue the national income subject any further.

We then turned to the estimates of the deficiency in the U.K.'s balance of payments with Canada during the first twelve months of the war. I told him that after allowing for repatriation in the amount of $191 millions (based on a total amount available of $237 millions, minus the then current estimate of our share of air training costs – $46 millions) we anticipated a deficiency of some $46/124 millions. He said that his estimates were approximately £16 millions. Having in mind that estimates cannot be absolutely accurate at this time, we were in substantial agreement. I pointed out that our repatriation commitment was a heavy one in the light of other war expenditures: that elimination of their deficiency by curtailment of purchases would affect our economic situation and necessitate a downward revision of the amount to be repatriated; and that we must ask them to cover the deficiency in the form of gold or U.S. dollars. Sir Frederick Phillips said that he considered our offer a generous one, and he was prepared to accept the situation as we outlined it, but that there was one point which worried him. We had taken a figure of $237 millions and deducted our share of the air training scheme costs for the first twelve months. Would we use the same figures and the same formula in succeeding years, when our share of air training scheme costs would greatly increase, thus reducing repatriation to much smaller amounts? I said that the figure of $237 millions referred only to the first twelve months of the war. The character and extent of our war effort in subsequent years were matters for later discussion, but the U.K. could rely on our cooperation to the limit of our capacity. He then said that, "There is no further problem."

Meeting at the Treasury, December 1st
Sir John Simon referred to the conversation which I had had with Phillips on the preceding day, and said he understood that everything had been settled

satisfactorily. He evidently wanted to discuss wheat. We thought it advisable, however, to go over the ground already covered with Phillips for the benefit of the others present. As you will have read in the Minutes, Sir John Simon then said that he considered our offer generous, and was prepared to recommend it to his Government. During this meeting at the Treasury, as well as in conversations with Mr. Chamberlain, Phillips and others, I took pains to say that in considering the maximum effort which we could make, we did *not* have in mind the maximum we could do in comfort, but rather what could be accomplished by dint of sacrifice. In conversation with Mr. Chamberlain on this subject, I added that Mr. King and George Watts had both told me that curtailment of consumption, import restrictions, etc. entered into our conception of the effort which we could make in case of need. I am referring below to some of the implications of this attitude. At the risk of labouring the point, I may say that I was firmly convinced that – while the English would not admit it – they had doubts as to whether Canada was prepared to make really severe sacrifices of the character referred to above. So long as they have some doubts of this kind, they tend to accept with some reserve statements to the effect that we are doing all we can, and therefore are unable to agree to proposals which they may make for additional contributions of one kind or another. I found it impossible to judge whether my remarks had any effect, but I am sure they did not harm.[19]

The arrangements agreed to in London were summarized by the Bank of England and given by Towers to Ralston as follows:

Our estimated net requirements of Canadian dollars for the first full year of the war vary between $240 and $320 million. Of this, the net amount the Canadians will be able to supply is, say, $200 million of which they have already provided, say, $100 million by repatriation. These figures leave a gap of $40–120 million which we shall have to provide in Cash (gold or U.S. dollars). They proposed a sequence along the following lines: (1) $100 million by the use of their existing balance which arose almost entirely from repatriation already done. (2) $45 million to be provided by cash (i.e. gold). (3) $65 million to be provided by a second repatriation or temporary accumulation of sterling balances. The total of these would be $210 million. The remaining amount of $30 to $110 million would be financed as to $35 million on the same basis as (3) and the balance by gold with the details to be settled when the $210 million is nearly used up. It was added that should Canada find it possible to increase her provision of dollars over and above the $200 million, she will do so.

JANUARY TO JUNE 1940

Such were the provisions that Canada had with the UK as it entered the fateful year of 1940. The financial arrangements detailed above were put into practice during the first half of that year.[20] The British were conscious, however, that their expenditure commitments in Canada were exceeding their forecasts. They did not take this up with the Department of Finance until the disastrous campaign in Norway ended the "phoney war" and the British forecasts were rendered obsolete.[21] Right up to the surrender of France in late June, British contracts placed in Canada were nearly all for food and raw materials, not for arms.[22]

At this time, attitudes in Ottawa were changing rapidly. Early in April (soon after the Canadian election), Norman Rogers, the minister of national defence, went to London to deal with a variety of matters relating to the Canadian forces and their relationship to the British services and supply authorities. He was there during the Norwegian campaign in April and the brilliant and devastating German invasion of Holland and Belgium. He arrived back in Ottawa on 17 May 1940, when that great battle was at its height. He reported immediately to the prime minister, who recorded in his diary for that day: "Clearly the [British] government from the time of Munich and perhaps before did not ever take seriously enough the German preparations."[23] Later that day Rogers reported to the Cabinet War Committee. He emphasized that the UK suffered from a thorough lack of preparation for mechanized warfare, both in equipment for the army and aircraft for the Royal Air Force. He went on to emphasize that the vital industrial centres in Britain, such as Sheffield, were concentrated and vulnerable to air attacks. The Germans now would be able to send fighters to protect their bombers from bases in Holland and Belgium.

After hearing Rogers's report (as well as being informed through other channels), the prime minister called for more decisive action. "The Empire is in extremis and we must say now what further steps we are prepared to take."[24] As a result, the War Cabinet decided immediately to form, in the field, an army corps of two divisions. It was further decided, in later meetings, that Canada would send another RCAF army co-operation squadron to the UK to back up the one already there, and would send the four available naval destroyers to England at once to help in defence of the United Kingdom itself. An army brigade with other support units would be sent to garrison Iceland. Smaller units would garrison the British West Indies. The one fully equipped and trained fighter squadron of the RCAF was also sent to serve with the RAF fighter squadrons in the defence of Britain.[25]

On 27 May 1940, King received a cable from Churchill saying that he now expected that France was going to give up altogether. The evacuation of the British Army at Dunkirk began on this day. King had also received a very secret message from President Roosevelt expressing concern about the danger to Britain itself and what might happen to the Royal Navy. Faced with this very serious crisis, King apparently recognized that further and more expensive action probably was going to be needed; he recorded in his diary that he felt the only way to get Ralston to "loosen up" on the Treasury was to let him know the inside information as he had it. He also felt that Rogers, the defence minister, and of course Power, the defence minister for air, should be informed. King told his ministers of Churchill's cable and Roosevelt's concern. "They were naturally well nigh stunned."[26]

This was the turning point. From this point in 1940 and on the Canadian services were permitted to make new expenditure commitments beyond what had been so far approved, and the recently appointed minister of munitions and supply, C.D. Howe, was permitted to approve contracts to produce arms and ammunition in response to British requests even though the means of financing them had not been worked out. These means of financing British requirements were to occupy the Department of Finance time and time again until the end of the war.

Similar decisions were being reached in London during the early summer of 1940, though on a much larger scale and with far greater risks. The British government decided in June that the risk of losing the war in the short term was so great that all their gold and dollar reserves must be committed to essential purchases of war equipment, munitions, and supplies, mainly from the United States. This was advised first by the chief of staff and then by the civilian advisers on shipping and other matters.[27] The British would place orders with the United States (and later would take over the contracts already placed by the French) that could only be paid for at the cost of all their liquid reserves and, indeed, perhaps would require the sale of marketable investments. They had to hope and expect that President Roosevelt would be re-elected in November for a third term, itself an unprecedented event, and that he could and would persuade Congress to provide Britain with what it needed to go on fighting. It was a desperate political gamble and an act of faith, which, in the end, of course, was justified and led to victory for the United Nations; it also led, however, to the loss of Britain's status as a great power.

FINANCING BRITAIN AFTER THE FALL OF FRANCE

A meeting was held in Ottawa in July 1940 between Towers and Clark on the Canadian side, and Phillips, Osborne, and others on the British side, to determine a financing plan for the second year of war, which was soon to begin. The British estimated their deficit for the twelve months beginning 1 July 1940 at $636 million Canadian, with a probable $250 million of that coming in the first six months (to 31 December). The Canadians were not willing to agree to a twelve-month plan at that time but would provide $150 million during the six months starting 1 August 1940, leaving the balance to be settled "in cash," that is, gold. During August, British needs were covered out of British balances and gold; the use of further Canadian financing began in September and involved repatriation of the four per cent Grand Trunk Perpetual Stock (guaranteed by the Dominion) in an amount equivalent to $85 million. There were British capital receipts from Canada for various other stocks, bonds, and mortgages coming due, and sales in Canada of other UK holdings that had been vested and sold by agents here, bringing the total repatriation as of 15 February 1941 to $315 million, of which $184 million had been completed by 31 July. The second-year program was to begin on 1 August 1941 and involved $131 million in repatriation to 15 February 1942, when the whole program had to be re-examined to take into account the effects of Lend-Lease arrangements.[28]

During the first year of war, the British had paid $185 million Canadian in gold for Canadian dollars, an amount almost identical to the amount of repatriation of securities ($184 million); Canada's sterling holding at year-end was not large. The British deficit in Canadian dollars had turned out to be higher than forecast, which was not surprising after the effects of the change in the war situation – that is, the end of the "phoney war" – in May 1940. Canadians now felt their own exchange position weakening. The Americans, meanwhile, were hoping to get more gold from the British; they did get some $65 million worth in the fall, but that was the last shipment during the war.[29] British expenditures for war supplies in both Canada and the United States were rising rapidly. Gold and US dollars were urgently needed for the UK's expenditures in the United States. Britain was liquidating her holdings of US securities to help meet her contractual payments. The American election of November 1940 precluded US measures to assist Britain, and after the election it took months, and a demonstrable stripping of marketable assets on the part of Britain, before the Lend-Lease Act could be passed and come into full effect. The Canadian government was going to have to finance Britain's deficit in Canada one way or another.

CONTINGENCY PLANNING

In the late spring of 1940 the Canadian government undertook a highly secret action that demonstrates the seriousness with which the financial situation was viewed at that time. On 5 June 1940, with the approval of the minister of finance, Towers initiated a study, first within the Bank of Canada, then later with the assistance of designated officers from several cabinet ministries, to assess the country's economic and financial situation with specific reference to problems that would arise in Canada if "communications with the United Kingdom were interrupted" to such a degree that "our trade with the United Kingdom would cease." This was a tactful way of expressing the possibility that Britain might be attacked and occupied by German forces. The study determined that should such an eventuality come to pass, the resulting economic and financial disruptions in Canada were likely to be very serious, marked by widespread unemployment and loss of markets for farm products. By mid-August, the initial analysis had been carried far enough to enable Towers to make a summary report to the prime minister including a half-dozen major conclusions. By September, the danger to the UK had been reduced by its brave and brilliant air defence so substantially that these contingency plans happily no longer appeared necessary.[30]

THE FRENCH GOLD

It did not involve the Department of Finance, but there was one serious dispute between Canadian and British authorities over gold during this 1940 period. It took place in August and concerned gold belonging to the Banque de France, which that bank had placed in the Bank of Canada for safekeeping. The British were rounding up all the gold they could from Allied governments and thought, because the French government had fallen under German domination, that they were entitled to borrow this gold to assist in the fight to liberate France. (The British intended to do likewise with gold held for France by the Bank of England.) There were US dollar balances involved as well, which the British had placed in the Banque de France's account with the Bank of Canada in New York to cover payments made on French orders for aircraft and armaments that the British took over in the fall of 1940.

Towers recognized that this was a very sticky political and legal problem and arranged for Phillips to consult the prime minister about it.[31] It was a frosty confrontation, which J.W. Pickersgill describes in *The Mackenzie King Record*.[32] King resolutely refused to give up the French assets that Canada held in trust and was not moved even by a direct cable appeal from Churchill.[33] Eventually, King's position on this matter was accepted by the British and the Americans.

UK RESERVES EXHAUSTED IN US

In late 1940, preparatory to negotiations for massive assistance from the United States, the British Treasury had to mobilize all of its available gold and US dollar balances and sell some of its less than readily marketable securities, in order to meet the payments due under contracts it already had entered into with the United States. Henry Morgenthau, Jr, told the British that the balances under these contracts would not be paid out of the Lend-Lease Act. Under these circumstances, there was no possibility at all of Britain's paying Canada in gold or US dollars. The Canadian government, in the persons of the prime minister and James Ilsley, were making month-by-month or even week-by-week advances in Canadian dollars to the British Treasury in exchange for sterling balances to be held in London by the Bank of Canada.

Early in December 1940, there was brief discussion of a more radical idea that Towers had suggested to Clark. The latter proposed it to Ilsley in a memorandum, being careful to make no mention that it came from Towers. Clark proposed that the government might make "a gift of $100 million to $150 million" to the government of Britain as assistance in continuing to finance its purchase of war requirements in Canada. One of the arguments in support of the idea was that it might help to influence opinion in Washington toward less onerous terms of financial assistance for Britain. Towers feared "that the United States might lay their hands on British assets all over the world as security for the loans they will make." He felt that this "would have most unfortunate results for the world post-war and in particular for the primary producers such as Canada who depend so greatly on the UK market." Clark's suggestion, which Ilsley raised in cabinet on 6 December 1940, was rejected out of hand by the prime minister, as might have been expected, for such a radical departure needed detailed advance consideration. Towers was told that it was too late to implement such an idea, as Parliament was adjourning immediately and would not return until early in the new year.[34]

Clark and Towers greatly underestimated the foresight and courage of Roosevelt and Morgenthau. Only a few days later Clark, who was in Washington, received from Morgenthau a very important secret message to be transmitted to King.

Before we had discussed anything, I told [Clark] that Morgenthau had said he had given him a special message for me. The special message was to tell Mr. King that he proposed whatever America did in the way of meeting Britain's needs from now on, should be done outright as a gift. He was not sure whether the President would agree to that. At any rate, it would not do to put forward the idea at the moment but it was what was at the back of his mind in getting to the bottom of the assets which Britain had and which we have, so that they could honestly state to Congress that Britain was not in a position to incur further obligations for war materials nor would she be in a position to pay them back.

From what Clark told him, King was convinced that there was an understanding between Roosevelt and Morgenthau on this point, and that Morgenthau was really representing the president's intention. All this was growing out of much-needed friendly relations between Canada and the US. This message from Morgenthau was the first hint of what would become the US Lend-Lease program.[35]

US LEND-LEASE FOR THE UK

Roosevelt himself developed the basic idea of how he would provide Britain with what she needed without payment. He called it Lend-Lease, a policy by which the US would lend matériel and supplies to its allies provided that after the war the US would be paid back in kind. The idea came to him on a "refueling" cruise in the Caribbean with his closest political adviser, Harry Hopkins, and a number of personal aides and friends. During this cruise, he received a long and very important letter from Winston Churchill, which brought home to the president just how dire the war situation was.[36] Roosevelt sold his idea to the press and the public himself. His most famous illustration of the concept was the analogy of a man who lends his garden hose to a neighbour whose house is on fire. Roosevelt wanted America to be "the arsenal of democracy" and "to take the dollar sign" off the transfer of what it produced. He presented his plan in the form of a bill to Congress on 6 January 1941. Getting this through both houses of Congress and their powerful committees, despite adverse votes by about one-third of their numbers in each case, was a great political triumph for the president.

Meanwhile, the British Treasury had to go through hell. They had to disclose all sorts of secret information to Morgenthau and his officers, who suspected them of holding back important items. Morgenthau and other senior officers of the administration felt that they had to pass on some of this secret information to the congressional committees. They also felt that on some occasions getting the necessary votes would require them to give the committees important and troublesome commitments; at times these ran contrary to agreements they had made with the British representatives. The largest and most serious was an undertaking not to appropriate under Lend-Lease any of the contracts that the British had already entered into and that required payments which Britain could not find the dollars to meet.

As a result, Britain, for the duration of the war, would be able to get arms and food from the US free of financial obligations. It was becoming clear that Canada would likely have to finance the whole of Britain's deficit with Canada, then forecast at $1.152 billion for the fiscal year 1941–42. Moreover, Clark forecast a deficit in Canada's balance of payments with the United States during the next fiscal year of $478 million.

CLARK APPRAISES EFFECTS OF US ACTION

Beginning in December, Clark went several times to Washington (apparently first on the urging of Towers) to consult the American secretary of the Treasury, Morgenthau, and other American officials, as well as the British, who were negotiating with the Americans about the Lend-Lease arrangements. The US–Canadian aspects of these discussions culminated in the very important Hyde Park Declaration of 20 April 1941 (to be recounted in chapter 5 below).

Clark returned from Washington on 21 March 1941 aware that a new understanding would have to be worked out to provide for Canadian financing of the British deficit in Canada. This would require some assurance that Britain would not shift its procurement of arms and food away from Canada to the United States. In addition, Clark proposed that arrangements be made at the highest level whereby Britain would obtain from the US under Lend-Lease component parts needed for use in equipment and munitions that Canada was producing for Britain. Clark recommended strongly that the prime minister should arrange to discuss these issues with the president himself. In the meantime, arrangements should be made with the British to carry on financing their Canadian deficit and no efforts should be made until later to get the Americans to agree that Britain be permitted to use gold or US dollars to pay Canada.[37]

The War Committee considered Clark's report and proposals on 21 March 1941. The prime minister said that he already had an invitation from the president for an informal visit. It was agreed that some kind of public statement would need to be made soon about financing British requirements in Canada. (Such did not occur until Ilsley's budget of 29 April 1941, which was coupled with an account of the Hyde Park arrangements, but Ilsley had made the main promise to the House of Commons on 20 March.)[38]

The subject was addressed again at the War Committee, on 27 March

1941, when Ilsley submitted the proposed text of a telegram to the British on the subject. The telegram, no. 46, was sent that night to the Dominions Office in London.[39] It summarized the situation created by the Lend-Lease Act, the cumulative deficit of the UK with Canada from the beginning of the war to the end of February ($737 million Canadian), and the means by which it had been financed, including $250 million in gold.

CANADIAN PROPOSAL TO THE UK

In the telegram, King said that Canada was now aware of Britain's difficulties in meeting their outstanding commitments in the US for the next few months and also that the US authorities were reluctant to allow the British to use any gold or US dollars to meet their deficit with Canada. He went on to say that he thought there would be a "far more appropriate opportunity" at a later date to negotiate with the US and that he was content to defer further representations to the US Treasury. The Canadian government had made US Treasury officials aware of Canada's large deficit in its payments to the US and the extent to which this arose from the purchase of components and materials in the US for the production of British war supplies in Canada. The telegram stated that Canada was prepared to continue meeting the United Kingdom's full deficit with Canada subject to the following conditions (my summary):

(a) To provide the Canadian dollars needed, Canada would repatriate securities at such times and in such amounts as appeared practicable; to the extent which that did not suffice, Canada would accumulate sterling balances.

(b) The Canadian government reserved the right to take up later with the US the question of the the reasonable amount of gold or US dollars to be transferred by the UK to Canada in partial settlement of their deficit with Canada, and the extent to which they would be prepared to offer the US component of British war orders in Canada to the UK as Lend-Lease.

(c) The Canadian government would be consulted about projects or additions of any importance to the program of purchases for the British account in Canada.

(d) There would be no diversion of British orders from Canadian to US sources in respect of munitions, farm products, or raw materials. In respect of foodstuffs that were produced in Canada, the UK would procure in Canada as large a proportion of its requirements as Canada could supply.

The telegram concluded by advising the British that "in view of the magnitude of the sterling balances which over a period of time it will probably be necessary to accumulate, we think it appropriate to adopt the arrangement originally suggested by the United Kingdom Treasury in October, 1939 ... that the sterling accumulated by Canada should bear an exchange guarantee at the rate ruling on the day the sterling was transferred."

DELAYED BRITISH RESPONSE

The British did not reply to this important telegram until six weeks later, after the Hyde Park Declaration was issued by King and Roosevelt. Britain took note of this declaration, and particularly of the method indicated for meeting the greater part of Canada's adverse balance with the United States. On the question of gold, Britain drew attention to its very large commitments in the US and elsewhere and said: "We shall for a long time ahead not have enough for our own primary necessities and no surplus available to send gold or United States dollars to Canada."[40] Britain confirmed the assistance already given by not diverting munitions orders from Canada to the United States. In regard to foodstuffs, it felt that it could not reasonably be asked to enter into so comprehensive a commitment as Canada requested. Britain thought that Canadian interests would be fully protected by the close relations already established between the British Food Mission in Washington and the Canadian Legation there. It went on to emphasize that the price factor would be more important than ever because of its recently announced stabilization of the cost of living. Finally, Britain sidestepped the question of an exchange rate guarantee by suggesting an obligation to consult each other before either side altered its exchange rate with the other.

No agreement was reached on the exchange rate guarantee, and the question was postponed; in any case, when the balances were converted into a non-interest-bearing Canadian-dollar loan, it became a moot point.

More difficulties arose during the summer of 1941 over the prices of foodstuffs. Canadian ministers and officials felt that with Canada undertaking to finance the whole of Britain's deficit in Canada, Britain could be more understanding of the need for some increase in the relatively depressed level of Canadian farm prices. US farm prices were rising. In the case of bacon, Canadian ministers decided that it was necessary for Canada to add a subsidy to the price the British were prepared to pay, under their contract to buy bacon in Canada, sufficient to bring the total price up to that paid by the United States.[41]

USE OF ACCUMULATING STERLING BALANCES

This question arose in June, and again in July, when, at the request of the minister of finance, the Cabinet War Committee considered the policy that Canada should follow for using its rapidly accumulating sterling balances, and what could be done to reduce these large balances. If they went on accumulating, the sterling balances would be an unmanageable and very troublesome war debt when the war was over. Ralston, the finance minister, submitted to the committee a lengthy memorandum from his department (almost certainly written by Walter Gordon under Clark's direction and after consultation with N.A. Robertson and Towers).[42] It indicated the large scale of the British deficit now being financed and the limited amount of Canadian government direct and guaranteed securities remaining in British hands and available for repatriation. Unless the government was willing to set up a large investment trust to hold other obligations and equities that were not relatively marketable, the repatriation of securities no longer would represent a substantial means of financing.

There was by that time a danger that Canada would be criticized for demanding payment from the British when the Americans were providing supplies on Lend-Lease without payment. If Britain owed Canada a huge debt in sterling at the end of the war, when Britain would likely have to continue with exchange controls, the currency would be of doubtful real value and might be an impediment to ongoing Anglo-Canadian trade. On the other hand, uncertainty as to the eventual settlement of this debt was making the British uneasy and cautious, notably in the purchase of Canadian foodstuffs, as well as in taking up US proposals to train British pilots in the United States. Ralston pointed out that there were other instances of financial bargaining and settlements that were definitely inconsistent with the broad approach that Canada was now taking to financing the British deficit.

The memorandum indicated that the minister and his advisers considered it unwise to proceed with repatriation of British holdings of various Canadian securities that were not readily marketable, and proposed that the government should reduce the growth of the sterling balances by measures that would yield Canada some material or political advantage. One such measure would be for Canada to pay the overseas (i.e., British) costs of the RCAF squadrons to be formed from Canadian graduates of the British Commonwealth Air Training Plan, and perhaps some Canadian ancillary troops serving with the British army. The memorandum suggested, however, that taking such measures should be conditional upon the UK's purchase of food from

Canada at prices that would be reasonable enough to eliminate any need for the government to subsidize the purchase.

It was agreed at the War Committee meeting of 20 June 1941 to repatriate the remaining direct and guaranteed obligations of the Dominion in the UK, and to ask the Economic Advisory Committee to consider proposals to reduce sterling balances and their relationships to the prices payable for farm products (in addition to some proposals for changing general economic organizations).[43] The Economic Advisory Committee considered this on 28 June and on 8 July reported in favour of the general principle advocated in the departmental memorandum, giving some additional supporting arguments. Specifically, the committee supported the suggestion that the government pay the full initial and maintenance costs of twenty-five proposed RCAF squadrons. It also agreed (although unfortunately in the absence of any representative from the Department of Agriculture) that if Canada assumed additional direct war expenditures of this kind from its sterling balances, it would be in a strong position to ask the British government to take a much more reasonable attitude in regard to the prices it was prepared to pay for Canadian agricultural and fishery products. It was also suggested that if such a program were agreed on, negotiations for the sale of farm or fishery products to the UK should be cleared through a central group or agency that would be able to view them as items in a general framework.[44]

On 15 July 1941, the War Committee once again considered this report and approved the general policy proposed in it. The committee also agreed that Ilsley, after consulting the minister of agriculture, should take up the subject of farm and fishery products with the British high commissioner. The British were forthcoming in regard to bacon, fish, apples, and eggs; the only foodstuff that remained contentious was cheese. At this time, and for months into 1942, the wheat trade was under discussion in Washington between the four major export countries and Britain, so it was not directly affected by negotiations between Canada and Britain about general financial arrangements surrounding agriculture and fish. The British gave some general assurances in early September of the kind requested by Ilsley, despite considerable misgivings in London.[45]

ALTERNATIVE MEASURES TO FINANCE THE UK

During the summer of 1941, thoughts in Ottawa began to turn to some substantial financing of Britain by way of gifts from Canada rather than loans or repatriation of assets. In July, C.D. Howe came to the conclusion that Canada should make a gift to Britain as a means of helping finance the British deficit in Canada. A few days after the discussion in the War Committee on 15 July, he wrote to Ilsley suggesting some uses of the sterling balances and adding: "In consideration for these adjustments, I would be disposed to make a substantial Canadian contribution to British purchases in this country as an outright gift ... I believe that the time to be generous with Britain is now, when the war is on, rather than in the post-war period when our people will be in a less generous mood." He enclosed a memo bearing on the situation from his deputy minister, G.K. Sheils, in which Sheils said: "An arrangement that would appear to be more generous to Britain would, in my opinion, be politically more acceptable in Canada and greatly beneficial to Canada's position in the British Empire. At the moment our reputation as cold-blooded bargainers is doing us a great deal of harm."[46]

Towers raised the subject with Ilsley on 6 August 1941 in a discussion of the whole problem of the repatriation of securities and the accumulation of sterling balances as solutions to the financing of Britain's requirements in Canada.[47] This discussion occurred after the War Committee had come to realize the futility of accumulating large sterling balances and was seeking ways to reduce those balances by paying more of the overseas expenditures incurred by the Canadian forces. Towers felt, as did Clark and Walter Gordon, as indicated in the department's memorandum to the War Committee in June, that there were important limits on the repatriation of securities. He favoured using the remaining Canadian securities held in England as a loose form of security for a Canadian dollar loan to cover about $500 million of the prospective deficit over the next twelve-month period, and he suggested that the deficit over and above that amount would be covered by a gift to Britain. He went on to argue that covering these further requirements as a gift would leave a much more satisfactory post-war situation, because Canada would wish to resume large-scale peacetime exports to Britain. He also argued that giving the British a gift of this kind would help Canada "in competing with lend-lease" in the US; the British deficit almost certainly would exceed the $500 million covered by loan, and there would be no incentive for the British to divert orders to the US since that simply would reduce the size of the gift from Canada.

Clark produced a paper, dated 25 August, on this subject, and Towers and Howe commented on it, but no copy seems to have been preserved. The comments from Howe and Towers implied that Clark proposed financing Britain during the third year of war (beginning September 1941) to the extent of fifty per cent of its estimated deficit by gift and fifty per cent by a loan secured by pledging Canadian securities. While both Towers and Howe were now sympathetic to the basic idea of making a large gift, they differed with Clark and between each other on various aspects of the proposal.

CABINET'S REBUFF OF 31 OCTOBER 1941

During September and October, there were continued exchanges between Towers, Clark, Walter Gordon, Howe, Ilsley, and Coyne. This was also the period during which the major economic policy decision to place a fixed ceiling on retail prices and strengthen wage controls was being debated and settled, so financing Britain was not the government's highest priority. Coyne, however, managed to find time in mid-September to write a lengthy and detailed paper on the possible solutions to the British problem, and the pros and cons of each.[48] Later, he wrote a memorandum, dated 29 October, in which he made a specific proposal applying to the period 1 September 1941 through 31 March 1943. He proposed a gift of the "tools of war" produced during this period, amounting to $1.300 billion. He also proposed that Canada cover Britain's other requirements, including the funding of Canada's sterling balances, by repatriation of the remaining government of Canada sterling direct and guaranteed securities, and a Canadian dollar loan, which would be secured by a pledge of other Canadian securities currently in UK hands.

At about the same time, Towers put forward to Clark and Ilsley a draft announcement of a plan to finance UK requirements.[49] This plan proposed that during the third year of the war, the government of Canada should provide the "tools of war" to Britain as a free contribution up to a value of $800 million. Secondly, there should be a loan of $700 million, in Canadian dollars, interest-free during the war, secured by a pledge of a roughly equal value of Canadian securities then owned in the UK (apart from those Dominion government securities being "repatriated"). This draft announcement included a review of how the UK deficits in the first two years of the war had been financed, and a variety of arguments for the proposed changes.

The substance of Towers's proposal was much the same as Coyne's, although the latter's covered a longer period and therefore involved larger figures. Ilsley presented the essential points contained in these proposals – clearing up outstanding British debts with a secured Canadian-dollar loan and financing future requirements with a large free contribution – to cabinet on 31 October 1941. He did not submit anything in writing and probably used the figures in Towers's memorandum, although King wrote in his diary for 30 October about "a couple of billions of dollars," which sounds more like Coyne's figures. In any case, it did not matter. This was the worst of all times to consider such proposals. King saw that his Quebec lieutenant and most influential political adviser, Ernest Lapointe, was so sick as to be nearly unrecognizable and was opposed to the proposal. King confided to his diary that he certainly felt more "used up" this week than at any time since the war began. "My nerves have gone completely ... as [has] the ability to do anything."[50] Lapointe died a few weeks later.

THE BILLION-DOLLAR GIFT AND RELATED MEASURES

By December 1941, Ilsley was ready to place before the War Committee his revised proposals for financing Britain in 1942 and reducing Canada's accumulating sterling balances. The background of these proposals, along with their relative pros and cons, were set forth in a departmental memorandum initialled by Walter Gordon, almost certainly with the approval of Clark and Ilsley.[51] The memorandum proposed that the remaining Dominion Government and CNR securities be repatriated (at an estimated yield of $295 million), that nearly all the outstanding sterling balances held by Canada be converted into a $700 million loan, non-interest-bearing during the war and secured by the hypothecation of the remaining British-held Canadian securities, and that Canada offer as a free gift to the UK "munitions of war" up to a maximum of $1 billion during the period from January 1942 through March 1943. In addition, Canada would offer to take over, at cost, Britain's investment in Canadian munitions plants.

These proposals were discussed at some length on 15 December 1941. Although he supported them, Chubby Power, the minister of national defence for air, also proposed that Canada should accept full financial responsibility for an additional twenty-five RCAF squadrons to be formed overseas. (This latter proposal was similar to part of the proposals made by the Department of Finance in June.) The War Committee decided that some of these proposals were desirable and asked Clark to consider overnight whether the Finance and air force proposals could be combined, and to attend the committee meeting the following day.

At that meeting, on 16 December, Clark expressed the view that the two proposals could be combined, and he urged that this be done in two stages: first the repatriation, the loan, and the gift, and second the buying out of the munitions plants and taking on responsibility for the squadrons. It was agreed that Clark should draft, for consideration at the next meeting of the full cabinet, an announcement of the first stage of these measures.[52]

Cabinet was not as forthcoming as the War Committee had been;

there was a serious division of opinion between the ministers. The prime minister was apprehensive about the total financial load that Canada was taking on. He was unwilling to offer this price package to the British Treasury, of which he wrote, "There was no more cold blooded body on earth." He asked for time to use the proposal as a bargaining tool with Churchill, who was to visit Ottawa later in the month.[53] King took the matter up with the British prime minister, but not in a bargaining context as he had intended.[54] Cabinet approved it, on 2 January, along with the rest of the war program for the next year. Ilsley informed the UK high commissioner and Gordon Munro, the senior UK Treasury representative in Ottawa, of the decision the next day.[55]

Now it was the British government's turn to wrestle with this proposal. They had already accepted in principle this last installment of the repatriation of the Dominion's outstanding debt. The gift of a billion dollars was most welcome both materially and politically. They balked at the idea, however, that Britain must put up its holdings of Canadian securities as collateral for a loan from another member of the Empire. Not only was there a serious difference of view here on the intra-imperial code of behaviour, but there were varying opinions on the serious risks that other parts of the Empire, notably India, which were piling up claims in sterling, might ask for some pledge of securities.

It was manifestly impossible, however, for the British Treasury, "cold blooded" though it might be, to turn down the package. Ingenuity and tact were employed to turn the "pledge" of securities into a "negative pledge" whereby during the war the loan would not be paid down by amounts equal to the earnings on the securities, but only by the amounts realized on any sales or redemption. The British wanted these terms of the loan to be secret during the war, but the Canadian government insisted on disclosing the main features to Parliament. In mid-January, King was annoyed to discover how much his colleagues, during his absence, had sacrificed to reach agreement on the loan, and he succeeded in toughening up some of the contingent terms of the understanding, though he did not include these tougher terms in his announcement in Parliament on 26 January 1942. In this speech, which included an announcement of the big gift to Britain, King summed up very clearly the essential reasons for the radical change in financial arrangements: "The advantages of the proposed financial plan are that it will avoid the growth to huge and unmanageable proportions of a war debt which might breed serious misunderstandings in the future; that it will definitely relieve Britain of any financial anxiety which might arise in connection with its Canadian sources of supply; and, finally, that it will bring our working arrangements into accord with the realities of the war situation."[56]

It was a sensible and practical package of measures that was a long time in the making. It required political courage, even after the US had brought in Lend-Lease, for the amount was much larger than the figures in the US program, its terms were less onerous, and a large part of Canada disliked any generosity to Britain. A survey of public opinion taken a few months after the gift was authorized by Parliament showed that fifty-six per cent of the people polled in Quebec were opposed to the action.[57]

In devising and negotiating these various measures to finance Britain in the 1939–41 period, Clark and Towers did a large part of the thinking and talking themselves, while others in the Department of Finance played only a supportive role. Ilsley, of course, took his wartime responsibilities very seriously. Having been persuaded by Clark and Towers of the desirability of financing Britain during the war, he was willing to support them in cabinet. During 1941, Walter Gordon assisted Clark in discussions with the Bank of Canada and External Affairs, and he also helped prepare the papers for the War Committee.

I worked for Clark in this general area during 1939 and 1940. I focused on statistics and forecasts, although I was encouraged to give Clark my views and suggestions in other matters as well. During 1941, I was busy with many other subjects, including our newly developed relations with the US Treasury; thus I was relieved that Gordon was able to work on financing Britain. In 1942, I was required to turn more and more of my attention to our financial relations with the British and American governments.

THE GIFT IN PARLIAMENT

The prime minister announced this package of measures in his initial speech in Parliament in 1942. It then had to be put into the form of a statute and passed by Parliament. Ilsley made his detailed statement on the measure in conjunction with a motion supporting the resolution. The leader of the Co-operative Commonwealth Federation, whose party supported the gift to Britain, called it "one of the most interesting and probably most significant statements that has ever been made in this house," while the official Opposition said that it was "not only a great contribution to the winning of the war but ... some contribution to the winning of the peace."[58] There was some annoying opposition from the Social Credit party and some minor opposition from two Quebec nationalists. On 27 March 1942, the bill was given royal assent and came into effect.

USE OF THE GIFT

No particular problems arose in connection with implementing the arrangements for the loan. The repatriation of UK-held Canadian securities was by this time a routine operation. (After the war, in 1946, the interest-free period of the loan would be extended to 1951, and through the proceeds of sales and redemptions, the British would gradually pay it off.)

For the dispersal of the gift itself, it was necessary to set up an operating procedure to ensure that the funds were used in accordance with the act that Parliament had passed. An order-in-council of 1 April 1942 laid down a procedure for issuing accountable advances to the appropriate British government account in the Bank of Canada, then receiving monthly a statement of expenditures from these advances for foodstuffs, raw materials, munitions of war and other expenditures by war departments, and other expenditures incurred in Canada arising out of the war.[59] Britain was spending more for these purposes than what Canada advanced, because it was using its own funds from exports to Canada and other receipts (which were pooled with the accountable advances). Inevitably, therefore, there was an arbitrary element in attributing the use of the gift to these categories. An additional provision of this order-in-council required an official quarterly estimate of the balance of payments between Britain and the rest of the sterling area. Authorities in Canada believed that it was essential to demonstrate the need for the gift to meet the deficit in the balance of payments.

One problem area was the gift's applicability to munitions of war transferred to other Dominions, notably Australia. The gift was clearly and legally given to the government of Britain to enable it to purchase various items "essential to the conduct of the war" and "the maintenance of the people of the United Kingdom." In this relatively simple arrangement (as compared with the legalistic complexities of Lend-Lease), there was no barrier to the transfer of these items by the British government to governments of other Commonwealth nations, provided that they were to be used for "the conduct of the war," and no condition would be specified as to whether these transfers should be in the form of gifts, loans, or sales. Britain sold some munitions of war to Australia and New Zealand, in exchange for payment in sterling. Since both of these Dominions were receiving Lend-Lease aid from the United States, it was to their advantage to acquire what they needed from that country rather than Canada, and thus economize their sterling balances. Australia in particular was also providing substantial reciprocal Lend-Lease to US forces on its own soil. Australia complained to the Canadian government about having to pay Britain for supplies from Canada; both External Affairs and Finance made it clear that this was something that Australia should take up with the British authorities. As a result of this, the chancellor of the exchequer waived payment in respect of Canadian supplies transferred in this way worth some $28 million. This waiver apparently satisfied the Australian ministers.[60]

There were a number of other anomalous transactions or possible transactions that Gordon Munro, the chief Treasury representative at the British High Commission, raised with Clark as constituting problems regarding the use of the gift. One of the most common questions was whether the Canadian government would prefer that Britain acquire certain items from the US under Lend-Lease (which was not as constrained by appropriations as was the gift) rather than deplete the money from the gift more rapidly by getting these items in Canada. Canada's answer was sometimes yes and sometimes no. Another question was whether Canada objected to Britain's provision of Canadian wheat, obtained as a gift, to US troops as reciprocal Lend-Lease; to that we had no objection. Clark took these items up with the finance minister, who raised some of them at council.[61]

The chief problem with the billion-dollar gift was that it was used up so quickly. It had been expected to suffice for the fiscal year ending March 1943, and perhaps somewhat longer. But by that month, Canadian production of war supplies was in high gear and was not yet being offset by large Canadian payments to Britain for the fighting supplies of an active army, nor for the operating costs of more than the original three RCAF squadrons. As a result, the billion dollars was being rapidly drawn upon. Frank Knox, a Queen's University economist who had come to Ottawa in the first years of the war, worked on the figures in the Finance Department during the summer of 1942. He warned Clark on 30 July that the 1942–43 appropriation would be used up sometime between mid-September and the end of November. In fact, it lasted until late in December.[62]

AIR TRAINING NEGOTIATIONS AGAIN

One of the major British obligations that came to light during the period in which the billion-dollar gift was in effect was the accumulated deficiency in British contributions to the British Commonwealth Air Training Plan. (This major program is described in detail in chapter 3 above.) The agreement originally was set to end on 31 March 1943, but by early 1942 it appeared that the need for large-scale aircrew training would extend well beyond that date. It would be necessary to have a new or extended agreement in place well before the existing one expired because of the need to place orders for more aircraft and supplies, and to coordinate the air training with other war plans. Moreover, there had been so many changes in circumstances during 1940 and 1941, notably the inability of Britain to spare her aircraft-making capacity and her decision to move more of the RAF training schools to Canada, that the existing agreement was becoming obsolete. Britain favoured extending the plan through rather informal arrangements, but Canada preferred to proceed by holding a short conference to work out a new agreement.[63]

Meanwhile, now that the United States and other countries had entered the war, the desirability of a broader, more general conference on air training was being considered and promoted. As early as 20 December 1941, the Permanent Joint Board on Defence recommended that the Canadian and US governments consider arranging a meeting of appropriate representatives of Britain, Canada, and the US to consider coordination of all aviation training programs in Canada and the United States. The US preferred to limit such a meeting to military officials, but Canada already had arranged a conference with Britain in May and suggested that the Americans might come to it. King took the matter up with Roosevelt when they met in Washington in mid-April and got the president's assent to such a conference. King suggested that South Africa might attend, as well as Australia and New Zealand. The president suggested the inclusion of other countries, including Norway, the Netherlands, and China, whose crews were training in the US.[64] King wanted the conference to proceed at a political level. The British delegation's concerns about the security dangers of such a large conference were addressed by careful limits on what was disclosed. Britain also suggested that a general conference be held first, followed by a smaller one to discuss revision of the British Commonwealth Air Training Plan. This was agreed to in Ottawa and Washington.

The general conference did not involve financial matters and need not be reviewed here. We may note that it was the first multilateral meeting of allied nations that were recognized as "United Nations" by right of their adherence to the United Nations Declaration of 1 January 1942. It covered a half-dozen subjects, which were reviewed briefly in its report of 22 May 1942.[65] This declaration gave rise to a Combined Committee on Air Training in North America, which, though slow in starting, eventually played a useful role.[66]

The second part of the conference, in which only the UK, Canada, Australia, and New Zealand were involved, ran from 22 May to 5 June 1942, when the new air training plan agreement was signed. The conference and the agreement were more concerned with manpower, terms of service, and the control and administration of the RCAF overseas, than they were with finance. These were the subjects of greatest interest to Power, the minister of national defence for air. About financial matters, Power's views were unorthodox. Just prior to the conference, he had said in Parliament: "Personally I think we should call the accounts all square, say that we have spent here so much, and that they have spent there so much, and let it go at that ... but of course that is unorthodox finance."[67]

Years later he was more forthcoming, writing in his memoirs:

I must confess that the financial conditions involved in the whole matter of air training left me pretty well confused ... At last I left such matters almost entirely in the hands of H.G. Norman, a partner in Price, Waterhouse and Co. in Montreal, who had come to the RCAF and the supervisory board of the Air Training Plan. I think he felt, as I did, that we were wasting a great deal of time and effort in endeavouring to clear up these complexities anyway, since it would be found after the war that the United Kingdom would not be in a position to make heavy payments in dollars. Financial matters would thus have to be settled finally in a rough-and-ready manner; and indeed they were.[68]

In retrospect, he was right. Canada, however, could not accept such rough-and-ready solutions in May 1942 even while dispensing the billion-dollar gift to Britain.

This part of the conference featured a financial committee, chaired by Power's representative, Harry Norman. The other leading member of the committee was the UK Air Ministry's Sir John Abraham, a very able negotiator. The committee came up with a draft report that estimated, on the basis of studies by the RCAF and the UK delegation, that the total cost of the plan for the extended period 1 July 1942 to 31 March 1945 would be $1.446 billion The relative usage would be split about half and half between Britain, on the one hand, and Canada plus Australia and New Zealand, on the other, making the best forecast of the probable use of all the schools by trainees from Canada, Australia, New Zealand, and Britain (and others for whom Britain accepted responsibility), based on current planning, and assuming it was possible to keep to these plans.[69]

The committee also assessed as carefully as it could the projected costs of the items Britain undertook to provide for use under the plan. These items were defined specifically, so that the UK could expect to obtain many of them from the US under Lend-Lease. They included aircraft, engines, spare parts, technical equipment, bombs and ammunition (other than UK or Canadian types manufactured in Canada), and gasoline and oil (other than supplies derived from Canadian wells). After reviewing a detailed survey by representatives of Britain and Canada, the committee estimated that the value of these categories to be supplied by Britain in kind would be about $670 million. The bulk of this was expected to be obtained as Lend-Lease and title of all Lend-Lease items was to remain with the UK.

The committee met all day on 27 May to prepare a report that included these various estimates and then said: "Consideration should be given by the proper governmental authorities, to the contribution in kind by the United Kingdom, whatever in the final event it may prove to be, being accepted as discharging its liability under the Plan, with the exception of such obligations as may be assumed in connection with the termination of the Plan."[70]

This proposal, combined with relatively simple formulas for charging Australian and New Zealand for their air training pupils, would of course have saved a lot of time and effort by rationalizing some of the complexities inherent in the British Commonwealth Air Training Plan, and perhaps the committee felt that the proposal would accord with Power's views and with the spirit of the billion-dollar gift. But Power and the government, and presumably Clark, who was keeping up with the progress from a distance, were not yet ready for such sweeping simplicity; indeed, implementing the proposal would have been unwise. Power held an "informal meeting" on Thursday morning, 28 May, during which he said that he and his colleagues found the draft financial report was entirely too indefinite with respect to the means by which the British liability to Canada (as administrator of the plan) was to be discharged (and, apparently, how it was to be determined).

As a result of this, Abraham and Clark arranged to meet on Saturday to consider a British proposal. That evening the financial sections of the Canadian and British delegations, along with Clark and B.G. McIntyre, comptroller of the Treasury, held a special meeting, after which Abraham sent Clark a proposed revised wording, which stipulated that the UK would accept a total liability of $723 million if the BCATP continued to operate until March 1945. Out of this emerged the key paragraph 14 of the final agreement, in which the UK accepted the $723 million liability and agreed to meet it so far as possible by furnishing planes and other specified items and by paying quarterly the estimated total of RAF salaries (but not allowances) for all RAF personnel, both staff and pupils, under the plan.

This financial arrangement was sufficiently orthodox for the government of Canada, and the agreement was drafted and signed. The first air training plan was terminated effective 1 July 1942; after the figures were sorted out, it was found that Britain owed Canada some $200 million. This remained as a book debt of Britain to Canada until the end of the war. Meanwhile, by December 1943, when about half of the extended period had expired, Norman was reporting to Clark a series of problems and changes which suggested that the UK contributions in kind were turning out to be much lower in value than expected. This was what had happened in the first stage of the plan. In late 1944, there was a review by Canadian officials, with Lord Keynes and other British representatives, of the rapidly growing British deficit in the financing of this second plan and its relation to other financing arrangements and policies.

THOUGHTS ON FUTURE FINANCING

The unexpected speed at which the billion-dollar appropriation for financing Britain was being used up meant that other measures were going to have to be worked out before the end of 1942 to cover the balance of the 1942–43 fiscal year and serve as continuing arrangements in future years. Before the billion-dollar gift was decided on, two provisional items had been approved for future action. One was the Canadian purchase of the British interest in munitions plants, a one-time operation that would involve perhaps $200 million. The second was for Canada to undertake to pay for the equipment and maintenance of RCAF squadrons overseas, which the British were still paying in accordance with the terms of the British Commonwealth Air Training Agreements, and which, for the twenty-five squadrons then formed or forming, would cost about $230 million a year. These items would neither cover the gap in the first quarter of 1943 nor provide a sufficient continuing source of Canadian dollars to Britain and other Allies seeking Canadian supplies.

Finance's idea concerning a continuing plan to finance Britain first appears in a letter from Clark to Robertson, who directed Canadian diplomacy during World War II. Commenting on Australia's complaint about not deriving any benefit from the billion-dollar gift, Clark indicated that in his view the revised arrangement for financing Britain should apply to all the United Nations. Robertson's closest colleague, Hume Wrong, acknowledged the letter and spoke sympathetically of this idea.[71] While it certainly was discussed in the department during the autumn of 1942, there appears to have been no correspondence about this proposal, and it does not appear among Towers's memorandums in the Bank of Canada archives.

There had been informal discussions with the British during June and July, during which this more general aid plan had been mentioned. These discussions also addressed the related question of Canadian representation on some of the combined boards that had been set up by the Americans and the British in January and in June. Finally, there was talk about the ability of the proposed United Nations body to provide relief for Britain.

In June, Clark had indicated that we might "generalize" a future gift to cover other allies, such as Australia, as well as the UK. Given the potential resources involved, this caused some concern among Treasury officials; Munro, their representative in Ottawa, urged London to take some initiative. The eminent British economist and civil servant John Maynard Keynes suggested that, at this stage of the war, it might be in Canada's interest to embark on some sort of lend-lease plan, but others thought it best to leave the initiative to Canada. By August, London decided that Phillips should talk to the Canadians before they decided on a scheme that would be relatively unattractive to the British. The aim of any aid plan should be for Britain to obtain contributions in munitions and food, not money, and to have the aid go to other allies as well as to the UK. When this was discussed, Clark indicated that Parliament could not be expected to legislate any new gift arrangements before early 1943. In the meantime, various interim measures might be necessary. Phillips reported Clark's feelings about representation on combined boards to London, and the Treasury lent its support to these efforts. Meanwhile, the UK balance of payments was supported temporarily by some special Canadian advance payments for naval and military equipment, thus prolonging until nearly the end of the year the period covered by the billion-dollar gift.[72]

CHAPTER FIVE

Scarce US Dollars and the Hyde Park Declaration

Early in 1941, with the war raging on in Europe, Prime Minister Mackenzie King stated that, financially, Canada risked being faced with "a greater burden than [its] people ... can be led to bear." The remarks came in the wake of the enormous defence purchases that Canada had made in the United States for equipment destined for Britain, and the growing scarcity of US dollars. Because of the complicated structure of international payments and the nature of continental trade, Canada's involvement in the war caused serious deterioration in the balance of payments vis-à-vis the US. The situation was exacerbated by the ratification in March 1941 of the Lend-Lease Act, which threatened to divert all British war orders from Canada to the United States. To avert a crisis, the Department of Finance, in conjunction with other branches of government, advocated a number of practical and innovative measures to control the flow in foreign exchange. While these early measures had some positive effect, more radical action was necessary.

As a result, in 1941 Canada negotiated a new economic arrangement with the United States. This would see the latter increase its defence purchases in Canada substantially, enabling Canada to make its own purchases of war equipment in the US. As this chapter notes, the negotiations leading up to the ratification of this new economic arrangement – the Hyde Park Declaration – were arduous.

Before the war, it was clear that Canada's participation in a major conflict allied with Britain while the United States remained neutral would lead to a Canadian shortage of US dollars. There were two reasons for this. The first involved the structure of international trade and payments. Canada characteristically had a deficit in her balance of payments with the US, which largely was covered by US dollars received from Britain as payment of her respective deficit in balance of payments with Canada. Britain, in turn, was largely dependent for her own supply of US dollars on the sales that sterling area countries made in the United States. The war clearly threatened to undermine this complicated structure of international payments. The second reason involved a predictable expansion in Canada's economy, including a substantial increase in imports from the US. These general circumstances could be expected to weaken the Canadian dollar; this would encourage an early outflow of capital from Canada, which would bring further pressure to bear on the Canadian dollar, resulting in a greater need for US dollars to support the exchange market. Canada's need for US dollars could be met to the extent that Britain was able and willing to pay Canada with gold or US dollars for net expenditures (including war expenditures) in Canada. There was no assurance, however, that Britain's ability to pay during wartime would be sufficient to cover Canada's deficit with the US.

As early as 1937, the Bank of Canada was considering the possible need for emergency legal controls over international payments (i.e., "foreign exchange control") in the event of war. By 1937, there were good grounds for thinking that war was probable. In 1936, Germany had shaken off the last shackles of the Peace Treaty of Versailles and her subsequent voluntary undertakings in the Treaty of Locarno. One year later, Germany was arming at high speed and was diplomatically and demagogically aggressive.

PREPARING EXCHANGE CONTROL

The quiet study within the Bank of Canada of the potential need for exchange control in war, and its broad practicability, led to a decision early in 1938 to prepare a detailed plan for such a control. Sydney Turk, chief of the Bank's Foreign Exchange Division, was relieved of much of his regular work to allow him to devote most of his time to preparing a comprehensive plan for solving the particular problems faced by Canada, with its high proportion of foreign trade and very close financial connections with the United States.[1] There had never been any exchange controls in Canada, even when there were informal or formal embargoes on the export of gold. Canadians had been quite free to buy and sell foreign currencies and other foreign assets. During the 1930s, European (most notably Germany) and other countries had developed elaborate and very restrictive controls, but these were poor models for Canada to follow given that it was a small, open economy. While Turk probably was aware that the British secretly were preparing controls for use in war, their plans – given the special role of sterling as an international currency and the almost sacred position of London as a financial centre – did not present a suitable model for Canada. Consequently, the plan that Turk developed, under the guidance of Graham Towers and Donald Gordon, was almost unique, developed patiently by a well-informed market man to fit Canada's particular circumstances.

It is not clear when Clark was informed of the Bank's planning. He said later that it was something that was only spoken about; nothing was committed to paper. He probably knew about it sometime in 1938. In any case, early in 1939, Turk's developed plan was shown to Clark and then to Dunning.[2] They agreed with Towers that the Bank should proceed to make all necessary preparations to put such a plan into effect on short notice. This involved, under the cloak of secrecy, the writing, and the duplication or printing, of many thousands of copies of detailed instructions and forms. Because all this could be done within the Bank (and the banknote printing companies) and at its expense, Dunning probably did not inform any other ministers. There was no need for anyone in the department other than Clark to know about it until the war had started, although the solicitor to the treasury may have reviewed the proposed order-in-council and regulations that Coyne had drafted.

INADEQUATE INITIAL EXCHANGE RESERVES

In retrospect, it is worth noting that while years of work were devoted to the preparation of controls, very little was done to strengthen Canada's gold and foreign exchange reserves in anticipation of war. In his 1939 report, Towers mentioned that the Bank had increased its foreign exchange reserves modestly in the years before the war, but that the total reserves of gold and foreign exchange had gone only from $186.4 million at the end of 1935 (the year the Bank was established and had the gold transferred to it from the government and the chartered banks) to $207.9 million at the end of August 1939. There was a further increase to $261 million by 15 September 1939, after two weeks of hostilities in Europe, before the control was established. (These last figures were in Canadian dollars and the devaluation of the Canadian dollar during September 1939 accounted for part of the increase in gold and foreign exchange reserves.) The $208 million held at the outbreak of war was only equal to about thirty per cent of the value of a year's imports and two-thirds of the annual flow of interest and dividends.

During 1937 and 1938, when the dangers of war were apparent, and Canada understood that the US Neutrality Act would prevent belligerent borrowing in the US in wartime, the Canadian balance of payments and Canadian credit standing were strong; surely it would have been prudent to accumulate more reserves even at the cost of some medium-term borrowing.[3]

In a memorandum dated April 1938, Towers reported that the advisability of acquiring additional reserves in the form of US dollars bought in the market had been considered in April–June 1937 and a program had been adopted that resulted in Canada's having $26 million US. They had reviewed the situation and decided that they should sell $5 million or perhaps $10 million of what they had bought in the previous twelve months. The reasons Towers gave seemed short-term, technical, and even trivial. Not a word was said about the possible need for reserves in the event of war. By early 1939, it was too late to borrow, according to the advice given by the government's principal underwriter in New York.[4] The relatively low level of Canada's reserves before the war was noted by the economist A.F.W. Plumptre in his 1940 book *Central Banking in the British Dominions.* Clark cited Plumptre's view on this to the US Treasury in early 1943 as evidence of the relatively low level of Canada's reserves at that time. I have found no evidence that Clark, who had many other preoccupations, ever gave attention during the 1930s to the low level of Canada's reserves from the point of view of war preparedness, although he was likely one of the people whom Towers consulted.

IMPLEMENTING EXCHANGE CONTROL

When Canada declared war on Sunday, 10 September 1939, everything was in readiness to impose exchange controls. It was decided that this should be done on the first weekend, so that officials at the chartered banks, who were to be the authorized agents in carrying out the implementation of exchange controls, could familiarize themselves with the details of the law and procedures. On the afternoon of Friday, 15 September, cabinet considered and eventually passed the order-in-council creating the Foreign Exchange Control Board and putting into effect, at midnight, the Foreign Exchange Control Regulations. Meanwhile, Towers and Gordon had the senior officers of the banks locked up in a room at the Bank of Canada studying and discussing the forms and instructions to be distributed by the thousands to the banks the next day. The order was signed and bankers across the country had a very busy weekend, but on Monday the system was in effect. Trade was moving and financial transactions were going ahead under the new system.[5]

The Foreign Exchange Control was the first wartime economic control to be introduced.[6] It was also one of the most comprehensive and complex, affecting the thousands of businesses engaged in export or import trade or trade in securities. It applied to all Canadian residents buying or selling foreign currencies or assets outside Canada. Inevitably, there were many questions and complaints about it, but it was introduced smoothly and effectively, thanks to the very thorough preparations that had been made. The exchange rate was fixed at approximately the level that the market had reached when the order was made.

The purpose of the order was simple: to control and to limit the export of capital from Canada by residents and non-residents. Permits were required for current account transactions, as well, to check them against evidence of the transactions so as to be sure that capital was not being exported in disguise. There were five basic rules: (1) permits were required for all payments by residents of Canada to non-residents; (2) permits were needed for the export of funds by travellers; (3) permits were necessary for the change of status of persons from resident to non-resident; (4) residents were required to sell to an authorized dealer all foreign exchange that they received; and (5) payment had to be obtained in a currency specified by the board for all exports of goods and services and securities, and for anything else of value anywhere transferred from a resident of Canada to a non-resident. Detailed regulations and permits were designed and applied based on these rules.[7]

While exchange controls applied by European and other countries during the 1930s had been used to restrict various types of currency transactions as well as to limit or prevent capital exports, the new Canadian controls were not intended, and with one exception (discussed below), were never used to restrict and prevent the outflow of capital. This simplified their administration and the public understanding and acceptance of them.

The Exchange Control Order required all resident Canadians, businesses and individuals alike, to report to the board all foreign exchange held by them at the time the order came into effect, and to use such exchange holdings only with permission of the board. The board was authorized to require all or any of such exchange to be sold to it. The order also required residents of Canada to declare all foreign securities that they owned at the time the control came into effect; these could be sold or bought within Canada but only exported for payment in US dollars. Canadian debtors with maturing obligations payable to non-residents in foreign currencies (other than sterling) could buy US dollars for this purpose.

FINDING THE EXPERT OFFICERS

When the exchange control was brought into effect, the main problem was to find expert officers to operate it. Towers and Gordon were the top managers. Both were men of outstanding ability but of very different temperaments. Towers was calm to the point of coolness, but supremely intelligent and incisive; Gordon was warm and gregarious, quick and tough, a good judge of people and an excellent operator. The two complemented each other excellently. They were responsible to and supported by a board with four other members: the deputy minister of finance; N.A. Robertson of External Affairs; Hugh Scully, the commissioner of Customs; and Dana Wilgress, director of the Commercial Intelligence Service. These board members did not participate in the day-to-day operation of the control. Between them and the staff was a management committee presided over by Donald Gordon, who was the chairman (alternate) of the board itself.

The executive and staff were assembled fairly quickly. The Bank of Canada was appointed the official technical adviser to the board; the Bank was an authorized dealer under the order and both agent and banker to the board. It was responsible for administration, staffing, and quarters. The Bank initially supplied senior and expert staff for the board out of its own staff, starting with Turk and his Foreign Exchange Division, but including others, notably J.E. Coyne, who was to serve as legal officer and adviser. Luckily, several capable executives had been hired to operate the Central Mortgage Bank, which was about to start business when the war broke out. Towers and the minister of finance decided not to start operations of this new institution, and those who were to run it were diverted to the Foreign Exchange Control, most notably the versatile David Mansur, who became assistant to the chairman. A number of able chartered accountants were recruited, and other professionals and businessmen volunteered or were requested to serve.

AN EFFICIENT, PRACTICAL OPERATION

In part because of its own good management and reputation, and in part because of the careful preparation of the plan and its various elements, the system went into effect quickly and smoothly. While there inevitably was some resentment and objection to this sweeping interference with normal business practices, the control generally was accepted as necessary and workable.[8] It was administered not legalistically but in a practical, functional way. As time went on, the details of the regulations were adapted to fit into normal business practices with the least interference necessary to achieve the objective. For example, resident businesses were permitted to hold controlled accounts in foreign exchange and to account for them monthly rather than on the basis of individual transactions.[9]

One feature of the board's regulations and operations should be noted. The world outside Canada (apart from enemy territory) was divided into two major areas for control purposes, and different regulations and policies were applied in them. One was the sterling area, as defined and organized by Britain, which included the British Empire other than Canada, Newfoundland, and Hong Kong (Newfoundland was brought within the Canadian control areas). For this sterling area, which had exchange controls patterned after the British, Canada had to supply Canadian dollars to Britain; it made sense, therefore, to permit Canadian residents to make capital payments to persons or businesses in that area. Imports of capital from the sterling area, however, were not helpful as they increased the overall deficit to be financed. Generally there was close co-operation between British and Canadian exchange-controlling authorities.

The other area was the dollar area – that is, the US dollar area – to which exports of capital were rigorously controlled and restricted, and from which imports of capital were welcomed and, if registered, new investments could be sold later for Canadian dollars. The United States did not have any foreign exchange control. To control capital payments effectively, current account transactions between both areas were subject to permits and controlled.

THE SLOW INITIAL LOSS OF RESERVES

Due to the "phoney war" during the autumn of 1939 and winter of 1940, the exchange control had an opportunity to develop without serious strains and without requiring special or severe action. During the later months of 1939, while war expenditures in Canada were rising fairly rapidly and the financing of Britain was being worked out on a modest basis, no early action to restrict current payments in US dollars appeared necessary. In the three-and-a-half months to 31 December 1939, private liquid reserves were running down and being taken over by the FECB so that official holdings increased, and the net impairment of the Canadian position was small.[10] The board's net US dollar holdings dropped, however, from a long position of approximately $55 million in early November to a short position of $2 million in early January. To some extent, this probably resulted from a nervous market, which, despite the controls, could expedite payments for imports and delay payments for exports. In any case, the drop was enough to alert those in charge of the board. In a letter to the finance minister, Towers included two final paragraphs in which he commented on this decline in the board's position (which was offset by a large increase in the government's US dollar balances), stating: "Our information is not sufficient to enable me to say that we are already losing ground in respect to US dollars, but the movement is not by any means reassuring, and serves as a reminder that the studies referred to above should be initiated at the earliest possible moment."[11] The studies he proposed were comprehensive reviews of Canadian imports to see what could be reduced or eliminated if and when there was a need to conserve exchange.

ENCOURAGING THE TOURIST TRADE

The board's first specific action was a positive one. In interviews with banks in the US, the FECB officers found little knowledge of Canada as an attractive place for American tourists, even in war. Few Americans realized that the exchange controls permitted them to finance trips easily and even at a discount through the acquisition of Canadian dollars in the unofficial, uncontrolled market in the US, where Canadian dollars were cheaper. Towers and his staff brought this subject to the advisory committee in March and argued that the government take vigorous action to persuade US tourists to visit Canada. (The details of the government's action in this regard are described in chapter 2.) This effort was successful, despite some difficulties arising from the US introduction of passport requirements at the border, prompting a fairly satisfactory volume of tourist business. Comparison with earlier years was complicated because the Bureau of Statistics was changing its estimates of tourist revenue from previous years, which had been found to be substantially exaggerated.[12]

CENTRALIZING EXCHANGE RESERVES

The next important action was to mobilize Canada's foreign exchange holdings more effectively. This apparently began with a memorandum dated 2 April 1940 sent by Towers to Clark and subsequently to Ralston.[13] Between 7 March and 30 March, the FECB holdings of US dollars had dropped $35 million to a net short position of nearly $33 million. It was possible that Canada could get through 1940 if it received the gold expected from Britain. There were so many chances for errors in forecasts, however, that Towers believed a policy founded on the expectation of breaking even would not be justified for 1940 and still less so for the duration of the war. Moreover, the FECB would not itself have enough US dollars to get through the next few months. It would need to buy gold or US dollars from the reserves of the Bank of Canada. These sales would show up in the weekly statements of the Bank and spark fears in financial markets. The Central Bank should normally hold on to the reserves, but at that time some of the reserves were going to have to be used and the decline would be visible. If the reserves fell under the purview of the FECB, however, their amounts and fluctuations would not be published and thus would not become known to the enemy. Towers proposed that the board should take over the whole of the Bank's reserves forthwith. He also proposed that the board, at the same time, should exercise its power to requisition foreign exchange holdings of all Canadian residents, except insofar as these were required in the near future for carrying on foreign business. Various orders-in-council would be necessary to transfer the gold to the board, to authorize the sale of government securities to the Bank so that Canadian dollars could be moved into the exchange fund to enable it to pay for the gold and foreign exchange, and to relieve the Bank of the statutory obligation to hold reserves.

Ralston approved Towers's proposals and took the matter to council, where the necessary orders were passed on 30 April 1940, effective the next day. Ralston then issued a lengthy announcement explaining what was being done.[14]

During May and June, the war situation in Europe changed so rapidly and disastrously that it was not possible to reassess the prospects accurately for rectifying Canada's shortage of US dollars. Towers sent a letter to Ralston in early June, pointing out the possible loss of exchange reserves in 1940 but noting the difficulty in forecasting imports for war purposes, the gold payments to be expected from the UK, and the uncertain state of the tourist trade from the US under these war conditions. He concluded that there was "a definite need now to reduce our requirements for U.S. dollars."[15] At the Department of Finance, W.A. Mackintosh was aware of the situation and was working on specific budget measures to deal with it.

BUDGET MEASURES TO CONSERVE FOREIGN EXCHANGE

Ralston's budget of 24 June 1940 addressed the foreign exchange situation. He was proud to report that in carrying out its work, the FECB had received "general and wholehearted cooperation from the people and business organizations of the country, and I may add, from the business organizations of the United States."[16] Still, more had to be done to conserve foreign exchange. Ralston went on to outline a number of measures that would be implemented to accomplish the task. The first was a "war exchange tax" amounting to ten per cent of the value for duty of all imports, dutiable or free, from non-Empire countries. This was not intended as a protectionist measure; steps would be taken to prevent unjustified increases in prices as a result of the tax. This was an emergency measure, of the type provided for under the war clause of the Canada–US trade agreement, and would end with the war.

Another tax was much heavier and more specific. It applied to sales of new passenger automobiles, whether made in Canada or imported, at rates of ten per cent on the wholesale value up to $700, and increasing progressively up to eighty per cent on the value over $1,200. The automobile industry was the one most readily diverted to war production, and even cars manufactured in Canada – particularly the higher-end models – required many imported parts.

Ralston said the government was trying to save exchange in the conduct of its own operations and "it may from time to time, in respect of certain classes of civilian imports, take other measures of a non-fiscal character for the purpose of meeting this vital need as circumstances seem to require."[17]

Ralston spoke approvingly of what the gold-mining industry was doing to increase gold production as a means of meeting the need for exchange, and spoke with some concern of the importance of the tourist industry as a source of US dollars.

RESTRICTING CANADIAN TOURIST EXPENDITURES OF US DOLLARS

The other side of the tourist trade – the Canadian tourists' expenditure of US dollars – had been receiving some attention among the officers of the FECB, at least during June. Donald Gordon wrote a memorandum dated 5 June 1940 suggesting a ten per cent tax on foreign exchange sold to Canadians for travel outside Canada. Coyne immediately responded with a critical memorandum arguing against the tax on grounds of ineffectiveness and inequity. He proposed a prohibition on the sale of US dollars for pleasure travel outside Canada, while business and certain other necessary travel might be permitted.[18] Coyne's view seemed to prevail, and he prepared a memorandum for preliminary consideration by the board in mid-June. With some approval there, he prepared a more specific proposal, which was approved Friday, 28 June 1940, and sent to Ralston, with a draft public statement to be made the following Monday.

The minister, however, would not be rushed; he took the potentially controversial proposal to council on the following Thursday, 4 July. Meanwhile, O.D. Skelton objected to taking this important action affecting the US without consulting its government, particularly as Canada had protested to the US about its imposition, without warning Ottawa, of passport and visa requirements on Canadians entering the United States. Towers responded quickly with a strong memorandum from Coyne. The council approved the FECB proposal to prohibit sales of US dollars to Canadians for pleasure travel to non-Empire countries. Ralston announced the new policy that night, saying, in essence, that to conserve the nation's supply of US funds for the purchase of war supplies, the FECB no longer would permit the sale of US dollars for pleasure travel or for unnecessary personal remittances.[19]

This was the first board action to bring any real administrative and enforcement troubles. Many Canadians evaded the prohibition by various devices and arrangements. Within a few months, the prohibition had to be extended to the sterling area because trips to Bermuda and the Bahamas had become frequent and were using up US dollars indirectly on transportation; furthermore, these trips often involved trips to the US en route, financed by one indirect means or another. Indeed, by autumn, Towers had to propose to Ilsley that to enforce the prohibition on tourist expenditures it would be necessary, in effect, to prevent the exit of Canadians from Canada unless they had good reason to travel.

IMPORT CONTROLS

As soon as the budget had been presented in late June, W.A. Mackintosh began serious work on "measures of a non-fiscal character" to restrict imports, which the budget speech had mentioned briefly and vaguely. He circulated a memorandum on the subject on 1 August 1940. The problem was discussed at the Economic Advisory Committee early in August;[20] Mackintosh circulated a draft report and sent forward (in Clark's absence) a report to council dated 21 August that made mainly procedural proposals. (These are detailed in chapter 2.) This report provided a framework for the interdepartmental discussion necessary to reach conclusions about prohibiting or restricting various categories of imports. Few records have been found of the subcommittee that was established or of the interdepartmental consultation. It seems certain that most of the detailed work was done in the Department of Finance, chiefly by Arthur Annis under Mackintosh's direction, in oral consultation with the departments concerned.

Ilsley outlined the principles followed in deciding on the restricted items when he presented the Exchange Conservation Bill to the House of Commons on 2 December 1940 (a speech that included an excellent summary of the balance of payments problems and the exchange control measures, but which explicitly avoided making public balance-of-payments estimates or figures for exchange or gold reserves).[21] Wherever possible, prohibitions of imports (rather than restrictions) would be used for simplicity of administration and equity. Prohibited items should be finished goods if possible, not parts or equipment required by Canadian industry. Durable goods for which the need could be met from stocks on hand would be prohibited, as would those items that consumers could do without in wartime.

There was a second part to the bill, specifying items for which imports would be controlled and restricted with increasing severity. The most important was petroleum and its various by-products. Canada was dependent almost entirely on the US for imports of oil, and the bill proposed rationalizing the importation and distribution of oil to meet Canadian requirements at the lowest cost. Later, gasoline was rationed. Other restricted imports included tobacco, automobiles and other motor vehicles, hardwoods, veneers and plywood, and natural silk.

Another measure that affected the department's work was a granting of authority to the minister of finance to enter into special financial agreements with individuals or corporations to assist them in developing new or expanded export trade. Some ingenuity was needed here to avoid the countervailing US duties on subsidized exports, so the measures implemented most often were special tax arrangements, notably more rapid depreciation rates. This provision in the act gave rise to a whole series of negotiations carried out by the department, chiefly by Eaton and Tolmie, to work out contracts of this kind.

Other measures affecting imports were a further increase in the heavy excise tax on motor cars and a twenty-five per cent excise tax on a wide variety of consumers' durable goods. More welcome was the removal of all duties on a list of British products to encourage what exports Britain was able to produce and ship under the very difficult circumstances to which she was then subject. Ilsley estimated the foreign exchange savings from the conservation measures at $5 million to $6 million a month (not a large proportion of non-war imports, estimated at $630 million for the portion of 1941 before these restrictions were imposed).

FOREIGN EXCHANGE CONTROL STAFF EXPLORE OTHER IDEAS

The relatively modest estimated savings arising from these restraints on imports caused some concern among the officers of the FECB, who of course were more conscious than others of the limited size of Canada's reserves and the potential demands on them as our purchases of war supplies in the US kept rising rapidly. Suggestions were solicited from among the board's staff for various ways of saving US dollars. They included restricting payments of one kind or another and changing the control regulations. The dozens of suggestions were analysed by technical officers and reviewed by a committee chaired by Donald Gordon. His committee prepared a report that forecast a very large deficit in Canada's US dollar accounts for the year 1941, "in the neighbourhood of $500 million, of which about $400 would represent war expenditure." Such a sizeable deficit would be very difficult to manage or to finance unless US dollars could be obtained either from Britain or by borrowing in the United States, which probably was meant to include assistance under the Lend-Lease legislation then being prepared.[22] In early 1941, ordinary borrowing by a belligerent country was still prohibited by the Neutrality Act. At several places in the committee's report, however, there were references to borrowing in the United States in some form.

The report went on to consider "measures of last resort." First, the restriction on imports as enacted in the War Exchange Conservation Act would be carried considerably further. The restriction would be extended at the risk of creating unemployment, rather than waiting for the war production program to provide alternate jobs. For example, the production of passenger cars in Canada would be prohibited, running the risk of some delay in transferring auto plants and their workers to war production. Second, the board would restrict some of the general activity that gave rise to substantial imports. The report proposed in particular a control over the creation of new plants and machinery for non-war purposes, since much of this was not essential and usually required a high level of imports. (A control of this kind was announced in Ilsley's budget of 29 April 1941, primarily for domestic reasons, and implemented by an order-in-council on 16 May.) Third, a variety of efforts would be implemented to promote Canadian production of various items that were then being imported or that could substitute for imports. This list included fruits and vegetables, imports of which were not at that point restricted, despite a strong demand for such restriction from Canadian producers. Ilsley had made clear in his speech introducing the import prohibitions that imports of US fruits and vegetables were politically sensitive; the US had vested rights under the Canada–US trade treaty, and the markets for such imports were already well established.

FECB internal reports also contained a variety of suggestions for dealing with payments to the US for services. Many of these would involve tighter administration and possibly "blocking" in Canadian dollar accounts of amounts payable to Americans for services being rendered currently or that had been rendered in the past. The largest item in this category was motion picture royalties and rentals, where some partial "blocking" of the Canadian income might be feasible. (Later in the war, a more imaginative and constructive arrangement in regard to motion picture royalties and revenues was worked out.)

During the preparation of the committee's report, officers of the board suggested a wide variety of changes to policies and practices in treating transactions with non-residents in addition to those already implemented. If an exchange crisis did arise, a number of these could be put into effect.

No urgent exchange crisis did arise in 1941, even though it was the year in which Canada suffered the largest depletion of its liquid reserves ($142 million US) and the largest net impairment of its overall US dollar capital assets and liabilities (about $200 million US).[23] To understand why there was no crisis, we must turn to the developments in the UK, Washington, and Hyde Park.

THE SERIOUS SITUATION IN THE UK

Britain's financial situation in terms of gold and US dollars weakened rapidly after the disasters in Europe in May 1940. The British government decided that it must get all the arms and aircraft it could from the United States. In his first message to Roosevelt as prime minister, after describing Britain's most urgent needs, Churchill stated: "We shall go on paying dollars as long as we can, but I should like to feel reasonably sure that when we can pay no more you will give us the stuff all the same."[24] As the last French government was falling, Purvis, the head of the British Purchasing Mission in the US, operating with a free hand from London and with the agreement of authorized French agents in New York, took over all French contracts in the United States as British contracts, on 17 June 1940. This would provide vitally needed arms most quickly but at a cost of some $600 million additional British dollar commitments.[25] The British warned the US authorities, both formally and in conversations with the secretary of the American Treasury, Henry Morgenthau, that they would be unable to continue paying cash and would have to rely on massive American assistance to continue. But no American assurances could be given, nor action taken, before the presidential and congressional elections in November. In the meantime, the British had to screen their new contracts very carefully; they had to gather up all the gold they could find from the "free" governments of the defeated European nations and from the Empire; and they had to sell some of the other assets they held that were marketable in the United States.

LEND-LEASE LEGISLATION

After the American elections of 1940, it took time to conceive and prepare legislation that would authorize large-scale assistance to Britain and her allies. The legislation then had to be passed through a Congress that contained a very large number of representatives and senators who were seriously opposed to intervention in the war. This opposition was supported outside Congress by a large and widespread minority of Americans, despite the fact that even Wendell Wilkie, the Republican who had run against Roosevelt, was strongly in favour of support for Britain.[26] Some of the opposing forces were well organized and well financed. Members of the American administration, and especially Morgenthau, believed it necessary to give the American people clear evidence that the British had come to the end of their financial resources. This required sifting through endless information from the British about the state of their finances, and also direct action on Britain's part, notably in the disposition of some of what the American public widely believed to be Britain's large holdings of US securities and business interests.[27]

What was Canada to do while the Americans were preparing their plan for lend-lease legislation, and simultaneously forcing the British to give them information and sell gold and other assets? Towers records that on 4 December 1940, "I again raised with Clark the urgent necessity for him to go to Washington and find out informally from Sir Frederick Phillips the approaches which he planned to make in respect to U.S. credit, etc."[28] Towers wanted him to urge Phillips to press the Americans to grant the British use of some of the dollars to be loaned to them for payments to Canada to cover at least a portion of their Canadian requirements. Clark did go to Washington, later that week, and saw Phillips and Morgenthau together and separately. The Americans felt the British were not disclosing information that was needed for an accurate appraisal of their position (and to satisfy congressional committees). Clark urged Phillips to disclose the British position fully and remove any American distrust.[29] Phillips did not disagree but was unable to assuage American suspicions. Nor was he able to get Clark to persuade King to release the French gold.

Clark had his own problem of disclosure. When he got to Washington in early December, he received a very detailed request from D.W. Bell, the undersecretary of the US Treasury Department. Bell asked for a vast array of statistics on Canada's balance of international payments with the US, the UK, and the sterling area, and its holdings of gold, US dollars, and other Canadian assets "possibly convertible into U.S. dollar exchange." Clark prepared a twenty-seven-page memorandum, providing all the requested information and more.[30] He handled the delicate question of French gold by excluding it from Canada's assets. He clipped to his page a short note giving the full facts of the gold, but stating these were French assets being held by the custodian of enemy property which, therefore, were not available for Canadian use. Clark's very detailed written information and willingness to discuss it with US Treasury officials won the confidence and respect of Morgenthau, with whom Clark lunched (apparently alone) on 13 December 1940. At this lunch, Morgenthau confided to Clark the nature of his intended assistance to the British and his difficulties in dealing with British officials. Morgenthau added that he liked Clark's attitude exceedingly well and that Clark had been of very great help.[31] It was fortunate that Clark gained Morgenthau's confidence at this relatively early stage, for it was to bear fruit later.

Clark's information showed that Canada was expected to have a net deficit with the US and other dollar areas of $448 million in the second year of war. This took into account war purchases from the US of $325 million, and a net surplus with Britain and the sterling area of $898 million. He indicated that a part of this surplus would be financed by a repatriation of Canadian government securities, but he expected that some would be paid by the transfer of gold or cash. In a presentation of evidence to a congressional committee, Morgenthau included a British requirement of some $620 million of gold or dollars to be paid to Canada; this was not helpful to the Canadian cause, as many Americans felt that they were being asked to make gifts to Britain while she was paying cash to part of her Empire.[32]

While the Lend-Lease bill was before Congress during January and February 1941 (when Finance and its minister were very busy with federal–provincial relations and other domestic matters), relatively little was being done about financial relations with the US. Some additional work was going on to improve and bring up-to-date the balance of payments forecasts with that country and with Britain. Concern was developing that Britain might divert orders to the US and away from Canada once Lend-Lease was in effect. Surprisingly little consideration was given in this period to whether Canada should seek or expect to receive war supplies from the United States under the Lend-Lease Act.

The state of the Canadian Atlantic coast defences, which were deemed inadequate, was discussed during the War Committee meeting on 26 February 1941. Priority had been given to the use of the Canadian air and naval forces for the defence of Britain and of the shipping routes approaching Britain. There was no disposition, however, to bring any of these forces back. At one point, when he saw the president, as he had been invited to do, King thought that he might arrange to have the US lend Canada some ships and some bombers.[33] This seemed to be contemplated not as a Lend-Lease transfer but as an informal arrangement. In any case, the council turned it down. It was agreed at that meeting, however, that Clark should go to Washington with the new senior counsellor at the legation, Hume Wrong, to discuss the situation with Phillips and other British officials, and subsequently with the US.

On 12 March 1940, the War Committee briefly discussed the Lend-Lease situation and its potential to shift British orders out of Canada to the US. In the course of this discussion, C.D. Howe, minister of munitions and supply, stated that "careful consideration should now be given as to whether Canada should not request that this legislation be applied to Canadian procurement in the U.S." Ilsley reported that Clark had been to Washington and seen Morgenthau and other US officials again. He thought it unlikely that the US would apply Lend-Lease to Canada until Canada sold at least some of its American securities in the United States to finance its purchases there. Morgenthau, however, was worried about the effects of such sales in the market. Ilsley also reported that the US was considering a proposal to provide the UK with various mechanical components under the Lend-Lease plan. These components would be sent to Canada for incorporation in war supplies and equipment manufactured for the UK.

Ilsley suggested that Clark attend the 13 March War Committee meeting. At that meeting, Clark reported on his discussions in Washington. He said that it would be a mistake for Canada to request Lend-Lease assistance at that point. Canada first should ask that the UK obtain under Lend-Lease the components to be used in Canada to produce war supplies for Britain. He also reported that the British were very worried about how to finance their large deficit with Canada. Clark said that Canada could expect to get no share of UK gold at this stage. The Americans wanted it all spent in the US on British orders that had already been placed there, and US officials had pledged in congressional hearings that all the gold available to Britain that year would be spent in the United States. Howe thought that Canada should be able to get some gold because Morgenthau was friendly to Canada.

At this meeting, Clark suggested that Canada eventually would have to apply for Lend-Lease to meet its gigantic undertaking in providing and equipping its own forces and producing supplies and equipment for the British. The big problem was the internal financing. Costs to Canada might be reduced by the Lend-Lease of production components to Canada for Britain, and even by Lend-Lease provision of orders on Canadian account. Clark said that he would prefer, however, to make his recommendations after further discussions with Morgenthau and the British. It was agreed that after further study, Ilsley and Clark would confer with Howe about what should be proposed to the United States.[34] King wrote in his diary: "We do not intend to avail ourselves of the Lend-Lease Bill but allow its advances wholly to Britain."[35] Nevertheless, from the context it appears that he did not intend to rule out taking Lend-Lease at some future time. Clark went to Washington again on Sunday, 16 March 1941, and remained there for five days. He spoke first to the new Canadian minister and old friend of Franklin Roosevelt, Leighton McCarthy; then with Hume Wrong, counsellor at the legation and a British Treasury official; then with US Treasury officials; and finally with Morgenthau. He also talked to British and Canadian representatives engaged in buying war supplies. He had brought with him Coyne, from the Bank of Canada, who was to remain for about five months as the financial attaché of the legation. Coyne essentially became Clark's agent in Washington.[36] Clark also took with him revised forecasts of Canada's balance of payments with Britain and with the United States, the prospective expenditures of the Canadian governments (including provinces and municipalities), and a revised forecast of the national income, all for the fiscal year about to begin.

When Clark talked to Morgenthau in mid-March he gave him an up-to-date report on the Canada–UK and Canada–US balance-of-payments prospects, and indicated the scale of financing that Canada required to meet its own war expenditures and the British deficit in Canada.[37] He noted that this was going to mean total government financing by revenue plus borrowing equal to fifty-six per cent of the gross national income as forecast for that year. Clark referred to the several questions he had put to Morgenthau at earlier meetings. In response, Morgenthau said that Canada should set up immediately its own organization to sell Canadian-owned American securities in the US, taking advantage of favourable market trends as they occurred. On the subject of gold, Morgenthau asked only whether US dollars would serve the Canadian purpose just as well, to which Clark said yes. As to whether the US would agree to offer American components of British war orders in Canada as Lend-Lease, Morgenthau said that this was now a question for Harry Hopkins, to whom the president had referred policy matters on Lend-Lease a few days before.

Clark wrote a report dated 21 March 1941 for the Cabinet War Committee. (See chapter 4.) Clark proposed that when the prime minister met the president in April he "should raise ... the question of securing a solution or at least an easing of our exchange problem with the United States, basing his arguments on the larger considerations and the more intangible factors in the long term relations between our two countries." He promised to prepare a memorandum highlighting the essential features of the problem and the type of argument that could be made.[38] Clark's proposal was accepted, and the prime minister asked to be thoroughly briefed.

While these new papers for briefing the prime minister were being prepared, Clark's advisers came to oppose a Canadian request for direct Lend-Lease assistance from the United States. On 12 March, N.A. Robertson had given the prime minister a memorandum about the problems involved in seeking aid under the Lend-Lease Act directly, on the one hand, and having the UK secure as Lend-Lease the US components for producing British war supplies in Canada, on the other. Robertson thought that the latter seemed a fair arrangement, but in practice it would be difficult to settle on an effective method of identifying the components in question. On 7 April, Robertson gave the prime minister a memorandum covering the more general economic relations between the US and Canada, including a recommendation that Canada seek some reductions in US customs duties as a means of increasing Canadian exports. The memorandum advocated more generally that Canadian–American trade positions be kept in mind as the US planned its defence production and purchasing programs, citing aluminum as a good example. In very general terms, Robertson's memorandum was moving toward the integration of production concept and US purchase undertakings that would appear in the Hyde Park Declaration two weeks later.

By this time, Howe had solidified his opposition to Lend-Lease. He wrote King a long, influential letter on 8 April with "a few thoughts on subjects that may come up in Washington."[39] About Lend-Lease, he was "strongly of the opinion that it is in the best interest of future relations between the U.S. and Canada that Canada should not come under Lend-Lease directly except as a last resort. Succeeding U.S. administrations would demand payment by Canada for such purchases, thus upsetting normal trade relations. It should be possible to avoid this direct Lend-Lease if the U.S. is cooperative."

Howe made several specific suggestions. First, the US could salvage the Canadian situation by purchasing certain war materials already in production in Canada, rather than setting up sources of production in the US (Howe's men in Washington had been considering this possibility).

Second, with the co-operation of the Americans, Canada could increase its production of aluminum greatly, thus providing Canada with US dollars and supplying a much-needed item to the US. Third, given Britain's considerable production of gold in South Africa, Canada justifiably could acquire some of it as payment from the UK to use in Canada's payments to the United States. Fourth, Canada could incorporate in its war production for Britain "components" given to Britain under Lend-Lease.

On 9 April, Clark sent three memorandums to the prime minister.[40] One was an up-to-date forecast of Canada's balance of payments with Britain. The second was an estimate of Canada's balance of payments with the US during the 1941–42 fiscal year. Clark expected that imports for war purposes would cost $428 million US (of which $244 million was for British production), and non-war imports would cost $525 million. He forecast Canadian exports of merchandise to the US at $475 million and sales of newly mined gold at $215 million. The net tourist receipts were difficult to forecast because of the uncertain war circumstances and some financing through the unofficial exchange market in the United States. There would be, as usual, some sales of US securities by Canadian owners and some investor purchases of outstanding Canadian securities. Clark's estimate of Canada's deficit, without US assistance, was $478 million Canadian. Against this, Canada's reserves of gold and US dollars at 28 February were only $312 million, and Canadian holdings of marketable US securities were about $275 million. This led Clark to endorse the proposal that Britain should obtain on Lend-Lease the US components needed for production on British account in Canada.

Clark's third memorandum was more interesting. It was entitled, "Should Canada Be Forced to Liquidate Her Holdings of U.S. Securities?" His answer was a resounding no. He concluded that it was better to find other ways to finance Canada's US dollar deficit, including the Lend-Lease to Britain of components. To this he now added what Robertson had mentioned in very general terms and Howe quite specifically: the deliberate purchase by the US of war supplies that Canada was "geared up" to produce. He felt this last idea should be explored carefully. His memorandum went on to say that Canada ultimately might have to consider getting war equipment and supplies under Lend-Lease for its own account. He hoped to avoid anything likely to damage goodwill between the two countries in future. Perhaps there would be no objection to such a scheme if there was a definite understanding that the US would take back from Canada in repayment specified amounts of war equipment manufactured in Canada for the US, such as trainer aircraft or guns or shells. (He went on to speculate that this might help to sustain employment in Canada after the war was over – a fanciful idea.)

Thus it happened that Clark, in rather a low-key way, and Robertson, in very general terms, came out in support of what Howe urged strongly and clearly: that Canada should meet its shortage of US dollars by selling war supplies to the US. Howe felt that the decision to do this should come from Roosevelt himself, and that the president should give instructions to the US procurement agencies. This idea appealed to King, who called Morgenthau in Washington on 17 April. The idea probably had come independently to Morgenthau; in any case, he was very much in support of it. He met with Clark, Coyne, and his own experts the next day, endorsed the basic idea, and said that he had outlined it to the president, who liked it. Morgenthau now wanted to discuss what Canada could supply and get on with working out the plan. In his minutes of the meeting, Coyne added parenthetically: "It was quite evident that the whole matter had come up, perhaps in very general terms, at a cabinet meeting."[41] Coyne's minutes also record that Harry White and Daniel Bell, both of Morgenthau's staff, were surprised that after eighteen months at war Canada would have spare capacity. Perhaps they had been over impressed by Clark's emphasis at earlier meetings on the scale and intensity of Canada's general economic effort. They probably were unaware that Canada had begun the production of arms and equipment really only after the fall of France ten months earlier and was still in the process of "gearing up." Morgenthau's conference notes indicate that Clark asked specifically whether the US would be prepared to buy supplies from Canada that the British, as well as the US services, needed. Morgenthau replied: "I think it would be both. I am sure we will buy every dollar's worth of your surplus capacity that you have."[42]

In Ottawa and Washington over the next few days, the Canadians, led by Howe and Clark, assembled tables of items that Canada would be in a position to supply to the United States. Clark gave these to Morgenthau on 22 April, and Morgenthau expressed appreciation for the prompt action.

THE HYDE PARK MEETING AND DECLARATION

Roosevelt and King, meanwhile, had their meeting at the president's estate at Hyde Park in upstate New York. After only a day's rest at the American resort city of Virginia Beach on the Atlantic Coast, King had gone to New York City. He met Clark and E.P. Taylor, one of Howe's "boys," who was representing the minister, for breakfast at the Harvard Club on Sunday, 20 April, and went over the papers they had for him.

King already had received by telephone from Howe a very favourable and encouraging report on the discussions with Morgenthau. Clark, along with Coyne and Wrong, had prepared a draft of a press communiqué that King hoped he could persuade Roosevelt to issue with him. King made a few revisions, including an increase in the upper estimate of what Canada might be able to supply to the United States.

There is no need to recount here the details of the meeting between Roosevelt and King, which has been described so well in *The Mackenzie King Record*.[43] In broad strokes, however, it may be said that both men had been briefed well and were in general agreement. Roosevelt accepted King's draft declaration with only two changes in one key sentence about US purchases, eliminating any reference to purchases required for Lend-Lease purposes but adding a reference to aluminum.[44] Roosevelt suggested that King give copies of their joint statement to the press at the railway station where King was boarding the train that night. King had what Roosevelt described as a grand Sunday.

The next day he met with the Cabinet War Committee, where he was congratulated by Howe. Then he met the press, making the most of the occasion and his good humour. Finally, on 28 April, he reported at length to the House of Commons on his visit to the United States and its results.

It is worth noting that earlier in the day of 28 April, Roosevelt had said, referring to what he had heard from Morgenthau: "Perhaps it might be going a little too far to have something manufactured in Canada for the U.S. to Lease-Lend to England." This was substantially different from what Morgenthau had said to Clark.[45]

SALE OF CANADIAN PRODUCTS TO THE US

There was much to be done to implement the two sets of measures agreed on in the declaration. Howe took charge of the arrangements for the sale of Canadian defence products to the US authorities. He had a new Crown company set up for this purpose: War Supplies Limited, with E.P. Taylor initially filling the role of president. The vice-president was J.B. Carswell; he had been representing the Department of Munitions and Supply in Washington as director general of purchasing in the United States. War Supplies Limited opened for business in Washington on 13 May 1941. By the end of July, it had received contracts for "defence articles" worth $200 million, nearly all of them British-type supplies to be provided as Lend-Lease to the UK. It took a long time, however, to produce these supplies and receive payment. By 3 December, shortly before the US entered the war, the firm orders of War Supplies Limited amounted to about $223 million, and estimated receipts in 1941 were only $6.6 million. Anticipated additional orders at that time were $50 million, and there had been discussions of a large order for merchant ships as well.

CANSHIP, CANEX, AND CANPAY

The arrangements for the Lend-Lease of components for Britain were initiated on 14 May 1940. The agreement recognized two categories of components. The first comprised those whose identity was retained and could be individually traced. The second comprised those that did not retain their identity. The UK agreed they would obtain the identifiable components from the US under Lend-Lease and send them to the Canadian manufacturers of the UK war supplies in which they were to be incorporated. These items came to be known as CANSHIP items. Canada, or Canadian manufacturers or their suppliers, would continue to purchase other components for cash, but the UK would compensate Canada by transferring other defence articles of an equivalent value that Canada otherwise would have had to purchase in the United States. These came to be known as CANEX items. A third category soon evolved, known as CANPAY, covering items that Canada purchased and paid for to get the benefit of US service priorities and prices.

Ruminations in London on the complexities of these relationships with Washington led D.H. Robertson render them in verse for his colleagues:

There's many a slip 'twixt the cup and the lip,
So we mustn't rely very much on CANSHIP.

Designed from the outset to plague and perplex,
This looks like the final demise of CANEX.

So back to the good old Victorian way
If you want any goods, you must prove you CANPAY.[46]

A copy of the Clark–Phillips agreement was given to Morgenthau, and he passed it on to Harry Hopkins, who was in charge of Lend-Lease policy. Hopkins queried Purvis, representing the UK, and Coyne about the proposed CANEX transactions. Hopkins was concerned about whether this process would imply that the US was taking over past contracts – a practice that Congress had been told would not be followed. Coyne assured Hopkins that no change to past contracts was involved, and Canada would complete payment for them in cash. Hopkins asked why Canada did not simply take Lend-Lease aid directly. Coyne's reply was twofold: he did not think that the US government wanted Canada to become a debtor under Lend-Lease, and the Canadian government was of the same view. Hopkins finally approved the arrangement and did not seem much interested in the distinction between CANSHIP and CANEX. It is worth noting, however, that he wished it to be agreed that no publicity was to be given to this arrangement.[47]

At the time of the May agreement, Canada thought that it probably would be necessary during the next twelve months to obtain about $220 million US worth of US components, of which about $120 million worth would be identifiable and thus potentially eligible as CANSHIP Lend-Lease orders.[48] In fact, nothing like that order of magnitude was obtained. CANSHIP requisitions placed up to 3 December, as reported by War Supplies, totalled only $16.7 million, and the total up to 15 April 1942 was only $20.3 million.[49] The reasons for this essentially were practical rather than political. Canadian defence contractors (and the Department of Munitions and Supply) were most anxious to fill their needs from the US quickly and surely; they did not want to go through the long, troublesome Lend-Lease process when they could buy directly from US businesses. The UK procurement officers in Washington could not be disabused of the idea that there were only limited appropriations for Lend-Lease and that these should be conserved for the UK's direct requirements. Neither the Canadian contractors nor the British officers in Washington had any direct incentive to go through the CANSHIP Lend-Lease requisitions routine.

The indirect CANEX procedure was more practical and was used more quickly. Requisitions of this type up to 3 December 1941 were about $69 million (but only about $5 million of this was for receipt in 1941), and the total value of requisitions placed up to 15 April 1942 was $123 million. While this procedure seemed more fruitful, it was a source of political concern in Washington. It was terminated in March 1943 after Canadian exchange reserves returned to more acceptable levels; later Canada paid the US the whole cost of the items obtained under the CANEX plan.

HYDE PARK'S EFFECT ON CANADA'S DEFICIT OF US DOLLARS

It proved difficult to forecast what the actual effect of the Hyde Park Declaration would be on Canada's deficit in payments to and from the US in 1941. On 17 May, just following the British–Canadian agreement on the Lend-Lease of components and the creation of War Supplies

Limited, Coyne forecast that the several measures would reduce the deficit with the US by $100 million. In his July forecast of the overall balance of payments for the year, he estimated that the Hyde Park measures would contribute $159 million. In a forecast from Ottawa in early November, he estimated that the Hyde Park measures, including some progress payments on the War Supplies Limited contracts, would contribute $93 million by the end of the year, of which the Lend-Lease of components would amount to $12 million. At the end of the year, Clark submitted a rather discouraging report to Morgenthau noting that Canada had experienced a bad fourth quarter and that the November forecast, therefore, had been optimistic. Canada's reserves had fallen during 1941 by $145 million US to a level of $185 million. The contribution the Hyde Park measures had made in cash during the year had been only some $61 million.[50] No progress payments on War Supplies Limited contracts had been received in December, as had been hoped, but they were promised for the first quarter of 1942.

As Coyne was about to leave Washington, he wrote a long, detailed letter to Clark about the allocation of responsibilities for preparing detailed quarterly balance of payments forecasts to be submitted to the US Treasury. Coyne suggested that the central responsibility for this should reside with the Foreign Exchange Control Board, which should be supplied with certain specific forecasts by the Department of Finance and by the Department of Munitions and Supply.[51] Clark informed Coyne that he did not agree to this central role for the FECB, saying that Towers and Gordon agreed. He added: "While I shall not place the reasons on paper, I trust you will be able to gather what they are." The inference was that there were pending organizational and personnel changes at the FECB; he probably had in mind the pending changes at the Wartime Prices and Trade Board, and the concomitant need to strengthen the management and staff of that board with persons from the FECB. The key decision on the new policy, however, was not taken by the government until 10 October and on the new FECB chairman until 7 November. As a result, Finance retained the main responsibility for the balance of payments forecasts.

There was no financial attaché in Washington during the last four months of 1941. This is probably why Walter Gordon visited Washington in late November to renew contact with White, Bell, and Coe of the Treasury and Lauchlin Currie of the White House. He found these US officials optimistic to a worrying degree about Canada's US dollar position. They raised various questions about Canadian plans for financing British requirements in Canada, which were then not quite decided, and about the possibility of Canada's removal or easing of its restrictions on exchange for tourist travel. There were also questions about the need for Canada to maintain its gold production and set priorities for supplies needed from the US for that purpose. Gordon urged some caution about assuming that Canada was "out of the woods" in regard to US dollars. On his return to Ottawa, Gordon emphasized to Clark the importance of his going to Washington soon and regularly, and putting our balance of payments forecasting on a routine schedule as quickly as possible.[52]

THE YOUNG RULINGS

An event on 21 November 1941 threw the whole Hyde Park program into confusion. Phillip Young, a senior officer in the office of the Lend-Lease administration, backed by an interdepartmental committee and bearing in mind congressional criticism of the program, made a ruling: "It is the policy of this Administration not to use Lend-Lease funds to make purchases in one part of the British Empire of complete defense articles destined for use in another part of the Empire." This judgment was included in a letter to Carswell, who had inquired as to the fate of a British requisition for Anson training planes to be purchased by the US in Canada. A few days later, Young elaborated on the restrictions implied in his ruling. He stated that while the Lend-Lease funds might be used to buy completed articles in Canada to be transferred, for example, to China, "if they are not effectively available in the United States," no such purchases could be made for Lend-Lease to the UK. Young continued: "Components of articles being made in the US for Lend-Lease to the U.K. may be purchased in Canada if: (a) they are not effectively available in the U.S.; and (b) if such parts do not constitute more than 50% of the value of the complete article."[53]

Carswell and Howe, furious about the ruling, went to Washington to press Morgenthau to have it changed. Howe argued that the ruling was against the spirit of the Hyde Park Declaration; had it been in effect earlier, it would have prevented most of the transactions already carried out and would have robbed the declaration of much of its effectiveness.[54] It should be recalled, however, that Roosevelt removed the specific reference to Lend-Lease in the declaration and that Hopkins wanted nothing said publicly about the CANEX arrangement. Coyne had warned Clark in August of the unfavourable atmosphere in Washington, saying that there were rumours that Lend-Lease officials were worried by the prospect of congressional criticism when it became known that they were purchasing munitions in Canada that in turn would be Lend-Leased to Britain. Carswell reported in a letter to Ottawa in October that "the atmosphere in Washington ... has changed considerably in the past three months," with the context of his letter indicating it was a change for the worse vis-à-vis the Hyde Park Declaration.[55]

For the next several weeks, Canadian officials pressed Clark to go to Washington to help win a more favourable ruling. Because of other urgent business in Ottawa, and the delay in the government's decision on the financing of British requirements in Canada, Clark was unable to make the trip until 30 December. He submitted two memorandums to the Treasury in advance of his trip. One was on the meaning and intent of the Hyde Park Declaration, arguing for a more favourable interpretation than that contained in the Young ruling. The other was the gloomy rumination on Canada's US dollar exchange position, discussed above.[56] Clark also noted in that memorandum several pessimistic factors he foresaw for 1942 in addition to the Young ruling. The first was a probable decline in tourist trade owing to gasoline rationing becoming necessary (in fact tourism did fall by about one quarter when rationing began); the second was a probable decline in gold production and sales, due to manpower and materials shortages (there was about a ten per cent decline in 1942 and a much larger one in 1943); the third was expected delays in getting steel to build ships that Canada hoped to sell to the US. On the other hand, 1941 saw an increase in Canada's merchandise exports to the US and in the sale of outstanding securities.

Clark's gloom was part of a general mood at that time. The war was going badly. Japan had attacked US fleets in the Pacific earlier in the month with shocking success and had delivered a severe blow to the Royal Navy a few days later near Malaya. Singapore was in obvious danger. The British had been suffering serious naval losses in the Mediterranean and army tank losses in North Africa. The immediate tragedies, however, were offset by longer-term reasons for optimism. The Russians had halted the German advance, although enormous battles were still to come. The Americans were in the war against Germany as well as Japan and had agreed that Germany must be defeated first. In the end, the prodigious industrial power and secure home base of the US was bound to tip the scales.

So it was with Clark's financial problems at the end of 1941. Canada's US dollar reserves were low and assistance from the Hyde Park Declaration was yet to make itself felt in any significant way. The financing problems in Canada, including the British deficit, were very daunting. Within about a year, however, Canada's US dollar position would be strong enough that the US Treasury felt it necessary to set an upper limit on the reserves that Canada might accumulate with US help. In Canada, the national income – now known as the gross national product – continued to grow under the demands of war, not only in dollar but also in real terms. Between 1940 and 1941, it increased by about fourteen per cent in real terms and between 1941 and 1942 by about nineteen per cent. Despite the increased demands of war, higher taxation, and savings, real personal expenditures on goods and services increased in those two periods by about six per cent and three per cent respectively.[57]

Looking back over this record, I am led to make three observations. The first is to wonder why Clark found it desirable to make such an issue of the high proportion of the national income that was being spent in Canada on the war. His argument was vulnerable, as White implied on 18 April 1940 when Clark emphasized Canada's capacity to produce more defence articles for sale to the US. The Canadian national-income statistics were poor at that time (far too low by later, more careful calculation), and there was capacity available to expand, as the record shows. What Clark needed was US dollars or gold, which Canada could no longer get from Britain except by US agreement or by selling more exports to the US, which it did. He was not asking for aid or having to justify any limits on our financing of the British. He must have been unduly impressed with Towers's initial memorandum on what we could afford in late 1939, or perhaps it might have been a general desire to impress Morgenthau with objective criteria. In any event, it worked, and Morgenthau continued to hold him in the highest esteem, notwithstanding the sophisticated skepticism of his staff (which recalls that of the British Treasury officials some sixteen months earlier in London).

The second observation concerns the utter failure, for practical reasons, of the very logical arrangement for Britain to obtain on Lend-Lease the US components that were needed for incorporation into Canadian war products to be sent to Britain (the CANSHIP items) and the political vulnerability of the two alternatives that were adopted: the CANEX items to be transferred by Britain to Canada in compensation for unidentified US components and the US purchase of Canadian-produced "defence articles" destined for Lend-Lease to the UK. Roosevelt himself saw the political danger of the second alternative and kept it out of the declaration, although he took no steps to prevent it from happening. Ultimately, however, CANEX resulted in the Phillip Young rulings in November and some weeks of consternation for Canadians. Hopkins saw the political dangers in the CANEX arrangement and asked that it be given no publicity. Morgenthau did not see the political dangers. Perhaps this was because he had other troubles, many of which concerned British programs. In the end, Canada did not need the CANSHIP transfers, and it got enough temporary assistance with the CANEX transfers before they were stopped. Canada ultimately could afford to reverse the CANSHIP transfers (i.e., pay US dollars from its "excess" reserves to wipe out the Lend-Lease obligation incurred by the UK). War Supplies Limited had received enough contracts before the Young rulings to meet Canada's US dollar needs in 1942 (along with the CANEX transfers). Canada's balance of payments situation changed so radically during 1942 and 1943 that a new political problem was created for Canada in Washington. (See chapter 6.)

The third observation is to note what a small part Ilsley played in working out these arrangements with the United States, even though his "opposite number," Morgenthau, was the key figure on the US side. The reason probably is found mainly in King's role and his views of Ilsley at the time. Ilsley had been minister of finance for only six months when the discussions in Washington began and had not yet proven his worth to King. Indeed, in his diary on 9 January 1941, King writes of him: "I find he is weak and not standing up sufficiently for the protection of the Cabinet as a whole in matters relating to public expenditures."[58] On the other hand, King had met and got along well with Morgenthau, essentially on non-financial political matters; he knew and kept hearing that Morgenthau thought highly of Clark and liked dealing with him, in contrast to the British Treasury officials.[59] Furthermore, as the series of discussions approached their climax at Hyde Park, the subject matter involved Howe more than Ilsley. Thus Ilsley remained in the background, working on the preparations for the critically important budget of late April and the complex and difficult Dominion–Provincial relations it entailed.

THE JOINT ECONOMIC COMMITTEES

It is appropriate to mention here another arrangement between Canada and the United States that was initiated in 1941: a pair of Joint Economic Committees, one apiece from Canada and the US, each consisting of four members. This project was active and ambitious when it began but lost its momentum in 1942 (at least on the Canadian side). The problem for the Canadian committee was that its tasks were taken on by other agencies and its members were diverted to other work. The initial idea came partly, it appears, from the Permanent Joint Board on Defence – a Canadian–American advisory board set up by King and Roosevelt at Ogdensburg, New York, in August 1940 to study joint defence problems. The board felt that it might be helpful to have "supply" representatives on each side of it.[60] At about the same time, the Wartime Requirements Board, chaired by R.A.C. Henry, a close adviser to Howe, considered the need for coordinating Canadian defence production with that of the US. This was discussed with

O.D. Skelton and Hugh Keenleyside of External Affairs; Keenleyside also discussed it with the US ambassador in Ottawa.[61] A proposal was put before the Cabinet War Committee in February 1941 that joint US and Canadian committees be established to study this matter.[62] Both Canada and the US approved the proposal by June 1941, and the terms of reference and membership were spelled out.[63]

The members of the Canadian committee were R.A.C. Henry of the Department of Munitions and Supply, W.A. Mackintosh of Finance, J.G. Bouchard of Agriculture, and Alex Skelton of the Bank of Canada. Professor Henry Angus, newly engaged by External Affairs, was the liaison officer on the committee for that department. Keenleyside, Angus's superior, was authorized "to sit with the Committee from time to time as occasion may render desirable." Henry was elected chairman of the Canadian committee but soon had to drop out due to serious illness; Mackintosh took over, first as acting chairman, then on a permanent basis. Carl Goldenberg took over as the representative from Munitions and Supply but was not nearly as close to Howe as Henry had been.

The US committee had members representing the Office of the Production Management, the Treasury, the Federal Reserve Board (Alvin Hansen), and the Tariff Commission, along with a liaison officer from the State Department and Adolf Berle, who were authorized to sit with the American committee in the manner of their Canadian counterpart, Keenleyside. Hansen, a distinguished professor of economics, served as chair of the US committee.

The curious relationships of these committees with External Affairs in Canada and the State Department in the US were unique and, we shall see, far below what was really needed.

The committees became very active soon after they were set up and held many meetings, both separately and jointly, during the latter half of 1941. They approved a variety of joint resolutions. Other early subjects of discussion involved coordinating export controls, allocating shipping space, setting priorities procedures and policies, comparing restrictions on civilian output, and eliminating tariff barriers to the trans-border movement of defence articles. One of the most important early recommendations was to set up a joint defence production committee. Both governments endorsed the creation of such a committee, and on 5 November 1941 the prime minister announced its inception.[64] The joint defence production committee met for the first time a week after the attack on Pearl Harbor that brought the US into the war. Roosevelt gave the committee his public blessing for its first joint statement on war production policies. The committee, renamed the Joint War Production Committee, functioned largely through subcommittees dealing with particular groups of products. These became effective coordinating agencies and reduced the potential role of the joint economic committees themselves.

There remained, however, a variety of specific subjects to which the joint economic committees turned their attention in late 1941 and the first half of 1942. They considered how the price of pulpwood in the US, which was higher than the ceiling price in Canada, could be prevented from creating a Canadian pulpwood scarcity. They studied the seasonal movement of woods labour from Quebec and New Brunswick to Maine and put forward a joint recommendation for exit controls to prevent a shortage of essential labour in the two Canadian provinces; following the imposition of these exit controls, the committees found it necessary to counter the serious shortage of woods labour that developed in the northeastern states. A good deal of attention was paid to the possibilities of collaboration in the field of agricultural production. The economic historian Warren James notes, however, that the problem of securing any significant readjustments in agricultural production was "so large and tangled that the [Joint Economic] Committees were content to confine their specific recommendations to relatively minor matters."[65]

The biggest and broadest of the joint committees' recommendations was Joint Resolution No. 6, dated 6 December 1941, just before the Japanese attack on Pearl Harbor. In it they urged the governments of the United States and Canada to invite the government of the United Kingdom to join in making a declaration "to collaborate with one another (after the war) in promoting full employment, increasing production, expanding markets, improving standards of living and fostering social security and economic stability throughout the world."[66] The resolution went on for several paragraphs, urging in effect the promotion of an international New Deal, to be commenced by the establishment of an international stabilization and development board. An undated draft of this declaration indicates its authors as Skelton and J.J. Deutsch, a special assistant at External Affairs, on the Canadian side and Hansen and C.P. Kindleberger on the US side. Mackintosh forwarded this resolution to King two weeks later, including with it a long memorandum, apparently from the Canadian committee, about the danger of autarky, which had been so prevalent in the United States before the war, the virtues of a functioning international market economy, and the pivotal roles of the US and UK in achieving these objectives.[67]

This was indeed a brave venture, made possible by the zeal of a select group of early Keynesian economists. It was, however, promoted at the worst possible time. Nothing further seems to have been heard of it, even by historians. It would be surprising if the US president, to whom the committees' resolution was sent just after the attack on Pearl Harbor, ever got to read it. The resolution appears to have far exceeded the committees' mandate.[68]

The work of the joint committees petered out in mid-1943. Keenleyside noted this in a critical memorandum dated 2 September 1943. He attributed the committees' lethargy partly to the transfer of their responsibilities, partly to the influence of the Joint War Production Committee and other agencies, partly to a weakness in the abilities of the personnel and their preoccupation with other tasks, and "above all" to some Canadian members' belief that the joint economic committees were not the best instruments for the tasks assigned to them. Keenleyside thought the committees could be revived, since by September 1943 interest in post-war plans was growing. Some Americans, including Berle, were agreeable to having the joint committees work on post-war industrial studies. In any case, Keenleyside felt the committees should be revitalized or disbanded.[69]

Mackintosh responded at Clark's request but with a sense of personal responsibility and as thoughtfully as ever. He argued in a long memorandum dated 8 October 1943 that these committees were not needed and should be disbanded.[70] There was a plethora of contacts with the United States authorities by that time, and the Department of External Affairs and the US State Department had no disposition to use the economic committees to bring about order and consistency among them. He suggested that all the myriad contacts between Canada and the US should be brought more fully under the eye of the Department of External Affairs, for which purpose there should be a strong new committee in Canada headed by a senior officer of External Affairs.

This memorandum was circulated not only in Ottawa but also to Hansen, the chairman of the US committee. By March 1944, the two governments agreed to announce, quietly, that the joint committees had served their purpose and would be dissolved. King, Howe, and Ilsley jointly put forward the formal order to dissolve the Canadian committee on 11 April 1944.[71]

Mackintosh noted in his apologia that quasi-academic studies such as those produced by the joint economic committees had more of a place in the looser American type of administration than in the cabinet government of Canada. Keenleyside and Berle were continentalists and theorists to a greater degree than others in their governments at the time, and the two were busy addressing the specific and urgent problems of the day. Canada had good representatives on the committee, but there really was no room or time for them to play the roles intended for them.

CHAPTER SIX

US *Economic Arrangements and Dollars Galore*

In the months following the Hyde Park Declaration, Canada witnessed its influence on the United States weaken significantly. The attack on Pearl Harbor on 7 December 1941 ended a tense period of uneasy neutrality for that country and launched it into an epochal conflagration that ultimately would transform its position in international affairs. No longer was the United States willing to isolate itself from global developments. Relinquishing its traditional isolationism, the US became more concerned with global than hemispheric issues. As a result, Canada lost its special status and became a junior partner in the Anglo–American–Russian alliance to defeat the Axis powers. Between 1942 and 1945, Canada had to lobby hard to be heard in economic matters in which it had an interest. The following chapter chronicles Ottawa's efforts, particularly within and through the Department of Finance, to be heard, specifically on the matter of economic relations with Britain and the United States.

The devastating Japanese attack on the US Pacific Fleet at Pearl Harbor early in the morning of 7 December 1941 extended the war around the world. Hitler's alliance with Japan led, albeit surprisingly, to his declaration of war on the United States thereby unifying that country.

The entry of the United States into the war with Germany, and that of Britain and the Commonwealth into the war with Japan, gave assurance to Britain of ultimate victory, at least outside Europe. It required the British, however, to reach agreement with Roosevelt, his vast administration, and the US army and navy on major strategic planning decisions and on the organizations by which such decisions would be made and put into effect. Churchill, along with experienced military advisers, lost no time in rushing to Roosevelt's side. Within a week of Pearl Harbor, he set off across the Atlantic on a new battleship, calmly preparing his points and papers. Roosevelt had him stay in the White House, alongside his invaluable adviser Harry Hopkins.[1] Churchill and

Roosevelt talked strategy calmly despite the dire defeats being inflicted on each of their nations' armies by the Japanese forces in the far Pacific. They studied papers, heard the results of the meetings of their military chiefs of staff, and decided on priorities and plans. Despite their differences, the brilliant, eloquent British leader and the consummate American politician got on well. They could not reach a decision about the Russian front except to agree to do what they could to aid Stalin and his enormous armies. They could do little to help the beleaguered Chinese, now more than ever cut off from outside support.

Their first and key decision was to confirm that the war against Hitler was to take priority over the hostilities against Japan.[2] There would, of course, be resistance and attack in the Far East, but not at the cost of the main thrust against Europe and North Africa.

The Canadians were not involved substantively in these discussions of strategy and organization, but King, alone among the leaders of the secondary allied powers, was invited in to join some of the conversations and to bring his three ministers of defence (but no military officers) for a briefing. As it turned out, much of King's attention had to be diverted to the minor crisis created by a free French naval force capturing St. Pierre and Miquelon without any North American warning or approval, thereby causing some diplomatic consternation about the Vichy reaction.[3] Churchill returned with King to Ottawa and made a famous speech to the hastily assembled Parliament, as well as meeting with the Cabinet War Committee.

THE COMBINED BOARDS

Little was said publicly about the strategic decisions taken at this Anglo-American conference, though the Americans did make some announcements about the huge numbers of tanks, planes, ships, and guns that they were planning to produce, objectives that had been increased substantially under the influence of the hard-driving Canadian-born Max Aitken, now Lord Beaverbrook, the only minister Churchill had brought with him. Churchill referred to Beaverbrook as "a potent impulse" behind the expansion of American production.[4]

What did become public knowledge fairly quickly had to do with the formation of combined boards of American and British officers or officials. The first and foremost of these was the Combined Chiefs of Staff Committee in Washington, consisting of the American chiefs of staff and the British chiefs of staff when they were there, or, more often, the three high officers who acted as representatives in Washington of the three British chiefs. Also included among the combined chiefs of staff were Field-Marshal Sir John Dill, representing Churchill as Minister of

Defence, and Admiral William Leahy, chief of staff to President Roosevelt.[5] The combined chiefs met some two hundred times during the war. These meetings were distinct from those of the joint chiefs of staff of each country, who met separately.

Below the Combined Chiefs of Staff Committee were combined UK–US planning committees both in Washington and London, composed of service representatives reporting directly to the combined chiefs.

Of more general importance were two Combined Munitions Assignment Boards, one in Washington and one in London. These two boards were immediately below the Combined Chiefs of Staff Committee and reported directly to it. The boards were chaired by powerful civilians – Lord Beaverbrook in London and Hopkins in Washington – and their members were senior service officers.[6] The role of these boards was to assign the monthly deliveries of finished munitions and war equipment to those forces and theatres of war where they were most needed strategically. They were not concerned with planning production or financing procurement but with taking the final decisions (subject to the chiefs and their bosses) as to where equipment was most urgently needed. They were to deal with both American- and British-produced supplies and presumably with what other countries were producing on behalf of the British and Americans (although this was not clear at the beginning).

A third set of these combined boards, also with Washington and London branches, was the Combined Shipping Adjustment Board, which was potentially of great importance given the shortage of shipping in 1942. As Charles Stacey comments, however: "It was not a powerful body, and in practice there was no real pooling of shipping resources."[7]

In January 1942, a Combined Raw Materials Board was struck and given the responsibility of planning the development, expansion, and use of raw materials under the control of the US and the UK. Stacey quotes the official British historians as saying that it was "perhaps the most successful of the Combined Boards."[8] There was already a U.S.–Canada Materials Co-ordinating Committee in May 1941; its US member was also on the combined board; hence the two groups were able to work harmoniously.

On 9 June 1941, the president announced the formation of two more combined boards. The Combined Production and Resources Board, which Hopkins helped to create at the suggestion of the British, was intended to assist in adjusting the production programs of the two countries to the needs of war. This mandate included responsibility for making decisions on the creation of new production capacity. The

Combined Food Board was set up to consider and formulate plans with regard to any food issues in which the US and the UK shared a common concern. It was also "to work in collaboration with others of the United Nations toward the best utilization of their food resources, and, in collaboration with the interested nation or nations, to formulate plans and recommendations for the development, expansion, purchase, or other effective use of their food resources."[9] This combined board included the US secretary of agriculture and the head of the British food mission in Washington.

Of the Combined Production and Resources Board, Stacey writes: "Investigators who have studied the subject seem unanimous that the Board never succeeded in establishing satisfactory relations with the U.S. military authorities and was unable to obtain vital information for them." He goes on to say that E.P. Taylor, who represented C.D. Howe on the board after Canada became a member, was dissatisfied with its failure to get military information and with the loose organizational arrangements on the American side.[10] (It should be recalled that the US military handled its own procurement programs, whereas in Canada we had a separate and efficient Department of Munitions and Supply.) The Combined Food Board, on the other hand, covered a wide and ever-increasing range of activities and was of considerable importance by the end of the war.

CANADA'S ATTITUDE TO THE BOARDS

From the beginning, leading Canadian officials, both civil and military, took a close and critical interest in these combined boards. They saw them not as necessary working arrangements between the two Allied great powers but as new international organizations from which Canada and the other lesser "United Nations" were excluded. Those concerned about the boards' exclusivity included Robertson, Wrong, and Pearson in External Affairs, Clark in Finance, Heeney in the Privy Council Office, the chiefs of staff in Defence, and Major General Maurice Pope, vice-chief of the General Staff. The prime minister tended to side with these officials. The federal ministers, apart from Ralston, were somewhat less concerned; they differed in their opinions on the subject and their opinions changed as time went on.

There was relatively little concern about the combined chiefs of staff. Clearly Canada could not aspire to membership within this nexus of major strategy-making. King, though he could and did meet with Churchill and Roosevelt from time to time and discussed some major issues, had little real influence on the major strategic decisions. In March, Major General Pope was appointed as the representative of the

Cabinet War Committee in Washington "for the purpose of maintaining continuous contact with the U.K.–U.S. Combined staffs and the combined planning committee ..." A few months later, when the US finally agreed to a Canadian joint staff being established in Washington, Pope became its chair. In his first report on the committee's work, Pope writes: "We would add that while we work closely with the British Staff Mission, we enjoy free contact with our U.S. colleagues and that the separate nature of our identity as a Canadian Joint Staff is well maintained."[11] This was what Ottawa wanted, and it was working.

Canada, which had no substantial merchant marine at this time, could not expect to participate in or even to influence the Combined Shipping Adjustment Board and paid no significant attention to it. The Combined Raw Material Board had as its American member W.L. Batt, a close friend of Howe, who sat with him on the U.S.–Canada Material Board. Howe regarded this close contact at the top as quite satisfactory, and there was no concern in Ottawa about this arrangement.

Attention was concentrated on the Combined Munitions Assignments Boards. On this subject, the diplomatic and cabinet history from late January until late October 1942 is one of the most convoluted and frustrating stories of the war. It is of interest here mainly because of the strong feelings of the deputy minister of finance, Clifford Clark, and his final effort to solve the problem in December.

The argument really started with a long analytical letter of 20 January 1942 to N.A. Robertson by Hume Wrong, written after he heard of the new boards from Field Marshal Sir John Dill.[12] In his letter, Wrong raised the question of how far Canada was entitled to go in pressing a claim to participate in inter-Allied bodies designed to coordinate the war effort. His own broad answer was as follows: "It is easy to state the general principle but remarkably difficult to apply it. The principle, I think, is that each member of the grand alliance should have a voice in the conduct of the war proportionate to its contribution to the general war effort. A subsidiary principle is that the influence of the various countries should be greatest in connection with those matters with which they are most directly concerned."[13] He went on to outline several alternative policies concerning Canadian representation on, or with, the various new bodies. The British were quick to propose in response that "the Dominions" should have their representation in London, and in particular at the London Munitions Assignments Board, which consisted of UK service representatives under the chairmanship of Lord Beaverbrook. "Dominion Service Liaison Officers should be taken into consultation by this Committee and its sub-Committees," wrote the dominions secretary to Canada's secretary of state for external affairs.[14] It appears that this was part of a plan agreed to with the Americans. Ottawa responded, saying that Washington was equally important. Meanwhile, the chiefs of staff emphasized their interest in full membership in the Washington and London Munitions Assignments Boards.[15]

Finance Minister Ralston (influenced by his chiefs) and, notably, the prime minister felt that Canada was entitled to full membership on the Munitions Assignments Boards by reason of the scale of its production of munitions and military equipment, which though much lower than either the UK or the US was by 1942 far greater than that of any other Allied nation. It was thought that this significant share in production – partly for use by the Canadian forces, mainly for transfer to the British forces, and in some part sold to the US – taken together with the "functional" principle that Wrong had enunciated, justified Canada's claim to membership on the board that would assign the deliveries of these munitions. There was a lengthy debate as to whether production intended for the Canadian services should be "pooled" for assignment; it was believed in Ottawa that the US military were reserving their own requirements from their production. There were also repeated debates about whether the munitions sold through War Supplies Limited to the US should be "pooled" by Canada for assignment; Howe in particular believed that pooling would inhibit the US services from purchasing in Canada. There was surprisingly little focus on Canada's ability to contribute to the essential role of these assignments boards in appraising relative "strategic need" for deliveries to the various services in various theatres of war, which had to be done in accordance with the decisions of, and information available to, the combined chiefs of staff.

After a good deal of argument, the British indicated that they were prepared to see Canada become a member of the Washington board. In Washington, Lieutenant-General Henry Aurand of the US army, who was active in the work of the Munitions Assignments Board (and reputed to be one of the senior officers most sympathetic to Allied needs) expressed a personal opinion that Canadian membership on the board would be acceptable and pooling at the board of all Canadian-produced supplies would be feasible.[16] In May, the ministers of finance and munitions and supply visited Washington with Clark and had further discussions with Aurand, who, as chief procurement officer of the War Department, reassured them that pooling their War Supplies Limited production would not reduce their US orders. Clark and the ministers returned to Ottawa satisfied with the discussion and supportive of the proposal.[17]

It seems that King, while visiting Roosevelt in April, had persuaded the president that Canada should be a member of the board. The president had said that he would tell Harry Hopkins, who was to be back in Washington the next week, that things should be arranged in this way.[18] Hopkins, however, had other ideas.

When the Canadian ambassador in Washington made a formal application to the State Department for membership on the Washington munitions board, Hopkins turned it down; he proposed instead that representatives of Canada be given full opportunity to present their needs and their views to the board, its staff, and the departmental assignment committees. He suggested that it was more important for Canada to be represented on the Combined Production and Resources Board and proposed that the Canadian ambassador discuss the idea with Donald Nelson, the American member of that board.[19]

This unexpected rebuff shook Ottawa, prompting the exchange of numerous papers and much discussion at the Cabinet War Committee. The discussion also addressed the question of how Canada could gain membership on the Combined Food Board. Eventually, Hopkins relented and asked his executive officer of the munitions board, Major General Burns, to offer full membership to Canada.[20]

This formal offer led to renewed debates about principles and procedures, because by now there were serious divisions of opinion among Canadian cabinet ministers. Canada's economic czar, C.D. Howe, was now opposed to pooling Canadian production for assignment by others, feeling that it could continue to be done informally in Ottawa with advice from the British and the Americans. He did not want his war production, which was mainly destined for other countries, to be assigned by boards on which Canada was represented by military officers rather than by his own senior civilians. Ralston disagreed, indicating that the military should take responsibility for assignment on the basis of "strategic need." (It was not clear how the Canadian officers were to get the strategic and operational information to make such judgments.) During these exchanges Clark wrote a very strong letter in response to a general review by Hume Wrong:

Personally, I can see no sound alternative to equal representation for Canada on the Joint Boards in those fields where Canada has much to contribute and is endeavouring to make that contribution her maximum. This point of view is not based on mere emotional resentment nor on mere considerations of national status and prestige (far less than most people, I think, do I place emphasis on status and prestige); on the contrary, it is based solely on the desire to find ways and means of securing the most efficient prosecution of the war and of laying the basis for a post-war world structure that will have some chance of safeguarding international peace and world prosperity. Over the last few months, there has been developing in my mind, an ever deepening sense of alarm, not only at the military course of the war, but also at the organizational developments, the ever-growing developing of an Anglo-American monopoly of the direction of all war activities (except those on the Russian front) and the [ever-]increasing evidences that Washington and London look to a future world authority based on the two, three or four great masses of power. There is nothing in past experience to indicate that the few large powers possess all the intelligence and the foresight or that in running a world they will be solely guided by unselfish devotion to the general, rather than the national, good. There is much in experience to demonstrate that without the full and equal participation in vital decisions of all interested nations, one cannot stir the mass of the people to the depths of effort and of sacrifice behind any cause however notable.

As Mr. Wrong says, the principle is clear – each of the United Nations should contribute to the direction of the general war effort in proportion of the value of its contribution to that effort. It is, of course, obvious that while the principle is easy to state, it is difficult to apply. I think we are probably guilty of not having thought through this problem long before this and of having clear-cut proposals to make. It is high time that we should formulate specific proposals which would represent the application to Canada's case of the principle just referred to. We should then take a strong line, and if we fail in our representations, we fail – but the responsibility is on other shoulders.[21]

The Canadian government had not thought "this problem" through, and the following two months were marked by indecision and frustration. After meetings with senior British officials and repeated discussions at the Cabinet War Committee, Canada made no decision to accept or reject Hopkins's proposal and never did join the board, nor did it pool its production for review there. It did accept membership on the Combined Production and Resources Board, of which Howe became the member, though he usually was represented by E.P. Taylor.

In July, the government had asked both Britain and the US to accord Canada membership on the Combined Food Board. The British found "difficulties" in this and suggested some alternative arrangements. In September, the Cabinet War Committee agreed to drop the request to have a member on this board, in exchange for assurances that Canada could have official representatives on all committees in which Canada had an interest.[22] In 1943, the situation changed, and Churchill and Roosevelt formally invited Canada to enjoy membership on the Combined Food Board.

The deputy minister of finance made one last attempt to get Canada on the Combined Munitions Assignments Board in Washington as part of the arrangements for the Canadian Mutual Aid program. It was not accepted by Canadian ministers.

I was not much involved in these discussions among my elders and betters. I do not recall having seen Clark's letter. It was written when the war was nearly at its worst and when Clark himself was tired and troubled by his bad back as well as the weight of his official duties. The contents of the letter undoubtedly were sincere, and I think Clark did want Canada to have increased status if not prestige. In retrospect, however, I think that he and the other officials involved in this dispute were getting too worked up. By the time Clark wrote his letter, Canada had been offered a place on the Production and Resources Board and a limited place on the Munitions Assignments Board, which, in my opinion, was the most that we could justify. Clark's concerns that the two big powers would reserve policy decisions for themselves in the future turned out to be wrong. Canada was fully involved in the preparatory work on the Bretton Woods institutions, the organization of the United Nations, commercial policy discussions, and ultimately the establishment of NATO. The United States' exercise of its power in 1947 and 1948 in establishing the Marshall Plan was done co-operatively in the general international interest. In my view, the combined boards were necessary arrangements for the two great powers (Britain still was one) to work effectively together. Hopkins's treatment of Canada was reasonable under the circumstances. The British, of course, still were trying to be the centre of an Empire that included Canada, but we were well aware of this and were able to deal effectively with them. After all, our three services were fighting essentially as part of theirs; we had no real alternative to this and had ourselves chosen to join them in 1939.

CO-OPERATION IN WAR PRODUCTION AND CONTROLS

Despite the concern and confusion in Ottawa about the US–UK Combined Boards, real progress and important results were achieved from the joint US–Canada institutions and arrangements initiated mainly in 1941, before the US entered the war. These arrangements concerned co-operation in planning and carrying out war production, from assessing requirements to letting contracts, and in determining the use of priorities, allocations, diversions, and deferments. Bilateral arrangements were necessary with regard to everything from basic raw materials and machine tools to finished munitions and equipment. Later, joint US–Canadian arrangements were extended to controls over essential civilian products and materials used to produce them. Some brief reference to this work is necessary to understand the general economic relations between the two countries.

Two major joint institutions were established for co-operation between Canada and the US. The first was the Materials Co-ordinating Committee (United States–Canada). This was set up in May 1941, shortly after the Hyde Park Declaration, which itself had called for co-ordination of wartime production. The committee was established in the US by the Office of Production Management, with the approval of the president, and in Canada by the minister of munitions and supply, Howe. Its purpose, as set forth in a letter from Howe, "would be to enable the pooling of the resources of the two countries to avoid shortages of supplies of metals, alloys, chemicals and other components of finished war products, in order that the best possible use could be made of the production of the two countries to take joint action when the curtailment of domestic consumption is necessary."[23] Committee members on the American side were the director of the Priorities Division and the deputy director of the Production Division of the Office of Production Management; on the Canadian side, they were the metals controller, George Bateman, and the power controller, H.J. Symington, of the Department of Munitions and Supply. These four officials had enough connections and influence to bring about the required co-operation.

This committee reviewed, and, when necessary, developed plans for expansion of mineral and other raw material production in the two countries. It dealt with the delicate and difficult problem of allocating scarce materials between the two countries. Information about requirements, production, and stocks was exchanged freely and stockpiles were shared. The vital synthetic rubber programs were treated essentially as one continental program through the committee's planning and coordination.[24]

The second joint institution in this field was first established as the Joint Defence Production Committee at the end of October 1941 but did not hold its first meeting until 15 December 1941, when it was renamed the Joint War Production Committee. At the December meeting, the committee made public recommendations to the president and the prime minister. These recommendations contained considerable detail; essentially, however, they elaborated on the central tenet that "achievement of maximum volume and speed of war output requires that the production and resources of both countries should be effectively integrated, and directed towards a common program of requirements for the total war effort."[25] The recommendations were approved by the Cabinet War Committee and publicly endorsed by the US president.

This committee met relatively few times as a complete unit but set up subcommittees in various fields of war production: tanks and automobile vehicles, artillery, small arms, chemicals and explosives, signal equipment, aircraft, naval and merchant ships, and conservation. These subcommittees consisted of the Canadian and American operating heads of the specific branches of the war production agency responsible for each respective field. There were many examples of the useful work of these subcommittees.[26]

No integrated war production program was developed for North America. The two programs described above were planned separately, but each had knowledge of and contact with the other. Moreover, the Canadian program was started long before the American one and was designed primarily to meet the United Kingdom's needs for equipment, which differed in very many cases from America's needs.

Canada's most urgent need in its war production relations with the US was to fit its requirements into the American system of priorities for items that were becoming scarce and of allocations for materials and products that were so scarce as to require limitations on deliveries. Such limitations were first required for machine tools in the fall of 1940. The demand for these tools associated with setting up production plants in the US to supply its own forces and Britain, combined with export demands from British and Canadian plants, had brought about a severe shortage. Canada had a controller of machine tools and a Crown company to acquire them and furnish them to war production plants in Canada. Prompt action was taken to ensure that Canadian requirements were integrated into the American allocation system, and Canada was well treated in this regard.[27]

To secure the necessary materials for Canadian producers of war supplies, Howe set up a priorities office and made arrangements with US agencies to give Canadian orders the priority that their nature and purpose justified. Although this objective was achieved fairly quickly where primary contractors were concerned, serious difficulties were encountered where subcontractors were concerned. "Blanket preference ratings" were introduced for US industries requiring supplies for repairs and maintenance or for the production of essential civilian goods or services. It took considerable time and effort to get this class of rating extended to Canadian businesses; this required the imposition of legal obligations on the purchasers to use the supplies only for the purpose for which they were assigned, with penalties for misuse.

On this general issue of priorities the economic historian Warren James concludes:

By the summer of 1942, the place of Canadian industry in the priorities system of the United States was well defined. The extension of priority assistance to Canadian industry on substantially the same terms as industry in the United

States was of great benefit to the Canadian war production program. In some specific cases parity of treatment was granted almost automatically, but serious difficulties were involved in the acceptance of parity as a matter of general policy. For the most part, the actions of war agencies in the United States were open handed and generous but there were other cases which involved continual intercession by Canadian officials over a long period.[28]

To get the benefit of US priorities and allocations, Canada had to agree to take action to restrict the use of scarce materials on a basis similar to that being imposed in the United States. This issue had first arisen in the Materials Co-ordinating Committee, with Canada agreeing that it was fair to have similar production restrictions in the two countries. The issue gained greater significance in connection with the priorities administered by the War Production Board. In 1942, Howe's Department of Munitions and Supply gave a formal undertaking to obtain similar results in the control of scarce materials, enforcement, and compliance as those being obtained in the United States.[29]

S.D. Pierce, a Canadian diplomat with lengthy experience in the Washington office of the Department of Munitions and Supply, wrote in 1945:

The official pronouncements, the committees, and the practical achievements do not adequately represent the degree of co-operation achieved. The intangibles have been equally important but more difficult to set out ... We both attach much more importance to facts and figures, the Americans perhaps more than we. They are fond of brass tacks, of talking turkey, and of claiming they are from Missouri. We do not take it amiss when the United States asks us to present facts and figures in support of a requirement, we do not feel that our prestige is lowered, or that it is beneath our dignity to corroborate our request. Since we were always in a position easily to obtain information about our war programme (because all war procurement, production, and distribution of critical materials were in the hands of the department of munitions and supply) and since our case was generally good, the facts and figures which were presented were generally all that was needed to establish our position. It was no handicap that we were a cash customer of the United States, and not the recipients of Lend-Lease, that we gave Mutual Aid, and that two-thirds of our war production was for others. It was of positive assistance that the United States was largely dependent on us for raw materials and our bargaining position was, therefore, very strong ... It is remarkable, though, how seldom we had to call on that strength. Then too, our war production, our price and other war controls, and our fiscal policy were highly creditable efforts, and the men with whom we dealt in the United States always felt that the materials supplied us would be put to good and efficient use.[30]

GOLD PRODUCTION POLICY

One field of production of considerable interest to the Department of Finance was gold mining, a field in which Canadian and American policy differed. Gold was a major Canadian export to the US before the war ($184 million compared with $906 million of total merchandise exports), giving strength to Canada's balance of payments and providing employment in a number of isolated towns that were almost wholly dependent on that industry. In 1941, when Canada's exchange reserves were low and declining rapidly despite the Hyde Park Declaration, exports of newly mined gold were earning about $185 million US a year.

It was therefore a matter of some concern to Canadian officials when, in July 1941, the newly established Joint Economic Committees took as the subject of one of their earliest discussions whether it was worthwhile to continue producing gold in the US and Canada when needs for labour materials and equipment elsewhere were becoming more urgent. This discussion continued off and on until 8 November, when a compromise was reached on a joint resolution that recognized that gold mining in general should be treated as a non-defence industry, but if the reduction of Canadian production resulted in a shortage of US exchange that was not offset by US purchases of defence articles, then particular modification of the priority system should be made to permit the continuance of production.[31]

In a decision at the end of December 1941, the US Office of Production Management put gold-mining machinery at the bottom of its list of priorities, and the Canadian metals controller made no recommendation for including Canadian mines in this list. At about the same time, the US Supply Priorities and Allocations Board, an inter-agency policy-making body, agreed that "in view of the military program only limited priorities and export licenses should be granted to the gold mining industry" and that "in granting priorities and export licenses for gold mining machinery, materials should not be allowed for expansion of production although minimum amounts for maintenance and repair may be provided."[32]

Canadian gold-mining policy during the rest of the war was in general accord with this decision. The scale of production was limited, and the gold mines were generally at the bottom of the list of priorities for getting materials and labour. However, they were permitted to continue to operate at these minimal rates, and where they had difficulties carrying on for lack of labour, enough manpower was diverted to them to continue operations. Production and exports of "non-monetary" gold declined fairly rapidly in 1943 and 1944 and by 1945 were less than half the 1941 level. In these years, gold was no longer needed for exchange purposes but the maintenance of communities dependent on gold production and of Canadian mining capacity remained important.[33]

In the United States, a very different course was taken. There was controversy over gold production during most of 1942, and by September there were serious shortages of labour in the non-ferrous metal mines. In October, under pressure from the War and Navy Departments and the War Manpower Commission, the gold mines were ordered to cease production, which they did, not starting up again until March 1944. Whether this drastic action accomplished much was doubtful. The official history of the closing of the mines reaches this conclusion: "The actual benefits in labor and equipment obtained through closing the gold mines were small in proportion to the economic distress and individual hardship that ensued."[34]

CANADA'S CHANGING DOLLAR SITUATION IN 1942

Howe and Clark had tried unsuccessfully in December 1941 to get the US administration to change the Young ruling, which barred the use of Lend-Lease funds to make purchases in one part of the British Empire (e.g., Canada) of complete defence articles destined for use in another part of that Empire (e.g., the UK). This ruling led Clark to visit the US Treasury on 30 December with Carswell of Munitions and Supply and to leave two memorandums with Harry White and his assistants. One memorandum gave a careful and gloomy view of Canada's US dollar position following a decline of $145 million in the net reserves in 1941. The other was a paper on the nature and purpose of the Hyde Park Declaration and why this did not justify the Young ruling. On this latter point, US officials argued first that the Canadian case was based on discussions preceding the declaration, and second, that Canada did not adequately take into account the implications of the president's action in deliberately removing from the draft declaration the reference to purchases from Canada being provided to others on Lend-Lease. White reported to Morgenthau that he did not feel justified in informing the Lend-Lease authorities that Canada's dollar position was critical.[35]

Secretary Morgenthau wrote to Clark in mid-January that he would raise the question of the Young ruling if and when Clark reported that Canada's exchange situation had worsened substantially. He thought such an eventuality was not imminent and wished to let the matter rest for the moment. Clark replied on 24 January that new forecasts showed that Canadian holdings of US dollars would run out by the third quarter of 1942; he also provided the details on which he based this forecast.[36] The US army, however, was placing a steady flow of orders with War Supplies Limited for Canadian products. Clark thought it best to have the change, if needed, arise from the actual behaviour of the US procurement authorities, rather than from his seeking to overturn the Young ruling. The matter was left in this state for several months. The regular balance-of-payments forecasts and statement of Canadian US dollar holdings showed some improvement, and Clark had no grounds for going back to Morgenthau. Louis Rasminsky, who later would become the governor of the Bank of Canada and at the time was making his mark at the Foreign Exchange Control Board, reported in April that War Supplies Limited was continuing to receive orders from the US army and navy. He warned the Canadian officials in Washington, however, not to see this as a solution to Canada's exchange difficulties.[37]

THE 1942 BALANCE OF PAYMENTS

Meanwhile, the Canadian balance of payments as a whole with the United States was continuing to improve. The year 1942 marked a turning point for a number of reasons, and Clark's concern in May over a potential shortage of US dollars proved to be needless. The chief influence on Canada's newly positive position was a large increase in exports to the US – up from $566 million in 1941 to $911 million in 1942, while imports only increased by sixty per cent. In addition, current war receipts from the US, largely arising out of expenditures by US forces in Canada, increased by $87 million while "other current payments" increased by only $17 million. As a result, the total current account balance with the US declined from a deficit of $318 million to $180 million. On the capital account (with all non-Empire countries, but predominantly with the US), the net sales by Canadians of outstanding securities to non-residents increased from $74 million to $156 million. Canadian liquid reserves, which had declined by $146 million US in 1941, increased by $133 million US in 1942. At the end of 1942, the total reserves (gold and US dollars) were $318 million and rising. As Clark pointed out at the end of that year, however, Canada had suffered, since the war began, a net impairment of its US dollar position and indebtedness, including liquidation of assets in the dollar area, of some $296 million, of which a net amount of $15 million occurred in 1942.[38]

DEVELOPMENTS IN WASHINGTON

During June 1942, the US Treasury gave a good deal of study to the Canadian exchange position and its relation to the large value of US munitions contracts, both those already placed with War Supplies Limited, and other orders then pending. This study resulted in part from information obtained through the Joint War Production Committee. Before the end of June, Harry White informed Morgenthau that if the current trend continued, by the end of 1942 Canada might have reserves of gold and US dollars totalling between $350 million and $500 million. Lauchlin Currie, the administrative assistant to the president, gave Roosevelt a memorandum on 1 July 1942 saying that Canadian reserves might increase excessively that year to a level that would be politically injurious to the American administration.[39]

It is remarkable that things had come this far within fifteen months of the Hyde Park Declaration, despite the utter impracticability of Lend-Leasing the UK components for production in Canada and despite the Young ruling. It may seem to us now that the US was unreasonable in being so concerned about limiting the size of our reserves, but at the time they were understood to be placing orders in Canada to help us avoid exchange trouble. In any case, they foresaw trouble with Congress and would have to be careful. They were also monitoring the reserves of other countries receiving US Lend-Lease aid.

Roosevelt sent Currie's note to Morgenthau. Morgenthau and his staff reviewed the orders that already had been placed and those being considered or proposed, and made assessments of the extent to which these orders were intended to support the Canadian exchange position as opposed to being placed for other reasons (usually because Canada already had the plant capacity and labour supply to enable particular items to be obtained quickly). Various policy alternatives were considered, including the possibility that the US would set a figure for Canadian reserves that, if exceeded, would result in the discontinuation of orders by the US. After this review, Morgenthau reported to the president that Canada would end the year with reserves no larger than it held at the outbreak of war. The situation was not out of hand, but the Treasury would watch it closely and propose a change in policy should that be needed.

At the time, the Canadian forecast of the increase in its reserves during the second half of 1942 was only $27 million, while the US Treasury estimated it at a minimum of $100 million. Morgenthau felt it necessary to scrutinize large contracts with Canada, and this was done over the next few months. The US authorities felt, however, that this did not occur fast enough. Currie suggested placing munitions contracts in Canada where desirable on supply grounds, but if it was decided that certain supplies were to go to the British, and Canadian US dollar reserves were adequate, the supplies in question would be diverted at the delivery stage by agreement between Howe and Charles

Wilson, vice chairman of the US War Production Board. Such supplies would be financed and provided to Britain by Canada rather than by the US under Lend-Lease.[40] This procedure would require some agreed on figure for Canadian reserves beyond which US orders would not support them. The Treasury, therefore, would have to take this matter up with the Department of Finance.

THE AGREEMENT ON CANADIAN RESERVE LEVELS

On 28 December 1942, Wynne Plumptre, Canada's finance representative in Washington, was called to see Harry White and was asked, in a formal manner: "What should be the accepted level around which Canadian reserves of gold and US dollars ought to fluctuate?"[41] Plumptre, a Cambridge-educated economist, was already aware of the proposed new arrangements mentioned above. White said that he hoped it would be possible to agree on this normal working balance before the end of January. He would welcome a discussion based on any figure Clark wished to suggest. Plumptre did not discuss the substance of the proposal with White, but in his report to Clark he suggested that the figure should be higher than the current level, which he regarded as inadequate. Clark decided to draw up a memorandum for discussion with White as soon as possible. The lengthy memorandum, dated 7 January 1943, suggested that attention needed to be paid to several general considerations affecting the level of reserves that Canada should maintain: (a) the vulnerability of Canada's international trading position; (b) Canada's large international debts, which at that time were owed mostly to the US; (c) Canada's probable post-war reconstruction needs; and (d) the desirability of being able to restore parity of exchange, eliminate various restrictions, and maintain a liberal commercial policy. Clark went on to supply facts about Canada's official and available private reserves at the outbreak of war, which totalled $390 million. He commented on the relatively low level of these reserves at the war's start, their subsequent decline, and recent recovery to $318 million. He then set forth two alternatives for White to consider. One would be to revert to the reserve level that existed immediately prior to the war. The other would be to accept a net impairment of $177 million in Canada's total capital position vis-à-vis the dollar area, but to permit Canadian reserves to rise by the amount of the subsequent decline in Canada's net position (both long- and short-term), which would be $119 million. This would give a working balance figure of $437 million. The average of the two alternatives would be $414 million. Clark suggested that Canadian reserves should hover in the range of $400 million to $430 million. He went on to suggest that, in agreeing on a suitable reserve level, the US should consider whether it was desirable to leave out of the calculation of future reserves any cash that might have accumulated from the net sale of securities – either US or Canadian – in the US by Canadians. Clark's thought was that these ordinary market sales of securities might be used to help pay off Canadian government securities maturing in the US within the next two or three years.[42]

Clark met White on 8 January 1943 and told him in some detail of the Canadian government's plan to introduce its Mutual Aid Program to finance the transfer of Canadian-produced munitions and supplies to Britain and other Allied nations lacking the means to pay for them. (See chapter 7.) He and White then went over Clark's memorandum.[43] About two weeks later, White discussed the subject with Plumptre. The proposal had been debated within the Treasury and also with the interdepartmental group that dealt with the reserve position of various countries receiving support from the United States. White said that the group had reached the conclusion regretfully that Clark's proposal was rather higher than they could support in the face of adverse criticism. He suggested, accordingly, a range of $300 million to $350 million. He said that the US had to keep in mind the ranges that they had accorded to other countries, including the United Kingdom. Moreover, it would be difficult for them to justify an aggregate reserve larger than what Canada had at the outbreak of the war. He said that the matter was still open for discussion, but Plumptre stated in a teletype that Canada would need to put forward a very strong case to get its reserves increased. Plumptre added that he thought the main difference between Canada and the US was that Canada was looking at its post-war position, which the US felt they could not use as a basis for wartime support. As for Clark's proposal to leave out of account the proceeds from the sale of securities, White said that they could not agree to this as a general principle but would be prepared to discuss specific cases when they arose.[44]

Clark responded to White through Plumptre, saying that while he thought his own points were valid, he did not think that the subject was one for bargaining, and he was prepared to leave the matter in the hands of the Treasury if they felt they must settle it primarily on the basis of comparison with other countries. He did ask whether in the next year or two US authorities would be prepared to have Canada pay off maturing or callable securities payable in US funds, up to the amount of the net proceeds of securities sales occurring after the date of the new arrangement. White had Plumptre inform Clark on 6 March that the range for reserves would be $300 million to $350 million, and that for 1943, receipts from the net sales of securities in the US might be used for the redemption of bonds in the US.[45] It was also understood that there would be no more CANEX Lend-Lease transactions.

This maximum–minimum balances arrangement was never communicated officially to the Department of External Affairs. The arrangement forced Canada, however, to expend a great deal of effort in trying, unsuccessfully as it turned out, to carry it out, and ultimately a great deal of money to buy its way out of it.[46] There were two main reasons for this. First, the use of variations in US purchases of Canadian munitions and supplies as a means of control turned out to be almost as impractical as Canada's using Lend-Leased components to make supplies for Britain. The vast machinery of US defence procurement could not be turned on and off at will, or even diverted, as Currie had proposed. Second, the improvement in Canada's overall balance of payments with the United States in 1942 continued with greater force through 1943. In that year, even wheat and other grains were sold in very large quantities to make good a deficiency of feed grains in the United States owing to a poor 1943 crop. These sales in 1943 amounted to $135 million (more than one-third the value of sales of war supplies and war materials). The US expenditures on war projects in Canada that year totalled $173 million compared with $26 million in 1942.[47] Even if the US management of purchases from War Supplies Limited had been carried out with full efficiency, it could not have kept Canadian reserves within the agreed on range.

In fact, there were serious delays and difficulties in regulating the volume of US purchases from War Supplies Limited. The Army, Navy and Maritime Commission (which bought merchant ships) had its own purchasing authority, its own appropriations, and its own reasons for buying; absent presidential intervention, neither the office of Lend-Lease (later the Foreign Economic Administration) nor the Treasury Department had effective control over it. In effect, the control of purchases (or the cancellation or diversion of contracts) had to be negotiated with the commission. It was also necessary to forecast the level of reduction in purchases that would be required or justified based on forecasts of the balance of payments as a whole.

The process began easily enough. Canada halted requisitions for CANEX transactions and cancelled, or transferred to CANPAY, requisitions and contracts of more than $70 million. Though the need to cancel or divert contracts was now officially accepted, differing views developed on each side about the process to be used. Clark visited Washington in early April 1943 for discussions with White and Currie.[48] He explained the reasons that Canada's dollar reserves at 31 March were $537 million – substantially above the agreed on maximum – before the process of adjustment started. White did not see any problem that required immediate action. (In fact, some of Clark's information was faulty and had to be corrected later.) Asked what procedure he favoured in handling the outstanding War Supplies Limited contracts, White said that he did not care which of the alternatives was used and asked what option the Canadians would prefer to see implemented. Clark's own preference was for outright cancellation of contracts, but the Canadian supply officials preferred Currie's earlier proposal: diversion of deliveries as the contracts were completed, with Canada paying for the deliveries instead of the United States. Some of the reasons were technical, but others arose from the Canadians' desire not to discourage the placing of new orders with War Supplies Limited. The US procurement officers were divided in their views as well. Some of them wished to retain control over the flow of supplies of particular items as long as possible and therefore favoured diversion rather than cancellation.

When Clark visited White again, in June 1943, it was evident to both sides that action was needed to reduce the US payments to War Supplies Limited. Clark suggested cancelling some $50 million of US contracts for production of UK supplies in Canada. He proposed that Canada take over the contracts and provide the supplies directly. This was agreed, but White wrote to Clark in July that the US procurement officials preferred to divert the deliveries to the Canadian Mutual Aid Board. That board immediately agreed to take deliveries. Morgenthau came back with a proposed list of supplies amounting to approximately $52 million. The list turned out to be faulty in a number of respects, because some items had already been cancelled, others were based on contracts that had been completed, and some items simply were overestimated.[49]

The problem of selecting a list was turned over to War Supplies Limited and the US procurement agencies. They came up with a list representing about $116 million (Canadian) and a new agreement to put it into effect by cancelling the contracts as of 25 September. Two days later, C.D. Howe wrote to Clark to say that Canada now had transferred to the Mutual Aid Board account practically all the US contracts for items destined to be Lend-Leased to Britain. He suggested that the remaining small contracts be similarly transferred; subsequently, Canada would sell the US supplies and equipment for its own forces. We should not be asked to cancel these contracts, Howe said, as they caused no political problems. Canada had taken on no new substantial US contracts for some time, except for additional quantities of items that it was already manufacturing. "If this could not be regarded as legitimate export business, our position would be rather hopeless."[50] Howe then recommended that Finance ask the US for a new deal as a matter of urgency. Clark agreed in general but said that he thought the US Treasury would not wish to have a new deal to replace the maximum–minimum balance arrangements before the end of the year.[51]

Howe was right in wanting a new deal, but he underestimated the variety of political problems in Washington. It was not only a question of Lend-lease to the Empire. The Treasury felt that it could give Canada no financial help – even with purely US contracts, as it was known to be doing under the Hyde Park Declaration – without a deal on maximum balances. Getting out was going to prove to be a painful problem.

When White saw the figures for Canadian reserves at the end of October, which again were higher than the Department of Finance had forecast, he wrote to draw this to Clark's attention. He suggested that they had better get together to see what could be done about these figures, which rose continually despite the large contract cancellations in September. Clark replied that he, too, was surprised and would go to Washington as soon as he had his facts together. Clark met with McIntyre (comptroller of the Treasury) and with Munitions and Supply officials to see what could or should be further cut from the War Supplies Limited program, which was then made up of items that the US wanted for itself.[52] The Munitions and Supply officials repeated what Howe had said: that it was time to get out of this deal. None of us at that time foresaw the very serious difficulties that we were going to have in the next four months in buying our way out of this situation.

Norman Robertson expressed concern to the prime minister, and also the US ambassador, about the anomalous position into which our financial arrangements had put us. We could not gain anything from additional exports to the United States (or elsewhere in the dollar area), and under the terms of the balances agreement, we could not reduce or remove our import restraints or restrictions on pleasure travel. Robertson thought that it was not in the interests of the United States or Canada to maintain such arrangements. The ambassador informed the State Department, which promised to explore the issue with the US Treasury.[53]

US MILITARY PROJECTS IN CANADA

There was another subject on which Clark needed guidance and authority from the government before seeing White in December. This concerned the substantial military expenditures that the US army (which then contained the air force) was making on its own defence projects in Canada, most notably on airfields and related facilities.

Two other large projects did not require attention at this time, though they involved the largest expenditures. The first was the Alaska Highway, which the US chiefs of staff and the president decided in February 1942 was essential for effective continental defence. The Canadian chiefs of staff did not share this view, nor did the senior Canadian civilian members of the Permanent Joint Board on Defence, but it was felt that Canada dare not block a project if doing so would run some remote chance of endangering the effective defence of Alaska. The Cabinet War Committee agreed on 5 March 1942 that the United States could build the road, with the US paying the whole cost of construction and maintenance. There were various conditions attached to the agreement.

The second major project was the Canol oil project, which was hastily undertaken by the US army in mid-1942. The project had three related objectives: (1) to search for additional oil in the Northwest Territories' neighbourhood of Norman Wells (and elsewhere in the Mackenzie valley); (2) to build and operate a pipeline (the Canol line) from Norman Wells to Whitehorse, with a capacity of three thousand barrels a day; and (3) to build a refinery at Whitehorse of the same capacity to produce fuel for the US air force, as well as for local requirements.[54] Ultimately, the American armed forces, which urged the project on a reluctant Canadian government, wanted a secure supply of oil products in the northwest to fuel defence efforts. US authorities had come to Ottawa to discuss the project a few days before Clark's December visit with White. The discussion covered various technical and diplomatic points but contained no suggestion that Canada pay a part of the project's costs.[55]

Once the project was completed, more than enough oil was found, and the refinery was operating as planned. The project, however, was a fiasco, costing more than five times its estimate, and was plagued by shoddy workmanship. Its deficiencies, exposed by a US Senate committee, chaired by Harry Truman, embarrassed the American military. When the pipeline was abandoned in March 1945 after thirteen months' operation, it left a festering scar across the Canadian northwest – as someone put it, a "junkyard monument to military stupidity."

There had also been suggestions at various times that Canada should pay for some of the airfields that had been constructed in that country for or by the US. No decision had been made on the matter. Heeney, the secretary of the Cabinet War Committee, wrote to Clark on 24 November 1943 suggesting that Clark have someone prepare a review of the various airfield projects, both current and future, that the War Committee might consider. Heeney noted the argument in favour of Canada's payment for these projects: that otherwise the US might claim some right to use them for commercial purposes after the war, notwithstanding agreements that the fields (if of a permanent character) would be turned over to the government of Canada following the end of hostilities.[56] Others thought, however, that the government of Canada would be criticized for paying the wealthy US for these airfields when it was under no obligation to do so.

Clark saw this as an opportunity to include something additional in his settlement with the US Treasury about terminating the maximum–minimum balances agreement. He had me prepare a paper for the War Committee listing and commenting on the airfields in question.[57] One group consisted of the bases at Mingan and Fort Chimo in Northern Quebec, Churchill in Manitoba, Southampton Island in Hudson Bay, and Frobisher Bay on Baffin Island, designed as part of a northeastern route to Europe (dubbed the Crimson Route). The second group consisted of the landing fields on the Mackenzie River route used in connection with the Canol project. A third group consisted of the eight or nine gravel landing strips on the Alaska Highway. The fourth and most important consisted of the bases on the northwest staging route, from the new base at Namao near Edmonton up to those in the Yukon near Alaska. These already constituted a major traffic artery on the way to Asia. Canada had built some of these airfields for the US but had not yet submitted bills for them. The US was in various stages of building others. The costs were difficult to estimate with the data available, but we estimated the total, to that point, at $30 million to $50 million. My memorandum recommended payment for the cost of the permanent facilities that Canada had already constructed but with qualifications as to the methods that could or should be used in valuing them.

The subject was discussed at the Cabinet War Committee on 2 and 3 December. The committee decided that the US should be told that Canada did not intend to request or accept payment for the construction of any permanent facilities or improvements made by Canada to airfields in northwest Canada, and wished to pay the US government for all construction of a permanent nature that the US carried out on air routes in northwest Canada.[58]

Clark saw Harry White in Washington on 7 December 1943. He gave White the details of Canada's exchange position and a long memorandum on the maximum–minimum balances arrangement and the operations under it during 1943.[59] These operations clearly had failed to carry out the purpose of the arrangements, for Canada's reserves at the end of November (including $96 million net proceeds of security sales) were $718 million, compared with the agreed on maximum of $350 million. The forecast figure for the year end, even excluding the proceeds of security sales, was $528 million – an excess of $178 million. Clark set forth a half-dozen reasons for this, including delays in the effects of contract cancellations, the unexpectedly heavy purchases of grain by the US, the larger than expected US expenditures on defence projects in northern Canada, and the large inflow of private US capital into Canada, both in the purchase of outstanding securities and in other forms.

Clark was anxious to get this matter settled quickly and made four specific suggestions for reducing Canada's reserves. The first was for Canada to make a payment on account of $100 million Canadian to the US government to cover most of the large accrued liability outstanding on CANPAY orders for military supplies. The second was to cancel two additional War Supplies Limited contracts for minesweepers and ammunition intended for Lend-Lease to the UK, amounting in value to about $20 million. The third was to pay a small amount for subsidies to develop some marginal base-metal mines and assure their production for US war requirements. The fourth was not to submit bills for expenditures incurred by Canada on US airfield development in the northwest, and to reimburse the US government for expenditures incurred directly by it for permanent or immovable airfield development in Canada. This proposal would be formalized by a diplomatic note in the near future. Like the Cabinet War Committee decision, it proposed to pay the US only for expenditures on our routes in northwest Canada. Clark thought that this might involve a total sum of $30 million to $50 million.

Clark noted that the estimated total involved in these four items would not bring the balances down to the agreed on figure, and he said that Canada would be willing to consider any specific proposals the US might wish to make. He suggested, however, that Canada no longer should expect the US to place contracts in Canada for exchange reasons alone. If this decision was made, it would follow that the maximum–minimum arrangement should be discontinued from the end of 1943.

White was not prepared to discuss any details of the merits or drawbacks of particular suggestions but did agree to study Clark's proposals. He made some remarks to the effect that the United States could not justify Lend-Leasing any Canadian manufacturing costs to the United Kingdom or other parts of the British Empire. To do so would lead to criticism in Congress and run counter to the best interests of both Canada and the United States. On the basis of this statement and what he learned from other quarters, Clark believed that all US procurement agencies had been advised two or three weeks before that this was the principle that should be followed in placing new contracts in Canada and adjusting existing contracts.[60]

Canada was not to get off as lightly as Clark had proposed. During the next few weeks, both sides studied diversions of more War Supplies Limited contracts. Clark visited White again on 28 February 1944, accompanied this time by Louis Rasminsky and Wynne Plumptre.[61] At this meeting, the US suggested a number of additional items for adjustment, most notably the reimbursement by Canada to the US of the value of all past CANEX deliveries, since the CANEX process always had been politically questionable in Washington. Another change (conforming to White's dictum prohibiting Lend-Lease of Canadian manufacturing) was the limitation of the Lend-Lease of petroleum supplies to the UK for the British Commonwealth Air Training Plan in Canada to crude oil content. It was decided that the US should take this up with the UK, which would have to make arrangements to have the oil refined. The biggest-ticket item involved the cancellation of a $63 million US navy contract for large flying boats made in Vancouver on behalf of the Royal Navy, and the reimbursement of the US navy by Canada of the $22 million in progress payments already made.[62]

On 6 March, Ilsley and Leighton McCarthy, the Canadian ambassador, met with Morgenthau, White, and Berle. Ilsley had come to the US for health reasons but took this opportunity to see Morgenthau.[63] By this time, Canadian reserves had increased by $65 million to a total of $661 million. As a result, the US officials, at the State Department's initiative, had some additional suggestions. These involved more US projects in Canada for which the Canadian government would pay. The projects included airfields on the Crimson Route in northeast Canada; an airfield near Mingan, Quebec (which had been a matter of some controversy); terminal facilities at Dawson Creek, the railhead serving the Alaska Highway; and the part of the telephone line from Edmonton to Fairbanks that was in Canadian territory. Ilsley said these new items would come as a shock to his colleagues in Ottawa, but White explained that his associates in the US Treasury had not realized that there were more airfields built by the US in Canada than those in the northwest. He thought that since Canada's reserves had risen so rapidly, the proposed addition of $42.8 million in reimbursement was not unreasonable. Ilsley promised a reply within two weeks.

Ilsley returned to Ottawa to discuss these matters with his colleagues. Clark visited White the following Monday, 13 March, to relate the tentative reactions of the Canadian ministers. Some of the new items were quite acceptable, but others would be difficult, partly because the Canadians always had doubted the wisdom of building the Crimson Route airports and the airport at Mingan. Clark urged that the maximum–minimum arrangement cease as of 31 December 1943, when Canadian reserves were $125 million lower than at 29 February. White pressed for settlement as of the end of February. In a memorandum to

Morgenthau on 14 March, White proposed that Morgenthau offer to settle as of 29 February, on the basis that the US would agree to consider as outside Canada's reserves the $109 million of net proceeds of security sales, provided that the government of Canada accept the items it had rejected the week before.[64]

Ilsley returned to Washington and, accompanied by Clark and Plumptre, saw Morgenthau, White, and Hickerson from the State Department on the afternoon of 14 March. Ilsley restated some of the Canadian objections to certain items, and Morgenthau said that, if Canada preferred, he could accept other proposals that had an equivalent effect on reducing the balances of payments. When Ilsley asked if the US would be willing to exclude net sales of securities from the reserve figures, White implied that the matter was negotiable. Ilsley said that he would like to get in touch with his government to see what they would be willing to do.

There was another meeting the following morning, but Ilsley had not received a response from Ottawa. During this discussion, Hickerson suggested the possibility of Canada's purchase of the Canol properties, which were still a highly controversial matter in Washington (and also in Ottawa, albeit secretly).[65] Morgenthau quickly dissociated himself and the administration from that suggestion. Ilsley promised that he would get in touch with his colleagues in Ottawa again and send an answer back via Clark. At long last, Ilsley himself left for a much-needed holiday with his brother in California, where it was hoped he could be effectively free from contacts and worry.

An answer from Ottawa did arrive later that day, but it was insufficient to enable Clark and White to reach agreement. Negotiations continued for another week, culminating in agreement on two detailed lists of measures. The first covered seven items or groups of items that would reduce Canada's reserves in total by $300.8 million. This included the disputed airfields and a large new item: a payment of $140 million by Canada for US tanks received by the UK under Lend-Lease and transferred in the United Kingdom to Canada. Many months later, this payment proved larger than was needed for the tanks and was applied to US-made aircraft transferred by the UK. The second list of items totalled $191.6 million and included measures that would reduce Canada's future receipts of US dollars (mainly cancellation of US contracts for Canadian-manufactured products to be Lend-Leased to the United Kingdom).

The Cabinet War Committee kept up to date with Ilsley and Clark's negotiations in Washington.[66] On 1 March, it decided the financial discussions regarding airports should be kept quite separate from any discussion of post-war finances. The bearing that the payment of building costs might have on claims to use the airports after the war was foremost in everyone's minds on both sides; this consideration, however, did not seem to influence Morgenthau's attitude. On 8 March, Ilsley and Clark reported on Clark's earlier discussions and on the ambassador and Ilsley's decision of 6 March, when the Americans had asked to have the Crimson Route and Mingan fields included. Howe thought that the American proposal for the Crimson Route should be resisted. He asserted that the route had no post-war value and that the US had constructed it against the unanimous advice of Canadian authorities. The discussion was adjourned until 10 March.

Despite serious criticism of some of these projects, the Cabinet War Committee decided that Ilsley and Clark should be given authority to make the best deal possible. They should try to include items likely to be of the greatest value to Canada, rather than those most embarrassing to the US government. On 15 March, the prime minister read to the committee Ilsley's telegram of the previous day summing up Morgenthau's main proposals. The committee simply noted all this with approval, in order that the negotiations might be concluded.

On 22 March, while Ilsley was relaxing at his brother's home in California, Clark outlined to the committee the items included in the schedules that he finally had negotiated with White. He drew attention to the large payment on account for tanks, the liability for which had only recently come to light and which would save Canada future payments. He also informed the committee that Ilsley intended, once this settlement had been completed and announced, to propose a relaxation of the severe restriction on the use of US dollars for pleasure travel in the US, and some relaxation of the restriction on imports under the Exchange Conservation Act. The Cabinet War Committee approved the arrangements negotiated with Morgenthau.

The results of these agreements were embodied in an exchange of letters dated 24 March between Ilsley and Morgenthau, which on both sides were cast in general and appreciative terms.[67] The substance of the letters concerned the secret schedules, initialled by White and Clark, of which the Canadian copies were locked in the securities deposit vaults of the department. Clark gave all those involved in making the specified payments detailed instructions about transferring contracts from War Supplies Limited to the Mutual Aid Board and other agencies.

Ilsley made a brief statement to the House of Commons on 21 April 1944 about these hitherto secret arrangements and how they related to the Hyde Park Declaration and its operation. He gave no figures, as the law required that the amounts of Canada's reserves not be disclosed, but he did mention the nature of the payments to be made, including the reimbursement of the US government for its expenditures on construction of airfields in Canada.[68]

The relaxation in the restrictions on tourist expenditures outside Canada (mainly, of course, in the US) was announced in the House of Commons on 18 May. Ilsley said that the foreign exchange situation was such as to permit that action, and the government attached importance to the resumption of normal friendly contacts between Canadians and Americans. It is worth noting here that Towers, as chairman of the Foreign Exchange Control Board, had recommended such action in a letter of 21 February, in which he emphasized how difficult it had become to enforce the travel restrictions.[69] Towers stated in that letter that evasion of the travel regulations was taking place on a large scale and that the board was powerless to put a stop to it without resorting to frequent searches of persons leaving Canada and much broader censorship of outgoing and incoming mail.

In the budget of 26 June, Ilsley carried the relaxation of restraints a step further by proposing the removal of Schedule 1 of the War Exchange Conversation Act, which prohibited the importation of a long list of goods into Canada.[70] He believed that the exchange situation no longer justified this discrimination against imports, but he warned Canadians that the supply situation outside Canada and various other restraints, such as price controls, would prevent any great wave of imports as a result of the prohibitions' removal.

Despite the special payments to the US in 1944, Canada managed to have an approximate balance in its current international accounts with that country and an increase of $278 million (equivalent in Canadian dollars) in its gold and US dollar reserves. The following year, 1945, Canada's exports to the US declined, but there were no special payments as in 1944, so again Canada had a small surplus on its current account with the US. To other non-sterling-area countries, however, Canada sent $534 million in exports in 1944 – much greater than even pre-war figures – while imports were only $111 million.

Although the surplus exports to these countries was financed to the extent of about $300 million by export credits, Mutual Aid, and relief, there was a total net current account balance of $504 million, and an increase in Canada's gold and US dollar reserves of $667 million (Canadian dollar equivalent), up to a year-end peak of $1.667 billion. Canadian gold and US dollar reserves declined in 1946 and 1947.[71] These figures indicate that it was much to Canada's advantage to buy its way out of the maximum–minimum balance arrangement, even given what seemed like a high price at the time.

After the negotiations of March 1944, little official war business was conducted between the Department of Finance and the US Treasury.

What remained to consider consisted of some details arising out of UK settlements for Lend-Lease supplies and settlements regarding US projects in Canada. There were, however, important discussions and negotiations about post-war arrangements to set up the International Monetary Fund and the International Bank for Reconstruction and Development. (These developments are the subject of chapter 9.)

In concluding this account of wartime relations with the US, we should note the fact that Clark himself, rather than his minister or his subordinates, did most of the reporting and negotiating with Morgenthau and White, both of whom respected and trusted him. He understood more about the United States and its attitudes and institutions than he did about their British counterparts, and more than the rest of us did. This, perhaps, was because of his years of work in the US during the 1920s, though he was working in the private sector then and the times were very different. He had many American friends and read more about the United States than he did about other countries. Whatever the reason, his ability to deal effectively with the Treasury Department was of real advantage to Canada at this important time.[72]

CHAPTER SEVEN

Mutual Aid to Allies

In late 1942, the home front began to receive some positive news from the war fronts. While the war had not turned fully in the Allies' favour, there was reason for cautious optimism. The Russians had virtually stemmed the tide of the Nazi invasion. In addition, the Canadian, American, and British forces were having greater success hunting the German submarines that had wreaked havoc in the North Atlantic since the beginning of the war. There was also some positive news from North Africa. On 8 November 1942, Allied Expeditionary Forces landed in French North Africa in the greatest amphibious invasion hitherto attempted. The French garrisons at Casablanca, Oran, and Algiers were overcome after brief fighting, and an armistice was arranged on 11 November. One day later, in the Pacific around the Solomon Islands, a three-day naval battle ended in a victory for US forces. One Japanese battleship and five cruisers were reported sunk, and twelve transports destroyed.

Despite these victories, the war was taking its toll on the Allied nations. Britain, particularly, was in need of food, raw materials, and munitions. Canada had plenty to offer by 1943. The domestic economy was firing on all cylinders. During the period between 1943 and 1945, the principal means by which Canada provided its allies with munitions and supplies was Mutual Aid. During the final two years of the war, the Mutual Aid Board allocated $2 billion worth of Canadian-produced goods without charge, most of it going to Britain and Commonwealth countries.

This chapter describes the intensive process leading up to the implementation of Mutual Aid in 1943.

As 1942, the year of crises, drew to its close, we had to turn our attention urgently to devising another major measure to succeed the billion-dollar gift to Britain. We were relying on the gift to finance Britain and indirectly to finance Canadian supplies on a small scale for Australia and Russia, but we did not regard a second similar "gift" of money to Britain as suitable or even feasible. This was partly due to criticism in Quebec, but there was another, more significant reason. Our minds were now on wider, more positive plans in which the government of Canada would play a more active role. We no longer thought of Canada primarily as a junior partner of a beleaguered Britain but as one of the United Nations, which included giants such as Russia and China, and distant dominions such as Australia, which had by then become not only the main American base in the South Pacific but a leader in the bloody battles against the Japanese in Papua New Guinea. We had learned about pooling and allocating munitions in light of strategic need; in the Department of Finance, Clifford Clark still hoped that our war production could earn Canada a full place on the Munitions Assignment Board in Washington.

On 9 December 1942, I wrote some notes for Clark about two key problems: devising the best means for maintaining the flow of supplies to the UK when the billion-dollar gift ran out and finding a sensible pattern of financial relations with Allied countries other than the UK and the US.[1] A few days later, Clark discussed these issues at a meeting with Sir Frederick Phillips of the UK Treasury. I was present for part of this discussion and supplied the two men with forecasts of the Canada–UK balance of payments. Clark outlined the nature of the broader problem we now faced – further financing of Britain – and mentioned the possibility of "pooling," which Phillips had suggested earlier. Clark said that he had not yet discussed the issue with anyone, even his own minister.

On 15 December, Clark put the finishing touches on a long and comprehensive memorandum entitled "Financial Arrangements with the United Kingdom (and Other Countries)," which he supplied to the minister of finance and other cabinet ministers.[2] In it he outlined the situation in detail and made several suggestions for dealing with the immediate financial requirements of Britain over the next few weeks. The memo's main proposals, however, dealt with problems that would be encountered over the long term: first, the purchase of British-owned war factories in Canada, which would provide sufficient operating funds for two or three months (following a British payment of $150 million US); second, the assumption by Canada of full financial responsibility for equipping and maintaining RCAF squadrons operating out of England; and third, the financing by Canada of the pay and allowances – and accommodation and maintenance – of all Canadians serving in the RAF.

Over the longer term, Clark's main "suggestions for consideration" were essentially as follows:

(a) The government should ask Parliament for a one-time war appropriation calculated to cover the needs of Canada's military program and the cost of surplus war production.

(b) Canada's production program should be based on Finance's estimate of the maximum munitions and supplies we could produce. This proposal was not intended to interfere with the established practice of determining the extent of the program based on orders placed by the UK, the US, Australia, Russia, and other Allied nations. However, in the absence of specific renewal orders, Munitions and Supply nevertheless might continue production if it was felt that certain products were likely to be needed by one of the United Nations.

(c) The first priority in claims on our war production would be the Canadian forces, unless otherwise determined by a committee representing the departments of National Defence and Munitions and Supply. Munitions and war equipment determined to be surplus once Canadian requirements were taken into account would be pooled for allocation to any of the United Nations in accordance with strategic needs.

(d) The only agency to make these allocations would be the Munitions Assignment Board in Washington. In these circumstances, Canada would be justified in insisting on full Canadian representation on that board.

(e) Canada's US dollar position should be safeguarded through an agreement with the US Treasury, which would recognize a stated amount of US dollar reserves (say, $350 million) as the minimum that Canada should maintain. For its part, Canada would recognize a somewhat higher amount (say, $400 million) as the maximum. American procurement authorities would continue to place munitions orders in Canada, which Canada would fulfill and deliver. If Canadian reserves of US dollars fell below the prescribed minimum, the US would pay Canada for the deliveries; if the reserves tended to exceed the maximum, we would provide the supplies free of charge, "even to the US."

At the Cabinet War Committee on 23 December 1942, James Ilsley raised the question of financing the UK and emphasized the urgency of establishing a plan for 1943 and after. He indicated the scale of financing required over the coming months and the next fiscal year and went on to mention the possibility of allocating Canadian products gratis to members of the United Nations, mainly the UK but also Australia, New Zealand, the USSR, and other Allies. The War Committee referred the question of general financial arrangements with the UK to a subcommittee composed of the ministers of finance, national defence, munitions and supply, and justice.[3]

This powerful subcommittee held three meetings. They undoubtedly had read Clark's long memorandum. It is likely that Clark, N.A. Robertson, and Arnold Heeney were present at some of these meetings. The subcommittee made a detailed report to the War Committee on 13 January 1943 accepting some, but not all, of Clark's suggestions. It recommended the following:

(a) Gifts of Canadian surplus war production should be made to other members of the United Nations, not just to the United Kingdom.

(b) The UK balance of payments deficit with Canada in the next fiscal year – to be financed by gifts of production, along with contributions of war material to other countries – might be on the order of $1.3 billion.

(c) To meet the requirement of the UK deficit in the first quarter of 1943 (after taking into account payments from the UK of $150 million US), the Canadian government should purchase British war plants in Canada, which probably would provide about $200 million Canadian.

(d) As of 1 April 1943, Canada should assume the costs of equipping and maintaining the thirty-five RCAF squadrons in the UK (in addition to the three squadrons for which Canada had been financially responsible from the beginning).

(e) Canada should accept responsibility for the wages and allowances, clothing, and personal necessaries of all Canadian pilots and other aircrew serving in the RAF, which would add about $35 million to RCAF expenditures in the UK during 1943–44. Some other minor payments to the UK were considered but not recommended.

(f) Canada might accept a more generous attitude toward the UK on the allocation of certain miscellaneous costs in Canada, for example in regard to camps for prisoners of war.

(g) The recommendations in (c) to (g) would reduce the British deficit with Canada by about $385 million.

To address the remainder of the problem, the subcommittee recommended that Parliament be asked to pass an act, somewhat similar to the US Lend-Lease Act, containing an appropriation of up to $700 million to cover the cost of surplus war materials and other supplies to be given free, or leased, or lent by Canada to any of the United Nations, in keeping with certain stipulated conditions. A board consisting of the ministers of munitions and supply, national defence, justice, and finance would be created to administer the act. (A "layman's draft" of a suggested bill was included.)[4]

The report made no mention of the Munitions Assignment Board in Washington or other assignment arrangements. It implied, however, that the proposed board of ministers would exercise assignment powers or authorize others to do so. Clark had failed to persuade the ministers that he should seek again to get Canada on the Combined Board in Washington. The real substance of his financing proposals had been approved, however, although the final proposed appropriation was not quite large enough. The "layman's draft" of the legislation was his, apparently written when he first heard the conclusions of the subcommittee's four ministers.

On 13 January, the Cabinet War Committee approved the recommendation of its subcommittee, reviewed the text of the draft bill, and referred it for redrafting by Clark, Robertson, Heeney, and the Department of Justice.[5]

The drafting and redrafting of the legislation went on for several weeks. In those days, such a bill had to be preceded by a resolution; in this case, the resolution was introduced on 12 February 1943. It provided for an appropriation of $1 billion rather than the $700 million stipulated in the subcommittee's report of 13 January. The increase was the result of extended bargaining in the Cabinet War Committee over the division of the limited total expenditures of $5.5 billion for the fiscal year 1943–44, a limit that Ilsley had set with King's strong support.[6] This was the highest level of expenditure authorized in any year of the war; indeed, the actual expenditure in that year, which totalled roughly $5.32 billion, was slightly higher than that of the following year, 1944–45, during which the Canadian forces were engaged more fully in the fighting overseas.

The resolution for the Mutual Aid Bill referred to the establishment of the Canadian War Supplies Allocation Board; when the actual bill was introduced in May, the name of the governing board had been changed to the Canadian Mutual Aid Board. The composition of the board included the ministers of munitions and supply, national defence, finance, agriculture, and justice. This last inclusion was considered important because it was necessary, in a potentially controversial area, to have the input of a senior cabinet minister from Quebec. Louis St. Laurent was in fact an active and constructive member of the board. The minister of agriculture was added to the board's composition after some wavering in cabinet about whether foodstuffs would be provided as Mutual Aid; it was decided that they should be eligible, just as they were eligible for Lend-Lease by the United States.[7] The key clause in the bill read as follows:

It shall be good and sufficient consideration for making war supplies available to any of the United Nations hereunder that the said war supplies are to be used in the joint and effective prosecution of the war, but no war supplies shall be so made available to any of the United Nations except upon terms and conditions approved by the Governor in Council or by regulations, and the Governor in Council may require, in respect of specific classes of supplies or any specific transfer of supplies under subsection one of this section, such payment or repayment in kind or property or such reciprocal action or provision of supplies or such other direct or indirect benefit as the Governor in Council deems appropriate.[8]

ROLE AND NATURE OF THE BOARD

One of the first considerations after the Mutual Aid Bill was drafted was the role and organization of the board itself. Knowing C.D. Howe's ability and desire to run things himself with his own officers, Heeney got the prime minister to make clear, at a meeting of the Cabinet War Committee, that the board was a committee of the Privy Council and should operate as such, with proper meetings of the ministers and minutes of decisions made by a secretary of the board provided by the Privy Council Office.[9] Howe did not oppose this arrangement and co-operated effectively as chairman, probably because he had a high respect for Ilsley, St Laurent, and Ralston. Heeney secured the part-time services of Captain Duncan McTavish, deputy judge advocate general of the navy and an eminent Ottawa lawyer, to serve as secretary. McTavish carried out his duties conscientiously but he was not at all acquainted with the subjects coming before the board and was so senior that he had forgotten how to keep detailed minutes. I attended all the meetings on behalf of the Finance Department. By virtue of my junior status, I was keen enough to scribble detailed notes about what went on; as a result, after most meetings I was able to help McTavish write or rewrite the minutes.

The board decided that those already doing the kind of work required by Mutual Aid would continue to do so. The Department of Munitions and Supply would place contracts for munitions and war supplies; Agriculture would do likewise for most farm products; and Trade and Commerce would be responsible for wheat and flour. External Affairs would receive the first applications from countries requesting Mutual Aid and would make the initial arrangements and draw up a formal diplomatic agreement detailing the principles and terms under which Mutual Aid would be supplied.

The accounts of the Mutual Aid Board were kept by the chief treasury officer of the Department of Munitions and Supply, A.V. Franklin, and his large staff. Their departmental accounts, complex beyond description, were closely interrelated with those of the board. Questions of financial policy and arrangements, particularly vis-à-vis the British, would continue to be handled by the Department of

Finance – in many cases by Clark himself, usually with my assistance. Frank Knox and Alec McLeod assisted us in assembling and analysing balance of payments statistics, which were essential in forecasting the Mutual Aid that would be available to Britain and Australia.

The Department of National Defence was responsible for determining its own requirements for munitions and military equipment and for reconciling these with the requests from applicants for Mutual Aid. National Defence was also the main source of advice to the board on strategic requirements. The Canadian defence services already included a munitions assignment committee, before which the various needs for assignable Canadian products were presented and assessed and the following month's deliveries settled on. In addition, a Washington advisory committee was established to serve the board. It consisted of senior Canadian officials in Washington, ranging from the chairman of the Canadian joint staff and the minister-counsellor of the embassy to various specialized officers including the financial attaché. This was a useful committee dealing with a wide range of questions. Later, a larger, more senior committee, the Joint War Aid Committee, was formed; it included members of the Canadian advisory committee in Washington and American officials concerned with US production and Lend-Lease problems and policies.

MUTUAL AID BOARD ADMINISTRATION

Howe was in charge of the administration of the Mutual Aid program and kept it small by getting assistance from others as outlined above. He selected Karl Fraser from his department's Washington office as director of administration. Fraser had the benefit of being familiar with the US Lend-Lease operations. George Heaseman, a senior officer in the Department of Trade and Commerce with long experience in Ottawa and abroad, soon was brought to the staff as senior assistant to Fraser. Three officers were seconded to the board staff from National Defence, the senior a colonel specialized in ordnance. There were a few other officers serving under Fraser from time to time. Stewart Mackay-Smith was one who kept well informed and with whom I maintained contact. He was the secretary of a large interdepartmental committee on Mutual Aid where many matters of procedure and special cases were discussed. Fraser was not a business-like operator. He did not write letters or memos when he should have done so, but trusted too much to telephone calls, of which he did not keep systematic records, even when they constituted commitments. His deficiencies were made good to some extent by Heaseman, but the latter did not always know what Fraser was doing.[10]

DIVIDING THE STERLING AREA

From the inception of Mutual Aid, Ilsley had made it clear that Canada intended to deal directly with the various countries that were to receive aid; he noted that in the past some assistance had been given to Russia by way of the UK and that the billion-dollar gift to the UK had enabled it to meet the Canadian dollar requirements of other sterling area members.[11]

Dealing directly with other United Nations countries regarding Mutual Aid, and having to take into account the balance of payments that these countries had with Canada, meant an increased workload for the department. We had to collect information from many sources to estimate the balances of payments for the sterling area countries – notably Australia, New Zealand, and India. We did not even try to take account of the ability of Russia and China to pay. (The way we dealt with them is outlined below.) Notwithstanding their relative ability to pay, neither of these countries required much from the Mutual Aid appropriation during the fiscal year 1943–44.

We had long discussions with the British Treasury through its Ottawa representatives Gordon Munro and Owen Williams, who were supported by Professor D.H. Robertson in London, about how we should allot our aid to parts of the sterling area. Munro, Williams, and Robertson felt that it was artificial and arbitrary to base aid levels on the balance of payments with Canada, especially given the UK's practices with other commonwealth nations. If these other commonweath countries had a deficit with Canada, London financed it; if they had a surplus, their sterling holdings increased. To be fair, we had to take other factors into account, for instance, the respective country's budget position, its overall balance of payments, and the size of its sterling reserves. The Treasury, and no doubt the Bank of England, felt that we were interfering in the central working arrangements of the sterling area. They were particularly sensitive about India, which already had accumulated very large reserves of sterling and had been paying off some of its sterling debt. Moreover, the British ruled India and directly bore much of the expenses of that country's military operations. On the other hand, India was basically a very poor country with little taxable capacity. As I wrote at the time: "Broad political considerations are presumably important in deciding what [India] should be required to pay for and what she should get free."[12]

The British Treasury recognized, however, that Canada had political reasons for wanting to deal separately with some parts of the sterling area, notably Australia, New Zealand, and the West Indies. They stated their regrets about our decision,[13] then co-operated by furnishing us with information to enable us to proceed, taking our bilateral balances of payments into account.

The Mutual Aid Board approved our general approach to the division of the sterling area for the purposes of Mutual Aid. Members of the sterling area other than the UK got less in 1943–44 than we had expected, because of delays in making the arrangements. Australia got only $21 million that year; Canada and the British had expected them to qualify for two or three times that amount. India got less than $1 million.

ACCOUNTING AND RELATED ARRANGEMENTS WITH THE BRITISH

The initial problem of dividing up the sterling area proved to be less of a hurdle than the accounting arrangements and rearrangements that we had to make with the British Treasury. We needed to take the large payments that we previously had decided to make for RCAF squadrons and equipment and supplies for the Canadian army overseas, as well as the commercial and various other payments of Canadian dollars that the UK was receiving, and channel this money back into payments for British arms and food. We were proposing that Mutual Aid be used only to finance the deficit in Britain's huge and complex balance of payments with us. Under the Mutual Aid Act, we were obliged to transfer goods (or services) but not money to the countries we were aiding. This meant that the goods first must be bought by the government of Canada or its agencies, and then turned over to the ownership of the United Kingdom. Since we could not tell precisely in advance how much money would be needed to finance Mutual Aid or how much of this money would be paid out of funds belonging to the British Treasury, we had to devise some means of channelling the British "cash" receipts into an account that could be observed and controlled by those making the Mutual Aid purchases. To make matters even more confusing, in July 1943 we decided, and the British agreed, that the government of Canada should take over all British munitions and supply contracts.[14]

The accounting problems involved in the Mutual Aid program were highlighted during a discussion between B.G. McIntyre, the comptroller of the British Treasury, and Karl Fraser, the director-designate of administration of the Mutual Aid Board.[15] Fraser proposed a solution to these problems that involved requiring the British to turn over their funds to the board – a proposal that the British, not surprisingly, did not like. McIntyre suggested radical changes in financial policy and arrangements that conflicted with the new Mutual Aid Act. When it became clear that the two had reached an impasse, the problem was passed down to Clark. There followed weeks of discussions with British Treasury representatives. The central issue involved determining the point at which UK money, for which these representatives had control and responsibility, passed over to the control of the Mutual Aid Board, and the degree to which that board was accountable to the various British departments and agencies of the Treasury.

Finally, early in August 1943, Clark and I hit on a relatively simple arrangement, which the British government was prepared to accept.[16] The normal surplus of British commercial and private financial receipts in Canada over their normal commercial and private financial payments would accumulate in the Bank of England's general account with the Bank of Canada. When the balance in that account exceeded an agreed on maximum, the excess would be transferred into a United Kingdom Suspense Account, owned by the UK government and held in the Bank of Canada. The government of Canada would pay into this account amounts payable to the UK by the Canadian army and air force. From this account there would be two types of payment. One type would be payments back to the Bank of England account, if it fell below an agreed minimum figure. The other, and principal, flow of funds would be payments into another new account, owned by the government of Canada but held and operated by the Mutual Aid Board to make purchases of war supplies (broadly defined) for the United Kingdom. This account was called the U.K. Cash Receipts Account and was managed by the Mutual Aid Board and its staff to pay for supplies ordered by the UK other than those supplies that were to be provided as Mutual Aid. The UK did not have to accept responsibility under their law for the management of this account. The Treasury would show in its books the transfers of funds from their Suspense Account to Canada's U.K. Cash Receipts Accounts as "payments to the Canadian Government for the purchase from the Canadian Government of war supplies." Clark insisted on this formula to prevent any misinterpretation. This arrangement was approved on 16 August at a meeting with Sir David Whaley, the senior officer of the UK Treasury in charge of overseas finance. The suspense account and the detail of its operation was the subject later of a formal memorandum of agreement between the two governments.[17] Although these arrangements sound cumbersome, they worked well once they came into effect, on 1 December 1943.

Between 31 March and 1 December 1943, it was necessary to continue operating with the old system under which the UK paid in cash for its war supplies. Britain had received cash from a variety of sources, including payments to the UK by the Canadian forces and from the sale of their war plants to Canada. When the Mutual Aid administration was ready to operate but agreement had not been reached on the two-account system described above, an interim arrangement was made by which the Canadian government paid monies that it owed to the UK into a temporary account held and operated by the Mutual Aid Board on behalf of the UK. This was called the U.K.–Canada Cash Account.[18] These monies were used with the approval of UK officers to meet obligations of the UK in Canada, including the purchase of war supplies before 1 December 1943. The total amount paid into and disbursed from this account was approximately $2.726 billion. After 30 November, a total of $59 million was placed in the U.K. Cash Receipts Account during the 1943–44 fiscal year, of which $31.5 million was disbursed for war supplies and the remaining $27.5 million carried over to the next year. In addition to these disbursements, $723.8 million was transferred to the UK in Mutual Aid during that year. To assist in making these large cash payments, the UK had on hand about $165 million from the sale of their war plants to the Canadian government and received about $70 million as a cash refund from what they had contributed to the working capital pool of the Department of Munitions and Supply; in the first quarter of 1944, they received a further credit of $170 million for progress payments that they had made on contracts for goods that they were to receive later as Mutual Aid or to pay for in cash at the time of delivery.[19] I believe that these complicated and non-recurrent payments in 1943–44 amounting to $405 million were not understood adequately by ministers and some of the key officials in other departments in forecasting what Mutual Aid would be needed in the next fiscal year, 1944–45, when such special payments would not be made.

MUTUAL AID TO RUSSIA

Canadian wheat, along with some other supplies, had been provided by Britain to the USSR during 1941 and 1942. The wheat shipments were eventually financed by a medium-term credit of $10 million, which Canada extended to the USSR in September 1942. This credit primarily covered wheat to be shipped after the agreement was signed.[20] Both the UK and the US were providing arms, munitions, and civilian supplies to the Russians pursuant to formal diplomatic agreements known as protocols. The second protocol was entered into in mid-1942 and spanned the twelve months beginning 1 July 1942. This protocol detailed the shipping tonnage to be made available for transporting "stores," and the amount of particular stores to be provided. Usually the amount of available shipping determined the amount of stores that the USSR actually acquired.

At the time that the Mutual Aid Bill was before Parliament, the government announced its proposed participation in the third protocol. Canada was unable to provide shipping tonnage, so it had to omit from its proposal any undertaking regarding tonnage to be made available to the USSR.[21] The supplies to be offered in this protocol by Canada were discussed with American and British officials in Washington by Fraser on behalf of the Mutual Aid Board. In July and later, the Mutual Aid Board approved allocations of $116 million to finance Russian requirements. The actual value of supplies, equipment, and services provided in the fiscal year 1943–44 – a period roughly corresponding to that of the third protocol – was only about $23 million. In June of 1944, the board reviewed the amounts that had been expended or "earmarked" for the USSR up to that time and decided that it should approve only an additional value of supplies and services amounting to $115 million for the fourth protocol in the year beginning 1 July 1944. The amount actually expended for supplies and service for the USSR in the fiscal year beginning 1 April 1944 was about $98 million, and in the period 1 April 1945 to September 1945 (the end of the hostilities), about $46 million.[22]

The largest items by volume provided to the USSR over the whole Mutual Aid period were aluminum and other base metals, valued at $32 million; these were followed by wheat and flour (supplied mainly in the form of flour) at $27 million; then came electrical, radio, and telephone equipment at $20 million; then automotive equipment and transport at $18 million. The big-ticket service item was repairing and servicing Russian vessels.[23] After the end of the war in Europe, Russia continued to receive some Mutual Aid from Canada, notably ten naval minesweepers, which were available because the Canadian navy required fewer than they had anticipated; Russia's need for the naval vessels resulted directly from the earlier hostilities.

The Russians had been receiving a lot of industrial equipment and had ordered much more before the termination of Mutual Aid on 1 September 1945. The Mutual Aid Board authorized the production of this equipment to continue on the understanding that the USSR would be prepared to pay for it on credit. Despite prolonged negotiation, however, the credit terms were never agreed on. The USSR was unwilling to accept the credit terms that Canada was offering its other allies, mainly the cost to the Canadian government of borrowing within Canada for the same length of time.[24]

MUTUAL AID TO CHINA

Logistics severely curtailed the amount and nature of arms and other war supplies that could be provided to China. Indeed, as the American historian Barbara Tuchman notes: "The effort to supply China, and the air and ground forces in China, presented the greatest logistic challenge of the war, probably of any war."[25] China's coast was cut off by the Japanese occupation, which in late 1941 extended to Southeast Asia. In early 1942, Japan seized Burma and cut off the road from India across north Burma. All that remained were the flights taking off from the Assam airfields and flying over the 20,000-foot Himalayas (known as "the Hump") to Kunming.[26] It was a difficult and dangerous route, flown by the us Air Transport Command, which strove to reach a monthly delivery target of 10,000 tons of munitions and supplies. Most of this was required to supply the Fourteenth (American) Air Force, which had been formed out of the earlier American volunteer group and was commanded by Major General Claire Chennault. It was hoped that this force eventually would be able to attack Japan by air from China, but the Chinese army was unable to protect its airfields against the Japanese infantry. Due to the nature and very limited capacity of the available transport, supplies sent to China during 1943 and 1944 were restricted to small arms and ammunition. Both the Americans and the British were ready to provide Lend-Lease arms where possible. Under the able and very dedicated leadership of General Joseph W. Stilwell, the American army was trying, unsuccessfully, to use Lend-Lease (combined with financial assistance) as a lever to induce Chiang Kai-shek and his predominantly corrupt senior officers to create some effective army divisions. Washington, however, took a much more relaxed view of Chiang's unwillingness to fight, which President Roosevelt seemed to feel was unimportant. Inside China, inflation was rampant and the condition of the peasants and common soldiers was appalling, except in the small remote areas controlled by the hardy, disciplined Communists.[27]

Despite this situation, the Canadian government wanted, for reasons of goodwill and with an eye to trade in the distant future, to provide China with Mutual Aid. In his first announcement of the Mutual Aid program, on 8 February 1943, Ilsley said: "We want to play our part in providing China with everything that can be transported to her so that she may strike back at Japan quickly and effectively."[28] Chinese representatives in Washington, led by T.V. Soong, the Chinese minister of external affairs, who spent much time in the American capital, quickly inquired as to what might be on offer. There were some preliminary discussions in Ottawa, and the Mutual Aid Board first addressed the question early in May.[29] The board approved in principle that Canada should provide supplies to China, within limits, if there was a satisfactory guarantee that the supplies could be transported safely. Soon after the Mutual Aid Act was passed, Soong submitted to Howe a list of supplies that China desired; the supplies totalled 60,000 tons and consisted mostly of small arms, ammunition, and artillery. Soong discussed this matter with Howe on 28 May and submitted a revised list. In July, the Mutual Aid Board approved a list of small arms, ammunition, and some small orders of artillery and anti-aircraft guns within a general allocation of $52 million for Chinese requests.

Both parties knew that it would be necessary for Canada to discuss the list of items to be supplied with American army authorities who controlled the transport into China. In preparation for such consultation, the Canadian and US governments established the Joint War Aid Committee during the summer.[30] As a result of consultations with the US War Department and members of this joint committee, the Mutual Aid administration agreed to decrease drastically the weight of the first shipments to China, limiting them to light artillery, ancillary equipment, and small arms and ammunition.[31] The revised offer was given to Soong in a letter dated 20 August. Soong was at the Quebec Conference where he had been invited to report on the Chinese situation. While the letter was not written in precise terms, it certainly assumed substantial reductions in the heavier items of equipment and the total weight of the program. It included with the light artillery some "ancillary equipment," the significance of which would became evident only much later.[32]

Back in Washington early in September, Soong protested to President Roosevelt that US officials had pressed Canada to cut back its proposed 60,000 tons of supplies to a total of only 12,500, to be placed in stockpile in India. "All that was before Quebec" and no longer applied, Roosevelt explained.[33] Notwithstanding Roosevelt's assertion, American army officials continued to oppose shipping artillery to India for Chinese use. The autumn brought further protests by the Chinese, along with efforts to get Canada to reinstate the items that had been eliminated from the program at the request of the Americans. There was some evidence that the US army wished to monopolize the provision of arms to China in order to exercise control over Chinese military programs and their operation.[34] Soong had hired Roy Peers as one of his staff in Ottawa. Peers had been on Karl Fraser's staff, which seemed to explain the detailed knowledge the Chinese had of the Canadian program and Canada's negotiations with the Americans.

After further consideration by the Mutual Aid Board,[35] a substantial shipment of Canadian-made arms and ammunition was assembled in Vancouver and sent in two ships, late in February 1944, to the Chinese ordnance officer in Karachi, which was outside US control. The goods would remain there for a year or more. When the British military mission in Washington examined the cargo manifests sent to them by the Canadians, they were surprised to find that the shipment included 644 trucks. By this point in the war, unlike small arms and artillery, military trucks were in short supply; the British were critical of Canada for shipping trucks that could not possibly be taken into China in the foreseeable future.[36]

After this unpleasant experience, Hume Wrong, second-in-command at External Affairs, wrote a highly critical memorandum for the Mutual Aid Board addressing the basic questions relating to aid for China. Besides recounting all the shipments and proposed shipments, Wrong declared that

reports from many sources support the view that the delivery of munitions to Chinese military representatives in India is not likely to hasten the defeat of Japan ... Apart from the reasons already indicated, the state of confusion, corruption and inefficiency now rampant in China, the virtual cessation of active operations against the Japanese forces and the inclination of many influential Chinese to regard the Chinese communist armies as the greatest menace, are general factors to be taken into account in deciding what more should be done in extending Mutual Aid to China.[37]

Howe and other ministers on the board referred this general question to the prime minister for his consideration. On N.A. Robertson's advice, King requested the views of the British Foreign Office and the US State Department as to whether it was wise to continue aid to China at that time. Both bodies thought that on balance it was best to continue.[38] King asked that the strategic need issue be referred to the Combined Chiefs of Staff Committee in Washington. Meanwhile, the board approved Howe's proposal to assemble a second shipment for Karachi. The combined chiefs of staff decided on 14 May 1944 that the general program should proceed but that all future shipments should include only small arms and ammunition light enough to be flown over the Hump. Since the shipment already assembled for dispatch included artillery, trucks, and other heavy items, the CCOS decision was troublesome. Howe and his administration urged that the proposed shipment go ahead, arguing that the CCOS decision did not really apply to it. External Affairs and American officials in Washington opposed the shipment, but Fraser somehow managed to get it passed through the Joint War Aid Committee.[39] At a meeting on 31 May, the Cabinet War Committee supported Howe, and the second shipment left Quebec on 15 June 1944.

Howe laid down the law at the Mutual Aid Board meeting on 5 June. He had backed up his man Fraser, as he nearly always did with his officials, but he was not going to stand for such controversy in future. Howe stated that future shipments to China would only proceed with the agreement of all concerned, including the Joint War Aid Committee in Washington. The board agreed and decided that the Chinese authorities should be informed that they could not expect to receive supplies that they were not going to be able to use.[40] The decision to curtail shipments to China was reinforced by a 29 July telegram from the Canadian ambassador in Chungking. The telegram outlined in frank detail the pessimistic views of two American generals – Stilwell's deputies – who thought that it would be impossible to move the stockpile of Canadian arms in Karachi in time for them to be used in the war against Japan. Moreover, these generals considered many of the arms in the stockpile to be unsuitable for use in China for various technical reasons; they felt that the real objective of the Chinese might be to equip a post-war army.[41] As a result of these allegations, Howe and External Affairs fell into agreement with Washington about suspending the Mutual Aid program for China, and the Mutual Aid Board did not need to deal with Chinese matters again for the next six months.

Meanwhile, the transport bottleneck over the Hump was being broken at the cost of furious land battles in Burma, with many casualties. These battles began with the stubborn resistance of British and Indian forces against a strong sustained attack by the Japanese against Imphal, on the eastern edge of India. For eight weeks, beginning in early March 1944, the Japanese repeatedly attacked the besieged defenders in fierce hand-to-hand fighting. The British, Indians, and Gurkas stood their ground with the aid of air-dropped supplies, slowly driving the Japanese back. In the north and northeast of Burma, three small American-trained Chinese divisions, along with a small American force, all under the personal command of General Stilwell, attacked the renowned Eighteenth Japanese Division. On 17 May, these forces drove the division off the airfield at the important town of Myitkyina, which was the northern terminus of the railway. Stilwell's forces, which by then included a British division, had a very hard time holding Myitkyina airport, despite the acquisition of more Chinese divisions from the east force in Yininan. The Japanese counterattacked repeatedly, and Stilwell was driven to such extremes as bringing in wounded Americans convalescing at the hospital at Ledo. The airfield was held and denied use by the Japanese, thus enabling the Air Transport Command to fly a more southerly route without fear of Japanese fighters. Their monthly deliveries increased to 18,000 tons in June and were up to 39,000 in November. By the time the Burma Road was reopened in January 1945, Air Transport was able to deliver more tonnage than the vehicles using the road could.[42]

The great improvement of transport routes into China enabled the stockpiles of arms in India to be cleared up early in 1945. In late March of that year, the Chinese asked Howe to reactivate the Mutual Aid program, and the board approved doing so.[43] The new list again included small arms, light artillery, and trucks. The US War Department advised the Joint War Aid Committee that it would have no objection to the shipment of small arms but that heavier items, including anti-aircraft guns, should be held back until a Chinese port was open. The committee agreed. It was decided not to wait for US approval in Chungking, so a third shipment confined to small arms was assembled and shipped in mid-May to Calcutta.

In the final year of the war, Ottawa decided that any proposal to send heavy items would be taken up by the Canadian ambassador in Chunking directly with General Albert Wedemeyer, the new American theatre commander in China. This process did not help. Wedemeyer let the proposals pile up and then, in June 1945, vetoed them all.[44]

While this may have forestalled further contracts for the production of heavy equipment, it did not prevent further transfers of aid to China. On 13 August 1945, when the Japanese were in the process of deciding to surrender, Fraser reported to the Mutual Aid Board that substantial progress was being made in meeting the requests of China and France from the surplus holdings of the Department of National Defence. Later, on 17 January 1946, the board was told that by VJ Day (when hostilities officially ceased), there were certain items that had been requested by China as Mutual Aid and that were so close to completion that it would have been uneconomical to halt production. It had been decided, therefore, that the items would be completed. The board authorized charging the cost of these items to Mutual Aid funds.[45]

In mid-September 1945, Mutual Aid approved two loans to China. The first was for $25 million, to be used for "ordnance" – essentially arms and ammunition in completion of the Mutual Aid program to be sold to China at a substantial discount. The second was for $35 million, for the purchase in Canada of reconstruction supplies.[46] Howe informed Soong of this before the latter's return to China. By this time, however, China was in turmoil and External Affairs succeeded in getting the Canadian ministers and the Chinese authorities to agree to postpone the shipments of munitions and the granting of credit until the outlook was clarified. By the end of 1945, President Truman had sent General George C. Marshall to China to mediate between the Kuomintang government and the communist forces. On 28 December, Ilsley wrote to General P. Kiang, director of the Chinese government supply agency in Ottawa, offering a loan of $35 million for post-war reconstruction supplies on the terms we were giving to

European Allied governments. He noted that "it is now expected and agreed that the weapons and munitions in the original program will not be purchased or shipped at the present time."[47]

Agreement on the terms of the loans was reached quickly. General Marshall succeeded for a time in quelling the struggle in China, and Robertson wrote to Howe, stating: "The internal political situation in China has improved markedly in recent weeks and I do not now feel that we can reasonably object to the shipment of the munitions in question so long as present conditions continue."[48] The $60 million export credit agreements were approved by order-in-council. The shipments were assembled and credit extended over the next three fiscal years while the Chinese civil war raged.[49] Small repayments on these loans were made up to 1950–51, but no further repayments were forthcoming. The People's Republic of China, with its new Communist government, was not prepared to recognize financial obligations incurred by a government with which it was at war. On the other hand, when Canada recognized the People's Republic in October 1970, it soon acknowledged and paid the Canadian guaranteed bank loans made to the Ming Sung Shipping Company to buy Canadian ships designed and built to ply the Yangtze River, ships that the Communist government had acquired after the revolution.[50]

In retrospect, it seems clear that none of the Mutual Aid provided by Canada to China was used against the common enemy: Japan. Nor did we succeed in our other aim, achieving goodwill. We got little thanks from Chiang Kai-shek and certainly could expect none from the People's Republic, against whom our arms shipments almost certainly were used, though in vain. Notwithstanding these failures, it was probably right to give aid to the recognized government of China. The United States did so on a huge scale and with the closest possible contact; Tuchman states the result succinctly: "China was a problem for which there was no American solution. The American effort to sustain the status quo could not supply an outworn government with strength and stability or popular support. It could not hold up a husk nor long delay the cyclical passing of the mandate of heaven. In the end China went her own way as if the Americans had never come."[51]

MUTUAL AID TO AUSTRALIA

Australia's concern over not sharing in the billion-dollar gift to Britain in 1942 had been one of the impetuses for Mutual Aid to other members of the United Nations. After Ilsley's first announcement of the program, on 8 February 1943, Australia was quick to inquire about it.[52] We were unable to answer their questions for the next few months.

Even when the act was passed, we still had to settle with the British how we were going to allocate the aid within the sterling area. Australia was the chief beneficiary of the rather rough-and-ready formula we adopted. It was based on current account balance deficits with Canada and supplemented by some consideration of its liquid assets and liabilities. In the case of Australia, this led us to a potential entitlement for aid on the order of $70 million for the fiscal year 1943-44, substantially more than it was feasible to provide quickly through our procurement and contracting arrangements. Thus, as of 1 September 1943, the Mutual Aid Board assumed responsibility for the undelivered portions of a considerable number of Australia's contracts with Canadian companies for the production of munitions and supplies. At the same time, the board undertook to pay for the training of Australian pilots and other aircrew, under the British Commonwealth Air Training Plan. For the seven remaining months of that fiscal year, these payments amounted to about $13.6 million. The remaining items provided as aid that year added up to only about $7.3 million in value, of which the biggest items were lumber, construction and repair of merchant vessels, and machine tools and related stores.[53]

By the fiscal year 1944-45, there were large deliveries of aircraft, automotive equipment, and mechanical transport, along with a wide variety of military and industrial supplies, and charges for both inland and ocean freight. The total in 1944-45 was about $55 million.[54] In the second four months of 1945, before the Japanese surrender, when the focus was on the war in the Far East, the amount of aid was at the same annual rate as in 1944-45, but the emphasis shifted away from air training, aircraft, and motor vehicles to radio and other electrical equipment and, of all things, paper.

In December 1944, an Australian delegation was dispatched to Ottawa to explain the rationale behind their requests for various supplies under the Mutual Aid program, specifically those for trucks and paper. The most important request was for motor trucks for civilian purposes, to replace those that had been worn out or converted to military uses. Trucks for civilian purposes were severely rationed and were needed urgently for food production and the transportation of food and war supplies throughout Australia. Given the important role that Australia was playing as a base for the war against Japan, the request was well justified. The paper was needed to package food to be sent up to Australian and Allied armed forces. The members of the board were impressed with the extent and nature of the Australian war effort and recognized the importance of meeting their requests, which were approved forthwith.[55] Canada had a large production capacity for trucks, and they were quickly sent in the next few months, but it took longer to divert the production of the grade of paper required, which was in short supply.

FORM OF MUTUAL AID AGREEMENTS

One political problem arose in connection with the Australian Mutual Aid program. Countries receiving aid were required to enter into a general agreement relating to the principles applying to the transfer of Canadian war supplies as Mutual Aid. Most of the terms of these agreements related to Canada's undertaking to furnish supplies and the receiving country's undertaking to use them in the effective prosecution of the war and not to sell them to others without Canada's consent; various other terms related to the specific transactions involved and to the return of the supplies under certain conditions. One clause, number ten, was patterned after Article VII of the US Lend-Lease agreements, wherein the US sought some general assurances of support for certain post-war endeavours. These included the expansion, by appropriate domestic and international measures, of the production and consumption of goods; the elimination of all forms of discriminatory treatment in international commerce; and the reduction of tariffs and other trade barriers. Recipients of Lend-Lease, including the United Kingdom and Australia, signed agreements containing this clause. Canada voluntarily subscribed to the declaration of policies in this clause in order to gain more standing in international discussions of the issues.[56]

When the Canadian Mutual Aid agreements were drawn up, they included this clause ten, which was, in effect, a mild reaffirmation of the declaration of policies in Article VII of the Mutual Aid agreements. In December 1943, the Australian high commissioner in Ottawa informed External Affairs that the Australian Labour government had refused to agree to the inclusion of clause ten in the Mutual Aid agreement with Canada. Apparently, Dr. H.V. Evatt, minister of external affairs and attorney general in the Australian Labour government, was concerned with the criticism that might be expected from the very strong protectionist elements in the Labour party should clause ten be included in the Mutual Aid agreements.[57]

While Canada was considering the Australian reaction, the government of India expressed serious reservations about signing an agreement including the clause, because it implied a reduction of tariffs. India could not afford this; their tariffs essentially were for revenue rather than protection. After receiving these two objections, the government approved a very mild form of the clause, which proved acceptable to both countries.[58] Because, in any event, Article VII of the Lend-Lease agreements would be the more serious commitment, there was no real drawback in making this concession. Canada did not have any minister as dedicated to the principles of post-war reconstruction as American Secretary of State Cordell Hull was, and we had nothing like the bargaining power of the US.

MUTUAL AID TO NEW ZEALAND

New Zealand normally had a much smaller deficit in its current account balance of payments with Canada than Australia did. Our estimate, made in May 1943, was that their deficit might be expected to be around $5 million per year out of total expenditures of about $35 million. The New Zealand authorities did not apply for Mutual Aid until mid-1944. The chief item they secured as aid in the fiscal year 1944–45 was an order of thirty-four Catalina aircraft for patrol duties in the South Pacific, costing about $5.6 million.[59] They also obtained a relatively substantial amount of wheat during 1944–45 and 1945–46, which they required by reason of drought in Australia, their normal source of supply. While they received some aid in the form of payment for the training of aircrews in Canada, this was small because New Zealand did most of its training closer to home.

AID TO FRANCE

In May 1943, when the Mutual Aid Act was passed, all of mainland France was under German control. Canada had ceased to recognize the Vichy French regime as being in effective control of its part of France because it yielded to German pressure to instruct the French armed forces in Africa to resist the landing of British and American forces in North and West Africa in November 1942. A French Committee of National Liberation was formed early in June 1943; it comprised an uneasy coalition of the military regime in North Africa, which had come over to the side of the Allies at the time of the landings, and the Free French under General de Gaulle, who was based in Britain but maintained scattered support of troops in some parts of the French Empire elsewhere in Africa. The committee also enjoyed the strong support of the French Resistance.[60]

It took the French Committee of National Liberation some months to organize effectively and gain some qualified diplomatic recognition, which the US State Department was very reluctant to grant. The Canadian government decided to act promptly to help this new coalition and through it the French in North Africa and the French forces that might help in the liberation of France itself. On 2 July 1943, the Cabinet War Committee decided in principle that Canadian Mutual

Aid should be extended to the French committee. When that committee was informed of the decision, through the British cabinet minister in Algiers, it was told the Canadian government would give prompt attention to requests for war supplies and for the training of French aircrews in Canada.[61]

Despite this prompt start in principle, it was to be many months before any Canadian supplies were shipped to North Africa. Much of the delay was due to lack of experience and indecision on the French side. Part of the delay, however, was due to the necessity to get approval from the Combined Boards and similar military, production, and shipping authorities in Washington at a period of intense activity there. It was easier and more understandable for the French to acquire military supplies directly from the US army and navy (with which the French forces were in contact) under Lend-Lease arrangements. A French naval mission visited Ottawa during 1943 inquiring about items that they needed, including the possibility of getting merchant ships. A wide variety of small items were ordered for them. There were army inquiries about materials for uniforms; cloth and clothing was one of the largest items transferred. The largest item of expenditure in the 1944–45 fiscal year was $7.7 million for six shiploads of wheat, to make up for a North African crop failure.[62] An allotment of $7.5 million to purchase supplies for the French was made by the Mutual Aid Board at its meeting on 13 December 1943, and another of the same size in April 1944.[63] On 14 April, an authorized representative of the French committee signed a formal Mutual Aid agreement that contained almost exactly the same terms as Canada's agreement with the United Kingdom.

Despite these formal steps, the progress in working out a firm program of aid was disappointingly slow. In June 1944, nearly a year after the first offer of aid in principle, the administrative officers of the board reported that there seemed to be confusion and duplication in the requests presented by the French to the US, the UK, and Canada, which required much time to sort out at the Combined Committees in Washington. At the same time, the administrative officers of the Mutual Aid Board forecast a total French program of aid costing $71 million: $6 million for the navy, $10 million for civilian supplies, and $55 million for the army.[64] This last figure, however, seems to have been a gross exaggeration. It may have included a rough forecast of the cost of equipping two infantry divisions for service in Europe, a proposal discussed informally in November 1944 after the provisional government of France was established.[65] This idea was received favourably by the Department of External Affairs and St Laurent later that winter. A formal proposal was not received, however, until mid-March 1945, after the Combined Chiefs of Staff Committee had approved support for a new, small French army. Canada could not equip these two divisions quickly enough to enable them to be of use in Europe, although we could meet some specific shortages from stock. Because of the rapid changes in Europe at that time, Mutual Aid production orders for French army supplies were not required. France was entitled to secure Mutual Aid for military purposes in the Far East after hostilities ceased in Europe, and Fraser reported to the board on 13 August that substantial progress was being made in meeting the program for France out of Department of National Defence surpluses. The small amounts of military supplies recorded as Mutual Aid to France for the year 1945–46 indicates that if some of the National Defence surplus stock was transferred, it was not charged to Mutual Aid.[66] By September 1945, of course, the need to fight Japan had ceased and there were huge surpluses of military equipment in Europe available at low prices.

There was debate at the Mutual Aid Board regarding supplies for civil use and the greater need to take into account other programs and the "ability to pay" the provisional government of France. Before the Allied landings in France in June 1944, civilian supplies were required for French North Africa; Canada furnished some of these, notably wheat. After the landings in France, military relief provided by the Civil Affairs units in the Allied armies met immediate civilian needs.[67] After the liberation of Paris in late August 1944 and the establishment of a French provisional government under de Gaulle, responsibility for civilian requirements passed over to that government and its prefects and local authorities. The bulk of France's overseas requirements for civil supplies in the later months of 1944 were obtained from Lend-Lease arrangements, because the French found the Canadian procurement processes slower and more difficult.[68] There were some special needs to which Canada attended, notably the provisioning and repair of fishing trawlers, as well as the construction of new trawlers, although this was regarded essentially for peacetime purposes and was offered only for credit or cash financing. Agricultural implements and fertilizers, however, were quickly available and were furnished as Mutual Aid.

The ability of France to pay for civil supplies had to be taken into account. The Banque de France had gold. French authorities also had US and Canadian dollar assets in North America, as well as an income in dollars from the purchase of such assets, in addition to an income in dollars from the purchase of francs for paying the troops in France. The Canadian assets of the French authorities (including the gold in the Bank of Canada), which had been placed under the aegis of the

Custodian of Enemy Property in 1940, were released back to them in late 1944, but it took until February 1945 for French officials in Canada to be given authority to use them.[69]

The Mutual Aid Board had a long discussion on 16 November 1944 about its policy to be adopted for Mutual Aid to France. The discussion began with five propositions: (1) The unfreezing of French assets in Canada and the US would not provide enough dollars to meet both the immediate need for relief and the long-term need for reconstruction. (2) France should be left with some working balances at the end of hostilities. (3) Canadian policy in regard to judging how much France needed to retain dollars had to be concerted with the US. (4) France should not get free relief supplies through Mutual Aid for which they would have to pay if they received them through the United Nations Relief and Rehabilitation Administration (to which they chose to be a contributor, not a recipient, of aid). (5) Requisitions should not be accepted for military supplies that would have to be put into production in 1945 or civilian supplies that could not be delivered in that year.[70]

After considerable discussion, the board decided on the following four principles: (1) All existing specific commitments should be met. (2) Certain strategically important military items could be sent as Mutual Aid either from production or surplus Canadian stores. (3) Requirements for the French navy would be eligible to be transferred as Mutual Aid. (4) Supplies for civilian use would be provided as Mutual Aid only if they were judged to be important in carrying on the war and could be supplied quickly.

These decisions were to be conveyed informally to the French by a group of senior officials from the board's staff and the departments concerned. With these as guidelines and the willingness of the French to commit their own funds to what was not eligible for transfer as Mutual Aid, a new and more efficient procedure was worked out, early in 1945, for placing orders for Canadian supplies. Time did not permit this improved processing to result in transfer of a large value of supplies during the period before Mutual Aid ceased operating on 1 September.

During June, the board was informed that US officials felt the conditions of the people in France, Belgium, and Holland were so serious that the US was prepared to send them large supplies of food and raw materials on a Lend-Lease basis. The Canadian Mutual Aid Board decided to stick to the policies and practices that they had adopted recently.[71]

What France really wanted at this time, mid-1945, was a credit of the kind that Parliament had made available under Part II of the Export

Credit Insurance Act in 1944. The amount provided by Parliament in 1944 for this purpose was only $100 million, and more than half of this already had been committed to Czechoslovakia, the Netherlands, and Norway. France wanted much more than $100 million itself. The Canadian government was quite prepared to give a large loan of this kind to France, but it would need to get an increase in its lending authority from Parliament. This legislation was passed in December 1945, increasing the authority to $750 million. On 9 April 1946, agreement was reached on a loan of $242,500,000 at an interest rate of three per cent and repayable in thirty equal annual installments. Meanwhile, in contemplation of this loan, short-term credits were extended to France under the standing authority of the War Appropriation Act in the amount of slightly over $82 million, which enabled total orders for Canadian goods to be placed amounting to about $188 million.[72]

MUTUAL AID TO OTHER COUNTRIES

From the beginning of the Mutual Aid program, it was recognized that India would present a special problem. Canada was buying very little from that country, the main item being tea. On the other hand, exports of war supplies to India in 1942 were very large: an estimated $168 million. These were paid for in Canadian dollars through both private channels – for example, Canadian automobile companies were paid by their Indian affiliates – and public, including some payments by the government of India and some by the UK government.[73] We never learned in detail what the plan or established practice was for dividing the costs of the Indian army between the British government and the government of India (which was made up of British nominees from the viceroy down, most of these being British senior civil servants). The government of India was supposed to be supported by the taxes (mainly customs duties) that it levied. We were told that the UK government paid all the costs of the Indian army except the costs of supplies made in India for the Indian army while it remained within the country's borders.[74] We asked why the government of India was paying for war supplies from Canada with dollars bought from the Bank of England. We did not receive a clear answer, but the British government suggested that motor transport, which made up the bulk of India's purchases, may well have been subject to special arrangements. The result of all this was that the government of India as such (or its Central Bank) had been paying off much of its debt to the UK and was accumulating large holdings of sterling balances in London. It was not providing Mutual Aid, or anything like it, to the hard-pressed British government. As a result, the British Treasury wished Canada to demand payment for its exports to India, be they for private or public use. To effect this, India would have to buy Canadian dollars in exchange for their sterling balances in London.

The first tentative suggestions for the distribution of Mutual Aid to Empire countries in the sterling area during the fiscal year 1943–44 included some $40 million for aid to India, which was much less than what might be argued for on the principle of meeting their balance of payments deficit.[75] I noted in a memorandum, however, that India was the most difficult case among all the countries in the sterling area and that considerations of high policy would have to be taken into account. They were. In 1943, neither the deputy minister of finance nor the Mutual Aid Board were prepared to agree to $40 million for India or to any other figure, with one exception: an Indian emergency. The harvest had failed in Bengal in 1943; there was famine there and in some adjoining provinces, which had already faced difficulties because food supplies from neighbouring Burma were cut off. The existence of the famine was public knowledge in Canada and officers of the Department of External Affairs had taken up Prime Minister King's suggestion that Canada might do something to help relieve the situation. It was discussed with the Indian agent general in Washington. He thought a gift of wheat not only would help but also would have important political effects. Shipping difficulties would be serious, in part because of the demands placed on vessels by military requirements in the Mediterranean.

Some ten days later, on 24 October 1943, King sent a cable to the viceroy of India offering a gift of up to 100,000 tons of wheat as Mutual Aid, "provided it may be found practicable to arrange for the shipment of this wheat to India from Western Canadian ports."[76] The viceroy cabled an immediate acceptance and said that he would try to secure the necessary shipping from the UK. King shortly thereafter received a telegram from Churchill asking him not to announce the proposed gift as at that time it would be wasteful to ship wheat from Canada rather than Australia, which was much closer. A news release, however, had been published in India already. A token shipment was sent on two Canadian ships carrying arms to India for China; this spurred the UK War Cabinet to order another 100,000 tons of wheat from Australia to alleviate the tragedy in India. Later in 1944, the shipping situation improved and Canada sent the remainder of its gift that year and in the year following.[77]

Because of the huge accumulations of sterling by India, ministers on the Mutual Aid Board, notably Ilsley and St Laurent, were critical of proposals to provide Mutual Aid directly to the Indian government rather than sending it through the British government. This view was consonant with the general views of the British government. So strongly did the Canadian ministers hold these views that even when the British Treasury got into a misunderstanding with the Indian Treasury and asked us to provide a large order of trucks to India as Mutual Aid, the board would not do it and insisted on India's paying for them in Canadian dollars obtained from the sale of sterling. Near the end of the 1944–45 fiscal year, the board decided rather grudgingly to finance one-third of the value of the military vehicles supplied to India, which were the budgetary liability of the government of India. This financing plus the wheat was to be the sum total of aid provided to the country. It amounted to a total value of about $15 million.

A token of Mutual Aid was provided to the British West Indian colonies as a measure of goodwill. During the war, these little islands, with which Canada had always had close commercial ties, imported essential goods amounting to much more than their exports to Canada; this deficit, of course, was financed by Britain as part of its requirements. With the approval of the British, Canada supplied to each of these colonies in both 1944 and 1945, as Mutual Aid, an amount of wheat flour equivalent in value to $1 per capita of their population. Flour was an essential food for their support during the war and thus eligible as Mutual Aid; its provision assisted in restraining wartime inflationary pressures in the islands. The total value of the flour amounted to about $5.6 million.[78]

BUYING FOR UNRRA

The United Nations Relief and Rehabilitation Administration was established by forty-four of the United Nations, which signed an agreement on 9 November 1943. It was designed to give aid to areas liberated from the Axis Powers. The Canadian government took an active role in negotiating this agreement and setting up the organization. (See chapter 9.) Parliament approved Canada's participation in the agreement by statute in May 1944.[79] This act authorized the payment of interim expenditures up to $10 million out of the 1943 Mutual Aid Act, with any additional money to be paid out of subsequent appropriations. The 1944 Mutual Aid Act authorized further UNRRA expenditures out of the appropriation of $800 million. The Mutual Aid Board and its administrators were responsible for Canada's financial contribution to UNRRA. In addition, it executed UNRRA's requisitions to use the remaining Canadian funds for the purchase of relief supplies in Canada. The nature of the procurement operation for UNRRA was similar to the operation of Mutual Aid. The minister of trade and commerce became a member of the board to deal with such problems. In November 1945, Trade and Commerce took over the administration and operational responsibility for dealing with UNRRA as the Mutual Aid operations were being wound down. The expenditure of Mutual Aid appropriation funds on UNRRA during 1944–45 totalled only $11,092,753.97, of which $7,644,500 was the cash contribution.[80] Many contracts were placed and deliveries made during the 1945–46 fiscal year by the Mutual Aid administration and charged to the Trade and Commerce funds from war appropriation before the actual transfer of operations to that department occurred.[81]

BUYING FOR MILITARY RELIEF

The first UNRRA council meeting, in November 1943, recognized the need for Allied military forces to provide food and other relief supplies to the civilian population of areas immediately following their liberation from German occupation. These operations had to be controlled in detail by army authorities to avoid interference with their military operations and to enable stockpiling and movement of supplies to be effected without revealing military plans. There were civil affairs units attached to army formations, and their general policy and preparations were controlled by the Combined Civil Affairs Committee in Washington and its various subordinate officers and committees. Canada first became aware of the importance of these operations at the UNRRA council meeting in November 1943 but became involved in serious discussions and negotiations during most of 1944. The chief problem for Canada was providing and financing Canadian supplies, especially wheat, for these services. The negotiation of the financial arrangements was carried out by the officials of the departments of External Affairs and Finance, principally in Washington, but also with the British in London. (See chapter 9.) Canadian expenditures for this purpose were to be taken out of allotments to the Canadian army from the war appropriation, and not from the Mutual Aid appropriation.

The general nature of these purchasing operations and shipment arrangements was similar to that for Mutual Aid; from the beginning, the funds for procuring the supplies requested by the Combined Civil Affairs Committee and its supplies committee were turned over to the administrative officers of the Mutual Aid Board.[82] The board itself was not, as such, involved in the financial negotiations, which were conducted under the authority of the Cabinet War Committee, chaired by the prime minister as secretary of state for external affairs.[83] In February 1945, as the financial negotiations in Washington with both the American and British authorities became more complicated and troublesome, the war committee decided that responsibility for military relief matters generally should be vested in the Mutual Aid Board.[84]

Military relief continued until the loading of supplies was completed in August 1945. Problems similar to those of military relief also arose in the British zone of Germany after August 1945, but the Canadian government, following consideration of the matter by the Mutual Aid Board on 13 September, informed the British Treasury that "we ... do not feel able to assume any new direct responsibility for the financing of relief supplies for Germany."[85]

The final report of the Mutual Aid Board shows total direct expenditures on military relief at about $85 million plus some Mutual Aid supplies provided to Britain, which diverted them to military relief. The two largest items by far in the relief supplies were $48 million for wheat and flour and $33 million for motor vehicles.[86]

THE INADEQUATE APPROPRIATION IN 1944

The original Mutual Aid legislation of May 1943 contained an appropriation of $1 billion to finance the operations it authorized.[87] Those of us working on Mutual Aid expected that further appropriations would be needed in later years, although their form and amounts were uncertain. It was difficult to forecast how much transfer of war supplies would be made, to what countries, and how much some of those countries, notably Great Britain, would be able to pay. In November 1943, when Canada agreed to participate in UNRRA, it was decided, as noted above, that expenditures arising from this participation should be met from the Mutual Aid appropriation. To authorize this on a continuing basis would require amending the Mutual Aid Act. Rather than including this authorization in the general war appropriation, therefore, a revising statute would be needed. This was announced in the speech from the throne on 27 January 1944. Nothing was said about the size of the appropriation, however, until 11 February, when Ilsley, in his major speech introducing the war appropriation resolution, said that it would be "less than last year" – that is, "less than a billion." Ilsley quickly added that the amount had not by that time been agreed on by cabinet.[88]

Cabinet reached a decision on 27 March 1944, a week after a discussion of the issue at a meeting of the Mutual Aid Board. At this meeting, Howe, St Laurent, and Ralston, who was acting minister of finance during Ilsley's lengthy absence because of illness, quizzed the senior officials thoroughly on the situation.[89] Clark and Hume Wrong were present to speak on the policy aspects of the proposed appropriation, while Karl Fraser, the director of administration; B.G. McIntyre, the comptroller of the Treasury, who had expert knowledge of the intricate accounting; and Carl Goldenberg, who was in charge of statistics at Munitions and Supply, were there to answer questions. I was present as acting secretary and an additional source of information. It was an examination for discovery, with only the briefest summary recorded. The minutes state that the facts and forecasts relating to the financial requirement for Mutual Aid and various possible courses of action in this regard were discussed at length. It was decided that such wide policy issues were raised by the discussion that the issue must be considered at cabinet.[90] This was one of the earliest cabinet meetings, as distinct from those of the War Committee, at which Arnold Heeney was present and made a record of the decision. The meeting was brief. Ralston, as acting minister of finance, described the financial position between Canada and the countries in the sterling area in receipt of Mutual Aid. He said that the total net deficit of the sterling area to be financed by Mutual Aid, plus the aid to be provided to others (Russia, China, the French Committee of National Liberation, and UNRRA), was estimated at $1.774 million. It was necessary for the government to decide what proportion of this deficit would be borne under the provisions of the Mutual Aid Act and what balance would be financed on credit. According to the cabinet record, it was decided that $800 million was to be the figure for Mutual Aid. King's diary indicates that the Department of Finance (presumably Ralston) put forward a figure of $850 million, while others were seeking to keep it at $750 million. The prime minister himself had fixed the figure at $800 million, and that figure was inserted in the resolution that King sent to the clerk of the House of Commons to appear as a government notice of motion the next day.[91]

I felt obliged to undertake the unpleasant task of informing the UK Treasury of the decision as soon as the notice of motion appeared. I phoned Owen Williams, the Treasury official in the High Commission office who was my normal contact there. I explained that the decision had been made public by the parliamentary process so quickly that there had been no time to prepare a proper explanation or answers to the inevitable questions this would raise in their minds. As I reported to my deputy minister in a memo, I told Williams – strictly off the record and not to be transmitted to London (though no doubt it was) – that I did not believe that there was any disposition on the part of the Mutual Aid Board to restrict the production of supplies for the UK or other Mutual Aid countries to $800 million; rather, the decision was meant solely to restrict the appropriation to that figure. Consequently, I thought, it would leave open the question of further measures to deal with the financing of additional supplies.[92]

The British were well aware of the very serious restriction that this $800 million could mean for them unless other financing was arranged. Their programs to obtain arms and food from Canada accounted for a large and vital part of what they needed to carry on the war. This news could not have been wholly unexpected; they had seen Ilsley's statement of 11 February, which said that the Mutual Aid appropriation would be less than a billion dollars. Now, however, the axe had fallen, and neither explanation nor alternative had been offered. Moreover, this impasse arose less than three months before the climax of the war in Europe involving the huge offensive landings onto the beaches of Normandy by British, Canadian, and American troops.

Gordon Munro, the senior British Treasury representative in Canada, had returned to London just before this decision. The Treasury had some months to seek a solution before additional sources of Canadian dollars were required, but they began work on the problem immediately. We in Ottawa did likewise. When ministers spoke of alternatives, they spoke of loans, despite the reasons Ilsley and other ministers had given publicly during the past two years for not using war loans to finance the transfer of arms and food to Britain. (The solution to the problem of financing Britain that year is explained in the next chapter.) In retrospect, one must ask how and why the government of Canada decided what it did in March, knowing that it would cause a crisis at an important time. The historical record is not complete, chiefly because the key decisions were taken in cabinet and there were no minutes of them. We are largely dependent on King's diary, some correspondence, a few memorandums, and inference.

The story began at a meeting of the Cabinet War Committee on 8 September 1943, the first meeting after the Quebec conference of Churchill and Roosevelt with their senior military staff. During this conference, the Canadian Cabinet War Committee had met with Churchill and some of his advisers, during which time Admiral Sir Dudley Pound had requested naval assistance from Canada. This request was under consideration at the September meeting. The minutes record that the prime minister emphasized that Canada had now reached the limits of her resources in her war effort. No new commitments involving additional calls on Canada's human resources and war supplies could be accepted. At the next session, Parliament would not be disposed to accept new commitments and, indeed, would be unlikely to renew the billion-dollar appropriation for Mutual Aid. The armed services should make their plans accordingly. Any new proposals should be confined within the limits of programs already approved.[93]

This policy was reiterated by the prime minister at the committee meeting of 21 October, during a discussion of the acquisition of an aircraft carrier from the UK. King was so frank in his statement that it is best to quote his own account of it, from his diary for that day:

I spoke plainly before the Chiefs of Staff, as well as colleagues, of the necessity of the Minister of Finance bringing in a budget this coming year which would reduce taxation and show reduced expenditure, pointing out that heavy taxation and outlays would raise such a feeling throughout the country that the government would certainly meet with defeat, and equally certainly that the CCF would come in its place, which would immediately take steps to reduce all the services and would see that this was carried very far in the post-war years. I wanted the Chief of Staff to realize not only what the position of the government was but their position as well in meeting the developments of the future.[94]

This attitude was reflected in the war appropriation approved by cabinet in the next few months and tabled in Parliament by Ilsley on 11 February. The total was down by $240 million, slightly over six per cent, from the total war appropriation for the previous year. Reductions had been made mainly in the allotments for army services and the navy, with only a small cut for the air force because of the deliberate expansion of its overseas squadrons and its assumption of the cost of pay and allowances for RCAF personnel serving in the Royal Air Force. The chiefs of staff and the ministers appear to have taken to heart the prime minister's warning. Incidentally, the actual expenditures in 1943–44 for the army, navy, and air force proved to be only seventy-five per cent, seventy-six per cent, and eighty-two per cent, respectively, of the amounts allotted to them from the war appropriation that year, and were in all three cases significantly less than the amounts allotted to them in February for 1944–45.[95]

The first decision on the amount of the Mutual Aid appropriation for 1944–45 (including UNRRA) was taken on 4 January 1944 on short notice, without any prior study by the Mutual Aid Board or the Cabinet War Committee or even the interdepartmental committee on Mutual Aid. It happened when it did as a matter of chance. On 30 December, cabinet, in the absence of the prime minister, had considered and deferred action on a proposed telegram to Australia about the wording of a disputed clause of the Mutual Aid Agreement relating to post-war trade policy. During the discussion, the ministers realized that they had made no decision about continuing Mutual Aid when the initial appropriation ran out; if it was not to be continued, the argument with Australia was not worth pursuing. Wrong, who had been called to the meeting by the presiding minister, reported what transpired to Robertson, who sent a memorandum on 31 December to the prime minister, first summarizing the events at cabinet and then giving what seemed to him the most important reasons for continuing Mutual Aid. Then he added:

It is pretty certain that if Mutual Aid is continued an appropriation considerably smaller than a billion dollars will be needed; perhaps half this amount might suffice to cover both Mutual Aid and the Canadian contribution to UNRRA. The need for Canadian munitions will probably fall off in the next year and our sterling expenditures with action impending in Western Europe are likely to increase. I think that it would be very desirable for Council to reach a decision on the next year's programme as soon as possible as a good many other things depend on this.[96]

Robertson's recommendation to continue Mutual Aid probably confirmed the prime minister's own view; after all, King was the secretary of state for external affairs, and to end Mutual Aid as the war was reaching its climax would have had disastrous effects on our international reputation and influence. However, Robertson and even Wrong, who normally attended the Mutual Aid Board, did not know enough of the very complicated flows of funds between Canada and Britain to realize that the requirements for Mutual Aid in the 1944–45 fiscal year almost certainly were going to exceed $1 billion, to which the payments to UNRRA were now being added. It certainly appears, in retrospect, that both the Mutual Aid Board and the Department of Finance should have given some detailed attention to the scale of the requirements by early December in order to inform the prime minister of the situation.

The problem stemmed, in part, from the diffusion of responsibility. Finance had invented the plan, and Ilsley had taken the original bill through Parliament, because it was essentially a financial measure, but Finance did not administer it. The board created a collective ministerial responsibility. The administration under the board was unable to cope with the accounting and balance of payments complexities in forecasting the future requirements. Very few of us realized the extent to which the burden of financing Mutual Aid in 1943 had been reduced by the repayment to the UK of its investment in munitions plants and of the initial and progress payments in their munitions contracts that were taken over by Canada in the summer of 1943. In a letter of 6 November 1943 covering the legislation to be prepared by the Department of Finance, Clark had informed the Privy Council Office that one of the bills would be to continue Mutual Aid or its equivalent but said that this would raise important questions of policy on which we needed direction.[97] We should have sought that direction sooner, but we were all very busy, especially Clark himself, who was giving a lot of thought to post-war programs, notably family allowances and their relation to wage control. As a result of lack of preparation, ministers were not adequately briefed when the prime minister took Robertson's advice and raised the subject of Mutual Aid in cabinet on 4 January. In his diary, King describes the gist of the discussion about Mutual Aid that day:

> In the afternoon, took up settling policy with respect to the Mutual Aid Bill. Decided after long and careful discussion to continue to have another Bill, not at the same amount but around 6 or 700,000. This to include monies to be needed for UNRRA. Mackenzie [minister of pensions and national health] and Angus Macdonald [minister of national defence for naval services] were pretty strongly opposed. Rest of Council seemed to favour recommendation to Finance Dept. for the following reasons: necessity of Britain having Canadian exchange to purchase agricultural products, etc., after the war. Otherwise danger of losing Canadian markets to Argentine and other countries. Necessity of keeping factories working on munitions so long as war lasted and change to peace-time commodities once situation permits. I took the position that we had given our word that Canada should stay in the war till the end. Also that ours would be a total war effort; that we would carry out this pledge until the enemy is defeated. It seemed to be based on a statement by Ralston that the war might be expected to end about October. Power feels from the extent to which the British are cancelling their orders for planes, dropping of men in Canada, etc. that it should be over much sooner.[98]

A memorandum from Heeney informed Finance on 5 January of the previous day's decision. He interpreted the result as implying that the figure to be requested was likely to be in the neighbourhood of $700 million. To those of us working on Mutual Aid, this figure appeared inadequate, but there was little we could do about it immediately, except to prepare the best possible information and forecasts of the likely requirements of the sterling area as determined by their prospective balance of payments deficit with Canada. On 17 January, Alec McLeod, my statistical assistant, made up a detailed set of estimates for the closing fiscal year 1943–44, and a forecast for the fiscal year 1944–45.[99] These estimates turned out to have underestimated the Mutual Aid that would be transferred in the last quarter of 1943–44; they exaggerated, therefore, what was left over from the first appropriation and available for the following year. Our inability to come up with a more precise forecast, due to lack of information, led us to delay efforts to seek a change in the amount suggested in Heeney's memorandum of 5 January. Before we could propose a larger dollar amount than that suggested by Heeney, we had to forecast the amount of arms and ammunition that the British were going to need from us in the very active year ahead, how much we would be able to produce for them, and how much we would be paying to the British for arms and ammunitions and other supplies and services required by the Canadian army and air squadrons active overseas.

During January, Ilsley and Clark were busy reaching decisions on the measures to be mentioned in the speech from the throne when Parliament opened on 27 January. These measures included many elements of the government's post-war economic and social policies. King asked Clark to help him draft the speech itself.[100] I had some conversations with Ilsley about the points he should make in parliamentary debates about Mutual Aid, but we did not address the size of the appropriation.[101] We did not have firm enough forecasts to make a strong case that Mutual Aid should be exempt from the general policy that favoured reducing the amounts provided for the Department of National Defence in the war appropriation. Ilsley succeeded in holding off a decision on a specific figure. He was able to announce in opening the debate on the war appropriation in the House of Commons on 11 February that although the final amount for Mutual Aid had not been settled on, it would be less than the total for 1943.

On 15 February, I sent Clark a memorandum reporting on several Mutual Aid problems. In a final report, I commented on the total Mutual Aid requirements for the next fiscal year and how they might be met. After noting the uncertainty of the forecasts, I stated: "Presumably it may be possible to gamble on substantially higher overseas payments and a somewhat lower munitions program than that at present in the production forecasts. In the event that this gamble did not work out, it might ... be necessary to come back early in 1945 for a supplementary Mutual Aid Appropriation, which might be a little safer than asking for anything approaching a billion dollars this year."[102] Clark did not pursue this last suggestion, and I believe he did not wish to propose relying on a supplementary appropriation when the government was carrying out King's general policy of restraining expenditures. We proceeded to collect the information needed to improve our forecasts.

In late February, Ilsley's health gave out. King records that Ilsley "finally spoke of the need to get away at once and I could see he was almost on the point of breaking completely."[103] King arranged to have him go to an UNRRA meeting in Atlantic City and then on to Washington, after which he would remain in the United States for a rest, probably at his brother's home in California. In fact, Ilsley had some important business to settle with the US Treasury. He returned to cabinet to discuss the matter on 8 March and went again to Washington to see Morgenthau. Clark finished the Mutual Aid negotiations with the US, and Ilsley went to California to rest. He did not return to Ottawa until 14 April, after the decision on the Mutual Aid appropriation had been finalized. Meanwhile, negotiations with the US and the urgent preparation of legislation kept Clark from dealing with the Mutual Aid appropriation.[104]

In March, others of us in the department were preparing revised forecasts of Mutual Aid requirements in the new fiscal year and discussing them with others concerned, in particular Fraser and his staff. The product of these discussions was Mutual Aid Board Document No. 63, which was before the board at its 20 March meeting. It showed an "apparent balance to be financed," by Mutual Aid or otherwise, of $1.8 billion. This was the paper on the basis of which the discussion between ministers and officials took place.[105]

I prepared a draft paper, dated 24 March, for the cabinet meeting on 27 March. It covered the Mutual Aid forecasts and the points of policy. Clark revised this and, I am sure, passed it on to Ralston. In this paper we concluded that the total of Canadian supplies that it would be necessary to finance during the fiscal year, by Mutual Aid or otherwise, would be not less than $1.5 billion. The memorandum also supplied the minister with background information and up-to-date figures on Canadian–UK financial relations during the war, along with arguments favouring a large Mutual Aid appropriation and arguments favouring a small one.[106] From the Department of Finance's point of view, this memorandum, plus whatever oral advice Clark may have given Ralston, completed the story of how the inadequate appropriation came to be made, and provided reasons for why there was no warning or explanation given to the UK Treasury before the result was published in the Parliamentary Orders of the Day on 28 March.[107] Although some of us working on the Mutual Aid program and the British Treasury went through a very worrying few months, the whole problem was solved in August without supplementary appropriations or a reduction in supply programs. (How this was negotiated and accomplished is explained in the next chapter.)

THE FLEXIBLE APPROPRIATION OF 1945

There was no lack of preparation in determining the Mutual Aid appropriation for the fiscal year 1945–46, which was expected to be stage two of the war, following the defeat of Germany but assuming active hostilities against Japan throughout the year. Canada's armed services were allowed by the government to play only a very limited role, which had not been clearly defined when the fiscal year began in April.[108] Following a series of negotiations, the Canadian government agreed that it would continue Mutual Aid to Britain and the sterling area on a scale necessary to finance the export of food and other civilian requirements at 1944 levels, and the export of arms and ammunition and merchant ships at reduced but substantial levels. (These negotiations are described in the next chapter.)

The British army, with air force support, was engaged in major battles with the Japanese in Central Burma until the capture of Rangoon in early May 1945. After that, it continued to be involved in rounding up defeated Japanese units in Burma and preventing them from joining the major Japanese forces to the east in Malaya, Siam, Indochina, and the Dutch East Indies. The strategic plans called for heavy British attacks on the Japanese in Malaya, Siam, and Singapore later in 1945.[109] Canadian Mutual Aid of arms was needed for these campaigns and for the less well-defined Commonwealth participation in the final attacks on Japan itself. However, Canadian participation in the war against Japan was expected to be small and mostly in co-operation with us forces and using us arms. Consequently, Canadian payments to Britain and others in the sterling area would be reduced a great deal after the end of hostilities in Europe and the repatriation of Canadian forces from Britain and Europe. Mutual Aid, therefore, would have to finance a much larger share of the supplies that Britain received from Canada. The Canadian government accepted this burden in principle, realizing that it might require total Mutual Aid expenditures of $1.3 billion in the fiscal year 1945–46.[110] However, uncertainty as to the role and expenditures of both the British and Canadian forces in a war in which the United States was by far the leading participant on our side and us-type weapons the predominant arms rendered more desirable a greater flexibility in the use of funds. Consequently, Mutual Aid funds would be lumped into the main war appropriation alongside expenditures on Canadian forces and other war requirements, and the costs of demobilization.

The parliamentary situation required other special features in the 1945–46 war appropriation. The life of the existing Parliament would expire under the BNA Act on 17 April 1945 and a new Parliament would have to be elected soon after. It was possible that there would be a change of government, bringing with it some changes in policies. Mindful of this, Ilsley, on behalf of the government, requested in the House of Commons on 3 April an interim war appropriation only, with sufficient funds to carry on for approximately five months until the new Parliament could meet and approve new appropriations. After reviewing the scale of expenditures in the past five or six months, he proposed a round sum of $2 billion, which would cover about five months, provided that there were no major changes in policies or rates of total expenditures. This figure included Mutual Aid expenditures, and those on UNRRA.[111] The official opposition did not oppose this war appropriation, and it was approved on 13 April, the day the prime minister announced that he would ask to have Parliament dissolved and would call an election for 11 June.

The use of the general war appropriation to fund Mutual Aid worked smoothly and effectively in the five months from early May to early September. It enabled the Mutual Aid Board to carry out its commitments and programs for the USSR, China, Australia, and France. It also made possible a rapid acceleration of financing of the supplies, both arms and food, being sent to Britain; during this time, the share of these supplies financed by British receipts from Canada fell off rapidly.[112] A large amount of the Mutual Aid that summer was wheat, for which the need was urgent. The largest items, however, were the expenditures on aircraft and parts, the construction of merchant ships (which were later returned to Canada), and naval vessels and equipment. The expenditures on shells and ammunition remained surprisingly high.[113] During this period, and especially in July, the Mutual Aid Board began to question seriously the need to supply some of the major items being produced or that the UK Ministry of Supply was requesting. At the meeting of the board on 12 July, Hugh Weeks, representing that ministry, outlined the programs that the UK was proposing to obtain from Canada during stage II of the war, which the chiefs of staff were now officially expecting to last for eighteen months. Howe and Ilsley questioned Weeks closely on several items; they were concerned about the comparison between the requests being made of the US and those being made of Canada. I was the only Finance official there with Ilsley, because Clark was very sick. The minutes record that I expressed doubts about Britain's overall requirements, given that total war, by then, was over; it seemed that the British services were still proceeding on the basis of total war. I questioned, in particular, the need to send the UK five thousand trucks each month, and to supply Mosquito fighter-bombers for use in Europe. Ilsley asked for a careful examination of the program.[114]

British representatives and the administrators of the board did review the program before the board's next meeting, on 20 July. Weeks made a lengthy statement at that meeting based on a document that had been prepared for the board.[115] He stated that as a result of the discussions, the total amount requested had been reduced from $1.1 billion to $915 million. The revision included reductions in the requested numbers of trucks and Mosquito aircraft. Two-thirds of the new order was made up of military vehicles, aircraft, naval transport ferries, and issuing ships and maintenance vessels. It should be noted that naval vessels such as these were required as a result of the strategic decision that the Royal Navy's participation in the final attack on Japan would necessitate a self-sufficient fleet; ammunition, stores, and maintenance could not be supplied by US naval bases.[116]

After the British representatives withdrew, St Laurent and Ilsley both stated that approval of this proposed British Mutual Aid program for the fiscal year 1945–46 would have to be considered by cabinet, and the board should not make any collective recommendation. They asked various questions of the officials present about the prospective costs of this program and Mutual Aid as a whole, as well as the expected costs of the activities proposed for Canadian forces in this stage of the war. I emphasized that it would not be possible at that time to estimate even within a hundred million dollars what Mutual Aid would cost for the fiscal year, though it was more likely to be closer to $1.2 billion than $800 million.[117] The matter was left for consideration by cabinet.

I am surprised, in rereading these records now, that there was no discussion of the likelihood of an early collapse or surrender of Japan. After all, the Japanese navy by that time had been defeated thoroughly by the US navy, and US aircraft had complete control of the air over Japan, enabling them to bomb the fragile Japanese cities to great effect. There was practically a complete embargo around Japan, blocking imports of food and oil. The Japanese army remained largely undefeated, however, and was the main source of political resistance. It would require intensive fighting in many places to destroy that army if the Japanese High Command refused to surrender.[118]

In Ottawa, only C.D. Howe and the prime minister knew that the atom bomb was now ready and that the US army air force in all likelihood would use it. Discussion of the prospect at the Mutual Aid Board would have been useless, and Howe and King would have been aware that immediate consideration of the British program at cabinet was premature.

The cabinet never did consider the British Mutual Aid program for 1945–46, which the board referred to it. Within three weeks, atom bombs had been dropped on Hiroshima and Nagasaki. Even before the bombs, the Japanese government was seriously divided over whether to surrender. On 10 August, immediately following the second atomic attack, there was a marathon session of the ruling Japanese councils, the cabinet, and the chiefs of staff with the emperor. At the end of it, the majority accepted the emperor's view that "the war must end" and sent word through Swiss authorities to the Americans. The Americans published the terms of surrender the next day, and once again there was bitter disagreement in Japan, with the army leading the opposition, even against the known view of the emperor. Following a conference with the cabinet and the chiefs of staff on the morning of Tuesday, 14 August 1945, the emperor repeated his decision and the cabinet formally accepted the terms of surrender. The news was received in Washington about 4 p.m., and the emperor broadcast it a few hours later to the people of Japan.[119] The formal surrender did not take place until 2 September when General Douglas MacArthur, who had been appointed supreme commander of the Allied Forces, arrived in Tokyo Bay on the battleship *Missouri* to hold the ceremony on the deck, safe from Japanese army fanatics. President Truman issued a decree designating this as VJ Day, exactly six years after the war began with the German attack on Poland.

TERMINATION OF MUTUAL AID

Both the Canadians and those countries receiving Mutual Aid clearly understood that the program was a war measure and would terminate when the hostilities ended. This limit was made clear in the legislation itself, in the statements in Parliament about it, and in the regulations that were passed under the act. When Canada informed the British government in late February 1945 that it would recommend to Parliament continuing Mutual Aid on the scale requested for the second stage of the war, pending the election of a new Parliament later that year, Churchill replied: "What a comfort it is to have your decision to see us through on Stage II."[120] While this implied more than Canada had undertaken, it certainly confirmed the British understanding that Mutual Aid was not expected to continue after the end of hostilities.

The formal Mutual Aid agreements between Canada and the governments receiving aid, however, did not make clear in explicit terms that aid would cease when hostilities were over.[121] This termination was implied in several articles of the agreements (e.g., Articles IV, VIII, and IX). But Article XI said that the agreement "shall continue in force until a date to be agreed upon between the two governments." This was consistent with the other articles cited here because the agreement included terms relating to the disposition after the end of hostilities of supplies delivered as Mutual Aid before the end. Unfortunately, it could be taken to imply that Canada would continue to provide war supplies until there was agreement between the two governments to stop. This became relevant in August 1945.

The first message from Japan, on 10 August, stating its willingness to surrender, provoked the Canadian government to take action that day to stop production of war supplies for its own forces upon the cessation of hostilities and to accelerate their demobilization.[122] In addition, the government directed the Mutual Aid Board and the Department of Munitions and Supply to review immediately the Canadian program of procuring war supplies for other countries, with the purpose of halting production on all items not required for relief and rehabilitation unless they were in an advanced state of completion and might have a substantial post-war value for Canada. Furthermore, the Mutual Aid Board should confer immediately with the UK, Australia, New Zealand, the USSR, China, and France regarding their continuing requirements for supplies from Canada and appropriate methods of financing them after the cessation of hostilities with Japan. The cabinet secretary was to call a meeting of senior officials of the departments of National Defence, Finance, Munitions and Supply (including Reconstruction) and the Mutual Aid administration to establish effective arrangements for carrying out these decisions.

The meeting took place Monday, 13 August; Mackintosh and I represented Finance. Later that day, the Mutual Aid Board itself met to hear a report from Fraser, the director of administration. He informed the board of some difficulties in dealing with the Russians, who had just entered the war against Japan a few days before, pursuant to an earlier agreement with the Americans. Fraser proposed that all countries receiving Mutual Aid be informed "that all shipments under Mutual Aid would terminate as of VJ day" (the date of which had not yet been determined). There was some discussion about what would constitute a "shipment," particularly as it had been formally agreed that in the case of Russia, items loaded in their ships were regarded as Russian property. It was agreed that cabinet would have to authorize any departure from the general rule.[123]

When the Japanese informed Washington late the following day, 14 August, that they were prepared to accept the terms of surrender, telegrams were prepared to be sent the next day to the UK and other recipient governments, informing them that Mutual Aid deliveries would cease "as soon as military victory has been achieved." This was taken to mean that day, 15 August.[124] The UK was surprised at this abrupt notification without warning or consultation. Clement Atlee, the new British prime minister, telegraphed King urging that the decision be suspended so that the matter might be discussed, particularly since the UK was negotiating with the United States about the termination date for Lend-Lease shipments. Fortunately, no public announcement of the Canadian action had been made. The UK high commissioner expressed the hope that the date of the official cessation of hostilities in the Far East could be moved forward, to the date of the actual signature of the instrument of surrender.[125]

The British (and others) received a similar shock early the following week over the termination of Lend-Lease. This applied to a larger range of supplies and was subject to much more detailed legislation, in which President Truman, as vice president, had been involved personally. Written notice of its termination was given the British in Washington on 20 August, and Truman announced it at a press conference the next day.[126] The provisions of the Lend-Lease law were more severe and farther reaching than the arrangements made in Canada. It would be necessary for the UK to pay the US for supplies already transferred but currently in British stockpiles or in transit. The US made some concessions, especially with regard to shipping services. The date on which Lend-Lease transfers would end was to be the date the Japanese formally signed the surrender. In September, the most important concession to the UK was made: the amount owing on Lend-Lease could be met on the terms of a credit to be negotiated, which eventually were the same as those on the post-war loan.[127]

At a meeting in Ottawa on 27 August, the Mutual Aid Board considered the British protests, along with a recommendation from Hume Wrong that the date for the end of Mutual Aid shipments should be the date of the actual signing of the instrument of surrender, 2 September. The board decided that the matter should be settled by cabinet, with a recommendation that Mutual Aid should continue until the date fixed by the president of the United States as the termination date for Lend-Lease. On 31 August, cabinet endorsed this recommendation as it applied to wheat and civilian requirements and agreed that certain specialized naval ships already under construction could be transferred as Mutual Aid early in September. Cabinet also agreed that ministers should meet with Lord Keynes of the UK Treasury early in September, when he would be in Canada on his way to Washington, to discuss interim financing of the wide range of supplies Britain would continue to need from Canada.[128] In accordance with these decisions, Mutual Aid transfers, with a few specific exceptions, ended at midnight on 1 September 1945, just before VJ Day. The Canadian government also waived its rights to reclaim or be paid for Mutual Aid supplies already in ships.

Ilsley, Howe, and St Laurent, along with Mackintosh and me, met Keynes and other UK Treasury representatives on 5 September to discuss the termination of Mutual Aid. This was an amicable meeting mainly because the Canadian government already had decided on the VJ Day termination date that Keynes wanted, and that it would waive its rights under Article VIII of the Mutual Aid Agreement to repossess supplies in ocean transit at VJ Day, although it would retain title, in general, to supplies that had been produced but not loaded. There was discussion of cancellation costs on contracts for the production of supplies that the UK had ordered. This subject had been discussed with Keynes several times late in 1944 and the first half of 1945, as in principle it could have led to the UK's ordering too much or cancelling too early in relation to Canada's economic interests. It also raised questions about Canada's passing of judgment on military needs. As the UK already had instructed us to cancel most arms contracts promptly after receiving our telegram of 15 August, and since there were advantages for the Department of Munitions and Supply in dealing with arms contracts on a general basis, it was agreed that Canada would bear all cancellation charges on the Munitions and Supply allocations from the war appropriation. There were a few exceptions, most of which occurred in those instances that the UK at first asked that the contract not be cancelled and later decided it should be. It was agreed that there would need to be a detailed examination of the ownership rights of the two governments regarding the large ordnance holdings in the major military depot at Longue Pointe, Quebec, from which most arms shipments to the UK had been made during the war.

Canada offered to continue to act on behalf of the UK government in the procurement of supplies, and if necessary to finance purchases on a temporary basis, pending the negotiation of a post-war loan. Keynes believed that little financing would be needed before the end of 1945 because of the amounts owing by the Canadian army and air force as a consequence of the settlements made in August 1944.

The results of these discussions were approved by cabinet on 5 September. Ilsley reported on them, and the other arrangements in connection with the termination of Mutual Aid, to the House of Commons on 7 September.[129] Official, detailed confirmation of the results of the discussions was set forth in a letter from Ilsley to the British High Commission on 13 September.[130] (Chapter 10 recounts the negotiation of the large post-war loan from Canada to Britain early in 1946 as well as the agreement on the final settlement of all outstanding war claims on each other by the Canadian and British governments.)

CHAPTER EIGHT

Financing Britain Further and Keynes's Visits

By mid-1943, the war finally turned in the Allies' favour. American, British, and Canadian forces had recently invaded Sicily. On 10 July, the Americans seized Gela, and British and Canadian troops drove along the eastern shore. By 22 July, half of Sicily was occupied. Then southern Italy was invaded. Within a year, the Allied forces were in Rome. At about the same time, Canadian, British, and American troops were landing in Normandy. The D-Day invasion of 6 June 1944 marked the beginning of the end for Adolf Hitler and Nazi Germany. Within two months of that invasion, France was liberated. Soon thereafter, Allied troops freed Belgium.

However, while the war across the Atlantic was going well, across the Pacific it was grinding on. The sobering thought that the defeat of Japan remained to be accomplished cast a pall over any Victory in Europe celebrations. Stubborn Japanese resistance was leading to heavy Allied losses. The fight for Iwo Jima, a speck of volcanic rock 750 miles from Tokyo, took nearly six weeks and brought more than 20,000 American casualties. The fight for Okinawa, which began on 1 April 1945, was even bloodier.

Within this environment, attention at the Department of Finance turned to financing "stage II" of the war: the fight against Japan. As in the past, officials in the small, overburdened department struggled with reconciling the national interest with its Allies' – specifically Britain's – seemingly insatiable financial needs. This chapter chronicles the department's efforts to finance Britain during the closing years of the war.

After the government had given notice to Parliament on 28 March 1944 of its resolution to request a Mutual Aid appropriation of $800 million for the fiscal year 1944–45, we in Finance began once more to consider what other new measures we might work out to finance Britain further in obtaining war supplies from Canada. Those of us in the department and on the Mutual Aid Board knew that the appropriation would be inadequate. We took it for granted that we could and would finance the other recipients of our Mutual Aid out of the $800 million appropriation; there was no alternative in their case. We could hope to find a different solution in the case of Britain, however, because we had so great a flow of payments and receipts and there was such a variety of at least theoretical possibilities of credits or payments in gold. Furthermore, we and the British could both hope that *in extremis* we could get a supplementary appropriation from Parliament later in the year. We dared not rely on that or even talk seriously about it, however; cabinet, armed with all the facts and forecasts, had just decided on the limited $800 million figure, probably with the overall 1944 budget in mind. The prime minister felt strongly, as we have noted in chapter 7 above, about the need for a popular budget in that politically important year.

The most obvious alternative was the first one seriously mentioned by Clifford Clark to the Mutual Aid Board at the next meeting on 31 March.[1] He spoke of using a loan or credit to supplement Mutual Aid and having the UK pay part of what was required in US dollars. Karl Fraser, the administrator of Mutual Aid, observed that some indication of the situation had been given to Gordon Munro of the UK Treasury before he departed to London earlier in March; it might be assumed that he would return with instructions on which further conversations could be based. After some further discussion, Howe and Ralston (the only two ministers present; Ilsley was away sick and Ralston was acting for him) decided that Mutual Aid funds should be used in the normal way for one month while the possibilities and future plans were discussed with the representatives of Britain.

We in the department did not formulate any specific proposals during the next few weeks before we heard from the British Treasury. We kept our forecasts up-to-date; indeed, one of the most sudden and substantial changes in British requests for Canadian production occurred at this time in urgent applications for increased amounts of artillery ammunition, which Canada was able to supply by shifting labour from aircraft production, which was declining, into ammunition plants that had been working below capacity.[2] In London, many possibilities were being discussed between Treasury and other officials.[3]

Munro returned to Ottawa late in April and soon discussed the situation with Clark. The latter reported on the conversation to the Mutual Aid Board meeting of 4 May. Clark felt that the UK authorities had the impression that there might be a further appropriation later in the year, making it possible to meet their requirements without recourse to credit arrangements. If no further appropriation was voted, Munro indicated, it might be necessary for the UK to consider cancellation or diversion of some of their Canadian contracts; the shortage of Canadian dollars was now, from the UK point of view, more severe than the shortage of US dollars. Clark reported that he had suggested to Munro that the UK might consider paying Canada in US dollars for the US content in Canadian shipments to the UK. Clark regarded this initial conversation with Munro as on the whole "inconclusive."

The first major move came in London from the British Treasury, and it was a positive one. Sir Wilfrid Eady and Lord Keynes had an important discussion on 18 May with Norman Robertson, who was in London with Prime Minister King for the Commonwealth Prime Ministers' Conference. Eady and Keynes suggested that Canada should pay the UK government for certain training services received by the aircrew of the Royal Canadian Air Force squadrons, and also should make more adequate payment for supplies furnished to the Canadian Expeditionary Force about to go into action in France. They proposed, in addition, that Canada should pay its share of the reserve stocks of arms and ammunition held by the UK to supply its own forces and the Canadian forces. Eady sent Robertson a note on these suggestions, which Robertson forwarded to Canada.[4]

Clark studied Eady's suggestions and prepared a paper on them early in June.[5] Eady had suggested that Canada should pay for "advanced training" and "operational training" provided by the RAF for Canadian aircrew to join RCAF squadrons operating out of the UK or later in Europe. Clark acknowledged that "there seems to be much to be said" for Canada to make these payments. A second suggestion from Eady was that the "capitation rate" paid by the Canadian Department of National Defence to the UK War Office to cover the cost of arms, ammunition, and supplies furnished to maintain the Canadian Expeditionary Force in the field should cover the estimated costs of maintaining that force in the role in which it was to be engaged, rather than on average costs of all army units. This was going to be important because the Canadian force was to be part of the armoured spearhead of the invasion and would be using great quantities of expensive arms and ammunition. Clark felt that this charge was one we should be prepared to pay. Eady's third proposal was that both the RCAF and the Canadian army forces as a whole should pay a share of the cost of the very considerable stockpile of arms, ammunition, and stores that were held by the UK in order to meet the needs of their own and the Canadian forces in the field. Eady estimated that the Canadian share of the cost of these stockpiles would be, roughly, $200 million for the RCAF and $50 million for the army.

Clark said that there was one serious objection to this proposal to pay for a share of the cost of the British stockpiles. Some of these supplies, for both of the services, had been furnished by Canada as Mutual Aid and some would have been paid for out of the billion-dollar gift in 1942. This at least should be reflected by a reduction in the claim, perhaps even eliminating the justification for the charge for the army. In his memorandum, Clark went on to argue that Britain should pay Canada US dollars for the US content of what Canada supplied to Britain. He estimated this to be roughly $250 million to $275 million a year and suggested making an agreed on estimate of it, which would be covered by periodic payments. (Recall that at this time in 1944 Canada's balance of payments in US dollars was strong; indeed, Canada had had to pay the US Treasury hundreds of millions of dollars to bring the US dollar reserves down to the agreed on level, as of early 1944.) Clark estimated that if Eady's first two suggestions were accepted, but not the one on stockpiles, and if his own suggested US dollar payments were made, it still would leave a fairly substantial gap in the financing of Britain's requirements in Canada during the fiscal year 1944–45. He suggested that this be covered by having Canada give a credit to the UK.

Clark accompanied James Ilsley to the Cabinet War Committee meeting of 14 June 1944. When this subject was discussed, Clark spoke extensively along the lines of his memorandum. Chubby Power, the minister of national defence (for air), stated that it had been agreed already that the number of RCAF operating squadrons overseas would be increased from forty-four to fifty-eight, which would involve Canadian payments to Britain of $200 million to $300 million for initial equipment and maintenance. The War Committee accepted Clark's advice and decided that:

1. Canada would accept the cost of advanced and operational training for aircrew entering RCAF operational squadrons.
2. Canada would accept a higher capitation rate for the Army, to be worked out by the EAHQ in London and the Department of Finance on the basis of the best estimate of actual costs.
3. The U.K. Treasury proposals on reserve stocks be rejected.
4. The U.K. be asked to make payment in gold or U.S. dollars for the U.S. content of Canadian War supplies furnished to the U.K.
5. An open book credit be granted to the U.K. to cover any remaining deficit.[6]

At the next meeting of the Cabinet War Committee, on 21 June, Power, in his continued effort to move Canadian aircrew out of the Royal Air Force into identifiable Canadian RCAF operating units, persuaded his colleagues, including Ilsley, to substitute expenditures on fourteen additional RCAF operational squadrons, in place of the

Canadian expenditure on advanced and operational training proposed by Eady and accepted by Clark and Ilsley. This was done in the counter proposal to be put to the British.[7]

These decisions, later endorsed by cabinet, were taken by Ilsley and Clark to a meeting with Keynes and Eady during the first few days of the International Monetary Conference at Bretton Woods, New Hampshire, which opened on 1 July 1944. The British were not prepared to agree with these Canadian counter proposals and succeeded in persuading Ilsley to defer action on them. This was the first meeting that Ilsley or Clark had had with Keynes, who was a remarkably persuasive man. He had been preparing his detailed notes to negotiate with the us for Lend-Lease during stage II of the war, after Germany was defeated but not Japan. Keynes gave Ilsley and Clark a full account of the very serious financial future of the uk and the importance of its not accepting loans from the us or Canada to finance its war requirements and of husbanding its meager gold reserves. Ilsley agreed that Keynes and Eady should come to Ottawa early in August after the monetary conference was over and they had had some time to rest. Ilsley and Clark, meanwhile, had to hurry back to Ottawa for one of the busiest summers in the history of the Department of Finance.[8]

After the exhausting weeks at Bretton Woods, Keynes arranged to have a leisurely holiday in Canada. He spent most of his time in Ottawa, with his wife, who scheduled his meetings and guarded his health. One event during the holiday is well worth noting. The 27th of July was the 250th anniversary of the founding of the Bank of England. After many, many years of criticizing the bank's policies, Keynes was now a member of the Court of the Bank. He showed that he had a sense of history and occasion; despite wartime austerity, he put on a sumptuous dinner that night at the Chateau Laurier for about two dozen of us then in Ottawa. After dinner, he made a speech – a beautiful, loving speech – about the bank, its history and traditions, and its practices and personalities. Only Louis Rasminsky and I can remember the occasion, but Clark and Mackintosh and Donald Gordon and others from the Bank of Canada (but not Graham Towers, who religiously kept July for a holiday) and Robertson and Wrong and Ilsley and perhaps a few other ministers were there. It was a long speech. The dinner and the wine were very good, so I remembered little of its content afterwards, except one significant detail that inevitably appealed to an overworked young officer of an overburdened department: the practice of the Bank of England always to try to have a few extra competent officers who could be spared for unforeseen tasks.[9]

AUGUST MEETINGS WITH KEYNES AND UK TREASURY OFFICIALS

Keynes and Eady (along with the UK high commissioner and Munro) had a long meeting on the morning of 1 August with Ilsley, Clark, Towers, Robertson, Wrong, and me (as secretary); in the evening they met with Howe, Ralston, Ilsley, St Laurent, and Gardiner, all senior and influential ministers meeting as the Mutual Aid Board, and several officials.

In the morning meeting, Keynes led off with a long, detailed exposition of the present and prospective international financial position of Great Britain and its relation to financial and other policies in stage II – the war against Japan after hostilities had ceased in Europe – and in stage III – the first few years after the war ended. He dealt in detail with the situation in respect to each of Britain's main creditors in the sterling area – India, Egypt, Australia, New Zealand, and the Crown Colonies – as well as South Africa, which paid its accounts to the UK in gold. He described briefly the position vis-à-vis the main neutral countries.[10]

Keynes emphasized that the UK would have to borrow as much as it could outside the sterling area but wished to avoid any such borrowing during stage II because it would need to use all its borrowing capacity in stage III. The UK hoped very much, therefore, that it would be able to continue to get Mutual Aid from Canada during stage II. He suggested at this point that in stage II, beginning in April 1945, arms and ammunition should not be charged to Mutual Aid but to the Canadian service concerned, which would transfer them without records to the UK counterpart service. This "pooling" process was being followed already between the UK and US services. Keynes was not yet ready to discuss the scale and nature of the British role in that part of the war or what they would wish to get from Canada. He and his colleagues felt that there were ways, in the meantime, to meet the deficit in Britain's accounts with Canada during the current fiscal year – before stage II – without an increase in Mutual Aid appropriation.

Ilsley and Clark asked a number of questions, which Keynes answered in detail. The minister was particularly concerned about how he could justify to Canadians the free gift of supplies to the UK when other countries in the Commonwealth and sterling area were selling them on credit by accumulating sterling balances. Keynes suggested a response to this question that seemed really too sophisticated for the minister to use. Keynes had said that with the exception of the Crown Colonies, these sterling obligations were going to have to be largely "blocked" and payable only in goods exported by the UK during future years long after the war. He felt that this type of war debt would not suit Canada's trade and financial interest.

The specific interim proposals that Keynes put forward included: (1) the elimination of taxes on Mutual Aid transfers just as other exports were exempt; (2) finding another way to finance the capital costs of ships, which were being charged to Mutual Aid, when the ships were only being lent; (3) the increase to a more accurate figure of the "capitation charges" paid by Canada to the UK for the maintenance in the field of the Canadian army units; (4) the payment by Canada to the UK of the costs of advanced training of RCAF aircrew; (5) payment of a share of the costs of reserve stocks and supplies in transit held by the UK to supply Canadian forces in operations. At the same time, the British did recognize that there was outstanding a balance of $200 million owing by the UK for the first period of the British Commonwealth Air Training Plan. There was a little discussion of some of these items but no decisions were reached. During this discussion, Keynes did say that Canada unquestionably had given the UK a much better deal than anyone else had; he could not deny, however, that in the UK's relations with Canada "one good deed leads to the expectation of another."

In the evening meeting with the five ministers, Keynes presented the essential facts of the situation more briefly than he had in the morning, concentrating on British policies and attitudes.[11] His government, said Keynes, felt that it could not afford to enter the post-war period with its gold and US dollar reserves below a level that they regarded as the essential minimum for economic and political security. In addition, his government had decided that it must not incur debts beyond its capacity to pay, and it would pay all debts incurred. Because it expected to need all of its available borrowing power to meet essential requirements from outside the sterling area in the immediate post-war years, the government felt it most important to persuade Allied governments that the UK must not be asked to incur war debts while the war lasted. If the UK reduced her reserves below the necessary minimum or used up her limited borrowing power before the end of hostilities, it would be necessary to restrict imports severely during the immediate post-war years, doing with fewer foodstuffs, for example, than would be desirable. The people of the United Kingdom naturally would feel that the great sacrifices made in the common cause should not result in that. Eady added that if the UK was left in a seriously weak financial position after the war, it would be unable to undertake its share of the obligations necessary for international security.

Keynes again suggested that Canadian authorities might consider in stage II, after the current fiscal year, a new type of arrangement for pooling the munitions (and military equipment) produced by each Allied country. These would be paid for by their own defence services but allocated for use by those forces by whom they were most required. If this was done, Mutual Aid could be much smaller and used essentially for foodstuffs. As for the current year, he and Eady were suggesting a number of proposals that they believed were in accordance with Canada's intention of meeting the full cost of her own forces, proposals that would enable the financing problem to be met with no increase in the Mutual Aid appropriation.

Some discussion of the information and suggestions put forward by Keynes followed (none of which was included on the record), but the ministers did not attempt to reach any decision on any of the matters. Keynes was a very fluent and persuasive man, with a surprising array of facts and figures at his fingertips. I had the impression that the Canadian ministers felt they needed to be cautious about taking decisions while under his spell.

The high commissioner of the UK submitted a Treasury paper dated 1 August 1944 that was to supplement these discussions in connection with the suggestions and comments made for dealing with the situation in the fiscal year 1944–45.[11] In a paper dated 7 August, Keynes summarized the major facts and figures that he had used in making his presentation; this summary appears in Volume XXIV of his collected writings.[12]

We in the department hurried to examine the proposals from these 1 August discussions and in the UK paper of that date in order to brief Ilsley on them. I prepared a long, detailed memorandum, dated 6 August, including an appraisal (and approval) of the British arguments. It is not clear whether this memorandum was revised or to whom it was sent. Towers sent over a strong memorandum on 10 August.[13] He supported finding some way of meeting the British requirements, possibly along the lines that they suggested. He argued that "it is most definitely in Canada's selfish interests that the United Kingdom should achieve this objective" – that is, to keep enough cash (gold and dollars) on hand to retain some strength and independence after the war and not get themselves into a situation where they would have to default on their obligations. Towers did agree, however, that Canada should not give up all claims to US dollars. We should try to get $100 million toward meeting what we spent in the US on Britain's account.

The UK proposals were put before a special meeting of cabinet on 14 August, which Clark and I attended. No paper had been circulated. Clark put forward the UK position and proposals, and we answered questions about them. Ilsley recommended that they be accepted, on condition that the UK would pay us US dollars equal to the estimated US content of Mutual Aid supplied to the UK and the rest of the sterling area that year. Cabinet approved these proposals in the following terms:

1. The payment by Canada of increased capitation rates for Canadian Army personnel overseas, calculated upon the estimated cost of Canadian formations rather than upon the average of U.K. forces; this principle to apply in respect of all active operations from the opening of the Sicilian campaign.
2. The payment by Canada of the cost of advanced training in the U.K. of Canadian aircrew who enter or have entered RCAF Squadrons; this principle to apply from the date of Canada's assumption of the cost of such squadrons [April 1943] or of their formation in the case of new squadrons.
3. The contribution by Canada of her fair share of the cost of reserve stores and stores in transit, drawn upon by the Canadian Army overseas and the RCAF overseas [several allowances and conditions were attached to this item].
4. The exemption of Mutual Aid supplies from the beginning of this fiscal year from sales and other excise taxes, and eligibility thereof for drawback of customs duties, etc. as in the case of other exports.
5. Payment to Canada by the United Kingdom in gold or U.S. dollars of an amount equal to the estimated U.S. content of Canadian munitions transferred to the U.K. (and the rest of the sterling area) under Mutual Aid. This is a condition of the Canadian government's agreement to items 1, 2, 3 and 4 above. It relates to Mutual Aid goods transferred during the current fiscal year and is estimated at approximately $90 million U.S. [later revised to $80 million].[14]

The following day, 15 August, we organized a large meeting in Clark's office, at which were present the resident and visiting representatives of the UK Treasury (Keynes and Eady had departed) and representatives of the interested Canadian departments and services. Clark read to them Heeney's letter summarizing the government's decision on the matter. There was a long, detailed discussion of the estimated amounts of the various items approved. It appeared that the additional Canadian payments that fiscal year would total $655 million, which would cover the estimated gap in the whole sterling area balance of payments for Canada, with $100 million to spare. The Canadian equivalent of the $80 million US payment, and the settlement of the tax exemption in the previous year on UK purchases through the Mutual Aid Board, plus a minor item, would increase the prospective surplus to about $250 million.[15] The UK representatives suggested that the first $200 million of any surplus might be used to pay off that amount owing by the UK for the first British Commonwealth Air Training Plan. There was, however, no effort to reach agreement on this suggestion because the probable residual amount was very uncertain given that the calculation was based on forecasts of many items on which those closest to the situation could make only an informed guess. The British representatives said that they would inform the Treasury immediately of the Canadian government's decision and they did so. On 29 August,

Ilsley received a cabled message of agreement and appreciation from the chancellor of the exchequer saying that the government of the United Kingdom agreed with the decisions and was prepared to proceed with working them out.[16] This broad agreement was a triumph of equity and common sense.

Reaching agreement on all of the details of these wide-ranging decisions took until February 1946; in the meantime, payments on account were made by Canada into the UK Cash Receipts account and were used to supplement the Mutual Aid appropriation. The longest delay was over the army capitation rates, on which there were interminable arguments between the Canadian Defence Department and the War Office. These parties did not agree until they were included in a broad settlement on which the two governments finally reached agreement. Another very troublesome item, which at the time appeared to be quite important, was the determination of the Lend-Lease content of what the Canadian services received from the British services, including transfers in the course of actual military operations. In principle, the British were to report these to the US and rebate the value to Canada, and Canada was to pay the US for them. Determination, reporting, and settlement of these transfers were not completed until months after the war, and it is not feasible now to determine from the files how much ultimately was paid to the US. (See chapter 6 above.) In the end, it proved to be a modest amount, chiefly for the initial supply of US tanks to the Canadian army and for US aircraft for the RCAF squadrons. Similar difficulties arose in determining the amount payable for Canada's share of the reserve stores both of the army and the air force. This, too, was not settled until months after the war.

These difficulties did not prevent Canada from making enough payments to solve the financing problem of the sterling area in Canada during 1944–45. Much had to be accepted on trust, on the basis of informal estimates and forecasts. This meant that several of us in the department had to monitor closely what Canada was estimated to be accumulating both as receivables and payables in our accounts with Britain. This took much time, and the building up of a network of contacts with trustworthy officers in Munitions and Supply, the three armed services, and the Mutual Aid Board, along with the comptroller of the Treasury's staff in Ottawa and London and the various UK Treasury officials. It was possible to do this because detailed parliamentary scrutiny and criticism were not hanging over us during these difficult years, unlike the situation in the US, where Congress monitored the decisions of federal departments.

CANADIAN SERVICES IN THE WAR AGAINST JAPAN

Canadian participation in the war against Japan, when hostilities in Europe were over, was taken for granted by the government, at least in early 1944. At that time, the minister of defence for air, with the support of the prime minister, began to seek the agreement of the British secretary of state for air on the complete "Canadianization" of Canadian aircrew still serving in the RAF when the war in Europe ended. The desire was to build up a larger RCAF under Canadian control that could serve against Japan in the Pacific as well as share in the occupation of Germany. Sporadic discussions also went on for some months with the Air Ministry and the British Naval authorities. Both these British services, which had been heavily engaged throughout the war in Europe, were interested in getting the assistance of their Canadian counterparts in stage II. The Canadian army was more modest in its ambitions. It was not at all clear where it could go or with what other army it could be associated. It was expected to provide a division for occupational duties in Europe, and to provide no more than a division with ancillary troops for duties in the North Pacific or even on the mainland of China. It did not want, nor did the government want it, to go to Southeast Asia, for which it would need tropical retraining and where it would be engaged in regaining colonial areas for the British Empire.[17]

Little was done or agreed on about plans for the war against Japan when the Commonwealth prime ministers met in London in May 1944.[18] After his return to Ottawa, King directed the Cabinet War Committee to refer the subject of the role and size of the Canadian forces in stage II to the chiefs of staff, supplemented for this purpose by the undersecretary of state for external affairs and the secretary of cabinet, both of whom were familiar with the prime minister's views. This group reported back within three weeks. The report noted first that from a purely military point of view, the simplest arrangement would be for the three Canadian services to continue to work in combination with the British services, as they had been doing, which would mean operating mainly in and around Southeast Asia. The report went on to say that from a Canadian and perhaps Commonwealth point of view, it might be better if the Canadians served in an "American" theatre, the North or West Pacific. However, while the British would seek and welcome Canadian formations working with them, the Americans would not request Canadian assistance, as they had ample forces of their own. As for the particular services, the army preferred to participate against the Japanese on their home islands or on the Chinese mainland, neither of which would require retraining under tropical conditions. The air force was prepared to accept the British suggestion of a large force of fifty-eight RCAF squadrons, but only on the understanding that no commitments had been made as to where these squadrons would serve. The Canadian navy would be glad to form part of the British fleet. The chiefs of staff, with Robertson and Heeney, concluded their report by saying that if Canada wanted its forces to operate against Japan in the North or Western Pacific, the matter should be taken up quickly with both the British and US governments.

King quickly informed Churchill of these matters. The British reacted as expected: they saw a possible role with others for our army division in the North or West Pacific but hoped that the Canadian navy would reinforce the British fleet in the Bay of Bengal or the Southwest Pacific and that the RCAF would be part of the main British effort from Southeast Asia or the Southwest Pacific. The British planners suggested large numbers in these Canadian forces.[19] After receiving the British views, each chief of staff discussed the subject with his own minister in late August and early September, before the Quebec Conference in September 1944.

The ministers discussed the issues at length in the Cabinet War Committee of 31 August. Immediately before that meeting, the prime minister talked to Major-General Maurice Pope, who had just returned from being chairman of the Canadian Joint Staff in Washington. Pope told King: "We were neither being asked nor were we wanted to take part in the war against Japan, so far as any existing need was concerned. It is apparent that the Americans want to make that fight themselves. It is also apparent that the British are having difficulty in getting a look in with them, but are most anxious to do so. Apparently they feel they must retake Singapore themselves to redeem face in the far east."[20]

At the 31 August meeting, the prime minister drew attention to the British view that large operations would be needed to conquer the main island of Japan. He agreed that Canada should have some forces with the Americans in fighting against Japan itself. He emphasized that a general election was immediately ahead and that it would be necessary to tell the public frankly what our contribution was to be; he was perfectly sure that the Canadian people would not agree to any contribution to the hostilities south of the equator. He said that it was going to be difficult to control the defence departments, but that the issues must be decided by cabinet as a whole.[21] There was no suggestion that the Canadian forces should not participate, but there was discussion as to where and in what role and what numbers, all of which would have to be worked out after the main decisions were taken by the US and the UK at the Quebec Conference.[22]

This general subject was discussed by cabinet on 6 September, after the prime minister had written strong letters to Ralston and to Howe urging care and economy in the decisions to be taken in connection with Canada's undertakings in the war against Japan.[23] At this meeting, cabinet all agreed that the Canadian services should participate in the war against Japan. There seemed to be a consensus in favour of one division's being prepared to go to Japan, with one to remain in the army of occupation in Europe. The proposed navy program was to be cut down fifty per cent, and the contribution of the air force to be made smaller than had been contemplated. The formal cabinet decisions also noted that Canadian forces should "participate in the war against Japan in operational theatres of direct interest to Canada as a North American nation, for example in the North or Central Pacific rather than in more remote areas such as South East Asia" and that the form and extent of the three services' contributions should be decided following the second Quebec Conference."[24]

At the US–UK discussions on 13 September, Churchill offered a British fleet to co-operate with the US navy in the war in the Far Eastern Pacific. The American navy was not enthusiastic about this, particularly Admiral King, the senior admiral, but Roosevelt accepted the offer. In due course, the combined chiefs of staff agreed that "the British fleet should participate in the main operations against Japan in the Pacific."[25]

Churchill attended the Canadian Cabinet War Committee on 14 September. King told him in that meeting that his government had to face an election soon and that their policies, therefore, had to be considered in light of what could be fought out on the platform. He then read out the careful decisions that they had taken about cabinet's preference for fighting in the North Pacific rather than the South. Churchill instantly said that the problem really was one of whether the Americans were going to take over the whole business themselves. He had had to tell the Americans that the British themselves had to regain some of the territories that they had lost, for example Burma and Singapore. The British had had to agree to fight under an American commander. He would have to ask the president about what part Canada could play. He asked King to let him have the memo that had just been read out and said that he would take it up with the president at once.[26]

The British and Canadian chiefs of staff then joined this meeting. There was no mention of an election, and Churchill told his chiefs what the Canadian policy was and that the Americans would have to be consulted. The discussion then got on to the specific services. There was no need of a Canadian army in the South Pacific. Only a token

Canadian force was needed even in the north. On the other hand, the British navy could be helped by the Canadian navy's sending out of a few ships such as one or two cruisers, one or two destroyers, and a carrier. They would be used in the North Pacific. As for fighting in the air, Churchill, on his own initiative, asked his chief of staff why they had put such a burden on the Canadian air force. He was told that the Canadian Air Mission had said that they welcomed it. Power intervened and said that nothing had been decided yet.[27]

After these meetings at Quebec, the plans of the individual services for their expected roles in stage II were worked out by their ministers and at meetings of the Cabinet War Committee during late September and October. These were to be included in the War Appropriation for 1945–46. Since only an interim, round-sum appropriation was eventually requested in March 1945, which by chance covered the period up to the surrender of Japan, these detailed items never saw the light of day.[28]

There was, however, a lengthy debate on the interim war appropriation in the House of Commons in April, before dissolution of Parliament. During this debate, on 4 April, King made a statement on the roles that the Canadian forces would undertake after the end of hostilities in Europe. Some of these related to the occupation of Germany by an inter-Allied army and to the protection of the Atlantic sea lanes. Regarding the action against Japan, King emphasized the vast distances of the Pacific and the limits that they imposed on the size of the forces that could be employed with advantages. "Canada's effort to maintain her just part in the further prosecution of the war against Japan will, as measured in numbers, necessarily be very much less than has been the case in the war in Europe," he said. King went on to emphasize Canada's role in producing arms and munitions needed in the war against Japan, and also in producing foodstuffs, raw materials, and other civilian requirements for relief and rehabilitation (as well as for Britain, which he did not mention).

King said that the specific roles of the three Canadian services would have to be determined with the UK and UK authorities in the light of the changing situation and the general strategy decided at the Quebec Conference. It had been agreed already that the Royal Canadian Navy would co-operate with the British Pacific fleet. Squadrons of the Royal Canadian Air Force would take part in operations against Japan in co-operation with the Royal Air Force. (These co-operative arrangements were of importance to Finance; they affected the payments likely to be made to the UK and, indirectly, the Mutual Aid required.) King said that it was proposed that the army would provide a force to operate with the US army. It would be reorganized and trained in Canada first before dispatch across the Pacific.[29]

Events moved so rapidly in the Pacific that very few Canadians actually served there. The Canadian cruiser *Uganda* served for a few months in mid-1945 with the Pacific Fleet of the Royal Navy before it had to return to Canada in late July to replace her crew with sailors volunteering for service in the Pacific in accordance with the new manpower policy that King also had announced on 4 April.[30]

PREPARING FOR STAGE II FINANCIAL NEGOTIATIONS

It was Canadian munitions, not men, that the British were seriously worried about in September 1944 when planning for stage II. Despite the satisfactory settlement with Canadian ministers in August, they feared, understandably, that practical political problems in Canada might do serious harm to their difficult international financial position during stage II.

The British staked their claim before the Quebec Conference. On 7 September, Churchill cabled King that they intended to ask the US for arms and ammunition on Lend-Lease during stage II, as well as foodstuffs and raw materials. More specifically, he said, during the first year of stage II, the UK planned to produce munitions at two-thirds of their current rate and would hope to be able to count on receiving munitions on Lend-Lease at two-thirds of the current level. Churchill said that he hoped Canada would do the same, with the details to be worked out later. His message included a reference to Canada's adopting of a "pooling plan" for the transfer of arms and ammunition between the armed services without charge, such as the US and the UK had adopted.[31]

Robertson sent a copy of this cable to Ilsley, inviting comment on it for the prime minister, who was leaving shortly for the Quebec Conference. In the absence of others in the department that Saturday, 9 September, I sent Robertson a short memo in which I said that to provide the UK with munitions on the scale proposed, plus food and raw materials for the first year of stage II, when our armed services were paying them much less than during the war in Europe, would require a very large amount of Mutual Aid or its equivalent. This would be, I said, probably in the neighbourhood of $1.1 billion or $1.2 billion, well above the level for 1944–45.[32] I would not have dared to add in this message that the UK were asking for this very substantial financial support for a large military program without any indication that they would explain it, let alone justify it, to Canadian ministers.

King gave Churchill no assurance in Quebec, or in the weeks after it, along the lines that Churchill mentioned. Obviously, ministers were going to have to study both the financial and other implications of this proposal as well as await some word on the outcome of British discussions with the Americans on Lend-Lease supplies and related matters. Moreover, the Canadian government had to assess the prospects for its general financial position in 1945–46, and to resolve its acute internal crisis over the reinforcement requirements for its army in Europe.

The first systematic and important discussion on Mutual Aid policy for stage II took place on 13 October 1944 at an informal meeting of the Mutual Aid Board.[33] Howe, Ilsley, and St Laurent were present. All three took an active part in the discussion, as did Hume Wrong and Sydney Pierce from External Affairs and Clark and I from Finance. It is not clear now whether Mackintosh was present, but he had written the main paper under discussion, entitled "The Place of Mutual Aid in Stage II of the War." This was an economic analysis of the problem of demobilizing most of the Canadian forces after the end of hostilities in Europe, and of reducing production and employment in war industries at the same time, without creating serious unemployment and frustration.[34] It was an excellent and comprehensive paper. It concluded that Mutual Aid, at least on the scale of the current year, was highly desirable in terms of Canada's own interests. It would enable demobilization, both military and civil, to be carried out at a manageable pace. It should be looked on as a transitional measure to attain satisfactory export programs after the war.

A second paper for the information of the ministers at the meeting was "Probable Sterling Area Requirements for Mutual Aid 1945–46," which I had prepared at Clark's request.[35] This paper gave detailed forecasts of what we expected the UK and other countries in the sterling area to ask us to supply, and their other payments to Canada. What was more difficult at that time was forecasting what we could expect our defence services to pay to the UK or other countries in the sterling area, and finally what we should expect the UK to do if we did not provide Mutual Aid (or its equivalent in pooling) on the scale required. I had estimated the scale to be about $1.2 billion for the year 1945–46, less whatever the Canadian defence services paid to the UK or other sterling area countries, which we estimated would not be more than $400 million.

In the discussion, Howe asked whether the British could be expected to maintain their objection to incurring new indebtedness to Canada during stage II. Clark said that he felt they would be adamant on this point. St Laurent asked many questions during the meeting, some of them quite fundamental, implying that Canada could change the basic nature of its economy so as to rely less on exports. He was answered on this fundamental point by Clark and by Pierce, and particularly by C.D. Howe himself, who felt very strongly that we would remain dependent on export markets. St Laurent later stated that the people of Quebec had accepted the principle that we should contribute supplies to the United Nations as part of our share in the war effort. Some participation in stage II could be justified to them on the ground that Japan must be crushed. At this point, Howe said that there was a strong argument in stage II for Canada to make its contribution in supplies rather than men, in view of the great distances over which operations would have to be carried out. He felt that we could not bargain at that time regarding post-war policies; rather, we should keep the flow of exports going. We should try during stage II, however, to have some of our supplies sold for cash or credit.

Ilsley had been impressed with Mackintosh's economic argument. He stated that the question was whether our fear of unemployment during demobilization was so great that we should continue Mutual Aid. His later actions indicated that he felt that it was, but in any case he was sufficiently impressed with the British economic arguments as presented by Keynes that he favoured the continuation of Mutual Aid.

This important meeting of the key ministers concluded that Canada should maintain its production of munitions during 1945–46 at about one-half its current rate and that an effort should be made to negotiate an arrangement with the UK that would permit this but that also would include some partial payment by credit or other means rather than wholly in Mutual Aid.[36]

A week after this meeting on Mutual Aid policy, External Affairs received from the British high commissioner a formal memorandum from the British Treasury dated 14 October 1944 and entitled "Arrangements for Supplies from Canada in Stage II."[37] This contained no new information of substance but was a detailed and formal proposal for pooling munitions and war services between the two countries, along the lines that Keynes and others had mentioned to us in August and September. In essence, the idea was that munitions, including weapons, ammunition, motor vehicles, and warships, as well as war services, including training (apart from the main British Commonwealth Air Training Plan itself) and inspection services, would be given freely by the appropriate service of the one country to the corresponding service of the other without any charges or accounting therefor. This would remove all such items supplied by Canada from Mutual Aid; their cost would be borne by the allotments of the war appropriation for the Canadian service concerned; on the other side, it would render unnecessary all accounting between the Canadian services and their British counterparts for munitions and war supplies overseas, such as the capitation charges for the army, the maintenance and capital costs of the RCAF squadrons, and the modest payments between the two naval authorities. Canada would continue to supply foodstuffs and raw materials as Mutual Aid. Various minor classes of transactions would be settled in cash, and the Air Training Plan deficits would have to be settled by negotiation.

There was some logic to this plan, as one would expect from one proposed by Keynes. Had it been proposed in 1943, in lieu of our complicated Mutual Aid arrangements with the British, the plan might have had held some attraction for us, and perhaps some material advantages, as well. As a plan to be introduced in 1945 to apply to stage II, however, when its advantages to Canada were about to fall drastically while remaining high to the British, it would attract suspicions immediately. Parliament would have to approve the plan, and it would not make the government's political task any easier, which clearly was Keynes's objective. Indeed, it inevitably would be regarded, in Ilsley's word, as "camouflage" (what would now be called cover-up, the most dangerous of political tactics). Keynes seemed unable or unwilling to recognize this – or to accept that it was Ilsley and his colleagues, especially Howe, St Laurent, and King, who must judge the political advantages and risks. Keynes seemed desperate to avoid a repetition of the inadequate appropriation of 1944, which was understandable, but the Canadian side had learned its lesson and paid for it. Keynes's repeated efforts to sell us this "gimmick" demeaned him in the eyes of our ministers (and Clark and me). We had a much simpler and better solution and a very favourable opportunity to use it, but he did not seem willing to consider it. He was, however, full of appreciation and co-operation when our measure had succeeded fully by the end of Mutual Aid in September 1945.

Keynes and Sir Robert Sinclair (of the UK Ministry of Production) had planned to be in Ottawa to discuss stage II requirements and financing in early November, during the American election. The two men learned from Munro that this would be inconvenient on the Ottawa end because Canadian ministers would not be able to give it their time and attention during the conscription crisis. Their visit was deferred to such time as they had finished their long and difficult discussions with the Americans on the same subject. These discussions included serious objections by the Americans on the same subject, and serious objections by the Americans to British plans to devote substantial resources to a program to start restoring their export trade, which would be vitally important to them in the immediate post-war period. In the meantime, Keynes sent to Clark, on 27 October, the key papers on their requirements as submitted to the Americans.[38]

After repeated delays in Washington, Keynes and Sinclair arrived in Ottawa on Tuesday, 28 November, when the conscription debate in Parliament was at its height. They had come from lengthy but ultimately successful discussions in Washington. They had obtained in Washington the assurance of the American supplies that they needed to carry on the war in stage II while relaxing their total efforts a little and beginning the drive to rebuild their export trade. The latter was essential both to solvency and to survival after the war as a major power.[39] The government in Ottawa had had no part in deciding the strategy and roles in the war against Japan. Yet it was now being asked to help underwrite a British effort that was appropriate to a Great Power but that Britain could no longer afford on its own.

Keynes was fit for the task. His abilities were best described in the words of Frank Lee, who was then one of the middle-rank Treasury representatives stationed in Washington and who had been through all the negotiations there. In a long letter to a colleague in London, Lee wrote:

On our side, of course, one name stands quite alone. Maynard's performance was truly wonderful. I think that occasionally he over-played his hand and occasionally wore himself out in struggling for points which were not worth winning. But in general he was an inspiration to us all: it is no exaggeration to say that we felt like Lucifer's followers in Milton, 'Rejoicing in their matchless chief'. His industry was prodigious, his resilience and continuous optimism constant wonder to those of us more inclined to pessimism, while I doubt whether he has ever written or spoken with more lucidity and charm ... And, of course, the impression which he makes on the Americans gives us an enormous initial advantage in any negotiation in which he participates.[40]

In Ottawa, the first meeting was with senior officials, on 28 November.[41] It covered, first, the nature and scale of projected UK requirements from Canada during stage II, which was taken to be our fiscal year 1945–46, and second, and mainly, a variety of special problems relating to supplies, past payments, and adjustment of claims. Keynes began with an informative description of their negotiations in Washington, essentially as background for these Canadian discussions. He then referred to a memorandum on the factual background, which Sir Robert Sinclair had drawn up after a preliminary discussion with the British and Canadian officials at an earlier meeting.[42]

This memorandum stated that the UK were planning to have a total strength in their army, navy, and air force at the end of the first year of stage II that would be about fifty-six per cent of the approximately five million that they had in late 1944. It would be necessary, they felt, to maintain India's armed forces at about their then level of two million. Munitions required for the British Services and other forces they supplied, including the Dominions, Indian and Colonial troops, and those of the European Allies, would call for a total volume of munitions production of about sixty-two per cent of the 1944 level (after allowing for the use of stocks likely to exist at the end of the German war). The UK planned to have its own munitions production at about sixty-six per cent of the 1944 level. This would involve a fall in the labour force engaged on such production to seventy-four per cent of the 1944 level, with hours of work reverting to normal levels. In the United States, the navy was planning to sustain munitions production at its peak, and the army (including the air force) expected their munitions requirements to be about seventy-five per cent of 1944. The US expected to furnish supplies available of the types required and not limited for financial reasons. The UK was planning to increase its exports in the year 1945–46 to sixty per cent of their pre-war volume, from the thirty per cent level of 1944.

The UK authorities were asking Canada for deliveries of munitions during 1945–46 at seventy-one per cent of the 1944 level, although this would imply a large decline in actual production of many items that take some time in production. The only categories that would not be reduced but increased in some cases would be ships, both naval and cargo, and aircraft, notably the Mosquito (wood frame), Lancaster bombers, and Harvard training aircraft (for use in the UK). The UK would hope to get about the same amount of food as in the preceding year (though they would gladly take more if Canada would pay for it). They would need fewer raw materials, particularly aluminum and some other metals, though they would wish to get more lumber for temporary housing and wood pulp to ease the paper shortage.

All told, the program of their requests from Canada for the UK and other sterling area countries, together with miscellaneous services and commercial exports to the sterling area, was estimated to cost some $2.1 billion in 1945–46, in contrast to $2.5 billion in 1944–45. Nearly $1 billion represented munitions and related war services, and another $1 billion was for food, raw materials, and non-war services. Offsetting this would be what they reckoned the sterling area as a whole would receive from Canada: about $400 million for exports and miscellaneous services. They would expect, however, that the payments that they received in connection with the Canadian services overseas would fall from the 1944–45 level of $1.165 billion (which included special non-recurring items) to about $450 million (including $100 million from servicemen's pay). After taking into account certain capital payments, they expected the sterling area would have a deficit of about $1.2 billion to be financed by Mutual Aid, "more than double the deficit which falls to be covered by Mutual Aid during 1944–45." (In fact, Mutual Aid in 1944–45 amounted to $673 million for the sterling area.)

There was some discussion at this large meeting of officials of the various items in Sinclair's paper, and Keynes pressed his inquiries about why the sterling area now appeared likely to get less Mutual Aid than the $600 million they were led to expect in August. It fell my lot to have to answer many of his questions and to emphasize the difficulty of forecasting how such complicated and uncertain accounts were going to turn out after another four months. Plans were made at this meeting for the others that would follow.

The second meeting of officials took place on 30 November, attended by the British with just Clark, Fraser, and me. Here a whole series of special subjects were reviewed: bacon and beef contracts; naval vessels; costs of prisoners of war and inspection services; relative UK–Canadian costs and prices for munitions; cancellation costs (at length); the UK Cash Receipts Account (to which it appears the British had agreed without Keynes's knowledge); railway rolling stock for India; possible payments by the UK in US dollars for the US content of Mutual Aid; and how to deal with the UK transfers to Canada of Lend-Lease supplies. This varied review enabled both sides to prepare for further work on these items, as well as to select those warranting consideration by the Canadian ministers.[43]

At a small meeting with Ilsley and Howe on 29 November, we were able to make faster progress on the main items.[44] Keynes and Sinclair summarized the proposed programs for 1945–46 (noted above) and argued that Canada was not being asked to maintain a greater effort in stage II relative to stage I than the UK and US were planning to maintain, and that in Canada's case the nature of the effort was economically convenient. Clark asked Keynes whether it would be possible logistically to deploy against Japan all the equipment and supplies they were planning to produce. Keynes responded that no one but the military authorities knew how it would be possible. Furthermore, both equipment and stores could pile up and the requirements could prove to have been based on pessimistic assumptions (as, in fact, they turned out to be). Keynes went on to outline his pooling proposal, which, he thought, might meet the Canadian political problem that would be involved in a substantially increased Mutual Aid appropriation. The two ministers gave this a cool reception. Ilsley said that it might appear to be an attempt at camouflage, which would be more dangerous than facing the issue squarely. I was given an opportunity to put forward my suggestion for a single war appropriation, large enough to include Mutual Aid, from which Mutual Aid requirements could be allotted month by month. Ilsley said that this ought to be explored and should be considered along with the alternatives.

Keynes was able to express his concern about the fact that the accumulating arrears of Britain's obligations were supposed to be met by supplying equipment obtained under Lend-Lease from the US. These arrears were apt to be piled on top of the $200 million deficit in the first plan. He hoped very much that some means of dealing with these accrued liabilities could be worked out, as well as the financing of the current requirement of the UK the following year. On the vexing questions of the Lend-Lease items transferred to the Canadian forces overseas, both sides hoped that some way would be found to avoid at least a substantial part of any obligation to pay the US for them. There was a lengthy discussion on the debts incurred by Britain to the countries holding large accumulated balances in sterling. Keynes explained the special circumstances that gave rise to the large balances held by India, Egypt, and the Crown Colonies. He emphasized that Australia and New Zealand were not accumulating large claims. The big holdings would have to be blocked and released by agreement. He thought that such claims on the UK were not what Canada would wish. Howe asked Keynes whether the UK would be prepared to accept a substantial long-term, interest-free loan, say for thirty years. Keynes answered that the UK was certainly hoping that Canada would make such loans to them immediately after the war, but the question was how often. There was a limit to what the UK could undertake even of this nature.

In concluding, Keynes said that if Canada was unable to provide aid to the UK next year on the scale proposed, the British would have to review their programs and see what they could do without. All were essential, in their view, but there were varying degrees of indispensability. Ilsley recognized that London would want to know what they could expect so that they could readjust their programs if necessary. It was difficult to say when Canada's decision could be reached. Referring to the current conscription crisis, Howe said that it was unlikely that a decision could be reached in the next few weeks.

Keynes apparently was depressed after this meeting and cabled to the Treasury in London, asking whether it was worthwhile continuing when no immediate decisions could be expected. Eady phoned back after consulting others in London and said that they could stay if they wished but should not agree either to borrow or to cut back their requested program.[45]

The most important meeting with Keynes was that on 1 December 1944 with the ministers comprising the Mutual Aid Board.[46] Ilsley opened it by saying that he wished his colleagues to hear from Keynes and Sinclair a summary exposition of the British proposals relating to their requirements from Canada in 1945–46 (which they were assuming would be in stage II of the war). In addition, Ilsley said, he would like to discuss special problems pertaining to Canadian financing of the UK and the rest of the sterling area: first, the pending large order for locomotives and other rolling stock for the Indian railways; second, the allocation of responsibility for paying costs arising from the cancellation of war contracts; and third, the contracts for the purchase of bacon and beef in 1946.

Keynes gave an exposition of the British plans for the size of their armed services in stage II, their own production of munitions and war equipment in that period, what they had arranged to get during that period from the US on Lend-Lease, and finally, what they would like to get from Canada. He emphasized the high degree of war mobilization that Britain had reached by 1944 and said that they felt the imperative need for some "moderate easement" in stage II. In addition, they must begin to rebuild their export trade, which they would require to pay their international bills after the war. In order to carry out the role in stage II that had been agreed on at the meeting of Churchill and Roosevelt with the chiefs of staff at Quebec in September, Britain would need assistance on a substantial scale from both the US and Canada. The US had not limited its assistance on financial grounds, but there were physical limitations arising out of the types that they were equipped to produce. The program being requested of Canada would permit a physical reduction in Canada's war effort that was fair by comparison with that of Britain and the US, and the nature of Canada's program would be economically convenient. It would include about as much food supplies as formerly; somewhat fewer raw materials but including more lumber and pulp and less metals; and a reduction in munitions to about seventy per cent of the 1944–45 level. Keynes went on to indicate that Canada would face a financial challenge. Financing the British requirements in Canada in 1945–46 would require a much larger amount of Mutual Aid – something like double the amount in 1944–45 – because Canada would be paying Britain very much less for supplies and services for her own services overseas in 1945–46 than it was paying in 1944–45. St Laurent raised some questions about the reduced load on the UK arising from the diminished demands of the Canadian services. Keynes acknowledged this but said that this reduction in the load was spread over the US and Canada as well. At Ilsley's suggestion, Keynes went on to outline his pooling plan for munitions, as an alternative to an increased level of Mutual Aid from Canada. Under this plan, all of the munitions made in Canada would be charged to the appropriations for the Canadian services, but the UK services would be permitted to draw their requirements from this pool. He gave various arguments in favour of this plan and they were discussed briefly. Keynes also mentioned some possible ways that Canada could pay for other items that might reduce the load on Mutual Aid. For example, ships might be purchased by the Canadian navy and loaned to the UK; Canada might pay the costs of maintaining prisoners of war in Canada, which the UK had been paying heretofore; and Canada might foot the cost of inspection of munitions production, of which the UK had been paying about $30 million a year. General McNaughton supported this proposal.

Brand of the UK Treasury said that the Treasury's underlying assumption was that Canada was "a full partner" of the US and the UK in the war against Japan. St Laurent questioned whether the Canadian people were prepared to agree that Canada's interest in the Pacific was sufficient to justify that assumption. Canadians had felt that in the European war, they should and would exert themselves to the full, but they did not feel that the same was necessary in stage II. Keynes said that both the UK and the US were going to be doing less in stage II; the real question was how much less and in what proportion the relaxation would be distributed. He argued that the British people had suffered a lot more so far in the war than those in North America. The question now, he said, was whether North America would help enough to enable the British to have a fair share of the relaxation that was going to be possible in stage II.

After this discussion, Ilsley mentioned as another alternative the lumping of Mutual Aid with the general war appropriation and allotting such funds as were needed for Mutual Aid from time to time. The meeting did not try to reach a decision on this central issue.

ROLLING STOCK FOR THE INDIAN RAILWAYS

Regarding locomotives and other rolling stock being produced for the Indian railways, Keynes emphasized India's very great need because of the war; indeed, it was given the first military priority. On the other hand, the equipment on order would last well beyond the war, although the Indian railway in general was suffering great depreciation as a result of the war. The US was supplying some rolling stock on a basis under which Lend-Lease would cover the difference between the original cost and the post-war value. Keynes did not ask for this equipment as Mutual Aid but as an approved purchase out of the British cash receipts account (which would increase the need for Mutual Aid in some other form). Howe suggested that this item might be covered suitably by a loan to India, as that would be the normal peacetime practice. No decision was reached on this item, which remained unsettled until after the end of hostilities.

CANCELLATION CHARGES

Ilsley brought up the lack of clarity over financial responsibility for the costs of cancelled contracts. The relevant documents relating to Canada's taking over of the former British contracts in Canada provided that cancellation costs on such contracts would be met from the UK Cash Receipts account, if and to the extent that there were funds available in that account. Beyond this limited extent, it was not clear that there was any undertaking or agreed on understanding as to the degree to which the UK would bear such costs.

Keynes emphasized that there would be large cancellations first when the war in Europe ended and again when the war against Japan ended. He argued that there was much to be said for Canada's bearing of the cancellation costs, since Canada could take into account the economic and social arguments for continuing production versus ending it or cutting it back. The British government did this with their own contracts at home. If the UK were to be responsible for cancellation costs on the Canadian contracts, it would want to cut them just as soon as the war requirements permitted.

St Laurent quickly pointed out the other side of the issue. If Canada was to be responsible for cancellation costs, it must take more responsibility in placing contracts, especially since there would be more chance of cancellation than earlier. Keynes agreed in principle but said that the cancellations normally resulted from decisions of the combined chiefs of staff "to whose decisions we are all subject." Howe intervened to argue that the responsibility that Canada would be assuming under this arrangement would include any decision to taper off production when that appeared likely to be sufficient. Sir Robert Sinclair suggested that this responsibility would have to be exercised by Canada in consultation with UK authorities. Ilsley thought Canadian responsibility for cancellation costs, together with Keynes's suggested pooling plan, would take the brake off requisitions by the UK in Canada. The Canadian government already was taking on a heavy responsibility in accepting requests and making commitments under the circumstances and was finding it exceedingly difficult to determine which requests were truly essential. General McNaughton took up this point. The difficulty arose, he said, from Canada's lack of information on strategic and operational requirements. If the Canadian government was to accept responsibility for putting supplies into production, or deciding whether or not production should be stopped or tapered off, it would need more information on strategic necessity and military requirements. Sinclair felt that this view was reasonable. The Canadian government should be given any information that it required to make a proper decision; also, General McNaughton and his officers should be able to obtain all the information they needed to know in order to ascertain the operational justification of UK requests. Keynes agreed.

While no decision was taken on this important point, the Canadians did not seem to be objecting to the views put forward by the British representatives. The matter came up again later as the German war ended, of course, and finally with the end of hostilities against Japan. In fact, it did not give rise to serious problems.

The relatively specialized and minor issue of bacon and beef contracts was discussed briefly and quickly settled. To get adequate production of meat for export to Britain, producers must be given adequate assurance at least a year ahead of the beginning of the year of delivery; contracts, therefore, must extend over two years. This conflicted, however, with the year-by-year financing arrangements now being made, and the UK Treasury had held up approval for orders for deliveries in 1946. Since both sides were satisfied that very high priority would be given to these meat exports, and some sort of financing arrangement for 1946 would be made, it was agreed that an arrangement could be made to place the necessary contracts in terms of prices and quantities, with the financial arrangements to be made at the time. Ilsley said that he would have to secure cabinet approval for such a special arrangement.

Clark and various financial and air force officers were present at a meeting held with Keynes on Saturday, 2 December, primarily to discuss the Air Training Plan obligations of the UK; the meeting was largely for exchanging information.[47] The main cause of the large deficit that was accruing in the 1942–45 plan was the fact that the cost of the aircraft, fuel, and other items to be provided by the UK "in kind" (largely under Lend-Lease) had been overestimated when the plan was agreed on in June 1942, while Britain had committed itself to meet a specified amount of the forecast total cost of the plan. Some detailed problems involved in winding up the plan in March 1945 were discussed. On the main issue, it was fairly well decided that the UK should not try to pay off its obligations under the Air Training Plans during the 1944–45 fiscal year because the payments required that year were already too heavy. Once again, the problem came up of how to determine the Lend-Lease components of what the RCAF and the Canadian army overseas were receiving. At that time, the amount was unknown and Canada's financial obligation to the US for it was by no means clear. Clark was anxious to get the matter settled during the war, but Keynes argued for keeping it open pending further investigation.

FURTHER CONSIDERATION OF PLANS FOR STAGE II AND THE PROBLEMS OF STAGE III

This was the last of this important series of meetings but by no means the end of the mutual search for means of dealing with the problems. As both sides had expected, the Canadian government took no early decision on either the form or the scale of the financing to be provided in 1945–46. A new and important element was entering into the consideration of the issues by senior officials and ministers. Meanwhile, several of us in the department continued to collect and analyse the facts and forecasts of the highly complex balance of payments between Canada and the sterling area as a whole, including the accumulation of unsettled war claims in both directions between the Canadian and British governments.

It was one of my tasks in mid-December to collect and summarize the various facts, issues, and arguments pro and con, which I did in a long memorandum entitled "Mutual Aid and Related Problems with the United Kingdom: Alternative Courses of Action."[48] There is no need here to recapitulate the facts and arguments. I came out in favour of providing what the British were requesting, but as Mutual Aid financing by periodic allotments from a general war appropriation. In doing so, however, I made the point quite explicitly that the British deliberately took on a bigger role in the Pacific in stage II than was necessary without consulting Canada, and did so knowing that a large part would be at our expense.

As early as 1 December 1944, work was being done in the Bank of Canada and the department on the financing of Britain during the immediate post-war years, its relations to British commercial policy, and also to the financing and trade arrangements with Britain during stage II of the war. On 1 December, Towers sent Clark a long memorandum that he had written a week before. In it he emphasized the economic importance to Canada of restoring and expanding our pre-war export trade with the UK during the immediate post-war period. For this it was vital that the UK should not discriminate in its import trade and in favour of the sterling area against Canada, as they had been doing during the war. For the UK to afford a non-discriminatory trade with Canada, it would need substantial assistance in the form of a very long-term loan at a low interest rate, with arrangements for deferring repayment in years when the UK balance of payment fell short of a defined test. To get this loan, the UK would be asked to avoid applying greater restrictions against imports from Canada, whether by currency or trade measures, than they were applying against imports from the sterling area. They would be asked to inform other members of the sterling area that they could buy Canadian dollars with sterling that they acquired from post-war current account surpluses with the UK or one another in order to make current account payments to Canada. These two conditions would permit us to develop our export trade with the sterling area as a whole on a non-discriminatory basis, though it would not involve requirements in regard to capital movements or the use of sterling balances held at the end of the war.

Clark studied these proposals carefully during December and organized a small meeting to discuss the subject in his office on New Year's Day with Towers, Rasminsky, Robertson, Donald Gordon, Mackintosh, and Hector McKinnon. By 12 January, Towers had revised his memorandum for wider consideration, calling it now "A Proposal for Averting a Breakdown in International Trade Relationships."[49] It contained further description of dangers that would be caused if UK policy became restrictive; he concluded by saying that "the upshot of all this is that the upper hand in British public life is being gained by those elements which are opposed to whole-hearted British participation in a co-operative effort to develop a large volume of world trade on a multilateral basis after the war." He contrasted this with the Article VII provisions of the UK–US Lend-Lease agreement, as well as what was in Canada's Mutual Aid Agreement with the UK. He sensed a danger of economic warfare between United Nations powers following the defeat of the Axis Powers. He then reiterated the importance to Canada of export trade with the UK and proposed target levels at which we should aim. He proposed, as a way to make this possible, a long-term loan of $1.2 billion, repayable at $60 million a year beginning ten years after the end of hostilities and carrying two per cent interest. In any year when payment of what was due would reduce UK reserves of gold and convertible currencies below a stipulated figure, payment would be deferred until the reserves rose enough that the payment would not have that effect. He argued that these favourable repayment terms were essential to meet the facts of the case. He envisioned other smaller but sizable credits to be granted to other Allied countries such as were being discussed already by the Department of Finance with Allied countries under the Export Credit Insurance Act, Part II.

The trade stipulations that Towers proposed for the loan to the UK were that the UK would not apply, or encourage other countries in the sterling area to apply, greater restrictions on imports from Canada than they would put on similar imports from the sterling area. Towers urged that whatever the US might be willing or planning to do, Canada should make constructive proposals to the UK along these lines. Only in this way, he said, "can we smoke out their true position and know where we stand as soon as possible."

Ilsley and Clark immediately arranged to bring these proposals and related issues before the principal ministers involved. They met in Ilsley's office in the early evening of 18 January. Howe, St Laurent, MacKinnon (Trade and Commerce), and McNaughton were there, in addition to Ilsley, along with Clark, Towers, Mackintosh (then Howe's man at "Reconstruction"), Robertson, Oliver Master, J.E. Coyne (then back at the Bank after his spell in the air force), and me.[50]

Clark opened the meeting by speaking of the immediate issue of the War Expenditure Appropriation for the next year, including Mutual Aid. He favoured including Mutual Aid, and Reconstruction as well, in the main war appropriation. This would enable the government to ask for a smaller total amount than if they were separated, which was a benefit given the uncertainty about when the war would end in Europe and when it would end against Japan. This question would be considered separately, Clark said; no decisions on it needed to be taken at that meeting. There was, however, an important aspect of Mutual Aid and other programs for the next year that should be brought now to the attention of the ministers most concerned, he said. This was the prospect for Canadian trade in the years immediately following the end of hostilities and the implications of this trade to financial relations between Canada and the United Kingdom. The developing prospects regarding the war against Japan justified urgent Canadian action to improve matters. Moreover, he could not properly recommend to ministers a substantial measure of Mutual Aid without drawing these potential trade problems to their attention. He suggested that Towers weigh in on the matter. Towers did so at considerable length, leading up to his proposal for a large long-term loan on favourable terms.

Howe recalled that Keynes had said that Britain did not want to borrow. Clark reminded him that Keynes had said that about stage II of the war. Towers brought up that he had asked Keynes unofficially what he thought the UK reaction would be to a proposal such as his. Keynes had said that he thought they would turn it down because Canada and the US would ask the UK, as a quid pro quo, not to discriminate in imports against them.

Towers went on at length about the problem of non-discrimination against imports from North America, especially by other members of the sterling area such as India, which had a huge accumulation of sterling. He had wondered, given that the United Kingdom was faced with these huge sterling debts, whether the US could be persuaded to accept responsibility for some of these debts arising out of the war, perhaps twenty-five per cent of them. This likely would be possible only if some political concessions were thrown in as well, such as a settlement with India on its political status. The value to the US of substantially improving the economic and political outlook after the war would far outweigh the amount of money involved. Towers then reverted to the Canadian situation. What was needed, he said, were export targets and their financing "if we are to have a sporting change of maintaining full employment."

Towers ended his exposition by saying that he had wondered whether he was being too pessimistic. He remembered, however, that he had felt the same about his dark views on the economic outlook in 1928 and 1930, and later about his similar views on European international affairs in the 1930s. In fact, over the past two decades, no pessimistic appreciation of the situation in advance had been within miles of being too pessimistic. Had we in fact realized how bad the outlook was, action might have been taken to avoid at least some of the series of economic and political disasters that had been suffered. He thought, therefore, that we should be thoroughly realistic in analysing the present outlook.

Towers was at his best in this kind of analysis and advocacy and he clearly impressed the ministers. Ilsley, McNaughton, and particularly St Laurent asked a number of questions, and Clark and Robertson made some observations.

Ilsley brought the discussion back to the immediate issue of Mutual Aid for 1945–46, and St Laurent observed that the situation now involved a fundamental change in attitude, away from strategic need and toward the other issues raised by post-war considerations. Mackintosh said that both the financing of the war and the helping of the transition to peacetime trade would be important objectives. Robertson thought there were other influences in the UK that would not want to discriminate against Canada and the US, and that any split with the US would be most repugnant to Churchill.

Ilsley asked whether any conditions should be attached to our Mutual Aid that year relating to trade policy. This was discussed at length, but several expressed the view that this wartime aid should not be subject to specific post-war policies. It would be important, however, to express the government's serious concerns about the outlook for trade policies in conveying to the British the decision about Mutual Aid. Several suggested that it would be desirable to discuss these matters informally with senior US officials, though one could not expect any commitments from the US on the matter. It was left that Clark, Towers, and Mackintosh (with Robertson) should set about drafting a message to the UK for consideration by ministers.

The meeting concluded with a brief discussion of the budget outlook for the next fiscal year, which was, of course, very uncertain, but

Ilsley and Howe thought the public were not going to be critical about the level of expenditures until the war was over.

When Robertson had finished drafting the messages to the UK, he took the subject up fully with the prime minister, showing him the proposed telegrams on 13 February. King later wrote in his diary that the telegrams set out the position clearly and he went over them carefully.[51] The next day, King took them to the Cabinet War Committee, introducing the subject as serious and urgent. There was increasing evidence of a tendency in Britain to meet their grave financial problems by fostering the development of trade within the sterling area and restricting purchases from outside that area. Such developments were a serious economic and political danger to Canada. The growth of rival sterling and dollar areas would cause serious restrictions in foreign trade and might well bring about a severe depression in Canada after the war. Such developments would affect Canada's position in the Commonwealth and on relations between UK and US officials of the several departments chiefly concerned, who had given a lot of thought to the problem and proposed a course of action outlined in the three telegrams to the British government. These King asked Robertson to read in full to the committee, after which Ilsley (who had brought Clark and me to the meeting) spoke briefly to say that if the war against Japan continued through the next fiscal year, the Mutual Aid required would be about $1.3 billion, of which $1.15 billion to $1.200 billion would be for the UK and other sterling area countries.

Considerable discussion (not recorded) followed these opening statements. The committee then approved the messages for dispatch, subject to a few minor drafting charges arising from the discussion, and also subject to the concurrence of St Laurent, who had not been present but was very interested in the subject.[52] A day or two later, St. Laurent met with the prime minister and gave his approval to sending the message, commenting that he thought it important that the US take a similar position.[53]

The decision about Mutual Aid for 1945–46 and the government's views about British trade policy were sent together in telegram no. 45 to the UK government on 23 February. A second telegram sent that day (no. 46) dealt with the immediate post-war trade and financial policies, including the suggestion of a large, long-term loan on favourable terms from Canada to Britain. A third wire (no. 47) was from the prime minister to the British prime minister emphasizing the importance that he attributed to the views on trade policy set forth in the other two.[54]

The telegram on Mutual Aid said that the government was prepared to recommend to Parliament the continuation for the time being of

Mutual Aid on the scale that had been requested. Pending a parliamentary appropriation for this purpose, which might be delayed by an election, the government would continue to place contracts and make other commitments in order to maintain the flow of essential supplies during the early part of the next fiscal year, in the expectation that Parliament would approve the policy that it had been decided to recommend. The message then went on to emphasize that Canadians had expected that Mutual Aid, together with similar arrangements extended by the US, UK, and others, would make it possible to transfer war supplies in such manner as not to "burden post-war commerce or lead to the imposition of trade restrictions or otherwise prejudice a just and enduring peace," using the words of the Mutual Aid agreement between the UK and Canada. It then expressed concern over "the implications of the policy being followed by the sterling area in discriminating against the purchase of Canadian products and in favour of purchases within the sterling area." Such a policy could be understood early in the war when the UK was so very short of dollars. While Lend-Lease and Mutual Aid had been developed, scarcities of shipping and supplies had been dominant. As these limitations receded after hostilities ended in Europe, the policy of restricting purchases more severely from Canada than from the sterling area would be certain to result in the diversion of trade from Canada to sterling area countries. If continued, this policy undoubtedly would set the pattern for the commercial policy of the post-war world. The message emphasized how badly these results would be viewed in Canada. Also problematic was the fact that such diversion would be building up vested interest in other countries. The message noted that it seemed reasonable to suppose that the UK would not want to build up more sterling debt than it already had by importing supplies that it felt were not essential enough to get from Canada. It did not appear necessary, therefore, for the UK to discriminate. After further argument, the message said that the government "urges the U.K. government to follow a general policy during the period Mutual Aid is in effect of non-discrimination as between imports from Canada and from the sterling area." It went on to request that the same policy be followed in other parts of the sterling area. It was a strong demand, even though it was not made an explicit condition of continuing Mutual Aid on the scale requested.

The message on post-war policy attempted to show an understanding of the British difficulties but urged that constructive, positive measures should be taken to meet them rather than a narrow, restrictive commercial policy. It was recognized that Britain would need large imports immediately after the war and would not have sufficient export earnings to pay for them. Credit would be required, therefore, and it was in this context that the Canadian government would be prepared to discuss ways of financing Canada's prospective surplus of exports to the UK and the rest of the sterling area, in such a manner as to encourage the largest possible flow of trade in both directions, without discrimination. Then the offer of a large-scale, long-term loan on favourable terms was made.

The reaction from London came in stages. The Canadian high commissioner wired immediately that these proposals had created an excellent impression at the official level and were warmly welcomed, being regarded as realistic, constructive, imaginative, and generous. The prime minister replied to King a few days later, expressing his gratitude for the financial proposals and the generous and friendly spirit that had inspired them. He took advantage of the opportunity to say, with no qualification, "what a comfort it is to have your decision to see us through on Stage II." Clark underlined and queried the last six words of this sweeping interpretation on his copy and wrote "What cheek" at the top.[55]

The official government replies came weeks later, on 21 March. The first concerned the immediate financing of the British requirements in Canada during 1945–46. It warmly welcomed the general assurance that Canada had given but went on to ask several questions. One of them, which must have been from Keynes, asked whether we were going to adopt his idea of pooling munitions (which we were not, as was made clear about two weeks later in Parliament). The government assumed on the strength of our telegram that the UK supply departments could proceed with the placing of orders in Canada in accordance with the program discussed in late November, and "consequential changes" would be introduced only after prior consideration.[56] (I was trying this time to get our ministers to ask the British to review their programs in light of the war situation and thought we should use this message as an opening. I continued this effort, and Howe took it up with Sir Robert Sinclair in a conversation on 3 April.)

We were most anxious to see their reaction on trade policy, of course, and it came in a telegram dated 21 March. Their reply was carefully written; it was friendly and welcoming but non-committal. They emphasized that the issues we had raised had to be viewed in light of their future relations with the United States, and here they could not expect any easy solution but could only feel their way gradually. They were pressing forward with the reconsideration of their economic controls as rapidly as the state of the war permitted, toward the long-term objective of freeing trade from the restrictions such controls involve. They said that it had been their "common aim" during the Mutual Aid period to regulate the demands made on Canada so as to achieve the maximum economy in the use of the Canadian dollars that thus were made available to them. They looked forward to co-operating with Canada in establishing conditions that would permit the removal of the wartime controls. There was no mention of the discrimination in favour of the sterling area, which had been the central point of our concern. However, they would welcome early discussion of co-operation in making the controls tolerable and free from permanently harmful effects. More specifically, they invited a group of the Canadian officials chiefly concerned with these matters to visit London for an informal exchange of views not only on the immediate problems but also on "possible ways of removing by administrative action particular difficulties which may arise."[57]

DISCUSSIONS IN CAMBRIDGE AND LONDON

After some delays, the visit was organized to take place late in May. Clark had said that he would be unable to go because of other business. In fact, he collapsed a few days after VE day (8 May) and was away from work until the end of the year. Mackintosh took his place on the visit, and Hector McKinnon went as our trade expert. But the dominant Canadian figure was Towers, whose incisive mind, fluent but precise speech, and dedication to the constructive solution of the British economic problem made him a fitting match for Keynes. The main discussions and their setting in Cambridge have been elegantly described in a fascinating essay by Douglas Lepan, who was representing the Canadian high commissioner.[58]

Nearly the whole of the discussions concerned the British post-war economic situation and their policy alternatives as presented by Keynes and supplemented by the knights and officers of the Treasury and the Bank of England. In these discussions, Sir Richard Hopkins, who had just retired as permanent secretary, was the senior; Sir Wilfrid Eady, the second secretary (in charge of external finance), was the most active; and Cobbold, executive director, spoke for the bank. This was the first, informal, and very highly secret presentation of what the British were planning to put before the Americans as soon as the war was over.

The substance of this discussion belongs in chapter 10 along with our Canadian discussions and agreement on the major post-war loan to Britain. Here we should take note only that the Canadian request for dropping discrimination against Canadian exports to the sterling area during the remaining war period while Britain's Canadian requirements were being financed by Mutual Aid was discussed and settled on 28 May in Keynes's room in the Treasury.[59] The formula proposed and accepted, after considerable discussion, was that when the goods were essential and when Canada had been a traditional supplier, there should be no discrimination as long as Mutual Aid continued. This was embodied in a letter from Keynes to Mackintosh, after approval by the chancellor of the exchequer.

Mackintosh took up these trade proposals with Ilsley in June, when it was clear that Clark would not be able to return to work for some weeks or even months. On 22 June, Mackintosh wrote to Munro at the UK High Commission stating that he had informed Ilsley of the proposed trade arrangements and that Ilsley had taken them up with his colleagues. The minister had told Mackintosh that he could inform Munro that the UK proposals were satisfactory. He had added two points. First, he assumed that since Newfoundland was in the Canadian dollar area, their exports would be covered in the arrangement. Second, the Canadian government might wish to raise at some future time the question of exports to Eire, should that become significant. The minister also wished to say that he and his colleagues appreciated very much the genuine effort that the UK had made to meet the Canadian position on this matter of trade discrimination. At the end of July, Munro furnished Mackintosh with copies of the detailed telegrams from London to the sterling area dominions and colonies asking them to follow this agreed on policy.

Thus it was that the trade discrimination problem that Canada had emphasized in continuing Mutual Aid for stage II was settled. The plan was modest in scope, because of its relation to the larger question of UK treatment of its imports from the US. Furthermore, and as things turned out, it was of short duration; fortunately for all concerned, including the Japanese, stage II of the war was far shorter than had been expected. The details of its end at midnight on 1 September, just before the signing of the formal surrender, have been described in chapter 7 along with the termination arrangements negotiated with Keynes on 5 September.

Our arrangement for financing Britain during stage II and the whole of the fiscal year 1945–46 worked out smoothly and harmoniously, despite the rather sour discussions of early December 1944 and Keynes's reiterated efforts to push us into pooling. The interim war appropriation of $2 billion sufficed for the five months from 1 April until early September, with only about $87 million of it unallotted. It was necessary for this period to allot $654 million for Mutual Aid at about an annual rate consistent with our forecasts for the year.[60]

Had the war against Japan lasted a few months longer, we would have had to allot substantially more to Mutual Aid from the war and demobilization appropriations and to have included it in Ilsley's forecasts of "additional amounts required up to March 31/46" in his tabulation of 28 September.[61] Had this happened, this aid probably would have been necessary for British army, navy, and air forces in Southeast Asia fighting to regain former colonial areas (including Singapore) from the Japanese army. This could have caused serious dissension in cabinet and perhaps expectation of trouble in the House of Commons as well. It might even have gone far enough to worsen Anglo-Canadian relations seriously, even though Canadian troops were not fighting in this area, as King had insisted they should not. Consequently, we must recognize that our success in financing Britain that year was partly due to luck.

CHAPTER NINE

Working up to Bretton Woods

Before the war, during the dark days of the Great Depression (1929–39), the international monetary system collapsed. In 1931, the British were forced off the gold standard and had to let the pound sterling depreciate in the foreign exchange markets. Many other currencies that were normally based on sterling followed it down or depreciated even more. While some Western European countries remained on gold for a few more years, they were forced later into devaluation. Others, most notably Germany, adopted extensive and rigorous exchange controls and used them to enforce bilateral clearing agreements in which the weaker countries were exploited. The United States, though holding most of the world's gold reserves, was plagued by waves of bank failures from 1930 to April 1931. As a consequence, the US voluntarily went off the gold standard and outlawed the gold clause in existing contracts.

After an almost comic gradual reduction of the gold value of the dollar during 1933, it was formally devalued in early 1934, down close to the extent of devaluation that the British pound had reached on the market.[1] While some relative stability was arranged between the US dollar, the pound sterling, and the French franc in 1936, other currencies either floated uneasily in the market or were subjected to severe controls over capital transactions and in many cases over trade and other current account transactions as well. Deliberate depreciation of currencies was frequently used to deal with domestic depression or gain a competitive advantage in trade. The international monetary system was broken and – perhaps more troubling still – no one had developed any promising ideas for widespread reform.[2]

This changed during the war as Allied governments worked on a plan to restructure the international monetary system. Canada's Department of Finance played an active role in this consequential reform. The small band of overworked mandarins at the department understood that Canada had an important national interest in setting up a well-organized multilateral currency arrangement. For many years before the war, Canadians had relied on converting its *current account surplus of receipts in overseas currencies into* US *dollars that could be used in meeting its chronic current account deficits in the United States. This system, however, had been undermined by the currencies devaluations of the Depression. As a trading nation, Canada would benefit from a stable international monetary order. This is what officials at Finance worked to achieve.*

This chapter recounts their efforts and sets the stage for the establishment of the International Monetary Fund and the United Nations Relief and Rehabilitation Administration. (These two institutions are discussed in greater detail in chapter 10.)

In 1941 and 1942, experts in positions of authority or influence in both Great Britain and the United States (and by good fortune in Canada, too) came to the fore on the issue of monetary reform.[3] As early as the beginning of 1942, in London, John Maynard Keynes, adviser to the Treasury, and in Washington, Harry Dexter White, assistant to the secretary of the Treasury, both had drafts of plans for a post-war international monetary system. These plans were the proposals of the experts themselves; they had no government approval, although both the British cabinet and the US secretary of the Treasury were aware of the nature of what was going on. In the latter half of 1942, the experts were beginning to exchange their drafts cautiously and informally. In Canada, Clifford Clark, the deputy minister of finance, received a copy of a draft of Keynes's plan in early September 1942 from Sir Frederick Phillips, the senior British Treasury representative in Washington.[4]

Keynes's plan, "An International Clearing Union," was to establish an international institution with its own international money, which he called "bancor," together with a code of conduct relating to foreign exchange rates and exchange restrictions. It would be based on the English banking principle under which customers of a bank may begin with a line of credit rather than having to make a deposit first. Initially, its members would consist of Great Britain, other members of the Commonwealth, and the United States, plus such others of the United Nations as wished to join.

In Keynes's scheme, each country joining the union would have its "quota" of bancor, proportional to its international trade. Bancor would be defined in terms of gold and would be accepted by member countries as the equivalent of gold in exchange for their own currencies. Member countries could acquire bancor by borrowing it from the union, up to the amount of their quota; they could acquire it as well in exchange transactions with other members who used it to settle their international accounts by transferring bancor on the books of the union. In this way, credit balances could be created and increased.

Bancor could be bought from the union by payment of gold, but the union would be under no obligation to pay gold in exchange for bancor. Limits were set in the draft agreement on the rate at which member countries could use up their borrowing quotas; these limits could be exceeded only with the approval of a governing board. That board could specify conditions that had to be met if the member country was to borrow more than the defined proportion of its quota, or to leave its debit balance at excessive levels more than a certain length of time. These conditions might relate to the exchange rate for the member's currency, or to restrictions on outward capital movements, or to repayment of part of its debit balance out of its gold reserves if it had them. If the member's debit balance continued to exceed three-quarters of its quota on average for more than a year, or was otherwise considered excessive by the governing board, that board could request it to "take measures" (which might include enacting domestic policies) to improve its balance of payments position.[5] If the member failed to reduce its excessive debit balance, it might be declared "in default" and no longer be entitled to draw on its bancor account without special permission from the governing board.

On joining the union, each member must reach agreement with the board on the par value of its currency in terms of bancor, which the member country must observe in gold or foreign exchange transactions. With certain limited exceptions, changes in par values could be made only with the approval of the board. No limits were to be set on credit balances of bancor, but a member with a credit balance exceeding one-half of its quota would be under an obligation to discuss with the governing board possible measures "to restore its equilibrium." (It was expected at that time that the United States would be the only major creditor, and its willingness to accept and hold balances of bancor would be all-important for the success of the plan.)

Keynes suggested, as a possible addition to his plan, using the union as an international bank for financing relief organizations such as the United Nations Relief and Rehabilitation Administration, which was then under consideration, or for financing commodity price stabilization programs.

LONDON CONFERENCE, OCTOBER 1942

In the Department of Finance, Clark and Mackintosh were very interested in this Clearing Union proposal. So, of course, were the Bank of Canada's Towers and Rasminsky, with their long experience in international monetary matters. Consequently, when the British authorities invited the Canadian Department of External Affairs to send several officials to a Commonwealth meeting in London in October for informal discussions of this plan, as well as some other post-war economic questions, Mackintosh, Rasminsky, and Hume Wrong of External Affairs attended and took an active part.[6]

No one at the conference attacked the principle of the Clearing Union proposal, and there seemed to be a general agreement that the idea was sound. The Canadians, primarily Rasminsky and Mackintosh, made a number of substantial points, which may be summarized as follows:

(a) They felt that it was unwise to use the Clearing Union either for financing relief operations or for financing buffer stocks used in commodity price stabilization schemes. Relief was charity, and the Clearing Union was intended to be used only for financing debits that with confidence could be expected to be repaid. Commodity stabilization schemes were going to be difficult enough to control, and if they were financed by the union, that would reduce the pressures to keep them responsible.

(b) The Canadians believed that the system proposed probably would be workable only if member countries normally needing to have debit balances in bancor had effective systems of exchange controls to restrict or stop outward capital movements. The draft plan provided that the union could require a member wishing to draw more than half its quota to impose controls on such capital movements, but Rasminsky felt that they would have to be more general. While Keynes agreed with this view, he believed that the Americans would not support a plan requiring such controls as a general rule. The paper as revised continued to recommend that the method and degree of exchange control should be left to the decision of each member state. This general policy was sustained through subsequent negotiations and appeared in Article VI of the Articles of Agreement approved at Bretton Woods.

(c) The Canadians also urged that the right to depreciate its exchange rate by five per cent, without the agreement of the governing board, of a member whose debit balance had exceeded one-quarter of its quota for at least a year, should be limited to one occasion only. A continuing right to devalue repeatedly could lead to an undesirable instability of rates. This change was made in the revised plan.

(d) The Canadians also argued that the governing board should have the right to be informed of the gold and foreign exchange position, both short-term assets and liabilities, of member states in addition to their bancor position. This would be essential if the board was to be aware of the true measure of the member's short-term position. This point was accepted and included in the revised draft, although apparently there had been earlier opposition in London to revealing to others the details of the assets and liabilities of countries within the sterling area.

(e) The Canadian delegates also argued that the provision in the draft plan imposing a charge of one or two per cent per annum on credit balances of bancor in excess of one-quarter or one-half of a member's quota would be an irritant to the United States, difficult to explain to Congress, without being substantial enough to influence a creditor member's policies. They proposed that it be removed and if the revenue were needed by the union, it be obtained by a small transfer charge on bancor. This view was not supported by other delegations, although the draft itself said: "These charges are not essential to the scheme." The revised text, dated 9 November, retained those charges on credit balances, and they were included in subsequent versions of the Clearing Union plan but not in the "Joint Statement by Experts" agreed on with the us Treasury in April 1944.

There was a good deal of discussion on the position of creditor members of the union and the means by which they could be persuaded or induced to accept large balances in bancor. This had been made serious by indications from American officials that the United States, if it came into the scheme, would have to set a limit on its holdings of bancor probably of the order of $4 billion or $5 billion. Almost all of those attending the conference were highly critical of persistent creditors in the scheme; the Canadians were the only ones showing some understanding of the American position. The attitude of the British led Rasminsky, in reporting to Towers, to say that one of his main impressions of the conference was "the extent to which the United Kingdom Treasury has acquired a debtor psychology."[7] The result of this prevailing psychology at the London meeting was to add a new section, Section III, to the revised draft, entitled "What Liabilities Ought the Plan to Place on Creditor Countries?" This section argued that these countries could and should use their own economic policies to keep the amount of their credit balances low. It was not very persuasive.

The British Treasury planned to send the revised version of the paper to us officials in Washington. The Canadian delegates in London suggested privately to Sir Frederick Phillips, who had been chairman, that Canadian experts, especially Clark and Towers, might do some useful work in bringing about a meeting of minds between the British and Americans. This conference in London was the last Commonwealth conference the Canadian experts attended that was devoted primarily to Keynes's proposals until Mackintosh discussed them in London on 23 June 1943.

THE WHITE PLAN: FIRST VERSION

On 24 December 1942, Clark received from Harry White his "Preliminary Draft of a Proposal for a United and Associated Nations' Stabilization Fund."[8] This very elaborate proposal led to the formulation and publication of a Canadian plan as a means to get some compromise between the American and British plans.

The White Plan, as first proposed (it was modified frequently during 1943 to take into account comments and suggestions), had the same basic objectives as Keynes's Clearing Union proposal. It did, however, differ in many important respects. Countries joining this fund had to make their basic contributions to it at the time of joining or soon thereafter; these would be paid partly in gold and partly in their own currencies. The fraction to be paid in gold depended upon the gold reserves of the joining member. (This was to be a bone of contention because no such gold contribution was required for the Clearing Union.) Each member would have a quota determining the size of its contribution, and its obligations would be limited to that, again in contrast to the Clearing Union proposal. The size of its quota would depend not only on its trade, as in Keynes's plan, but also on its gold and foreign exchange reserves and its national income. The total of all quotas would amount, as was suggested, to "at least 5 billion dollars." These various provisions were expected to make it much more acceptable to the US Congress than the virtually unlimited liability to accept bancor under the Clearing Union proposal. On the whole, however, the Stabilization Fund proposed by White would be a very much smaller source of credit to deficit countries than Keynes's Clearing Union.

White's original Stabilization Fund would have important powers. It would determine all exchange rates between member currencies and a member could only propose changes in its rate to correct a "basic disequilibrium." Such changes would require approval by the executive committee of the board of directors by a four-fifths majority of the votes; the number of votes were weighted, depending mainly on the size of the member's quota, which would give the US much the largest voting power (but not to exceed twenty-five per cent); in effect, the US would have a veto on all changes in exchange rates. The same sort of veto would apply to many other decisions of the fund.

Deficit countries would have the right to buy foreign currencies from the fund that they required, up to specified limits, to meet a balance of payments deficit on current account, but not to finance the export of capital. Indeed, a country drawing on the fund's resources under certain conditions might be required to impose exchange restrictions on the export of capital. If the deficit country wished to buy foreign exchange for its currency from the fund beyond specified limits (e.g., 150 per cent of its quota), it could be required to adopt and carry out economic policy measures to correct the disequilibrium in its balance of payments. This (and the corresponding provisions in Keynes's plan) was the beginning of the fund's power of "conditionality" in providing credit, which was to provoke considerable debate in subsequent redrafting of the proposals and was later to be developed to a high art in the operations of the International Monetary Fund and be a source of international and domestic controversy.

White's plan was much more explicit than Keynes's about the problem relating to countries with large creditor positions in their balance of international payments on current account, which would cause the fund to use up its holdings of that currency. The plan called on the fund to make a report to the creditor country, warning it that its currency was getting scarce and suggesting means of alleviating the shortage by balance of payments measures. The fund, meanwhile, would use some of its gold to buy more of the scarce currency – or borrow it. If the scarcity persisted, the fund would declare that currency as officially "scarce" and would ration its limited supply among those requiring it. Such action, of course, might require countries to discriminate in their use of that currency. There was no requirement that the scarce currency be revalued to a higher par value, and countries requiring it could not pay more for it in the market than the authorized rate.

The monetary unit of the fund was named the "unitas," equivalent to $10 US of the then current gold content. This was, however, purely a unit of account for the fund, used for keeping its books and not intended to circulate even between central banks. The plan contained policy obligations that member countries would be bound to observe: they must maintain their exchange rates; they must not enter into new bilateral clearing arrangements; they must co-operate with the other member countries who were seeking to control international capital movements; they must furnish the fund with such information as it required for its decisions and operations and take into account the views of the fund on monetary or other economic policies likely to lead to serious disequilibrium in its own or other countries' balances of international payments. Countries already having controls and restrictions on international payments for other than capital transactions, including discriminatory restrictions, were allowed to retain them for a transitional period but were required to end them when circumstances permitted.

It is not feasible to go into the White Plan's many pages of detail. On the whole, it provided for a small, very powerful international organization effectively controlled by the US. It was a very important proposal to those of us in Ottawa concerned with international finance; we felt that it was much more likely than Keynes's Clearing Union to become the initial form of the post-war system. The problem was how to appraise it and to influence White and others in Washington to make it more effective and more acceptable to the British and the Europeans.

WORK IN OTTAWA IN EARLY 1943

In the Department of Finance, Clark designated Mackintosh as his chief assistant on these monetary plans at a time when we were all very busy on other matters (e.g., on Mutual Aid legislation and operations). I was to assist Mackintosh. We had help from Wynne Plumptre, our man in Washington, who proposed in January that we prepare a Canadian plan as an illustration of our views.[9]

The most important work was done by Rasminsky, at the Foreign Exchange Control Board, in consultation with Towers. Rasminsky did most of the drafting and did it very well. His experience during the 1930s with the Economic and Financial Section of the staff of the League of Nations had qualified him both in understanding international monetary processes and problems and in writing clearly about them. His wartime work in senior positions in the Foreign Exchange Control gave him a detailed knowledge of foreign exchange markets and the problems involved in controlling them. His abilities in this field were recognized quickly and were respected by both the British and American experts.

In January and February of 1943, those of us in Ottawa designated to work on these currency plans studied them in detail, along with some papers we received from British officials about the White Plan, including, in particular, a detailed comparison of the Keynes and White plans as they stood at that time. This comparison included many critical comments on aspects of the White Plan, although in the end the paper concluded that many of the faults could be corrected.[10] This accorded with our own views in Ottawa. By mid-March, Rasminsky had prepared his considered views on the two plans and sent us several papers on them, including, in particular, a list of questions that we should raise with the Americans about their plan when we had an opportunity to do so.[11] These were discussed on 27 March at a meeting of Rasminsky, Mackintosh, and five other officials.[12] It was agreed that we should seek a discussion with the American experts, during which we should ask questions and discuss the answers.

An opportunity to do this soon occurred. Clark was in Washington on 6 April seeing White on other business, and White asked him if the Canadians were ready for discussions on the Stabilization Fund. Two days later, Ilsley sent a letter to the US secretary of the Treasury saying that he was ready to send officials to Washington the following week. He suggested a possible three-cornered meeting with British officials in Ottawa, but the US Treasury preferred a bilateral discussion. As a result, Mackintosh, Rasminsky, Plumptre, and John Deutsch had six meetings with Harry White and other American officials.[13] The question-and-answer tactic proved successful; amicable discussions took place on many points of substance arising out of the American responses to the Canadian questions, and these ranged over most of the important parts of the White Plan, beginning with its total size (which the Canadians thought was much too small), then touching on: the way in which the fund might use the gold received in contributions; the excessive role proposed for the fund in fixing exchange rates; the way in which the fund and its members would operate in exchange transactions; the obligations of the fund in regard to a currency that becomes "scarce"; and whether the US could justify the need to have the power to veto so many types of decisions of the fund. On many matters, White expressed his appreciation of the Canadian comments and suggestions, which clearly seemed intended to make his fund more workable. At the end of the last meeting, he said that he would like to get together again with the Canadians after discussions with others.

In April, the Americans published the latest version of White's preliminary draft, and the British government, more reluctantly, published the latest version of Keynes's Clearing Union proposals. This permitted public study and comparison of the two plans. One such study was published by the *Economist* newspaper of London on 1 May 1943.[14] This early publication permitted some parliamentary and congressional scrutiny and discussion of the proposals before governments were committed to them, as well as some expert comments by academics and bankers. It also, however, probably made it more difficult for both the US and the UK to compromise their versions in reaching an agreed on plan, which of course was vitally necessary. In any case, this publication encouraged us in Ottawa to proceed with the formulation of an unofficial draft Canadian plan as a contribution to the process of international negotiation of a final agreement.

Rasminsky had made progress already on such a draft before the long meetings with the Americans in April. He expedited this work after these discussions. By 20 May, he had a draft ready for discussion, which he distributed with a letter of that date, and which was discussed at the Bank of Canada on the night of 25 May. The paper was in two parts. The first was "General Observations of Canadian Experts on Plans for Post-War Monetary Organization," containing general observations on the need for a post-war organization and comments on the British and American proposals. The second was a "Summary of Proposals of Canadian Experts," giving the main lines of the draft Canadian proposals and comparing them with the US and UK plans. After the discussion at this meeting, and with others in Ottawa, Rasminsky revised his draft and the final revision was dated 9 June.[15] Mackintosh, meanwhile, had sought the approval of the minister of finance to produce and circulate to experts of other countries a paper of this kind. Ilsley took Mackintosh's memorandum (dated 2 June) to the Cabinet War Committee meeting that day and secured its approval of the action proposed.[16] On 3 June, he instructed Plumptre in Washington to tell White that we would be ready for the discussions on 15 June and to intimate to him that our suggestions would take the form of an integrated plan.[17]

THE CANADIAN PLAN

The "Tentative Draft Proposals of Canadian Experts," as the prime minister thought the plan should be called, cover ten pages of fine print, which it is impractical to summarize here. In his memorandum to Ilsley of 2 June, Mackintosh describes it tersely as follows:

The main features of the Canadian plan would be
(a) the adoption of the American form, i.e. a Fund;
(b) the enlargement of the Fund by larger contributions and by agreed lines of credit to the Fund;
(c) the elimination of the United States veto through providing in less objectionable ways for safeguarding the interests of the United States and other creditors;
(d) modification of the rigidity of the United States plan without accepting the complete flexibility of the United Kingdom plan;
(e) various detailed amendments designed to make the plan completely multilateral and to make the operative sections workable.

What Mackintosh did not say, though it was true, was that the wording of these proposals, Rasminsky's wording, was clear, precise, and persuasive. White's proposals were not. The paper presenting the

Canadian plan included five pages of "General Observations of Canadian Experts on Plans for Post-War Monetary Organization." These observations emphasized the need for an international monetary organization that could grant short-term credits as part of a post-war system that would include other financing for relief and rehabilitation and for long-term foreign investment. The post-war reforms would have to include, as well, improvements in commercial policy and more stable primary product prices. While many economic problems would have to be solved, it was convenient to begin with the monetary arrangements. It would be better to create an international monetary organization that could provide short-term credits to countries needing them to meet temporary balance of payments deficits than to rely on bilateral credits. Canada expected to have a current account surplus in its international payments after the war and regarded an international plan such as that proposed as a good means of providing its trade customers with temporary credit to meet their needs. Creditor countries would not be giving their money away by pooling it in the manner proposed; it would be a business investment, not an act of generosity. Moreover, the fund created should be big enough to meet the need. There would be less real risk to the interest of the creditor countries in establishing a fund whose resources were unnecessarily large than there would be in establishing one whose resources were too small. If the proposed organization functioned well, it would have at its disposal more information about the international financial situation and the causes of disequilibrium than had ever existed before. It would be in a position to offer informed and disinterested advice to its members. Any member who felt its national interests were being jeopardized by the actions of the organization would be free to withdraw from it on short notice and settle its outstanding accounts.

This paper by the Canadian experts was circulated very quickly to the experts in other countries who were working on these monetary plans. It was published on 12 July, when the minister of finance tabled it in the House of Commons and made a statement about it and about the international discussion of experts that had led up to it and the most recent June discussion in which it had been used.[18]

Rasminsky had sent a draft of it to Keynes as soon as that was authorized, early in June. Keynes and other British Treasury officials regretted and criticized the action of Canadian officials in producing and circulating a paper of this kind at that time, even though they agreed with many of the observations in it and much of what was proposed.[19] They seemed to feel that Canada should take a Commonwealth view and accept the leadership of the United Kingdom. Canadian officials did not share this opinion and felt that it would be useful to put forward their views when those differed from what the UK was saying. They felt, in particular, that the lack of any limit on the liability of creditor countries to provide financing (except the sum total of the quotas of all the debtor countries) made the Clearing Union proposal a non-starter in the United States.

MULTILATERAL WASHINGTON DISCUSSIONS

The Canadian paper was first used at a large meeting of experts from the United States, the United Kingdom, Canada, and fourteen other countries (including those from governments in exile), which took place in Washington on 15–17 June 1943. White of the US Treasury was the convenor and chairman. He had received copies of the draft proposals of the Canadian experts and included them on the agenda, along with a revised draft of his paper on the Stabilization Fund. A detailed agenda in terms of the subject matter of various important sections and subsections of his revised paper was used to guide the discussion. Detailed minutes were made of these discussions.[20] Efforts were not made to reach decisions or a consensus on the various points discussed, and there were many criticisms of the Stabilization Fund plan.

This was an intellectual and diplomatic operation rather than in any sense a negotiation and was well conducted for its purposes. Canada sent a high-level expert group: Towers, Clark, Rasminsky, Deutsch, and Plumptre. Attending for the UK were its senior Treasury representatives residing then in Washington: Sir Frederick Phillips (who died a few weeks later), Professor D.H. Robertson, and Professor Robbins. The US group included White and Bernstein from the Treasury, Goldenweiser and Gardner from the Federal Reserve Board staff, and Professors Viner and Hansen from outside.

It is not possible or necessary to summarize the discussion here. The Canadians acquitted themselves well and made frequent references to their draft proposals. They were supported on numerous points by UK experts. The British experts frequently referred to the merits of their Clearing Union proposal, apparently to keep it in the running despite US opposition to it. White said at the end that the discussion had clarified the various proposals and problems and narrowed the area of disagreement. Within a week of the conclusion of this large and non-committal meeting, White began the serious negotiation with the British by telling Phillips what the US considered essential conditions for a "synthesis." This would lead to a US–UK negotiation (noted below).[21]

White and his group revised their Stabilization Fund proposals after the June discussions and dated their revision the 10 July version. They sent copies of it to us in Ottawa and to others who had attended their meeting. That was a very busy summer in Ottawa on domestic issues (and Mutual Aid to allies), so Clark did not get around to writing a letter to White on the latest version until 29 July.[22] In this letter, he commented on several important details, including the gold portion of the required contributions to the fund, the right of a member to change its initial exchange rate within limits, the adjustment of voting rights to reflect the net use the member of the fund had made of the member's currency during a year, and a reduction in the majority of votes needed to approve a change in an exchange rate. White replied in some detail to Clark on 1 September but said that they were not planning to make further changes in their draft at that time.[23] In fact, it was only two weeks later that the minister of finance received a very friendly letter from the secretary of the US Treasury thanking him for Canada's help and enclosing a printed revised draft.[24] This clearly was the draft that they intended to use in beginning their main negotiations with the British.

NEGOTIATIONS BETWEEN THE US AND UK, 1943

The major negotiations between the Americans and the British began on 14 September and continued until 9 October. Theirs were the only two governments whose support for a post-war monetary plan was essential. In these negotiations, the Americans clearly had advantages over the British because the latter were financially much weaker in 1943 than the Americans were. Those who knew the British financial situation (as some of us did in Ottawa) realized that the British were going to be very dependent on American help when the war and Lend-Lease ended. The British had some advantage in Keynes's outstanding ability to negotiate. He had arrived in Washington in time to begin in mid-September. He was pleased with the progress that they had made by mid-October, as he reported officially to the UK War Cabinet in a memorandum dated 13 October; attached to that memo was the agreed on draft statement of principles to be used later in preparing articles of agreement to be put before an international conference.[25] There were other related documents as well. The "Draft Principle" was not a final agreed on draft. It included several important parts on which there was both an American and a British version. The choice between these versions, or changes in them, was going to require political approval in London by ministers.

Much progress was made by the UK and US Treasuries in reaching agreement on unsettled points by correspondence and diplomatic discussion during the period between mid-October and late December.

The British government decided in late December, therefore, to invite the governments of the Dominions and India to send qualified delegates to a Commonwealth conference to consider these monetary proposals and some other post-war economic matters. To enable these delegates and other officials in their governments to prepare for the conference, the British high commissioners delivered to the appropriate officers copies of Keynes's report of 13 October noted above and its attached papers. On 3 January 1944, the secretary of state for dominion affairs sent four lengthy telegrams to each of the Dominions summarizing the progress made up to that time in reaching agreement with the US Treasury on a draft joint statement of principles for the establishment and operation of an International Monetary Fund.[26] Rasminsky went to work on these reports very soon after their receipt in Ottawa and sent to Finance and External Affairs his analysis and summary of them and a third paper suggesting the position that Canada should take on these detailed proposals.[27] These were discussed among those of us working on the subject in Finance, External Affairs, and the Bank of Canada before the delegation left for the conference in February.

DISSENSION IN THE BRITISH GOVERNMENT

Having received reports on the monetary negotiations in Washington and afterward, the British War Cabinet asked Richard Law, minister of state for the foreign office, who had been in Washington with Lord Keynes and his delegation, to prepare a report for the War Cabinet on the issues arising from those negotiations that ministers should consider and decide on. This would have to be done in time to be reflected in the discussions with Commonwealth representatives at the conference to be held in late February and also to be prepared for discussions in the British parliament after the publication of the Joint Statement by Experts.[28]

The Treasury was expected to draft much of the report that Law would submit, and it was in preparing this report that serious differences of opinion became evident within the Treasury and between the Treasury and the Bank of England. Most of the Treasury officials supported the results of the negotiations that Keynes's delegation had carried on with White and the US Treasury Department, which were embodied in the "Draft Joint Statement by Experts on the Establishment of an International Monetary Fund." Now that the hour of decision had arrived, however, the officials of the Bank of England came out clearly in opposition to the central features of the plan, though their objections were clothed politely as "technical issues." Within the

Treasury, the opposition was led by Sir Wilfrid Eady, joint second secretary, the senior officer primarily responsible for international finance, but who only recently had been transferred to the Treasury. He was supported by other senior Treasury officials but not by a majority. These officials felt strongly enough on the issue, however, that with the approval of the chancellor of the exchequer (the minister in charge of the Treasury), their minority view was included in the report submitted by Law to cabinet, as well as the view and argument written by Lord Keynes as leader of the delegation to Washington.[29]

When the War Cabinet met after receiving Law's report and a dissenting memorandum from Lord Beaverbrook (then Lord Privy Seal in the cabinet and champion of Empire trade), it decided to set up a committee on external economic policy, including the chancellor, Beaverbrook, and four others. This committee held six meetings, which Keynes described in a letter as "a complete bedlam." It reported on 18 February, with Lord Beaverbrook again dissenting. He recommended that discussions should proceed (with the Commonwealth and with the Americans) on the basis that Britain eventually would see its way clear to enter into the proposed post-war arrangements provided that there were special arrangements for a transition period after the war and that Britain received assurances as to financial assistance from the US before committing herself to the monetary fund. The War Cabinet approved this report of its committee on 24 February.[30]

The opposition to the International Monetary Fund proposals by the Bank of England and the minority of Treasury officials was based on a variety of details, ranging from annoyance over having an international body selling and buying sterling to serious concern over what sort of management the Americans would appoint for the fund. The more fundamental objection, shared by them and Beaverbrook and a few other ministers, was that the monetary fund agreement would prevent Britain from maintaining indefinitely after the war a currency and trading bloc based on the use of sterling and the retention of Empire trade preferences and other trade discriminations, with only a minimum use of US dollars and financial assistance from the United States.

In preparation for the final cabinet discussion, Keynes gave to the chancellor of the exchequer a relatively brief memorandum constituting a devastating attack on this sterling area bloc proposal of the Bank of England. He made the case that without substantial financial help from the United States, the people of Britain would have to endure "extreme austerity in domestic consumption in the early post-war period, probably involving a level of consumption below what it is now, and the very opposite of our expansive domestic policy, coupled with a high (though not perhaps a comparable) standard of discipline in the rest of the sterling area." He went on to say: "We shall end the War owing to all our friends and close associates far more money than we can pay. We are in no position, therefore, to set up as international bankers, undertaking large and not closely defined liabilities, unless we can secure a general settlement on the basis of temporary American assistance followed by an international scheme ... The Bank [of England] is not facing any of the realities."[31]

THE COMMONWEALTH DISCUSSION IN FEBRUARY 1944

The meeting in London, which began on 23 February and ended in mid-March, was intended to inform the representatives of the dominions and India of recent developments in regard to the International Monetary Fund proposal and provide those representatives an opportunity to ask questions and make comments on the proposal. In addition, it involved discussions about the talks that had taken place between the UK and the US on post-war commercial policies, and there was a brief session about the American proposals for an International Bank for Reconstruction and Development. The Canadian delegation was headed by Mackintosh and included H.B. McKinnon for trade and tariff subjects and Deutsch from External Affairs.[32]

Discussions on the monetary fund proposal were extensive. They began with a detailed statement by Keynes. He reviewed the main features of the White Plan and of his Clearing Union plan, and of the lengthy negotiations that had taken place in Washington in September and October, and later, through diplomatic channels, between the UK Treasury delegation headed by him and the American delegation headed by Harry White. There was considerable discussion of these matters with the representatives of the other Dominions and India. The Canadians were already well informed on these negotiations and appear to have said relatively little, being prepared to accept the agreement that had been reached by mid-February with the Americans on a proposed joint statement that had been distributed to the delegates (and to the governments they represented). Keynes reported after the conference was over that the Dominions had caused no trouble. They had asked for some drafting changes, and several wanted larger quotas.[33] They preferred the form of the US proposal that included an international monetary unit of account to be termed unitas, but the UK felt it necessary to accept the alternative version "without any new-fangled monetary unit," because the Americans said that this would greatly ease the gaining of congressional approval.

The major problem for Canada in accepting this final Anglo-American proposal was carefully considered in Ottawa at the time, and was the subject of a telegram to Mackintosh in London from Robertson on 2 March.[34] This problem was the final section in the proposed joint statements that dealt with "Transitional Arrangements." It provided that the agreement by a member country to make its currency convertible into other currencies in the market, and the agreement not to impose restrictions on international current account payments or engage in any discriminatory currency arrangements, would not become operative until that country was satisfied as to the arrangements at its disposal to facilitate the settlement of imbalances of international payments during the early post-war transition period by means which would not unduly encumber its facilities with the fund. Thus these transitional provisions would permit a member country (notably the UK) to retain, and adapt to changing circumstances, exchange regulations that had been in operation during the war. The fund could make representations at any time that conditions were favourable for the withdrawal of some or all of such restrictions. The United Kingdom had made clear to the Americans and the Canadians that it would need to make use of these transitional powers. This was of great concern to Canada because it meant that for some years the British would be able to continue the wartime discrimination in trade and other current account transactions in favour of the sterling area and against Canada. Thus these transitional arrangements would defer for an unspecified period much of the benefit Canada could expect from the establishment of the International Monetary Fund. (In fact, the trade discrimination lasted until February 1961.)[35]

The authorities in Ottawa concerned with these matters, the Bank of Canada and the departments of Finance and External Affairs, recognized, however, that with a fund as small as that proposed and one that could not then be increased greatly, the British really had no option; they needed to retain these powers to control their balance of payments on current account, if necessary by discrimination. There was no use in a Canadian attempt to block those transitional provisions if the Americans were prepared to accept them. Robertson's telegram to Mackintosh told him that this risk in the transitional arrangements had to be accepted and that he need not seek to have them changed. It suggested that they might ask the British how they intended to operate under this transitional clause, and whether they had considered the effects that their actions might have on the US Congress.

JOINT STATEMENT BY EXPERTS

The result of the long negotiations between the Americans and the British was the "Joint Statement by Experts on the Establishment of an

International Monetary Fund." Apparently, the US Treasury Department and the UK Treasury had agreed secretly that neither would agree to a change in these principles without the consent of the other.[36] The Canadian prime minister tabled a text of this joint statement in the Canadian Parliament on 2 April, the same day that it was published in Washington and London.[37] He made a short statement to the House of Commons referring to the earlier published plans, including the Canadian one. He said that he was glad to announce that as a result of discussions among experts of the United Nations, there was a consensus of opinion among those participating on the need for an International Monetary Fund and a statement had been drawn up of the principles that should govern its constitution and operation. He made it clear that the government was not committed to the substance of the principles. The secretary of the US Treasury published the statement with a brief explanatory introduction. The UK government published it the same day with a lengthy introductory note by "U.K. experts" (undoubtedly Keynes) that compared the joint principles with the earlier published UK plan for an International Clearing Union, explaining and justifying the differences. It was argued that "it has proved easier to obtain agreement on the mechanism of the proposed fund which has the appearance of being closer to what is already familiar. It was therefore no longer necessary to introduce a new international unit." This concession to the Americans on unitas was given at this eleventh hour and only to get agreement in time to hold the Bretton Woods Conference in July, when the Allied armies were fighting on the Western Front.[38]

A few weeks after the publication of the joint statement, the US State Department issued invitations to the governments and governments-in-exile of the United Nations to meet at a major international conference in Bretton Woods, New Hampshire, beginning on 1 July 1944, to consider proposals for establishing an International Monetary Fund and an International Bank for Reconstruction and Development.[39] The US Treasury invited experts from a select group of countries (including the UK and Canada and others who had participated in earlier discussions) to meet in Atlantic City, New Jersey, on 19 June as a drafting group to prepare for the Conference. The British and European delegations were unable to get there until 24 June because of military restrictions on shipping arising out of the D-Day landings in Normandy in early June. The result was a rather messy series of meetings reviewing the agenda for the conference and exploring potential disagreements. White, in charge of the US delegation, had several conversations with Keynes and was concerned to find that the British had some specific proposals that the US could not accept, about which he warned Secretary Henry Morgenthau, Jr.[40] The most troublesome of these was the result of the last-minute request by the chancellor of the exchequer to Keynes to change the agreed on wording of the proposed paragraphs relating to changes in par values of currencies in such a manner as to recognize the sovereign right of a member country to change the par value of its currency. (This had become an issue in London.) The draft that the British brought with them was unacceptable to the American officials, and Rasminsky agreed with the American view on this point at a meeting of Commonwealth experts on 25 June.[41] It was decided then and there, however, that it would be desirable to withdraw the troublesome sentence promptly and replace it with something less provocative. Settlement of this troublesome point was achieved during the conference itself. It is clear that Rasminsky played an important part in the behind the scenes process.[42]

THE BRETTON WOODS CONFERENCE

It is not feasible or necessary here to give an account of the Bretton Woods Conference of 1–22 July 1944. It was a huge international gathering, in the midst of war, at which two very detailed agreements were successfully worked out: one on the monetary fund and another on the International Bank. It took hundreds of people working under extreme pressure long into the night to accomplish it, operating without votes but by consensus. There is a detailed summary account of the conference, insofar as it involved the IMF, in the official history of the IMF,[43] and another more detailed formal account of the proceedings and documents published by the US State Department.[44]

Canada contributed very effectively to the conference with a very small team, essentially Rasminsky, Mackintosh, Deutsch, and Plumptre. The minister of finance and his deputy and the governor of the Bank of Canada put in a token appearance on the opening day, 1 July. They went over the main issues with those who were going to participate and designated Mackintosh to act as head of the delegation.[45] Then, after a brief meeting with British Treasury officials on quite unrelated current bilateral problems, they hurried back to Ottawa. During the conference, Clark received a few phone calls from Mackintosh or Rasminsky to report on special points that had come up and seek his views on the line to be taken. On these occasions, Clark usually consulted the Bank of Canada, Robertson at External Affairs, and me before replying. Ilsley, our minister, was too busy on parliamentary work to put his mind to these technical post-war matters.[46]

There is no doubt that Rasminsky was the star of the Canadian delegation; indeed, he was one of the outstanding members of the whole conference. He was made the reporting delegate of Commission I, summarizing the detailed substance of the main discussions on the IMF. He also was appointed the chairman of the drafting committee, which dealt, among other matters, with the decisions of the Special Committee on Unsettled Problems. These two committees had to meet late into the nights, when the sessions of the main commission were finished, in order to produce precise solutions for the controversial sections.[47]

The Articles of Agreement of the International Monetary Fund (and those of the International Bank for Reconstruction and Development – see below) were approved *ad referendum* by consensus at the end of the conference on 22 July. They were to enter into effect when formally approved by governments of the participating nations having quotas equal to sixty-five per cent of the total quotas set out in schedule A of the articles.

In Canada, as in most member countries, the Articles of Agreement required legislation by Parliament. This was provided in the Bretton Woods Agreement Act, passed in December 1945. The United Kingdom also passed the necessary legislation in that month, having deliberately waited until after the agreement for large post-war loans from the United States to the British government had been signed. (See chapter 11.) By the end of that December, enough formal approvals of the articles had been recorded to bring them into effect. Most of the year 1946 was taken up with organization and preparation, so it was only in March 1947 that the IMF began to operate. It is now well known that Towers was the American government's first choice to be managing director of the fund, but he was unwilling to accept the post, partly because he did not like the top-heavy executive board organization and partly because he did not find White, who was to be the powerful American executive director, congenial.[48] Rasminsky became the first Canadian executive director, on a part-time basis with a full-time alternate. He remained in this post for many years, with a succession of alternates, and played a leading role in making the fund effective.

THE WORLD BANK

In contrast to their many activities in developing the proposals for the International Monetary Fund, Canadian officials did not take a leading role in working out the plan to establish the International Bank for Reconstruction and Development. Canada traditionally had been a borrower not a lender in the international capital markets. Apart from Towers, hardly any officials in Ottawa had any experience in foreign investment. Moreover, the Americans and the British worked out their ideas on the bank over a relatively short period between November 1943 and June 1944 while we few in Finance were very busy on other urgent matters. Little attention had been paid before that time to the possible post-war need for joint international action to finance the development of underdeveloped countries, most of which were still colonies or protectorates. We did not give the bank proposal a high priority.

The first thing we saw suggesting an international bank was a premature proposal hastily made public by the US Treasury on 8 October 1943 after a newspaper report on the subject had appeared, based on an earlier and obsolete memorandum. Copies of this were sent to us from our embassy in Washington with a dispatch describing the circumstances.[49] We read this hasty effort but did not take it seriously, as we expected they would revise it. We did not have long to wait.

THE US PROPOSAL

On 24 November, Morgenthau, the secretary of the US Treasury, published and distributed to finance ministers of the United Nations a paper entitled "Preliminary Draft Outline of a Proposal for a Bank for Reconstruction and Development of the United and Associated Nations."[50] This included a long foreword by Morgenthau himself on the background and purpose of the proposal, which reads in retrospect as though it was introducing the Marshall Plan of 1947. The draft proposal bad been prepared by the technical staff of the Treasury and other departments, headed up by Harry White. White intended that this international bank would be the companion institution to the International Stabilization Fund, the monetary plan that the Treasury Department originally proposed in 1942 and was, in late 1943, negotiating in detail with Keynes and UK Treasury officers. This November proposal on the bank was the only one published by the US Treasury before the Bretton Woods Conference in July 1944. Although its clumsy drafting and confusing details were severely criticized by Keynes and others, the substance of the proposals constituted a progressive and, indeed, generous measure on the part of the American administration. The main form and functions of the institution proposed in November eventually were incorporated in the bank's final Articles of Agreement with some changes of emphasis and much clarification. The bank proposal appears to have been prepared by the Treasury with more input from the State Department and other institutions than was the case with the fund proposal.[51] It was discussed in the early months of 1944 on a number of occasions with representatives of Latin American governments.[52]

Morgenthau said in the foreword that "the primary aim of such an agency should be to encourage private capital to go abroad for productive investment by sharing the risks of private investors and by participating with private investors in large ventures." Later in the foreword, he said: "One great contribution the United Nations can make to sustained peace and world wide prosperity is to make certain that adequate capital is available on reasonable terms for productive use in capital-poor countries." The formal statement of purpose of the bank incorporated and extended these views of the secretary of the Treasury. The Treasury proposed, however, that the resources and facilities of the bank should be used only to benefit its member countries, and that only countries that joined the monetary fund could be members of the bank.

The proposed capital of the bank, amounting to about $10 billion, would be subscribed by its member countries, with the proportions to be settled by a formula to be agreed on. It was expected that the US share would be about one-third of the total. Only a part of the subscribed capital would be paid up; the remainder, a substantial part, would be held as a surety fund to meet obligations of the bank either under its own borrowings in the capital market or under guarantees. The initial payments to be made on shares would be twenty per cent of the amount subscribed, payable in part in gold, the fraction depending on the gold and exchange reserves of the member. The remainder would be paid in the "local currency" of the member, to be loaned only with the approval of the member. Member countries whose gold reserves increased in future years would be expected to repurchase with gold a small fraction of their local currency subscriptions. There were a variety of detailed provisions in the plan relating to how and under what conditions the local currencies held by the bank could be used in making loans. All currencies were formally equal under the terms of the proposal, but many, of course, were much weaker than others, and at the beginning almost all currencies other than the US dollar were not convertible into others in the market. Insofar as the bank could issue its own securities to borrow convertible currencies in the capital market, these local currency difficulties could be avoided. Insofar as the bank was able to operate by guaranteeing securities issues in markets whose currency was convertible, the "local currency" difficulty could be avoided further. These problems relating to currencies and their use, without mentioning the US dollar, gave rise to misunderstanding of the bank proposal, especially by the British and later by Canadian and other Commonwealth officials.

The lending powers of the bank, under the American proposal, required that all loans it made had to be guaranteed by the government of the country in which the project or program being financed by the loan was located. The loan also had to be approved by a "competent" international committee that investigated the project or program being financed and found it would serve, directly or indirectly, to increase the productivity of the borrowing country and that the prospects were favourable for the repayment of the loan. A loan could be made or guaranteed by the bank only if the borrower otherwise could not secure the capital under conditions that in the opinion of the bank were reasonable. The local currency needs within the borrowing country normally would have to be financed largely from domestic sources; the bank would furnish the foreign exchange required. Borrowers would have to agree to pay interest on the loans, and repay the principal, either in a currency acceptable to the bank or in gold. When repayment was made in currency, the amount repaid must be equivalent at the time of repayment to the original gold value of the loan, plus interest.

Authority for the operation and management of the bank would be vested, under the proposal, in a board of directors that would include a director from each member country. Decisions of the board would be taken by a system of weighted votes, with the number of each member's votes being based mainly on the amount of capital stock it subscribed. This comprehensive board would appoint a small executive committee, whose members (or alternates) would have to be continuously available at the head office of the bank and who would receive "appropriate remuneration" from the bank. This executive committee would take decisions by weighted voting, if there was not a consensus. The board would delegate to the executive committee the power to make loans or guarantee loans. The board also would appoint a president of the bank, who would be given charge of its operating staff and who would be an ex officio member of both the board and the executive committee. This proposed organization was broadly similar to that proposed for the International Monetary Fund. In their final forms, the two organizations were almost parallel, although in fact the executive board of the fund was relatively much more powerful and in the bank the president and the senior staff were more powerful. In each case, weighted voting became more and more important as the number of member countries increased as a result of decolonization first in Asia and later in Africa.

Such were the main features of the US Treasury Department proposal received by the Department of Finance in Ottawa in late November 1943.[53] We had some discussion of it among ourselves but not much. Unfortunately, the department's file on the subject cannot be found, but our few important activities and ideas relating to the bank proposal can be traced through the main file of the Department of External Affairs and the Rasminsky papers in the archives of the Bank of Canada.[54] These sources show that we had no discussion with US Treasury officials on this subject until the Bretton Woods Conference in July 1944, at which Mackintosh served actively as a member of Commission II, which dealt with the bank proposal.

COMMONWEALTH MEETING MARCH 1944

The important discussion of the bank proposal from the Canadian viewpoint was the one that took place in London on 14 March 1944 during the Commonwealth conferences on post-war economic questions.[55] Keynes had prepared a lengthy paper on the subject, which was distributed to the delegations a week before the discussion.[56]

The first half of Keynes's paper, paragraphs 1 to 16, was highly critical – indeed, was derisory – of the American draft proposal. It charged that the plan made no distinction between creditor countries that could afford to lend and debtor countries that could not. The reason for the omission, Keynes stated, was essentially political since the United States itself was the country most able to finance long-term loans, but its Treasury Department did not wish to be suggesting that the US should be chiefly responsible for financing the bank that it was proposing. Keynes stated that to escape this obvious difficulty, there were many peculiar provisions in the draft, "obscure and devious devices," that needed revision to bring it back to common sense.

Keynes went on at length to illustrate these "devices" and how they worked. Most of his illustrations referred to the use of "local currencies" received in the subscriptions and the limitations on their use. The main means by which the local currency problem could be avoided, Keynes said, was by the bank's guaranteeing of loans to be issued through the normal investment channels in the capital market in a country whose currency was needed by the borrower. If the bank later needed to make good its guarantee, it would use the currency that country had subscribed. Keynes did not seem to have noticed the other, less elaborate way of the bank's avoiding of the local currency problem: by borrowing itself in the capital market of a member country whose currency was fully convertible into other currencies that it would be free to lend as required. This was clearly authorized in paragraph 15 of Part II of the US proposal, which Keynes must have chosen to ignore. It was not highlighted in the subsidiary clauses of the US paper, which is understandable because it would probably only be feasible on a substantial scale in the US capital market.

Keynes pointed out other implications of the bank's attempt to use its supply of local currencies received in capital subscriptions. Some of these amounted in effect to making "tied loans," usable only in one or a few member countries. He was much opposed to such loans being made by an international body, as he emphasized in describing his paper to the conference.[57] In retrospect, it seems that Keynes was unfairly critical of the American plan, and in such strong terms that he probably condemned it in the minds of some members of the Commonwealth delegations, perhaps including Mackintosh.

In the latter part of his paper – paragraphs 17 to 21 – Keynes was much more appreciative of the US proposals and constructive in his suggestions. He felt strongly that loans from creditor countries (those with a surplus in their international balance of payments on current account) to debtor countries needing them in the early post-war years were essential to avoid widespread economic chaos and human suffering. It was also essential, however, that the loans made should be such as would achieve "the purpose desired," by which he meant this broad purpose, not just the financing of a project. To achieve this broad purpose, two conditions must be satisfied: first, that the proceeds of the loan must be "free exchange" that the borrower may expend in any market, and second, that no member country should be obligated to subscribe directly or indirectly to such loans unless its own monetary authority approved. If such approval was given, the loan could be made by the government of the country or by the lenders in the capital market of that country.

Given these conditions regarding free exchange, what should be the role of the international institution? Keynes thought its first function should be to make an expert appraisal of projects for international loans, the priority that ought to be accorded them, the reliability and technical competence of those who would handle the projects, and the prospects that the borrower would be able to repay the loan. The second function of the international institution, he wrote, should be to guarantee the repayment of approved loans and to have an internationally subscribed fund adequate to make good on such guarantees. These broad principles were what Keynes and the UK Treasury proposed to submit to the US Treasury Department.

Mackintosh spoke as the Canadian delegate in the discussion of the International Bank proposal at the Commonwealth Conference.[58] He said that the American proposal of November was not clear as to the role of the organization and the part that it would play in rehabilitation. According to the minutes of the meeting, he said that he agreed entirely with Keynes's criticisms. The context, however, does not make clear whether he meant Keynes's biting criticisms in his paper (described above) or the much milder and more constructive things

Keynes had said that morning in opening the discussion.[59] It was probably the latter. Mackintosh thought that the guarantee feature was perhaps the most promising. He stated that the Canadian financial authorities did not expect Canada to be a large foreign investor after the war, but that it might have some available current account balance for that purpose. The Canadian authorities would welcome a sound international institution. He then went on to ask some questions about the prospects of private financing after the war.

Delegates from Australia, New Zealand, South Africa, and India all spoke. The Australian delegate said that he found the US proposal unsatisfactory and would like to see a clearer picture of the functions of any such bank. He was dubious about the value of a guarantee given by a bank such as the one proposed. Keynes responded to this, arguing that a guarantee by a bank of the size and nature proposed would be quite reliable unless the bank guaranteed too much, beyond the value of the capital pledged by members whose credit was gilt-edged.

The Indian delegate thought it certain that his government would agree with Keynes's general approach. He raised a number of detailed points that Keynes thought inexpedient to discuss at that stage. Sir Wilfrid Eady of the UK Treasury thought that it should be made clear to the Americans that the UK authorities were not prepared to take part in a conference on the American proposal as the basis of discussion. He went on to speak in some detail on the various types of post-war projects that might need financing in the reconstruction period. He thought that large projects such as transport and electrification might require outside capital, which the bank could usefully supply. He gave a number of other more specific points that he thought should be taken home to the Americans.

After some discussion of specific points, which included Mackintosh, it was agreed that the kind of approach that Keynes and Eady had put before the meeting should be sent to the Americans as the views of the UK, but it could be said that they had been discussed with "experts" from the dominions. Eady said that they would proceed on that basis, if their ministers agreed, but they did not intend to publish any UK document on this subject, nor would they enter into any conference on the details of the American proposals.[60]

THE "BOAT DRAFT" AND THE COMPOSITE PROPOSAL

In April, the British sent some "suggestions" to the US Treasury Department about its bank proposal, to which the Americans replied.[61] This may have cleared the air somewhat, but it failed to get either side to change its position before June. Meanwhile, also in April, White invited Clark in Ottawa to arrange for Canadian officials to meet US officials in Washington to discuss the proposal. Recalling the severe criticism of the US paper at the Commonwealth meeting, Clark asked that any such meeting be deferred until mid-May. This suited White, but the meeting was overtaken by events and never took place.

The American uncertainty about the ability to get any agreement on the bank proposal was reflected in the terms of the formal letter from the secretary of state of the United States to forty-four governments inviting them to a conference at Bretton Woods. It described the conference as being "for the purpose of formulating definite proposals for an International Monetary Fund, and possibly a Bank for Reconstruction and Development."[62] Other evidence indicates that US officials were doubtful about the wisdom of including the bank on the conference agenda right up to the time of the meetings in Atlantic City in late June.[63]

Lord Keynes resumed work on the bank proposals early in June. He may have been worried by the possibility that the Americans now would drop a proposal that was potentially of substantial importance. On 9 June, he sent a message to the chancellor of the exchequer that began with a strong paragraph in favour of proceeding with work on a compromise proposal on the bank. He wrote: "The importance, not only from the point of view of the European countries, but also from our own point of view, of a Reconstruction Bank in the position of being able to make or guarantee loans, being organized at as early a date as possible, scarcely needs stressing. Failing this there will be the strongest pressure on us to make advances far beyond what we can reasonably afford."[64]

Keynes then went on to outline a compromise proposal for the bank, conceding much to the American Treasury in form but changing in substance what was needed to meet British requirements.[65] This paper emphasized the relatively small role of the loans to be made from the currency subscribed to the bank (over which the member country would retain control) and the larger role to be played by loans made with a guarantee from the bank (for which a fee of about one per cent per annum would be charged) and especially the loans made in "free exchange" borrowed by the bank itself in capital markets of creditor countries able to export capital.

The chancellor approved the delegation (to be led by Keynes) proceeding on these lines. The British delegation went by boat, the *Queen Mary*, to New York, en route first to the agenda meeting in Atlantic City and then on to Bretton Woods for the 1 July opening of the conference. On the boat, the members of the delegation, after discussion among themselves and then with members of the seven other delegations on the boat, reworked the American proposals for the bank into a form that embodied the principles that Keynes had put up to the chancellor.[66] This "Boat Draft" was a major improvement in both clarity and precision, with a few changes of substance. It was put before White and other members of the American delegation at a meeting on 24 June. Professor Robbins, a member of the British group, describes this meeting in his journal as follows: "This went very well indeed. Keynes was in his most lucid and persuasive mood; and the effect was irresistible."[67] From then on, members of the American and British delegations co-operated in producing a composite proposal, which was put before the conference on 6 July as document number 169, marked "not to be attributed to any particular delegation." It had, however, marginal notes indicating the origin of various articles and paragraphs in the earlier American and British drafts or as "new" or derived from the latest conference draft of the International Monetary Fund articles.[68] This draft was put before Commission II of the conference, of which Keynes was chairman and Mackintosh was the member representing Canada. It was of great interest to many of the delegations – probably of more interest than the IMF articles. The Europeans, including the Russians, and the Chinese saw it as a major source of funds for reconstruction, while the Latin Americans and other less-developed countries wanted it for development. The articles were neutral on this issue.

One final word about the bank should be added. Despite the emphasis laid by Keynes and the British Treasury on the important role of guarantees in the prospective operations of the bank, and the acceptance of this by the Americans and others, including Canada, the bank never did use guarantees in practice to any important extent. After the initial management appointed in 1946 was replaced in 1947 by officers familiar with the American bond market, their first concern was to test the market for bonds issued by the bank itself. This proved to be very good, and the bonds soon were given a very high rating. Serious study was then given by the management to the relative advantage of having the bank borrow directly or give its guarantee to securities issued by those seeking its assistance. The main points at issue were the practices and preferences of the US capital market, in which nearly all its issues would have to be placed during the 1940s and 1950s. The decision was taken to finance the bank, and its loans to its members, by the issue of its own bonds, both long-term and medium-term, and also, as time went on, by short-term securities in which central banks invested.[69]

During its first ten years of operations, the bank made some use of guarantees in arranging for the participation of commercial banks and other institutional investors in financing parts of loans made mainly from the bank's own funds. It discontinued this practice in 1956 when the reputation of the bank's lending was well established and private participation in loans continued on a substantial scale without guarantees.[70]

CHAPTER TEN

International Institutions

The Department of Finance played a subtle yet active role in the creation of the international monetary system that emerged after World War II. Not uncharacteristically, the Canadian contribution lay in finding the middle ground between the American and British positions. In discussions on international monetary reform, which began in earnest in 1943, Canadians exhibited an independence of mind and action. They were not willing to be bullied or coerced. Rather, they acted as good Anglo-American mediators, making sure that any continuing arguments between the United States and the United Kingdom did not stop the formation of those international institutions that would stabilize currencies and foster international trade.

Members of the department – particularly W.A. Mackintosh, Clifford Clark, and Bryce himself – understood what was at stake. Mackintosh had once stated that Canadian post-war prosperity would rely on the ability to restore international trade. Only then would Canadians be assured of a "high and stable level of employment and income" – a phrase enshrined in the Liberal government's 1945 White Paper. Bretton Woods proposed a par-value system, which would provide for a system in which currency stability would become the norm: currencies would be pegged against the US dollar, which in turn would be convertible into gold at the rate of $35 US per ounce. It was hoped that this new system would put an end to the competitive devaluations of the 1930s.

This was particularly important for trading nations like Canada. The stabilization of international exchange rates would aid international trade and anything that fostered international trade would be of enormous benefit to Canada. By helping establish the International Monetary Fund and other international institutions that sought to rationalize trade, Finance officials created the environment that produced a post-war economic boom. There was no return to the depressed economic conditions of the 1930s after the war, as many had feared, and for this, Canadians have members of the Department of Finance to thank.

Canada played a significant role in "shaping the peace," to borrow a phrase from the historian John Holmes. As a rising middle power, Canada attempted, with some success, to get recognition for secondary states such as itself. It demanded proportional representation in the new world order. It was willing to recognize that its influence was less than that of the United States, but it wanted the Great Powers to admit that its influence was greater than, for example, Egypt.

This chapter chronicles the formation of a number of international institutions and the role of Canadians, and more specifically, the Department of Finance, in their creation.

As the tide of war turned in favour of the Allies early in 1943, more and more attention was put to the shape of the post-war world. International co-operation was regarded by many as the key to a lasting peace, and the mid-1940s gave rise to what since has been described as "a relatively Golden Age of international political inventiveness and institution building."[1] The Allied governments and their officials drew up plans and began a round of negotiations and conferences that resulted in the formation of new international organizations, including the United Nations, the International Monetary Fund, the International Bank for Reconstruction and Development, and the Food and Agriculture Organization. The United Nations Relief and Rehabilitation Administration was the first of these international organizations to be established during the war years, though unlike the others, it was never intended to be permanent. It was important, however, not only for the work it actually accomplished, but also because it was seen as establishing a pattern for subsequent and more enduring institutions.

Canadians were vitally involved in this process of institution building, a consequence, in part, of the country's desire for what it considered appropriate recognition in the new organizations. Canada was also important as a supplier nation, a role that was most significant in terms of its participation in UNRRA. In addition, through the course of the war, Canadian officials had become known and respected by their British and American counterparts, which enabled the Canadian delegations to play a somewhat stronger role in what were often largely "ABC" (American, British, Canadian) negotiations.[2]

Canadians had a large stake in international co-operation, not only for the purposes of defence, but also to maintain the foreign trade vital to the economy. Canada's strong ties with both Britain and the United States made multilateral co-operation attractive. After all, it was clear that it would not be in Canada's interests if, in the absence of international agreements, differences between the UK and the US forced it into closer integration with one country at the expense of relations with the other.[3] Idealism regarding international co-operation was of necessity accompanied by calculations of national self-interest.

Clifford Clark had strong views on what Canada's role should be in international institutions. Along with some of his colleagues in Finance, he was actively involved in the discussions in Ottawa. Full Canadian representation on these new bodies, with the attendant fiscal responsibilities, had to be balanced against the still heavy demands of the war effort and plans for domestic post-war programs. The question of what constituted a fair contribution, in terms of Canadian participation and finance, is a common thread running through the discussions leading to the formation and operation of these international organizations.

UNRRA

The United Nations Relief and Rehabilitation Administration was established formally in November 1943 after several years of talks. The first commitment to bring relief to the peoples and countries devastated by the war was made by Winston Churchill in the British House of Commons in the dark days of August 1940. While refusing to allow supplies through the blockade, he did promise aid for areas as they became liberated, guaranteeing that the "shattering of the Nazi power will bring them all immediate food, freedom and peace."[4] Minor steps soon were taken by the British, but it was clear that co-operation among the Allies was essential. Accordingly, in September 1941, representatives of Britain and the Dominions, including Canada, and of Belgium, Czechoslovakia, Greece, Luxembourg, the Netherlands, Norway, Poland, the USSR, Yugoslavia, and the Free French met in London and established the Inter–Allied Committee on Post-War Requirements. It was agreed by all of the delegates except the USSR's that a bureau should be established by the government of the United Kingdom that would coordinate the estimates of post-war relief requirements prepared by the Allied governments and then present proposals to the committee. The USSR, however, could not accept the idea of a central bureau under the control of the government of the United Kingdom, pressing for an international body based on the principle of equal representation.[5]

In the following months, data were compiled on provisional relief requirements and other preparatory work done by the British bureau while proposals were discussed for the establishment of a United Nations relief and rehabilitation organization. In January 1942, the

USSR submitted a plan to the Allied governments for the establishment of an international organization to deal with some of the problems concerning the economic life of post-war Europe. Unofficial recommendations then were submitted by the British to the US government in February.

The British and USSR proposals were considered by the Americans, who made their suggestions known in May. In June 1942, the Canadian government agreed in principle to the draft US proposal but reserved the right to raise the question of Canadian representation at a later date, arguing that the country's participation was important in view of its probable post-war position as a major supplier of foodstuffs. This was the beginning of "much work and many headaches" for the Canadian Mission in Washington over the arrangements and negotiations that led to the formation of UNRRA.[6]

Canada's struggle for representation in UNRRA took place at much the same time as its negotiations for a place on the Combined Boards in Washington, and the same basic principles were involved.[7] Canada wanted representation on these bodies commensurate with her contribution, and it was in the course of these discussions in 1942 and into 1943 that the Canadian version of what came to be known as the functional principle crystallized and became the approved policy. Prime Minister King explained the idea in the House of Commons in July 1943: "A number of new international institutions are likely to be set up as a result of the war. In the view of the government, effective representations on these bodies should neither be restricted to the largest states nor necessarily extended to all states. Representation should be determined on a functional basis which will admit to full membership those countries, large or small, which have the greatest contribution to make to the particular object in question."[8]

The Canadian government wanted to be on UNRRA's Central Policy Committee, which largely would control the organization and decide how it would operate. The committee's membership, however, was limited to the Big Four: China, Britain, the US, and the USSR. The Russians and Americans argued that if Canada was to be included, then Poland, Brazil, and possibly other nations would demand membership. Britain was more sympathetic with the Canadian position, a view influenced by the fear that the Canadian war effort and financial aid to Britain would be prejudiced if Canada's views were not accommodated.[9] A compromise eventually was suggested: Canada would name the chairman of the proposed Suppliers Committee, with a clause in the UNRRA agreement that would stipulate that the chairman of that committee would be invited to sit in on the meetings of the Central Policy Committee when it considered supply questions. This compromise was rejected forcefully by Clark in a letter to Norman Robertson dated 3 March 1943.[10]

It seems to me there is only one answer to be given by us, and that answer should be given now: Thank you, boys, but count us out! We are still trying to run a democracy and there is some historical evidence to support the thesis that democracies cannot be taxed without representation. We have tried to lead our people in a full-out effort for the war, and we had hoped that we could continue to lead them in such a way as to get their support behind the provision of relief and maintenance for battle-scarred Europe in the post-war years. We will not be able to secure their support for such a program if it, as well as the economic affairs of the world generally, [is] to be run as a monopoly by the Four Great Powers.

Clark argued that any compromise would be dangerous because it would set the pattern for post-war economic organization as well as for post-war political organization. He concluded his letter with a warning: "Any Canadian government that accepts such a compromise would soon be brought to realities by the public and would deserve what they would get."

The discussions continued in both Washington and Ottawa. Lester B. Pearson, who was the Canadian minister in the United States and was involved in these negotiations, comments on them in his memoirs: "The most violent opposition to the 'compromise' regarding UNRRA came from our Deputy Minister of Finance, Clifford Clark, a very real power in Ottawa in those days. He was emphatic we should have nothing to do with any relief convention which did not put Canada in an equal position in every way with the Big Four. He had little or no appreciation of the obstacles in the way of achieving this."[11]

The issue was resolved in the Cabinet War Committee early in April 1943. James Ilsley was against the compromise, arguing that if Canada withdrew from its position on UNRRA where the Canadian argument was strong, claims on other international organizations would be hopelessly prejudiced. Despite his objections, the compromise was accepted. As King comments in his diary: "It was important to consider how the Canadian people would view the rejection of a proposal of this kind with its possible consequences and repercussions as against refusing to participate at all because not given full recognition ... Before going into the Cabinet, I had felt the only thing for us to do was to accept. We would have gained nothing by refusing ..."[12]

The UNRRA agreement was signed on 9 November 1943 in Washington. The signatories agreed, in order to provide relief to occupied areas immediately upon their liberation, to establish an international organization that would "plan, coordinate, administer or arrange for the administration of measures for the relief of victims of war in any area under the control of any of the United Nations through the provision of food, fuel, clothing, shelter and other basic necessities, medical and other essential services."[13]

Once established, UNRRA consisted of a council of all members, which was to meet every six months, and the Central Committee of the four Great Powers. The Central Committee controlled policy between sessions but had to submit its decisions for confirmation by the council. The Standing Committee on Supplies, chaired by Pearson, advised the council, Central Committee, and UNRRA administration on policies regarding the provision, transport, distribution, and financing of supplies. In addition, two regional committees were set up, one for Europe and one for the Far East, composed of representatives of the governments in the areas concerned.

Executive authority would be vested in the director general, who would be an American citizen. Herbert Lehman, a former New York governor, was the first to hold the position; he had been director general in waiting since his appointment by President Franklin Roosevelt in November 1942 as the director of the Office of Foreign Relief and Rehabilitation Operations.[14] When Lehman resigned in March 1946, Fiorello LaGuardia, the former mayor of New York, was appointed to take his place.

FINANCING UNRRA

The first session of the UNRRA Council began in Atlantic City, New Jersey, on 10 November 1943, the day following the signing of the agreement. Over the next three weeks, the various committees and subcommittees established the administration's organization and formulated the broad policies that were to govern its work. On signing the agreement, member governments were committed to contribute to the resources needed to enable UNRRA to accomplish its purposes. Provision was made for two separate types of contribution: administrative and operating. The budget for administration was drawn up by the director general and was subject to approval by the council, which determined the proportions to be paid by each member government. The operating contribution was to be determined both as to size and character by the member governments themselves, but the obligation to pay either type of contribution did not become legally binding until the appropriate constitutional bodies of each government chose to make it so.[15]

In the course of the discussions on the financing of relief, some general principles were agreed on. The first principle was that the acceptance of relief should not result in a burden of indebtedness; countries without resources would not be called on to pay for relief. The second principle was that those countries with financial resources would be expected to pay for their own relief. The chairman of the Committee on Financial Control was empowered to appoint committees to examine the situations of countries in order to determine their eligibility for assistance from UNRRA and their ability to pay for relief supplies. The third principle was that all countries, including those that had been overrun by the war and those that had not, should contribute to UNRRA's administrative expenses. Both donor and recipient countries then would be shareholders in the enterprise and be equally entitled to be heard in the UNRRA councils. The final principle was that the financial plan must be acceptable to the American Congress since the US would be providing the bulk of the resources.[16]

A financial plan had been drawn up by Harry White of the US Treasury a few weeks before the conference began. He proposed that each contributing country should appropriate a sum equivalent to one per cent of its national income for the purchase of relief supplies, ninety per cent of which would be spent on purchases within that country and ten per cent outside.[17] The idea had some obvious advantages by providing a substantial fund in a relatively straightforward manner. Under this plan, it was expected that contributions would total $2.5 billion, of which the United States would give $1.4 billion.[18]

The plan also had some deficiencies. As Clark commented, it would be easy to make some objections based on the different degrees to which countries were already devoting their resources to the war, or the possible necessity of monetary transfers if each country could not make available appropriate domestic supplies equal to the amount of its levy, or the difficulty of determining national income on any kind of comparable basis.[19] The British reaction to the proposals was mixed. They welcomed the US Treasury proposals because they involved a larger American contribution on a basis that probably was acceptable to the American public. They were concerned, however, that the UK contribution under the formula would be beyond its capacity to pay.[20]

When the first UNRRA Council session convened at Atlantic City, the US Treasury's financial plan, after considerable debate, was adopted without any substantial alterations. Each member country whose home territory had not been occupied by the enemy agreed to commit itself to donate the equivalent of one per cent of its national income for the year ending 30 June 1943. Ninety per cent of the contribution would be in the form of a credit in local currency to permit UNRRA's director general to procure goods in that contributing country. The remaining ten per cent would be in a currency that could be spent outside the contributing country, the so-called free funds.[21] The national income formula was adopted because it was a convenient means of assessing the potentially largest contributors: the United States, United Kingdom, and Canada. The concept of national income was familiar to these governments and had been used by Canada, for example, in the early months of the war in determining the appropriate Canadian contribution to the war effort.[22] It was fully recognized when this formula was adopted, however, that UNRRA could not expect much more than token contributions from some of its member governments. Accordingly, the financial resolution included a clause for "governments in special economic situations," which allowed those governments that found the one per cent formula onerous to contribute what they could.[23] Canada's contribution under the UNRRA formula was $77 million on the basis of its national income for the year ended 30 June 1943. In accordance with the financial plan, ten per cent of that amount, $7.7 million, was available in funds that could be used by UNRRA for purchases outside of Canada. The first instalment of $50,000 (US) was authorized on 5 April 1944 from the appropriation of the Department of External Affairs. The second portion of these "free funds" was provided under the UNRRA Act, which authorized the expenditure of an amount not exceeding $10 million for the purposes of Canadian participation in UNRRA. The UNRRA Act had to be amended in 1944 to authorize the provision of "commodities, services and equipment required by UNRRA."[24]

At the end of the 1944–45 fiscal year, Canada had fulfilled its responsibility in the payment of the free funds. The bulk of the contribution, however, was in the form of a credit against which UNRRA could draw to pay for Canadian goods and services. A division of the Mutual Aid Administration was formed on 1 May 1944 responsible for obtaining UNRRA supplies through the same agencies as Mutual Aid. Up to 30 September 1945, $55,844,918 of Canadian goods and services had been committed, leaving about $13 million for future UNRRA purchases. In addition, Canada was an important source of supplies beyond those financed by Canada; UNRRA free funds of about $51 million had been applied to the purchase of Canadian supplies and services as of 30 September 1945.

The third Council session, in August 1945, discussed the need for more money; it was proposed that UNRRA must request a further contribution or dissolve itself owing to lack of funds at the end of 1945. The resolution was passed on condition that terminal dates for UNRRA operations were established, those dates being the end of 1946 for shipments to Europe and the end of March 1947 for shipments to the Far East.[25]

The second Canadian contribution was equal to the first, $77 million, and was authorized in December 1945. In November, the Canadian procurement division of UNRRA had been transferred to the Department of Trade and Commerce because Mutual Aid shipments for the most part had ceased and its administration was being wound up.[26]

After the US and UK, Canada was the third largest contributor to UNRRA, providing $154 million. These three countries provided ninety-four per cent of the total operating contributions. The countries contributing the remaining six per cent were more significant than anticipated, as sources of supply for scarce commodities. Voluntary contributions from non-governmental sources in contributing countries, including, for example, clothing drives, amounted to approximately $210 million, making up about six per cent of UNRRA's total resources, providing a much valued, tangible proof of support for the work of the organization.[27]

Canadian individuals made significant contributions to UNRRA operations. The Canadian government actively assisted the administration of that body in recruiting qualified staff for senior positions, including: Andrew Cairns, who headed the Food Division at the UNRRA headquarters in Washington; Major General Charles Stein, who was the deputy chief of Finance and Administration at the European Regional Office in London; and Captain Lawrence J. Lismer, the director of Accounts and Audits, Bureau of Finance and Administration, at headquarters. Brigadier C.M. Drury was the chief of the UNRRA Mission to Poland, whose task involved a delicate political situation and a needy population due to widespread devastation in the country.[28]

UNRRA's activities were wound up in 1947. Its work was continued by the United Nations International Children's Emergency Fund and the International Refugee Organization, as well as through other arrangements for economic rehabilitation, including, most notably, the American Marshall Plan. Although UNRRA's initial inspiration had been concern over the fate of the starving of Europe, it was active primarily in the Far East, Eastern Europe, Italy, and Greece. The countries of Western Europe – the Netherlands, Belgium, France – could afford to finance their own relief and rehabilitation, and one of UNRRA's basic principles was that it would aid only those unable to pay.

The decision to aid Italy had not been easily reached. There was a strong feeling in the council and administration that UNRRA's first responsibility was to the liberated Allies and that aid to Italy would disperse already strained resources. A limited program was approved by the council in September 1944. It began early in 1945 when the country was still divided, with Allied armies controlling the south and Germans controlling the north. The scope of UNRRA's activities in Italy was expanded the following year in light of Italy's continued need and, more importantly, the Berlin declaration that paved the way for Italy's entry into the United Nations.[29] In Germany, UNRRA's activities were limited to assisting displaced persons; the Allied military government distributed relief supplies at a minimum level to prevent disease and such disorders as might "endanger or impede military operations."[30] UNRRA was active in Austria, however, because it had been accepted, in the Moscow Declaration of October 1943, as the first victim of Hitler's aggression and an area to be liberated. UNRRA was invited by the Allied Control Council for Austria in December 1945 to take over responsibility for relief and rehabilitation supplies.[31]

MILITARY RELIEF

The scope of UNRRA's work was defined during the council's first session at Atlantic City late in 1943. It was agreed that UNRRA was to be an emergency organization; its goals were limited to immediate relief and rehabilitation and were not to include long-term reconstruction.[32] In addition, the signatories recognized that immediately after a territory's liberation, the distribution of civilian relief, food, medicine, and other needed supplies would be under the control of the military authorities. It was estimated that the period between liberation and before UNRRA assumed responsibility might be about six months. Immediately after the conference's end, however, difficulties arose about the division between civil and military responsibility for relief and rehabilitation. The American president issued a directive to the US army in December indicating the possibility of a substantial extension of military responsibility beyond the six months contemplated when UNRRA had been organized. In January 1944, Pearson wrote to Robertson describing a recent conversation with British officials in Washington who reported that in the view of the British War Office, UNRRA was little more than window dressing because there would be very little for them to do. A further indication of Britain's lack of commitment was their intention to have its one per cent of national income promised for relief include all forms of relief, both military and UNRRA. The attitude of the British military was illustrated by the refusal of its Combined Civil Affairs Committee and chiefs of staff to discuss the relationship between civil and military relief at the higher levels of authority. UNRRA's director general was told "somewhat curtly" that two colonels would be made available for such a discussion.[33]

The Canadians were concerned about these developments. As a combined operation, military relief was under Anglo-American Control. The Canadian government was reluctant at this point to hand out free military relief supplies to be distributed by the armies of the US and UK without having some part in the process. At the same time, the government felt a commitment to UNRRA and wanted the period of military relief to be kept as short as possible.

Britain's announced intentions regarding the financing of relief disturbed the Americans, who then wanted to establish some kind of formula for military relief. They suggested that each country (Britain, the US, and Canada) should pay for the supplies originating in their respective territories according to the allocations of the combined boards. Neither the British nor the Canadians were inclined to accept this proposal. The Canadians objected that it was unlikely that its government would be prepared to undertake such a blind commitment because it did not participate in the planning of relief activities during the military phase and the length of the military period was uncertain.[34] Furthermore, Canada had the potential to be a major source of supplies for military relief but to a degree well beyond its capacity to finance them. The American proposal was unacceptable to Canada, therefore, because it could lead either to paying a disproportionate share in the total cost of military relief or playing a much reduced role as a supplier.

Canada did not want to be seen as shirking responsibility for relief, and discussions on the financing problem continued in Ottawa through the spring of 1944. Officials from External, Finance, National Defence, and the Privy Council Office, in consultation with Pearson and Wynne Plumptre in Washington, established several principles on which to base the Canadian position. It was agreed that any Canadian contribution should be in proportion to the Canadian share in the invasion of Europe. It was also proposed that relief in the military period should be treated as analogous to contributions to UNRRA, for which a limit was set to each country's financial contribution rather than as Mutual Aid contributions, which were financed entirely by the country from which the supplies originated.[35] Canadian representation on the Combined Civil Affairs Committee of the Combined Chiefs of Staff in Washington was suggested as a possible condition for Canadian participation. This committee had been charged with responsibility for military relief.[36] This condition was of great importance to Clark among others in Ottawa. They argued that "it would be politically unjustifiable for Canada to provide military relief under present circumstances in which Canada has no control over the allocation, disposition or distribution of such relief, and no access to the moral credit or financial returns obtained for such relief in liberated territories."[37]

At its meeting of 17 May 1944, the Cabinet War Committee discussed the military relief proposals developed by their officials. At the end of the month, the Canadian position was explained to the UK and US governments. Canada would make provision for financing any orders that might be placed in Canada for military relief but the ultimate cost would be shared by Canada, the UK, and the US. Canada's share would be approximately eight per cent, which corresponded to the proportion of Canadian forces participating in the liberation of Europe. Canada also requested representation on the Supplies Committee of the Combined Civil Affairs Committee with the Canadian representatives to be invited to CCAC itself when relief questions were under discussion.[38]

While the discussions on how to finance military relief continued, the progress of the war made a resolution increasingly essential. The Canadian government made some provision for this interim period by authorizing expenditures up to $5 million for military relief chargeable to the War Appropriation for Army Services. The Mutual Aid Board made the expenditures under arrangements satisfactory to the Department of National Defence.[39] The authorization of these funds came none too soon. Italy had surrendered to the Allies in September 1943, but the long fight to liberate the country from the Germans was to last for many months. In the wake of the fighting, the Italian population was in need, sometimes desperately, for food, medical supplies, and water.[40] The liberation of France began with D-Day on 6 June 1944, and throughout that summer the Soviet army advanced westward through the Balkans and into Poland. It is important to note, however, that in countries within the operating areas of the Soviet armies, responsibility for civilian relief in the military period fell to UNRRA. In the Balkans, for example, provision was made in April 1944 for UNRRA's participation in the military relief programs.[41]

Canadian direct involvement in military relief operations was through the Civil Affairs service under the direction and control of the Supreme Headquarters Allied Expeditionary Force. Basic detachments consisting of four officers and six other ranks, sometimes supplemented by specialists, were attached to army formations and were responsible for administration, public health, and safety, as well as supply, food production, and relief, in the newly liberated areas. Three hundred Canadian officers and four hundred other ranks were attached to these detachments, often remote from the operations of the Canadian field army and entirely divorced from Canadian control.[42] It was intended, however, that Civil Affairs staff should be predominantly of the same nationality as the commander of the formation to which they were assigned, so Canadians were attached to the detachments serving with the First Canadian Army. Canadian civil affairs staff, for example, assisted in the evacuation and subsequent care of civilians evacuated from Boulogne and Calais in September 1944. In Italy, some thirty-five Canadians served as Civil Affairs officers with the Allied Commission controlling the operations of the Allied Military Government and supervising the administration of the areas handed back to Italian jurisdiction.[43]

In October 1944, the governments of Canada, Britain, and the US formally agreed on the arrangements for financing military relief. Supplies up to a total of $1 billion were to be financed by the three governments. Payment in full was to be requested of the governments or controlling authorities of the liberated or conquered areas receiving military relief supplies. It was expected, however, that some of the governments would not be able to pay for all the supplies received; the prospective deficit was limited under the agreement to $400 million, of which Canada's share would amount to $32 million. The total to be financed by the three countries without a new agreement would be limited to $1 billion. It was impossible to say that the supplies Canada would be required to finance initially would be limited to eight per cent of the $80 million, because the placing of orders in Canada would depend on the availability of supplies.[44] Canada's position as a supplier of goods could lead to the assumption of more than its share of the burden while its lack of economic power relative to Britain and the US could make it more difficult to collect payments from recipient countries.

Clark found this arrangement a source of great concern. He suggested that Canada should restrict its own purchases of supplies to the three per cent of the total military relief and should ask the UK and US to purchase the additional supplies when Canada was designated by the Combined Boards as a source. Canada had become involved in military relief in the first place, however, precisely because the US and UK had refused to buy in Canada for this purpose. Furthermore, the apparent intention of the agreement with the US and the UK had been that each country should finance the supplies obtained from it. Limiting Canada's interim financing of military relief, therefore, would be difficult.[45]

It then was suggested that Canada should ask the other two countries for a firm commitment that they ultimately would reimburse Canada so that the final outlay would be only eight per cent of the net loss. Clark did not like this idea of a guarantee when it was first suggested. He must have been persuaded, however, because a few days later he wrote to Robertson advocating such an assurance. Clark argued that he did not see how Finance could recommend to the Treasury Board the allocation of further funds for the procurement of military relief supplies unless the Canadian government was assured by the US and UK that it would not be left to bear a disproportionate share of the risk of non-payment by the recipient countries.[46]

Discussions focusing on the Canadian request for a guarantee continued into the new year. The British were sympathetic, yet by the end of January no official response had come from London. The Americans, while unable to give Canada a guarantee of eventual reimbursement if it had to pay more than the agreed on figure of eight per cent of the ultimate net loss, seemed uninterested in discussing alternatives. Plumptre, the financial attaché at the Canadian Embassy in Washington, was intimately involved with the negotiations. He reported that "there was a happy assumption that relief supplies would continue to flow to Europe whether or not financial arrangements were concluded. There was no willingness to come to grips with the actual statistics of what supplies were flowing, at what cost, from whom, and whether to paying or non-paying destinations."[47]

Canada's orders for military relief by late January 1945 had exceeded the limit of what it expected to be its share of the ultimate costs. On 13 February 1945, Canada notified Britain and the US that it was forced, reluctantly, to suspend further financing of military relief supplies.[48] A month and a half later, however, Canadian officials were embarrassed to discover that the United States, rather than Canada, had borne a disproportionate share of the burden of interim financing. Supplies to the value of $1,058,200,000 had been or would be delivered up to 30 June 1945. It was estimated that 76.8 per cent had been provided by the United States, 18.2 per cent by the United Kingdom, and only 5 per cent by Canada. Unless obligations for additional relief supplies were accepted, Canada might have to make a contribution in US dollars to meet its share of military relief.

Under these circumstances, Canada decided to send 150,000 tons of wheat to Europe as military relief at a cost of $10 million. This decision was made by the Mutual Aid Board, which, on 28 February 1945, had been assigned responsibility for military relief policy.[49] Canada wanted an outlet for its wheat surplus and there was no doubt that the wheat was badly needed in Europe. This commitment, therefore, satisfied the claims of conscience and self-interest. At the same time, the British proposed a compromise that would meet the Canadian demand for a guarantee. Each supplying country would give an undertaking to the other two not to regard the liability of any recipient country to itself as having been discharged until the liability to each of the other countries had also been discharged, and to hold all receipts in suspense accounts until this discharge had been accomplished. In early April, the Americans notified Canada of their approval of the proposal and Canada resumed the financing of military relief.[50]

Under the original military relief agreement, maximums of $400 million net losses and $1 billion total supplies had been established. In April, it appeared that Canada had reached the net loss figure. The military relief situation was further complicated by the approaching defeat of the Axis powers. The determination of the Allies to accept nothing less than unconditional surrender resulted in their taking complete responsibility for feeding the populations and rebuilding the economy of Germany, Austria, and Italy, as well as the liberated territories. The potential cost of military relief seemed to be mounting rapidly.

Canada wanted to revise the military relief formula to reduce the burden. As Clark wrote to Robertson, however, the issue was subject to divergent pressures:

I do not think we can enter a new fiscal year with a huge potential liability hanging over us on which no limit can be set and about which very little can be said. We must somehow budget for whatever provision is made, and the strain upon our budget is going to be very severe at a time when many Canadians will be expecting a considerable reduction in War expenditures. On the other hand, I do not suppose the victorious Allied powers can let the people under their control starve to death merely because they are unable to pay for what they require.[51]

Clark argued that Canada's share under the existing formula was more than could be justified on the basis of each country's relative capacity to bear the cost. A more equitable formula would put Canada's share closer to the arrangement under UNRRA in which the ratio of Canada's burden to the US was 1:17. Clark argued that Canada, however, should pay no more than the same amount per capita as the US – a ratio of 1:12 of the absolute amount borne by the Americans. Clark suggested that if military relief were to continue, Canada should be asked to cover no more than five per cent of the ultimate cost.

In May, representatives of the Canadian, British, and American governments met in Washington. The British were anxious to reduce their financial commitments, while the Americans were wary of any dramatic increase in their share. A new formula was agreed on: the US would take on seventy per cent of the costs, Britain twenty-five per cent, and Canada five per cent.

Agreement on this formula was short-lived. The British, who were increasingly hard-pressed financially, had hoped that the formula would apply to all of occupied Germany as well as to all other areas receiving military relief, but the Americans considered their responsibility in Germany to be limited to their zone of occupation. In July, the

British presented a formal *aide-mémoire* to the Department of External Affairs requesting Canada, as a joint occupier of the British zone, to accept responsibility for the initial financing of relief supplies for that area. They asked Canada, in addition, to put this as a separate item in the appropriations to be repaid later by Germany rather than having it met from the UK share of the Mutual Aid.[52]

Canada, with little inclination to accommodate the British and commit resources to a program over which Canada had little or no control, was slow in responding to the British request. On 10 August 1945, the Americans came to Britain's aid, proposing to revise the formula so as to increase the US share of military relief by four per cent and extending this formula to relief supplies furnished to Germany and Austria.[53] The final formula, accepted by the Canadian government on 13 September 1945, thus was US seventy-four per cent, Britain twenty-one per cent, and Canada four per cent. The original formula (US sixty-seven per cent, UK twenty-five per cent, Canada eight per cent) was to apply to losses up to $400 million, while the revised formula proposed by the US would determine the shares for the losses above $400 million.[54]

With the termination of military relief as of the loadings of 31 August 1945 by the combined military authorities, Canadian policy on relief finally achieved the simplicity intended at the time of the signing of the UNRRA agreement in November 1943. Now only UNRRA would receive further contributions. Other countries and agencies desiring Canadian goods and services were invited to negotiate with the proper commercial authorities. Responsibility for UNRRA was transferred to the Department of Trade and Commerce on 1 November 1945. In the end, Canada's share of military relief was approximately $95 million out of a total supplied by the three countries of $1.725 billion.[55]

Canadian direct involvement in the provision of military relief was the most memorable during the liberation of Holland. In April 1945, the Netherlands District came directly under the operational command of General Henry Crerar of the First Canadian Army, which included responsibility for Civil Affairs. In the western part of Holland, which contained the most heavily populated areas as well as the largest cities, the Dutch were close to starvation and there were shortages of food, fuel, and medicine. At liberation, it was reported that a state of "acute general starvation" had been avoided by only two or three weeks.[56] The distribution of food to the civilian population was, therefore, a pressing responsibility. Another priority was re-establishing the electric power system, which was needed for the water works and to operate the pumps essential for flood control. The task was complicated because the normal supply route for the coal needed by the power plants was by inland water transport and the canals were blocked and the railway and roads restricted. Civil Affairs staff also assisted in maintaining or restoring public health facilities, monitoring the number of cases of infectious diseases, and evaluating the need for doctors, hospitals, and medicine. They also assisted in reopening banking facilities and maintaining law and order. When necessary, they regulated the movement of the population.[57] The emphasis in Holland, as in military relief operations elsewhere, was to pass the responsibility for relief to the civilian authorities as soon as possible. Within three months, the Dutch authorities had taken charge, though large numbers of Canadian troops remained in Holland awaiting demobilization.[58]

The settlement of Canada's claims for payment for its share of military relief costs did not immediately follow the end of the war. Canada waited until Britain and the United States, both of whose claims were much larger, had had an opportunity to settle their accounts. In addition, it was expected that by waiting a few years, these countries would have had some time to re-establish their battered economies, putting them in a better position to pay their debts.

The settlement with Holland was made in 1948. Along with Canada's claim for military relief, there was the large Dutch counter-claim against Canada to settle, arising from the long stay of Canadian troops in Holland. To these issues was added the question of the forty million old guilders and seven million new guilders acquired by the Canadian troops. Canada accepted the Dutch arguments for compassionate treatment due to the extensive war damage suffered by the country and agreed to reduce its original claim for military relief of $14 million. In the end, the Dutch agreed to pay Canada $5.7 million, to be paid in Canadian dollars in payments spread over ten years.[59]

In the spring of 1950, two years after the United States had wiped out almost all of its claims and one year after the British had made its settlements, James Sinclair, the parliamentary assistant to the minister of finance, went to Europe accompanied by Clarence Read, a Department of Finance official, to try to collect what they could on the military relief accounts.[60]

Settlements were complicated by the nature of the military relief program; carried out as it was in the turmoil of the war, accounting for the goods received was not always accurate. Formal contracts were not usually signed with the recipient countries because there may not have been a real government at the time to carry on negotiations. The obligation to pay was, in fact, moral rather than legal.[61] Under these circumstances, it was not expected that payment in full would be received for all of the claims.

Adjustments were made to the military relief claim regarding Belgium and Luxembourg because those governments had better accounts of the goods received than the US, UK, or Canada had of what had been sent and could show deficiencies in quality or quantity in the goods received. Belgium settled Canada's outstanding claim with one payment in American dollars of $7,106,000 in the first half of 1950. As for Luxembourg, its effective system of price control had made goods purchased in that country less expensive than those bought elsewhere; consequently, Canada further adjusted the claim. One payment of $365,000 was made, as compared with the original claim of $439,000.

"Blocked payments" were arranged in several countries. These were payments made not in American dollars but in the local currency and were usually subject to some restrictions. In France, for example, $4 million payable in French francs was deposited in a Canadian account in France to be used for the purchase of property or equipment for the Canadian embassy or its local operations.[62] A more restrictive arrangement was made in Italy where the debt was large but where the country's political and economic troubles had led both the United States and Britain to wipe out their debts completely. The agreement stipulated that the "nominal" payment of $1.3 million out of the total claim of $28.4 million was to be used in Italy for the purchase of property or for scholarships for Canadians studying there. A blocked payment was also arranged in Yugoslavia where it was agreed that $150,000 out of the total claim of $226,000 would be paid to Canada in the local currency and used to maintain the embassy's operation. These discussions were described by Sinclair in his diary as the "best humoured negotiations," but the most interesting part of the trip to Yugoslavia was the pleasant interview Sinclair and Read had with Marshal Tito. They discussed the war, Tito's break with the Comintern, and other subjects.[63]

The visit to Greece was highlighted by an hour-and-a-half visit with the king and queen. Sinclair was charmed and reported in the diary that "he is a fine fellow and she is out of this world."[64] The discussions regarding terms for settling the debt with Canada were inconclusive, but the trip was satisfying because of the gratitude of the Greek people for Canadian aid. As Sinclair later reported to Parliament, "If we get no other payment out of Greece than that gratitude, I think Canada will have been well repaid."[65]

FOOD AND AGRICULTURE ORGANIZATION

The first of the wartime international economic conferences was proposed by President Roosevelt in February 1943. The announcement came as a surprise; no one in Washington was aware of his plans.[66] The purpose of the conference was to provide an opportunity for the exchange of views and information and to seek agreements in principle on post-war co-operation in solving food and agriculture problems. After some initial confusion in establishing the date and agenda, it convened at Hot Springs, Virginia, on 18 May 1943.

The conference was a success, at least in the sense that it achieved all that possibly could have been expected of it. Few questions of policy were decided; any issues on which disagreement seemed likely were pushed aside.[67] An interim commission was established to continue the work of the conference, with Pearson as its chair. This commission drew up a formal constitution for a permanent organization and prepared a declaration in which each signing nation recognized its obligation to collaborate with the others in raising nutrition levels and improving agricultural production. In addition, technical reports were prepared by experts in the fields of nutrition and food management, agricultural production, fisheries, forestry and primary forestry products, and statistics.[68]

Finance officials were not the primary Canadian participants in the FAO; Agriculture, Fisheries, and External Affairs were the departments most vitally concerned. The draft declaration and constitution prepared by the interim commission in the form of two reports were referred to the Economic Advisory Committee by cabinet on 8 February 1944. A subcommittee consisting of representatives of the departments most concerned and including Mitchell Sharp from Finance was formed to examine these reports and then make recommendations to the committee.[69] Early in April 1944, the committee made its recommendations. They proposed that the first report, the declaration, be accepted officially. The second report, including the proposed constitution, was recommended for approval subject to certain amendments. They suggested including an explicit reference to the desirability and advantages to be gained from international trade and proposed a new paragraph to be inserted in the report. While recognizing that some countries might decide that their circumstances justified "restrictive devices," the committee proposed that the new organization should declare its intention to promote the reduction of barriers to international trade in food and agricultural products and the adoption among member nations of commercial policies that would lead to greater international economic collaboration and the expansion of international trade.[70]

The EAC was reluctant to accept the suggested wording on commodity arrangements in the report. The interim commission had recommended the establishment of an international authority to coordinate and supervise the administration of individual commodity arrangements. In the view of the EAC, such commodity agreements would be between governments and conflicts would be inevitable if an independent authority attempted to supervise. It was proposed, instead, that an international body be charged with responsibility for examining and reviewing commodity arrangements and reporting to governments on the extent to which they conformed to agreed principles and were achieving the justifiable objects of such agreements.[71]

These comments on trade and commodity arrangements reflected discussions of the issues conducted with the British and the Americans since mid-1942. In the case of the Food and Agriculture Organization's constitution and declaration, the amendments proposed by the Canadian government were not accepted. The interim commission's response was that the suggested paragraph on trade could lead to trouble with the US Congress and might also rouse suspicions on the part of other nations regarding the organization's potential interference with their tariff and trade barriers. The section on commodity arrangements was the result of a hard-fought compromise, and the Canadians were asked to reconsider. They did not consider the proposed amendments to be vital to the success of the new organization and agreed that they might be withdrawn if there were serious objections.[72]

Two additional issues of particular concern to Finance were discussed in the report on the FAO: the method of financing the organization and the taxation of its employees. The interim commission had suggested that the FAO staff be accorded "diplomatic privileges and immunities," including the exemption of official salaries from income tax and privileges with respect to the purchase of goods free of duties and taxes. This suggestion raised a general issue relevant to the treatment of the staff of other international organizations. The subject had already come up in reference to UNRRA, which had also proposed that its official salaries be free of tax, whether or not the employees were considered ordinarily resident in Canada. The Canadian government recommended that the general subject should be discussed with the appropriate authorities in the US and UK and that an international convention should be adopted and then applied to the staff of all international organizations. The members of the interim commission regarded this as reasonable, and the British proposed an amendment to the relevant section that allowed for common treatment for the employees of all international organizations.[73]

The proposed scheme for financing the organization was accepted with some misgivings by the Canadian government. The commission had decided to establish a maximum share of twenty-five per cent of the costs, apparently because the American delegates believed that they could not get Congress to accept a larger contribution if the

United States was to have only one vote like all other members. The interim commission had also proposed that the share of the occupied countries, given their special difficulties, should be scaled down temporarily by one-third. Compensation for these reductions would be through increasing the shares of those member nations subject to neither the maximum nor minimum limits.

According to the Canadian government, some departure from the principle of making assessments on the basis of each member's ability to pay was justifiable; the government argued, however, that a distinction should be made between the principles applied to determining administrative costs and the more substantive costs incurred for projects that nations would undertake collectively – for example, relief through UNRRA.

The Americans then proposed an amendment that the maximum and minimum limit to contributions be written into the constitution. This was opposed by Clark among other Canadians as a dangerous and troublesome precedent. They suggested that Canada should refuse to agree unless a proviso was added that the limitations would apply only to the administrative budget and not for carrying out special and substantive functions. In the end, the apportionment of expenses was not part of the constitution and was left subject to change. Canada was sixth in terms of the size of its contribution, paying 5.06 per cent, while the United States paid 25 per cent, the United Kingdom 15 per cent, China 6.5 per cent, and France 5.69 per cent.[74]

The USSR participated in the Hot Springs conference and the interim commission, and some of its suggestions for changes in the report and constitution were incorporated into the final document presented to the establishing conference in Quebec late in 1945. In spite of its part in drafting the constitution, however, the USSR withdrew from the organization after the constitution had been accepted.[75]

PLANNING THE INTERNATIONAL ECONOMY

While meeting at Placentia Bay, Newfoundland, in August 1941, Roosevelt and Churchill agreed on the Atlantic Charter, a statement of common principles and war aims. Included among its vague but impressive phrases was a declaration of the commitment of the two leaders to "fullest collaboration in the economic field" and the promotion of mutually advantageous economic relations. Six months later, on the signing of the Lend-Lease Agreement, this commitment to post-war economic collaboration was reiterated in its Article VII, in which Britain and the United States agreed not only on the general objective of bettering world-wide economic relations but also on reducing tariffs and other trade barriers and promoting measures to expand trade and employment.

Article VII also pledged to eliminate all forms of discriminatory treatment in international commerce, an aim clearly incompatible with the maintenance of the British system of preferential tariffs. Before the agreement was signed, Roosevelt reassured Churchill that the US was not using Lend-Lease as a trading weapon against the principle of Imperial preference and that the British were no more committed to the abolition of their high protective tariffs.[76] The British preferential system, however, continued to be a major point of discussion in the subsequent commercial policy talks.

In both the United States and the United Kingdom, policy-makers were putting great emphasis on the political and economic importance of liberal trade policies. They believed that it was important, in capitalizing on the co-operative spirit among the Allies, to initiate a program for the reduction of trade barriers as soon as possible. Independent planning by both governments as well as the commitment assumed on the signing of Article VII led to a series of exploratory talks followed by more concrete proposals.

It should be noted that questions of commercial policy were only some of the topics covered in the Article VII discussions. International monetary arrangements designed to make multilateral payments easier and to assist in the achievement of some equilibrium in the international balance of payments were a necessary complement to a less restrictive trade policy. Both subjects – international balance of payments and trade policy – were discussed, often at the same meetings. The evolution of monetary arrangements leading to the creation of the International Monetary Fund and the International Bank of Reconstruction and Development at Bretton Woods was largely independent of the talks on trade, though their architects did envisage an international environment of multilateral trade and domestic full employment.[77]

While irritated at their exclusion from negotiations on policy questions of such direct concern and at the US linkage of trade policy and Lend-Lease, Canada was glad to see the UK and US attempting to work out new international trade arrangements.[78] In the series of informal discussions and organized conferences that followed, Canada attempted to ensure that its views were heard and, when possible, participated in discussions of international economic policy.

TALKS ON TRADE

The United Kingdom made the first move after the signing of the Lend-Lease agreement. In May 1942, the Dominions Office in London informed Canada and the other Dominions of the purpose and nature of the upcoming, but as yet unscheduled, Article VII talks. The talks at this stage were to be "informal, exploratory and non-committal." Their purpose was "to survey the whole field of post-war international economic reconstruction, to define in broad outline the problems which will confront us and to determine if possible the methods of approach which seem best calculated to facilitate a solution of these problems." The Canadian response was to press for participation, arguing that Canada was "the extreme case of the effects of the repercussions of U.K. and U.S. relations" and that any decisions made at these talks would be of most critical importance to the country.[79] Canada's concern was unimportant at this stage, however, as differences in opinion in Washington made any talks with the US unlikely until after the American elections in November. In the interim, Britain proposed an informal exchange of views and ideas with the Dominions on questions of post-war economic policy. Hume Wrong of External Affairs, Louis Rasminsky of the Foreign Exchange Control Board, and Mackintosh of Finance were the Canadian representatives at the talks held in London in October and early November 1942.

Only one of the thirteen meetings held in London was devoted to a discussion of post-war commercial policy; proposals for an International Clearing Union occupied half of the representatives' time, and national income statistics, post-war relief, and the international regulation of primary products competed for space on the agenda.

The discussion on commercial policy was general and discursive as no proposal had been prepared prior to the meeting. It was accepted in general that the United States would press strongly for the abolition of British preferences and that some form of multilateral negotiations on trade would be preferable to bilateral arrangements. The Canadian representatives supported the suggestion of a "bold positive approach" to commercial policy but noted in their report that some of the UK representatives were far from optimistic that the US would take any real action.[80]

One of the Canadian concerns at the talks in London in October was to avoid giving the United States the impression that a common Commonwealth front was being formed on economic matters. From the Canadian point of view, direct talks with the US officials were a necessary complement to the Commonwealth discussions. As part of this process, Canada and the US had a formal exchange of notes defining the objectives of post-war international economic policy. Canada was reluctant initially, because the formal note was very similar to Article VII, which had been signed by other nations as a quid pro quo for lend-lease supplies; Canada was wary of any appearance of direct involvement with lend-lease. It was suggested by Mackintosh, however, that by participating in the exchange of notes, Canada could ensure its involvement in the discussions on economic policy that countries signing the agreement were committed to undertake at an early date and also ensure its inclusion in any post-war conversations. The War Committee approved the terms of the draft note, and the formal exchange of eighty-one notes took place on 30 November 1942.[81]

The next move on trade policy came from the United Kingdom. In April 1943, the British proposed a joint meeting of experts from the Dominions and India to discuss post-war monetary and economic policy preliminary to their conversations with the United States. Clark wrote to Wrong that "the subject matter is so important that we must participate in any conference that is held." The Economic Advisory Committee prepared a report as a basis for instructions to the delegation.[82]

The talks, held in London between 15 and 30 June 1943, were informal and friendly. All of the meetings were devoted to the discussion of post-war commercial policy and specifically to the program circulated by the United Kingdom. It was proposed that a multilateral convention should be negotiated establishing a Commercial Union and embodying a commercial code. Adherence of all friendly countries to this convention would be invited, the benefits of which would be extended only to members. Under the convention, protective tariffs would be reduced but would be subject to exception if approved by the Commercial Union. Provision was also made for a quasi-judicial, fact-finding body, under the union, to which aggrieved states might appeal on matters of discrimination or non-compliance with the code.

The Canadian delegation supported the proposals in general, though with some reservations. As a result of the discussions, the United Kingdom put forward some amendments to its draft, including a suggestion of the Canadian delegation: a clause reserving for consideration the question of special provisions to meet the temporary needs of infant industries.[83]

The UK revised its *aide-mémoire* to the US government again after the meetings in London, proposing a broader approach to involve bilateral discussion of the whole field of economic relations, with the object of obtaining broad UK–US agreement on an orderly agenda for the discussion of Article VII. Great importance was put in the revised *aide-mémoire* on achieving prior agreement between the two governments on economic issues before they were discussed in a wide international field. These modifications were regarded with concern in Ottawa. Once again, Canada felt excluded from negotiations.[84]

Agreement beyond general statements of principle between the UK and the US was a long way off, however, as was clear at the talks between those two governments held in Washington in the fall of 1943. The governments agreed broadly on the need for a multilateral convention on commercial policy, supplemented by an international trade organization, but as discussions became more specific, differences between as well as within the two delegations became apparent. On the relation between trade and employment, for example, the US State Department emphasized the contribution that trade liberalization could make to the maintenance of high levels of employment. They were more inclined to regard trade restrictions as a cause of the Great Depression than their colleagues in the US Department of Commerce, who tended to see it the other way around: that high levels of income and employment were a precondition of international trade liberalization. The British were more inclined to the Commerce view, putting more emphasis on the contribution that the maintenance of high levels of employment could make to the liberalization of trade than on the contribution that the reduction of trade barriers could make to employment.[85]

The discussions on tariffs and preferences were probably the most contentious. Article VII of the Lend-Lease Aid Agreement had pledged to reduce tariffs and eliminate preferences, but the problem was to how to go about it. The US was determined to achieve the elimination of Imperial preferences and made a distinction between tariffs and preferences. The British, however, made less of a distinction between the two and wanted to devise a formula to reduce both kinds of barriers.

There were some grounds for optimism at the end of the UK–US talks. Agreement had been reached on the broad outlines of policy and on the need for some form of international trade organization. The discussions, however, had been only at the expert level and on general principles; it was clear that serious problems would arise when the issues were reduced to more specific obligations.

After the meeting in the fall of 1943, there was a lull in the UK–US negotiations, a result of British concerns and division on questions of commercial policy. In the interim, the US approached Canada and proposed "confidential exploratory conversations in the near future between officials of our two countries, for the purpose of reaching general agreement on an orderly agenda for future discussions of a more definitive character looking towards the implementation of the principles set forth in the Exchange of Notes of November 30th, 1942 ..."[86] The US approach was received by the Canadians with guarded enthusiasm. There was a feeling that the time was right to talk to the Americans about a trade agreement that could be the first major instalment of the multilateral program. It was proposed that Canada tell the United States that it was willing to negotiate a trade treaty that would exchange free entry on important products; the question of British preferences, however, would be left to multilateral convention. It was important that both the UK and the US be aware that the Canadian proposal was to be additional to a multilateral convention. As Mackintosh wrote in mid-December 1943, Canada had a great deal to gain from a UK–US agreement. Although both the UK and the US were needed by Canada as customers, the best arrangement, in Canada's view, would be multilateral, where neither could apply undue pressure on the country.

The Canada–US conversations took place at two sessions in January and February 1944. As with previous discussions on commercial policy, there was general agreement on the principles to be followed. It was agreed that a convention should be negotiated by the US, the Commonwealth countries, the Soviet Union, and a few other states. While other nations might join, the terms could not be altered to suit them; if they refused to join, such countries would be denied any benefits of the commercial convention. The establishment of an international trade organization was discussed, as well. Robertson, the head of the Canadian delegation, expressed strong views that Canada was entitled to a full share in any international commercial body and that there was no merit in arrangements limited to the Big Four, whose dominance in the political sphere Canada had accepted reluctantly.[87] The Canadians suggested that a formal connection should be established by the commercial policy organization with existing international bodies and that when appropriate, they should function closely.

On the contentious issue of Imperial preferences, the Canadians proposed a multilateral reduction in most favoured nation rates, a reduction that in itself would eliminate a great many preferential margins and reduce every one of the remaining margins by at least one-half. In the opinion of the Canadian group, this would go a long way toward the "substantial abolition of preferences" recommended in Article VII. The US group did not accept the Canadian proposal, arguing that the extent of the tariff reduction suggested would need to be accompanied by the simultaneous substantial abolition of preferences. It seemed clear, they said, that a significant proportion of the Imperial preferences would remain. The US group would find it difficult to defend a convention providing for drastic tariff reductions that allowed an important segment of the preferential system to remain until negotiated away in supplementary bilateral agreements involving still further tariff reduction. They argued that such a convention would be susceptible to the criticism that the United States had used up almost all of its bargaining power without achieving the desired objective.[88] Both groups agreed that further study was required.

A Canadian–American trade agreement, which Canadian officials had talked about the previous December, does not appear to have been discussed at the talks early in 1944. The idea, however, was not forgotten. In March 1944, during the course of Commonwealth commercial policy discussions, Robertson noted in a letter to Clark that the gap between the UK and US positions was widening and that a more continental approach to trade might be necessary:

> In general, objectives seem to be shrinking and receding. It seems to me that, as the multilateral programme becomes more modest and more remote, we shall have to look more seriously and more quickly at the specific problem of Canadian–American trade relations. I had envisaged a bilateral agreement with the United States, supplementing a general multilateral tariff reduction, but if effective multilateral action is to be indefinitely deferred and, when achieved, prove modest, then I think we may have to look at the question again from the continental viewpoint.[89]

This pessimism about the future of multilateralism was echoed by Clark. In May 1944, the Canadian officials involved in the formulation of commercial policy – Clark, Mackintosh, McKinnon, Master, Deutsch, and Wrong – agreed with Robertson that it would be advisable to recommend a "six months hoist" of negotiations and not to attempt to produce a statement of principles at the expert level. Until the United Kingdom formulated its policy and the US elections were concluded, further negotiations were likely to be conducted with such caution and rigidity as to be pointless and harmful. It remained desirable, however, to advance, clearly and vigorously, the Canadian view regarding a comprehensive international approach.[90]

Early in 1945, UK and US officials in London resumed discussions. By February, they had reached a considerable measure of agreement on a draft multilateral convention. In July, Robertson led a Canadian delegation at talks with the Americans in Washington and Ottawa that focused on the ways to achieve tariff reductions. The Americans were unable to accept horizontal cuts, arguing that Congress would be critical and there would be serious difficulties in bringing the other trading nations along. The goal should be to work out a "multilateral plan under which tariff reduction could be carried out selectively," possibly through a bilateral–multilateral approach. The Canadians argued that the American approach would be hopelessly inadequate and that the timing for decisive action would never be better because the whole world trade system was in flux. In addition, a horizontal cut would eliminate the preferences problem substantially.[91]

In September 1945, the British and the Americans resumed their discussions, which culminated in "Proposals for Consideration by an International Conference on Trade and Employment." These proposals were in two parts: "Proposals Concerning Employment" and "Proposals Concerning an International Trade Organization." The employment provisions reflected the large measure of agreement between the UK and the US on the importance of tying the reduction of trade barriers to complementary measures in the employment field. It was stated that the attainment and maintenance of "approximately full employment" by the major industrial and trading nations was "essential to the expansion of international trade" and "to the full realization of the objectives of all liberal international agreements." Domestic programs to expand employment "should be consistent with realization of the purposes of liberal international agreements and compatible with the economic well-being of other nations."[92] In addition to agreeing on these general principles, each country was committed to take action to achieve and maintain full employment, but not through measures likely to create unemployment in other countries; they also agreed to participate in the international exchange of information and ideas on employment issues.[93]

The proposals on an international trade organization included the contentious issue of preferences. The formula eventually adopted maintained the general commitment made in Article VII of the Lend-Lease agreement but left the final details vague. The elimination of preferences by the UK was pledged, but the commitment was only to enter "arrangements for action" leading to a final settlement that was mutually advantageous. The US negotiators had rejected any proposals for automatic tariff reduction through some pre-arranged formula. They were prepared, instead, to conduct traditional bilateral negotiations at a large conference where different sets of negotiations could be conducted simultaneously. Despite the American experts' view that an across the board approach to tariff reduction would be desirable, the traditional system of bilateral bargaining for reduction of tariffs was retained because a pre-arranged formula could not possibly be acceptable to the US Congress.[94]

The American action was a disappointment to the British and dampened hopes for a dramatic approach to multilateral trade. Later events were to show that the optimism of the middle years of the war was misplaced. In February 1946, the UN Economic and Social Council set up a preparatory committee to prepare for a planned UN conference on trade and employment. At meetings in the fall of 1946 in London and from April to August 1947 in Geneva, the committee discussed a "suggested Charter," circulated by the US, for an International Trade Organization. After revisions, the draft proposals were presented to the UN conference on Trade and Employment that met in Havana in November 1947. This conference, attended by most of the members of the United Nations, but not the Soviet Union, produced the Havana Charter for the proposed ITO in March 1948.

In mid-1947, negotiations for the reductions of tariffs took place among the twenty-three countries of the Preparatory Committee. At the same time, the General Agreement on Tariffs and Trade was drawn up. Based on the draft ITO Charter, GATT was considered to be an interim document that would be superseded by the charter once it was ratified by its signatories. It was adopted by the twenty-three countries of the Preparatory Committee on 30 October 1947 just before the Havana Conference. The ITO was never established, largely due to the opposition of the US Congress, although the British had lost their enthusiasm for the organization, as well. GATT has at least partly filled the gap that the ITO was intended to fill.[95]

THE UNITED NATIONS ORGANIZATION

The United Nations was probably the best known of the international institutions established during the 1940s, but the story of its development has been described well elsewhere. Suffice it to say here that Canadian involvement was largely through the officials of External Affairs, with the Department of Finance playing a very minor role. In the formal and informal interdepartmental discussions of the UN in Ottawa, senior Finance officials, including Mackintosh and me, were active participants, but the bulk of the work was the responsibility of Robertson, Pearson, and others from External. Finance officials assisted in drawing up the formula for contributions and became active in the UN administration once the organization had been established. Sidney Pollack of the department, for example, regularly attended and maintained a close interest in the work of the General Assembly and the various specialized agencies, watching for extravagance and urging economy.[96]

CHAPTER ELEVEN

The 1946 British Loan and Settlement

In 1945, Europe lay in ruins. Some Europeans questioned whether the Continent had the will to regain its former prosperity and importance. At war's end, the British prime minister, Winston Churchill, asked rhetorically: "What is Europe now? A rubble heap, a charnel house, a breeding ground of pestilence and hate."[1] There was ample justification for his pessimism. Almost forty-five million people had been killed between 1939 and 1945. The material cost of the war was also enormous, perhaps $1 trillion in military expenditures and twice that in property losses. All across Europe, great cities had been reduced to rubble.

The war had had an especially devastating effect on Britain's finances. The once-great power had lost £3 billion in war damages and £4 billion in overseas assets. To make matters worse, its external debt was increased by £13 billion despite higher taxation at home. Through Lend-Lease, Britain became a dependent of the United States, a nation that had emerged from the war as the new economic powerhouse. Britain, as Churchill pointed out, was on the verge of "bankruptcy."

The final chapter in the history of the international operations of Canada's Department of Finance thus witnessed a strenuous effort to "save" Britain by putting it back on a sound financial footing. The small band of supermandarins in Ottawa acknowledged that Canadian prosperity relied, in part, on the economic health of its long-time ally. Canada had always counted on Britain for markets, technology, and capital. With Britain and the rest of Europe rebuilding after the war, Canadians would find markets for their exports. There was a legitimate fear, however, that without financial aid, Britain would turn inward, embarking on a policy of trade restriction and discrimination in favour of the sterling area. In an effort to prevent this, Department of Finance officials worked on a financial package that would overcome Britain's post-war balance of payments problem.

This chapter details the Herculean efforts of those officials in this undersized and overworked department to meet Britain's financial needs and to restore economic stability to the international marketplace.

The billion-dollar loan made by Canada to Britain in March 1946 had its origins in August 1944. Early in that month, during discussions of British requirements of Mutual Aid supplies from Canada, the ministers on the Mutual Aid Board and senior financial officials learned from John Maynard Keynes the full measure of the UK's international financial difficulties. In part, these difficulties were immediate: the need for more arms, munitions, and food in that fiscal year 1944–45 and extending into the period we called stage II of the war, when hostilities in Europe were finished but the war against Japan continued. In part, the difficulties were foreseen. By mid-1944, it had become evident that Britain would face very large deficits in its balance of international payments for several years after the war was over.[2] Keynes gave us the details of Britain's gold and dollar reserves and of its very large sterling liabilities to India, Egypt, Eire, Palestine, and the Crown Colonies, as well as the much lesser amounts owing to Australia, New Zealand, and some Latin American and European nations with whom it had special payments arrangements. His rough estimate was that Britain's total international current account deficit in the first three post-war years would be at least $5 billion US, which it would have to finance by loans or other forms of assistance. These deficits would be caused in part by continuing military expenditures, in part by the reduced levels of receipts of interest and dividends resulting from the sale of overseas assets, and in large part by the delay to be expected in rebuilding its export trade, which had been much reduced by the war. Keynes and his colleagues were telling us this to demonstrate that Britain would need to keep all of its borrowing power to use in this post-war period and therefore needed Mutual Aid or other current assistance during the war.[3]

TOWERS'S FIRST SUGGESTIONS

Among those who heard Keynes's presentation on 1 August 1944 was Towers, the governor of the Bank of Canada. He took it very much to heart and studied the implications for Canada of the UK's expected post-war predicament. By late November, he reached very serious conclusions, which he outlined in a memorandum dated 25 November and circulated to Clark, Robertson, and a few other senior officials.[4] After a discussion with these officials on New Year's Day 1945, Towers revised his memorandum for consideration by ministers. Ilsley arranged a meeting on 18 January of the principal ministers involved to whom Towers's paper had been sent.[5] It was entitled "Post-War Commercial Policy Prospects: A Proposal for Averting a Breakdown in International Trade Relationships." It emphasized the vital importance to Canada of restoring and expanding her trade with the UK as soon as possible after the war, and the danger that British politicians would succumb to the temptation to maintain policies of trade restriction and discrimination in favour of the sterling area, policies that were being advocated by some leading political figures. The expected shortage of dollars arising from the massive deficits that Keynes had forecast was playing into the hands of these restrictionist ministers. Towers felt that financial assistance by Canada, as well as the United States, would be needed to head this off. Canada should start on this course immediately by offering Britain the assurance of a large post-war loan on easy terms. He proposed offering a loan of $1.2 billion, repayable over a period of twenty years beginning ten years after the end of the war and carrying an interest rate of only two per cent. Moreover, in any year in which payment of what was due would reduce UK reserves of gold and convertible currencies below a stipulated figure, payment would be deferred until the reserves rose enough that the payment would not have that effect. Towers argued that these special repayment terms were essential to meet the situation. In return for this loan, Canada would ask the UK not to discriminate against imports from Canada and to indicate to other countries in the sterling area that they need not discriminate against imports from Canada.[6]

THE CANADIAN PROPOSAL OF FEBRUARY 1945

The ministers present at Ilsley's meeting approved Towers's proposal and asked that it should be put in the form of a draft telegram to the British government, for consideration by the prime minister and the War Committee of the Cabinet. The latter approved sending it, on 23 February, along with another message agreeing to continue Mutual Aid for six months on the scale requested by the UK, including any part of that period after hostilities in Europe were over but were continuing against Japan. Canada would need to have a general election during that period, but war and Mutual Aid expenditures would be authorized in advance in a lump sum appropriation to be allocated month by month as required. A third message, sent on the same date, from prime minister to prime minister, emphasized the trade policy concerns of the Canadian government.[7]

The initial reactions from London were friendly and appreciative. On the current Mutual Aid, they warmly welcomed the assurances that Canada had given (which they exaggerated) and asked a few questions. On the post-war loan proposal, a later reply was sent on 21 March.[8] It, too, was welcoming, but it was non-committal. It said that post-war proposals had to be considered along with Britain's relations with the United States. It suggested that these might best be discussed orally with a few Canadian officials. After some further delay, when it became evident that Clark still was unable to get away from Ottawa, it was arranged that Mackintosh would take his place and go to London in May with Towers and H.B. Mackinnon, who would cover the trade policy aspects. Douglas LePan, from the high commissioner's staff in London, would join them.

THE CAMBRIDGE TALKS

The discussion on post-war problems and policies took place in Cambridge on the weekend of 19–21 May.[9] These dates permitted Keynes to use as his speaking notes the printed memorandum he had prepared in consultation with officials of the Treasury and with the chancellor of the exchequer, which had just been circulated to the cabinet. The personalities at this meeting, including senior Treasury and Bank of England officials, as well as its unique setting in King's College, have been noted in chapter 8, where the relationship to then current British trade policy was recounted. Here, we are concerned with the proposals relating to Britain's external financial situation in the first few post-war years and the kinds of assistance it would seek from the American government and others. These were described in an account written by LePan and taken back to Ottawa by Mackintosh, and later in more detail in the elegant memoir written by LePan and published in his book *Bright Glass of Memory*.[10]

Keynes outlined the three alternative policies, as he saw them, that would be open to the United Kingdom. The first he called "Starvation Corner," by which he meant a policy aimed at a maximum degree of self-sufficiency. Under this policy, full employment would be impossible and the international financial role of London would be destroyed beyond repair. Some extremists in London wanted this as something that would be good in itself, but others, more moderate, felt that the UK might be forced into this easily by the inability to make satisfactory arrangements with others, notably the United States.[11] Elsewhere in his cabinet memorandum, Keynes had written of the need to keep this option just plausible enough to use it as a bargaining tactic.[12]

The second policy Keynes named "Temptation." It was the policy of least resistance. It would be based on large-scale borrowing on easy terms and "it seemed likely that the United States would be only too accommodating in this matter." For this policy, dollar loans of from $5 billion to $8 billion would be necessary to tide the UK over the transitional period. The US probably would be willing to lend at an interest rate of 2 per cent or 2.5 per cent, and to allow very flexible terms of repayment. As a condition of such loans, it would expect the UK to move quickly to make sterling convertible, at least for the current earnings of the sterling area. This would mean gradually converting sterling debt into dollar debt, which would be very difficult for the UK to pay off because of the difficulty of increasing their exports to the US. The US, meanwhile, would become the chief supplier of goods to the sterling area. Sooner or later, this would lead to bankruptcy. "When its meaning became clear, it would seem an outrageous crown and conclusion to all that happened during the War."[13]

In place of this, Keynes proposed "Justice." In his cabinet paper, he described it as approached by "a general reconsideration of the proper burden of the costs of the war," but this underlying aspect he did not mention in the meeting with the Canadians.[14] Rather, he emphasized the implications of it for relations with the sterling area creditors, on the one hand, and the North Americans, on the other. He would ask the United States for a free grant of $3 billion, as a sort of refund or retrospective lend-lease of Britain's wartime purchases in the US before Lend-Lease began – expenditures that built up the arms and munitions industries there. He would ask the US, as well, for a line of credit of $5 billion at one per cent interest. Given this support, Britain then would approach the various members of the sterling area with proposals for dealing with their accumulated balances in London.[15] Not all would be asked to bear the same proportion of the burden; broadly speaking, however, they would: be offered about one-quarter in immediately convertible currency; be asked to cancel about an equal amount; and be asked to fund the remainder of their balances over a long period, with interest at about one per cent per annum, and accept payment of their capital instalments in the form of special shipments of capital goods. These arrangements should be worked out by separate negotiations with each of the countries concerned, but the United Kingdom should make it clear that if any country did not agree to some cancellation, it would not be entitled to any freely convertible balance at all.[16]

The UK would ask South Africa, which had done well financially out of the war and contributed very little, for a contribution of £50 million out of its accumulated gold reserves. In the case of Canada, the Treasury intended to propose, as part of this general settlement: (1) a final Mutual Aid appropriation to take care of the $600 million of book debt resulting from the Air Training plan deficits and the supply of Canadian tanks to the British forces;[17] (2) an option on a loan of $500 million on the same terms as the US line of credit;[18] and (3) the continuation of the existing Canadian dollar loan. This was made in 1942 and was being paid off by sales of Canadian securities.[19]

Keynes stated that these proposed measures still would leave the United Kingdom with between £2 million and £2.5 million of overseas indebtedness. They would be the only country in the Alliance that would end the war with substantial overseas debts as a result of it. He thought that these obligations, however onerous, were supportable. LePan reports that Keynes concluded by saying that if the proposals were accepted, "the sweet breath of justice would be felt to be blowing" by the people of the United Kingdom.[20]

When Keynes invited Canadian comments on his proposals, Mackintosh said that he was pleased to see agreement on the whole agreement between authoritative Canadian and British opinion on the final objective of post-war economic policies. He also was pleased to hear the Treasury's view that the transitional period should be as short as possible, because the Department of Finance in Ottawa had come to the same conclusion.[21] Towers carried on most of the Canadian end of the discussion. He argued first that it might be easier to get a line of credit of $8 billion from the US with elastic terms of repayment than to secure acceptance of the proposals that Keynes had described. Keynes, and more forcefully Sir Wilfrid Eady, replied that under such an elastic arrangement, the United Kingdom would always be at the mercy of the United States financially, coming cap in hand to Washington for concessions. Eady went on to emphasize that without an outright contribution, the UK could not expect to reach a solvent position. In regard to such a contribution, both Mackintosh and Towers said that it would be wise to link this with the highest political objectives, and even with some minor territorial adjustments that, though unimportant in themselves, might be highly gratifying to the United States.

In regard to Canadian policy, Towers emphasized that one of the dangers that would arise for Canada, if the United Kingdom did not succeed in reaching a settlement enabling it to participate in a multilateral system, would be that the country inevitably would be drawn more in the direction of the United States. If a multilateral system could not be arranged, American opinion might be more receptive to closer relationships with Canada. Keynes asked what Canada's attitude would be if proposals such as his were rejected by the US. In that case, would Canada be prepared to accumulate sterling balances in London? Towers said that if the UK proposals seemed reasonable to Canadian opinion (as, in his own opinion, they were), it was likely that Canada would go a long way to make possible the continuance of trade on a large scale with the UK. Special arrangements with the UK, however, could not be thought of as a long-term solution. Ultimately, the difficulties of such an arrangement almost inevitably would cause a closer economic relation between Canada and the United States.

LePan, in his memoir, mentions that at an earlier stage of this meeting's discussion, some "intermittent fencing" was going on between Keynes and Towers over the possibility that Canada would accumulate sterling.[22] It began in reference to Canada's February offer of a loan with realistic and flexible terms of repayment. Keynes asked whether the same objectives could not be reached more efficiently if Canada simply agreed to accumulate sterling, because flexible terms of repayment might have disadvantages. Towers remarked dryly that accumulating sterling might have some disadvantages, too. That Keynes's suggestions of this nature were premeditated is evident in a reference in his cabinet paper to the possibility of an arrangement "by which Canada agreed to hold sterling, receiving in return the freedom of the sterling area, and (in truth) half entering it."[23]

In its splendid setting and the disclosures made, this May meeting showed the respect and trust with which Lord Keynes and the British Treasury officials regarded their friends in Ottawa. Later, Keynes twice sought advice from Towers regarding his negotiations with the Americans. The first time was in Ottawa when he was on his way to Washington. Keynes had received a cautious mandate from the new Labour government to seek "Justice" without asking for it. Keynes talked over with Towers the tactics to be used in the initial presentations to the Americans. Towers was critical of what he was told and suggested a more structured and conditional approach. Keynes expressed interest in these suggestions, saying that he believed he could follow that line. Later, in October, when the Washington negotiations seemed to be stalled, Keynes invited Towers to come down to Washington. Towers complied and assessed the situation quickly. He emphasized the value of a waiver on repayments if circumstances warranted it, an approach Will Clayton had proposed.[24] In the end, this turned out to be very important, despite misgivings in London about its implications.

THE ANGLO–AMERICAN NEGOTIATIONS

Those of us in Ottawa concerned with these international financial arrangements were not aware of the course of the Anglo–American negotiations. Furthermore, apart from Towers, we had no influence on them. A brief account of them here is desirable, however, to clarify the Anglo–Canadian negotiations that followed early in 1946.

Keynes, as head of the Treasury mission, and Lord Halifax, the British ambassador, opened negotiations on the financial agreement in Washington on 13 September, with the Americans headed by Fred Vinson, the new secretary of the Treasury, and Clayton, undersecretary of state for economic affairs. The British had for months examined and re-examined their own international financial situation and how they should present it and proposals for American assistance. They had not studied adequately the American situation, American public opinion, and American political personalities and their views. The British delegation expected far too much. They had not heeded the advice of their own Treasury representatives in Washington, nor the timely warning by the sensible and sympathetic Clayton in London in August. The British public, after rejecting Churchill in favour of the Labour party in the 26 July election, looked forward to some relaxation and new social measures after six years of bearing the burden of war. As for the American public, "in their view, it was high time to end the controls, reduce taxes and return to 'normalcy' ... surely the rest of the world, with the assistance the United States had already given, would now be able to look after itself."[25]

Keynes was, as usual, an optimist. He had persuaded the new Labour government to give him a mandate to seek the course of "Justice," but the ministers did so with caution and a decision that he was not to ask directly for a "grant-in-aid." He and his negotiators (at his request) should be given no discretion on the main issues and what they agreed should be *ad referendum*.[26]

The first few days were spent with the "Top Committee" on a brilliant exposition of the British situation by Keynes, during which he answered many questions and gave detailed facts, estimates, and opinions. The next two meetings were in the Finance Committee, a smaller group, where Keynes outlined the two broad policy alternatives open to the United Kingdom.[27]

The first was to carry on with a minimum of prearranged assistance from the United States or others, and would concentrate trade and payments mainly within the sterling area and countries with which payment agreements were concluded. Such a system, though filled with discrimination, would have considerable advantages and was not without its advocates in the United Kingdom. Keynes, however, emphasized its disadvantages.

The second solution would have as its aim the complete elimination of the discriminatory elements in the sterling area system – insofar as current account transactions were concerned, at any rate. Part of this alternative would involve some settlement of the huge sterling balances owing to India, Egypt, and other countries in the sterling area. Keynes outlined the possibilities that he saw for negotiating the funding into serial long-term obligations of a large part of those balances, the cancellation of another part, and the freeing of a part for immediate use or for conversion into other currencies required to meet trade deficits. The Americans felt that some reduction and settlement of these debts would be required if the US was to provide Britain with substantial assistance. They urged Keynes to be more specific.

Keynes went on to indicate the reasons that the UK required new financial assistance from the US, in addition to the settlement of Lend-Lease. The UK estimated that it would need to be able to draw on a sum of $5 billion in the next three to five years; various contingencies might require another billion dollars.[28]

After these general and non-committal talks, Vinson proposed that they meet in smaller groups. On 26 September, Keynes and Halifax had an important discussion with Vinson and Clayton. The two Americans said that they accepted the British proposals regarding the liberalization of the sterling area and dealing with the sterling balances. They said that to get a proposal approved by Congress, however, they must rely on the advantages to the United States of facilitating and liberalizing international trade, not on comparative past sacrifices or efforts. (So much for "Justice"!) While they seemed to accept the possibility of an amount of $5 billion, they felt sure that a loan with interest was the solution most likely to be acceptable to Congress.[29] A grant-in-aid certainly was impossible.

Bargaining began and continued for more than two months. On 9 October, on instructions, Keynes urged that $2 billion of the assistance be in the form of a grant, but he failed to move Vinson and Clayton. Moreover, the two Americans insisted that an interest-free loan was not practical politically. When asked what they had in mind, Clayton suggested "an untied loan of $5 billion repayable in 50 annual instalments beginning in 5 years with an additional annuity of $50 million p.a. to cover interest."[30] There would be a clause permitting the waiver of interest payments based on a liberal test of the UK's ability to pay. On being informed of this, the chancellor of the exchequer, Hugh Dalton, rejected Clayton's proposal as inequitable. He also disliked the waiver proposal because it involved the possibility of continuous friction. He suggested asking for an interest-free loan repayable over fifty years. When this instruction was put to Clayton and Vinson, on 15 October, they made no progress whatsoever.

From this point on, the negotiations became complex because of the relation of the loan discussions to commercial policy discussions, which the Americans insisted must go along at the same time: the Lend-Lease settlement negotiations, which were complicated but not so difficult, and the various conditions to be attached to the loan, as well as its terms. Regarding these terms, there was great difficulty in getting London to recognize that the Americans would insist on interest because they were sure that Congress would insist on it. The

Americans were prepared to be generous in regard to a formula to waive interest where the facts of the British situation justified it; London was opposed to relying on such a waiver clause, partly for fear of the future friction with the US that it might cause, and partly because its existence or its use might do damage to the financial reputation of London. On the Lend-Lease settlement, the negotiations proceeded well; the amount payable was reasonable and the terms were to be the same as those of the main loan.[31]

There were numerous disputes over the conditions attached to the loan. There were many arguments over the sterling area, the way it operated, the way it should be described officially in documents supporting the loan, and what was to be said in the loan agreement about the intentions of the United Kingdom in settling its sterling liabilities. The delegation had difficulties with its own government, and with the Americans, on all of these.

A final crisis came in late November. From the beginning, in August, Keynes had advised ministers, and believed that they had agreed, that the UK should accept an obligation within a year of the effective date of the loan agreement, to make the current earnings of members of the sterling area convertible into dollars or other currencies to the extent that they were needed for meeting deficits on that member's current accounts. This had been discussed with the Americans and agreed. At the last moment, the chancellor instructed the delegation not to accept this condition. Keynes, by this time, was in a state of almost complete exhaustion. He had wanted at several points to resign but had been dissuaded by his colleagues. He rallied to defend this pledge of convertibility by the end of 1946. Among his several arguments put to London was the certainty that Canada would insist on this convertibility as a condition of its assistance, even if the US did not.

In the end, London gave in on this point, as well as on many others that they had urged on the delegation. The final consent came after the UK government had sent Sir Edward Bridges, the top Treasury official, to lead the delegation in the final meetings, along with Keynes and Halifax. Keynes again had to be talked out of resigning. The Americans, however, were greatly offended by the parachuting in of Bridges at the last moment, for they held Keynes, as well as Halifax, in high esteem, and decided that they would make no concessions to him. Bridges got nothing, and the net result, according to one of the British team, was "exactly as expected, humiliation." London, however, was now convinced they had the best deal possible, and it was quickly approved and signed on 6 December.

The amount of the loan had been determined by US president

Harry Truman at $3.75 billion, splitting the difference between Vinson's and Clayton's judgments as to what they could get Congress to approve. In addition, in a separate agreement, there was a credit, on the same terms, for $650 million in settlement of Lend-Lease supplies; $118 million of it was payment in full for supplies "in the pipeline" when Japan surrendered, and the balance for surplus stocks and property in the UK at the end of the war. This undoubtedly was a good bargain, as Eady later told us in Ottawa. The loan agreement contained the disputed clause (no. 7) undertaking the convertibility into other currencies for current requirements, of sterling received in current transactions by all sterling area countries, not later than one year after the effective date of the agreement.[32] In another clause, both the UK and the US undertook not to discriminate against imports from one another (with minor exceptions) if they imposed restrictions on imports. The rate of interest on the loan was two per cent, applying after 1950, and there was a clause (no. 5) on the waiver of interest in any year when the UK found it necessary, in view of international financial conditions and the level of its reserves, and when the International Monetary Fund certified that on average, over the preceding five years, the UK's international income from exports plus her net receipts from "invisible" current transactions in her balance of payments was less than the average annual cost of imports to the UK in the years from 1936 to 1938, adjusted for changes in the price level. This waiver would not be requested or allowed unless there were proportionate reductions in the aggregate releases of sterling balances held by the sterling area creditors of the UK before the effective date of the agreement. In clause 10 of the text of the agreement, the UK declared its intention to make agreements with the countries concerned to settle the disposition of accumulated sterling balances in three categories of treatment – one part to be released and made convertible into other currencies at once, another part to be similarly released by instalments after 1950, and a third category of balances to be "adjusted" as a contribution to the settlement of war and post-war indebtedness.

One sub-clause of the agreement (6.ii) was of direct relevance to Canada and came as a complete surprise to us in Ottawa. It said that the UK would not arrange any long-term loans from governments within the British Commonwealth before the end of 1951 on terms more favourable to the lender than the terms of this line of credit. This, of course, would set these US terms as the upper limit for our negotiations with the UK. The surprise caused serious resentment in Ottawa. Canadian officials other than Towers had been informed rather meagerly of the British–American negotiations. Through various British officials, Pearson and others in the Canadian legation in

Washington learned something, from time to time, about the course of the negotiations, but nothing of the difficulties between the delegation and London.

Immediately after the US agreement had been signed and announced, several of the senior British officials came to Ottawa for meetings at which they explained the US loan agreement and answered questions about it. The main meeting was with Ilsley and senior Canadian officials on Saturday, 8 December. Sir Edward Bridges was there but said very little. Brand gave a rather summary account of the agreement, supported by Harmer of the Treasury. Brand emphasized that the US offered the waiver of interest but that its working out took much time. Sir Percival Leishing of the Board of Trade spoke about the trade discussions and the US proposals for an International Trade Organization with suitable rules. The UK had associated itself with this proposal, in a general way, in a public statement. Much of the discussion in this field concerned quantitative restrictions on imports, which were foreseen as the major problem of the transition period. Ilsley asked a few questions. In response, Brand explained that the US was giving the UK more favourable credit terms than others got because of its role in the war, its loss of overseas assets, and the time it would need to demobilize and organize for exporting, and also because the US was interested in having the UK co-operate in creating the international trade system that the US wanted.

On Sunday, there was a more technical discussion of the loan agreement and its implications between the British officials and Mackintosh, Rasminsky, and me. (Clark was still absent on sick leave.) Later in this meeting, Mackintosh raised some questions relating to the prospective UK and sterling area balance of payments with Canada and its relation to a Canadian loan. He asked if they felt that the Canadian loan should be approached from the point of view of that deficit or as part of the whole picture. Harmer, who did most of the speaking for Britain in that meeting, said that they hoped it would be approached as part of the whole, particularly as that would help with convertibility. It would also help in Congress. They would like to have the Canadian loan untied, "except statistically"; in fact, it would not involve other currencies, but the UK should be able to sell Canadian dollars for sterling. Rasminsky noted the exchange control problems that this would raise. He also asked if Canada did not prefer to lend directly to other sterling area countries, to which Harmer replied that the UK would like to borrow enough itself to cover the sterling area needs. My notes record the remark, "Possibly we would agree from time to time on the rate of release," but do not show who said this.[33] In any case, that was not settled until 1949.

There was a second Sunday meeting, at which Robertson, Mackenzie, and Mackintosh discussed trade negotiations with Leishing, Bridges, Brand, and Harmer. This discussion related chiefly to whether, when, and where there should be Commonwealth discussions, or UK–Canadian discussions, on the US trade proposals. Mackenzie used the occasion to press for an interim trade arrangement to permit at least token Canadian exports to the British market. Leishing showed a reluctance to agree to such discussions, and Bridges emphasized the difficulty of taking any action until after the British loan agreement was approved by the US Congress.[34]

THE EADY DELEGATION TO OTTAWA

By late January, the Treasury in the United Kingdom was ready to send a delegation to Ottawa to negotiate a large, long-term loan from Canada to supplement the American loan, which had begun its long passage in Congress. Keynes had decided that he could not come, and the chancellor of the exchequer decided that Sir Wilfrid Eady, joint second secretary to the Treasury (in charge of overseas finance), and C.F. Cobbold, deputy governor of the Bank of England, should head up a small delegation, which would include A.T.K. Grant and Edgar Jones of the Treasury, and Bridge of the Bank, along with secretarial staff.

Eady and Cobbold had been highly critical of the Anglo-American agreement and its negotiation. Douglas LePan, of the staff of the Canadian High Commission, relayed some information to Ottawa on their attitudes and aptitudes, concluding with the sentence: "From what I have said, you will gather that, in my view, it is the less tractable, and I might almost say less sensible team of advisers which is going out to Ottawa."[35] The delegation was intended not only to negotiate a loan but also to settle a wide variety of outstanding claims and counter-claims arising out of the war. This would include some rather dubious and ill-defined claims and one major item: the combined deficits in the agreed on British share of the costs of the 1939, and later the June 1942 British Commonwealth Air Training Plans, which together amounted to $425 million. (See chapter 3.)

The delegation arrived by air at Dorval on Friday, 1 February. Eady and Cobbold made a side trip for a few days' work in Washington, while the rest of the group proceeded directly to Ottawa to meet with Canadian officials on preliminary statistical work before Eady and Cobbold met with the Canadian ministers on 11 February. There was a large preparatory meeting of Canadian officials on 4 February with these other members of the delegation, who were joined on the British side by Gordon Munro and Richard Bell, the Treasury representatives on the staff of the UK high commissioner.[36] We planned the agenda for meetings that week on the facts and figures to be used in the principal discussions the following week, including balance of payments forecasts, details of the status of the 1942 loan, and other figures relating to the international financial position of the United Kingdom. Most of our time at that meeting, and at subsequent meetings that week, was spent assembling and discussing items and categories of items to be taken into account in the settlement of claims and counterclaims. (These are recounted later in this chapter.)

Shortly before Eady and Cobbold arrived, the prime minister held a preparatory meeting with Ilsley, C.D. Howe, and Louis St Laurent, together with three senior officials: Clark, Robertson, and Towers. King's account of this meeting does not indicate that they reached any conclusion, other than that he would like to be present at the main discussions, but not as chairman.[37]

THE BRITISH–CANADIAN LOAN NEGOTIATIONS

The negotiation of the Canadian loan to Britain began on 11 February and the agreement was signed and published on 6 March (along with a separate agreement on the settlement of war claims). This was less than thirty per cent of the time taken for the British–American negotiations. It was possible to reach an agreement like this more quickly in Ottawa for a variety of reasons. Canadian ministers and officials already knew much about the British situation from earlier discussions and reports. The US already had made the ruling on the issues of sterling convertibility and trade policy that were important to us. We had no need or desire to get into the question of what the British should do about their sterling balance obligations. A year earlier, the Canadian government had decided in principle that it was prepared to make a large post-war loan to the UK with a postponement of payments due, under some specified conditions. From the first, we were willing that the loan should be about the size that the British requested in their initial presentation.

On the other hand, we faced some problems that had not come up with the Americans. We were sensitive about the large holdings of Canadian securities in British hands; Canada was a very large international debtor and conscious of it. Should we be lending on easy, non-commercial terms when we owed so much at market rates? We already had outstanding a large non–interest bearing loan to Britain that was negotiated in the midst of the war as part of a package that included the billion-dollar gift, and we were not disposed to give it up. We also had some $425 million of well-established British obligations owing to us under the British Commonwealth Air Training Plan agreements of 1939 and 1942, in which we already had paid our agreed on share. On the other hand, while most Canadians were more prepared than the Americans to recognize British requests for "Justice," Canada had a large French-Canadian minority, including a large proportion of the members of Parliament making up the government's rather slim majority. The French-Canadians did not share the majority's sympathy for the British, whom they saw as a Great Power that had taken Canada into two European wars and that now was striving to remain a Great Power when it could not afford to be one. These French-Canadians had to be persuaded that help to Britain was based on Canadian interests in the future, rather than on gratitude for past action. It was for this reason that St Laurent, minister of justice and future prime minister – a man of great intelligence and integrity, but hard of head as well – took a prominent part in the negotiations.

The opening phase of the negotiation consisted of two-and-a-half days of discussions between Eady and Cobbold, on the one hand, and the ministers designated to meet with them, on the other, with Ilsley as chairman and including St Laurent and James Gardiner; the prime minister was also there as "an observer."[38] Canadian officials present included Clark, Towers, Robertson, and Mackenzie, with several others, of whom I was one. Malcolm MacDonald, the UK high commissioner, was also present, as well as the other members of the delegation listed above.

The first day – Monday, 11 February – was taken up mainly with long expositions by Eady, and later Cobbold, of the British predicament, along with its statistical foreground and historical background. In essence, the British had so reduced their export trade because of war requirements for men and production, had accumulated so much short-term debt to the members of the sterling area, as well as some debts to other countries, and had had to dispose of so much of their overseas assets, that they would have great difficulty getting through the next few years without large-scale assistance from Canada, as well as from the United States. Given such help, they could restore their trade on a multilateral basis, make sterling a convertible currency at an early date, and have a chance to make some kind of mutually acceptable settlement of their huge liquid liabilities to India, Egypt, Ireland, Palestine, the Crown Colonies, and other countries in the sterling area. Without such help, they would be forced into severe trade and currency restrictions and discrimination, perhaps of the extreme type that Hjalmar Schacht had practised successfully in Germany during the 1930s. They had been promised a good deal of help from the US government but it was not sufficient to meet their needs.

The US agreement had just been sent to Congress for approval, where it was to have a very long and difficult passage. Canada was expected to provide proportionately more assistance and on more generous terms, and to do so before the decision of Congress was reached on the US agreement. Little did we realize in February that it was only the growing fear of Russian hostility that would get the US loan through the Congress, months later.

Eady described the expected balance of payments deficits of Britain and the sterling area as a whole in 1946, and the prospects for 1947 and 1948. The British were hoping for equilibrium by 1949, and a surplus by 1950. They were bound by the US agreement to make sterling convertible within one year of the effective date of that agreement (which turned out to be 15 July). They knew that Canada wanted sterling convertibility, and they would need Canadian help, as well as American, to achieve it. Britain would have to pay its debts later, including those to the sterling area, out of the proceeds of its exports. Eady also spoke of the large scale of British government expenditure overseas, most of it being military expenditures and some for relief. He referred to Britain's responsibilities for maintaining law and order, including the occupation of Germany. Unless Britain was financially strong, it would not be possible for her to be strong in her external relations. Eady ended up by requesting, on behalf of the British government, a loan of $1.25 billion, interest free. As the meeting was about to adjourn for the morning, King said that he had been much impressed by the presentation, which reminded him of Lord Curzon's review of foreign affairs at the Imperial Council of 1923. He also said (according to my notes): "We recognize the UK's sacrifice and will go as far as we can [to help]."[39]

In the afternoon, Cobbold spoke, almost lovingly, of the sterling area, its banking origins and subsequent evolution, its vital role in the war during foreign exchange control, and its immediate problems. One of its defects, however, was that it had made it too easy to accumulate enormous UK indebtedness to various members of the area. Now, its central liquid reserves (gold and dollars) had been restored to a level that was reasonably satisfactory, if means for financing the expected deficits could be arranged. He and Eady then answered numerous questions. Several issues were opened up. St Laurent wanted further consideration given to the relation of UK holdings of Canadian securities to the form and terms of a loan. Ilsley raised and discussed the problem that would arise if Canada approved a loan and the US Congress then rejected the US loan agreement. Towers asked what the justification was for Canada to finance, on these special terms, the needs of the other members of the sterling area who were not in the special position of the UK. These questions were held over to be dealt with later.

When the discussions resumed on Tuesday, Cobbold responded to questions asked the previous day by giving figures for UK holdings of US and Canadian securities. The total value of British holdings of Canadian-dollar securities was estimated at $770 million and of Canadian securities denominated in sterling, $480 million, along with direct investments valued between $200 million and $300 million. The aggregate amounted to about $1.5 billion Canadian. Total holdings in the US were estimated at $875 million US. It was not feasible at that time for the British to estimate meaningful market values outside North America, but they estimated the total net annual income from all countries at about $390 million US, of which $44 million was from Canada. St Laurent then asked whether it would be possible to arrange that Canada would get the returns payable to UK holders of Canadian assets – equivalent to $44 million US per year, by Cobbold's figures – and retain it as a return on the two outstanding debts: the 1942 loan and the British Commonwealth Air Training Plan deficits, plus a new loan to Britain equal to the difference between the amount of these debts and the roughly $1.5 billion value of the British-owned assets in Canada. As the assets were sold or redeemed by their British owners, the debts would be paid off. The British government, meanwhile, would pay the holders of the securities amounts in sterling equivalent to the interest, dividends, or profits earned by the investments.

This suggestion came as something of a shock to the British delegation and a surprise to the Canadian officials. It led to a very spirited and frank discussion on both the economics and the equity of that proposal, and of Eady's request of the day before. The British obviously were most anxious that the terms on which they settled with Canada the disposition of the 1942 loan and the British Commonwealth Air Training Plan debt should not prejudice their ability to get a favourable settlement of their vast sterling obligations incurred during the course of the war.

One important problem was settled in the discussions that day. Eady said that he thought the UK government should not be asked to accept a clause saying that the Canadian loan agreement was contingent on congressional approval of the US loan. The government could accept a general consultation clause, however, such as there was in the US agreement. This would provide that either government should be entitled to approach the other for a reconsideration of any provisions of the agreement if, in its opinion, the prevailing conditions of international exchange justified such reconsideration. They also would be prepared to agree, on the record, that the failure of Congress to approve the US loan would make it necessary to consult under that clause. Ilsley asked whether the UK delegation would be prepared to state this publicly. When Eady confirmed that they would, it was decided that the matter would be handled in this way.

At the morning meeting on Wednesday, 13 February, Eady made a lengthy, considered reply to Louis St Laurent's personal suggestion of the day before concerning the use of British-held Canadian securities. Eady spoke from an *aide-mémoire*, which he left with us.[40] It argued that the most direct effect of this arrangement would be to reduce, by some $55 million, the gross annual income of Canadian dollars that otherwise would be available to pay for British imports from Canada and thus would worsen the difficulties already foreseen on both sides in financing this trade in the following years. Second, the arrangement would prejudice UK arrangements and negotiations with other creditors very seriously. It would require renegotiation of the US credit because it would give better terms to the lender than the Americans had given. It would be a very dangerous precedent in negotiating the tolerable settlement of debts owed to countries in the sterling area. Finally, and most importantly, Eady's document argued, the arrangement would set back rather seriously, both directly and indirectly, the commonly shared approach of Britain and Canada to post-war international trade and financial policy.

Later in this meeting, Clark raised again the question of whether Canada should lend directly to other members of the sterling area on commercial terms. Cobbold replied that these countries had the right to use sterling at that time and would have it under the Bretton Woods agreement and under the convertibility arrangements being planned. Consequently, Australia, for example, was not likely to find it to her advantage to make separate arrangements with Canada. This question came up later in the negotiations. In the end, Canada did not wish to restrict the amount of credit to the UK in order to lend to other parts of the sterling area instead.

That same day, immediately after the end of these initial meetings with the British delegation, cabinet gave its first attention to what had been raised. Ilsley reported on the substance of the discussions. St Laurent was satisfied with the answer that he had received to his suggestion and questions about UK holdings of Canadian securities. King was much impressed with the seriousness and sadness of a situation that had forced "a great world power, like Britain, [to be] really suppliant for help to restore its place as a producing and manufacturing exporting country."[41] There was some discussion of possible propositions that might be put to the British delegates, which were to be thought over by ministers and the experts within the next day or two.

Clark lost no time in following up this discussion. He saw Eady the next morning, 14 February, and told him that the government would not press the suggestion made by St Laurent. On the other hand, the government would not accept the proposal that Eady had put forward on Monday. The ministers' view seemed to be that Clark and Eady should have a frank talk to see whether they could narrow the area of disagreement. Clark put forward two possibilities for discussion. One was to wipe the slate clean of war debt, including the 1942 loan and the British Commonwealth Air Training Plan deficits. In addition, the Canadian government would be prepared to buy from the UK all of its Canadian securities. This complete cancellation of war debt would help them with their negotiations with the sterling area countries. The alternative proposal would be a credit for their new cash requirements on the same terms as the US loan, a negative pledge of their Canadian securities against the whole debt, and continued elimination of interest on the 1942 debt. An undertaking would be required, however, to see that the proceeds of sales and redemptions of their securities would amount to $100 million a year.

Eady felt that neither of these proposals would be acceptable to his government. For several reasons, he objected strongly to the repatriation of securities. He also expressed the hope that the BCATP debts could be cancelled. Clark reported: "I expressed great surprise [and] pointed out that the two sides were further apart than even I had realized."[42] The two agreed, however, to talk the matter over with their colleagues and meet again that afternoon. British records show that Towers and Clark put forward the first alternative again that afternoon, but neither showed enthusiasm. Eady reported to the Treasury: "In spite of the great attraction of complete cancellation, we felt bound to reject this both on its merits and because of its obvious and immediate reaction in Congress."

Eady and his delegation saw Ilsley on Friday 15 February and again urged the case for a non-interest bearing loan, this time on the grounds of equity. Eady said: "If it is felt necessary to insist on the same terms as in the Washington agreement, a great constructive opportunity will have been missed." He went on to say: "If it is proposed that U.K. investments in Canada have to be sold to finance our purchases of food, etc., in Canada, we are certain that such a proposal would be rejected by public opinion of all kinds in the U.K. It would tear up established associations, and both politically and commercially this would be very grave."[43]

Eady said that the solution for which UK ministers hoped would be that claims and counterclaims at 28 February would be cancelled, with the exception of the 1942 loan, which would be merged into a new loan with $1.25 billion of new money, to be repayable in fifty annual instalments, beginning in December 1951, and free of interest. Eady went on to argue, on economic and philosophical grounds, the case for such a solution. He concluded by referring to the defence and security burdens of the UK and its important role in preventing political dangers in Europe, saying: "Our policy in such matters can only be hesitant and incomplete if all the time we are haunted by anxieties over our overseas financial position."

At Ilsley's request, Eady put his case into writing. He sent the letter to Ilsley on 16 February. In it he said that the British would be willing to leave the 1942 loan separate and interest-free, and that it should be repaid by the proceeds of sales or redemptions of UK securities, provided that sales of securities by UK residents for the purpose of switching into other Canadian securities should not require repayment of the loan. He also referred in his letter to Ilsley's asking if they could suggest any action on their part that: (a) would hold out prospects of immediate benefit to Canadian manufacturing interests, and (b) make it plain that they would follow up the lead given by Canada and expect their other creditors to recognize an obligation to assist in the early improvement of financial and lending conditions. Regarding (a), Eady said that they could consider the plans for manufactured imports that had been under discussion between M.W. Mackenzie and the UK Board of Trade if the Canadian government thought that it would be helpful. (This was the token import plan.) Regarding (b), he said that he had no doubt that if the agreement were on the lines suggested, the chancellor of the exchequer would announce in parliament "the significance which the U.K. government attached to the agreement, both in regard to the trade interests of Canada and also to the pattern that the U.K. government would expect to arrange in its negotiations with its sterling creditors."

This was the first counter proposal from the UK after the initial discussions and the arguments in support of it. Cabinet was to consider it on Monday the 18th. Ilsley sent a copy of the letter and the enclosed memorandum to the prime minister, who read it carefully on Sunday. It made King indignant. He spoke strongly about it in cabinet on Monday, reading parts of it and saying: "They must take us for a lot of infants and children to present a document of that kind to a government."[44]

St Laurent was not present and King insisted that no final agreement be reached without the whole cabinet having a chance to discuss the matter fully. It was understood, he said, that there was to be no interest-free loan. Indeed, he had come to feel that they should take the position that they could not get a loan through the Canadian Parliament on terms less favourable than those of the US agreement.

Later that day, Towers came to see the prime minister. Speaking from notes and aware of the discussions of the previous week, Towers expressed his view that even with the assistance of the US loan, the international financial situation of the UK was very serious and would not enable the British to follow a reasonably expansionary economic policy such as we hoped. He urged on the prime minister, therefore, the view that the Canadian loan be non–interest bearing and that the deficits of the BCATP be written off. The prime minister recorded in his diary: "I confess that Towers' statement did not impress me. What did impress me was that as Governor of the Bank of Canada he was really under the influence of the large financial banking world. It was clear he was influenced by their environment."[45]

The next evening, Tuesday, King was in a friendlier mood when he hosted a government dinner for the delegation. He spoke separately, however, to each of Eady, Cobbold, and Brand, giving them to understand that, in contrast to their memorandum, they could not adopt a "take it or leave it" attitude.

The next morning, Ilsley, St Laurent, Towers, Clark, Robertson, and I met again with the senior five in the British delegation.[46] Ilsley told them that an interest-free loan was out of the question. St Laurent proposed a new loan on which the interest would be three per cent payable in sterling, which would be held or invested in the UK. This might, he thought, require some consultation with the US. This rate, however, would mean no sacrifice to Canadian taxpayers, as that was Canada's borrowing rate. Eady immediately said that the US would disagree, even if the waiver of interest was included. The American people did not understand the transfer problem. He said that their response would be: "No, it is three percent, not two percent, and you are pulling a fast one." He went on to speak about the burden on the British taxpayers and consumers. If Britain was really driven to it, they could produce much more food at home, at higher cost, but saving the foreign exchange. Ilsley then raised an alternative that I had suggested: a variable interest rate, dependent on British export earnings, with a ceiling of more than two per cent. Eady said it would not be practical to run the top figure above this rate; it, too, would start the argument again in the US.

Eady was quick to see an opening here, however. He suggested that we should accept the problem with the taxpayers regarding the new loan, and take it on the US terms, but wipe the slate clean on the debts incurred during the war, which Canada had already financed. St Laurent quickly responded that there was a substantial difference between the war debts since the 1942 loan and that loan itself. It had been tied up with the package that included the billion-dollar gift and was a substitution for the further repatriation of securities. He did not see how Canada could write off that loan.

This set off a long and free-ranging discussion of the relative external indebtedness of Canada and the UK, the prospects for some writing-down of the sterling debts, and the effects of various possible actions on future trade and convertibility. St Laurent said: "Canadians don't want for all time to be a debtor country." Brand said that future trade was what was really important. Eady professed fear of resentment in the UK against North America and its effects on policies. The high commissioner raised some political arguments, including the just-disclosed Igor Gouzenko revelations about Russian espionage in Canada, which illustrated the political dangers. Supporting the UK and Western Europe would help keep Russia in check. After this long discussion, Ilsley suggested that the Canadian government should make a specific proposal now. He would try to get one ready for cabinet to consider on Thursday.

That afternoon, Ilsley met with Clark and, probably, other officials. The basis of a compromise had begun to emerge. Both Eady and St Laurent now seemed prepared to agree to a new loan on the US terms, but Eady required some writing-off of war debts, while the Canadians were unwilling to write off the 1942 loan or meld it in with the new loan. Clearly, the possibility of compromise hinged on cancelling the $425 million of BCATP debts. This was the package that Ilsley proposed. It was recorded, with supporting arguments, in a memorandum dated 21 February, probably written by Clark, and a one-page summary table suitable for discussion at cabinet.[47]

Ilsley did not succeed in getting cabinet agreement to his proposal at a meeting on 21 February. St Laurent opposed it on two points. One was acceptable to Ilsley: that the 1942 loan should continue interest-free only until December 1951, when its future would be discussed. The second was much more difficult: to ask for payment of the BCATP debts in sterling, to be invested by Canada in Britain. The cabinet conclusion said that the sterling received for the BCATP debts would be settled on a basis not less favourable than that accepted by other Allied sterling creditors.

St Laurent's new proposal was to be given to the British delegation by Ilsley on Friday morning. When he received it, Eady said that he thought the package would be regarded in London as "wholly unacceptable." Ilsley suggested that it be discussed later that day, 22 February, with the other ministers. This was quickly arranged, and St Laurent and the prime minister were there with Ilsley. This meeting was the climax of the negotiations, and quite unpleasant. The meeting began with Eady on the offensive. He said that his government had not expected to be asked for two per cent interest from the United States and expected it even less from Canada. They had hoped, in both cases, for an agreement for which they would not need to apologize. That was also the reason for asking for cancellation of the war debts. What Eady seemed to miss was that at no time did the Canadians feel that full cancellation was possible. When Ilsley referred to cabinet's proposal to accept payment of the BCATP debt in sterling, to be held for possible cancellation later, Eady rounded on him, arguing that it was hard to compare the BCATP debt with debts owed to members of the sterling area. In the first place, they were owed mainly to countries who were not in the war. In the second place, the government of the United Kingdom would have to defer payment of them and to scale them down. That would be very difficult politically. His government would be disturbed if the result of such action had to satisfy the government of Canada as well. Canada's role would not be helpful and would be misjudged. Eady went on to say that the proposal made to the delegation would leave the British facing substantial war debts: $560 million in the old loan of 1942, $425 million for the BCATP deficits, and accrued miscellaneous liabilities, say, $150 million on balance. This would add up to more than $1.1 billion in all, nearly the amount of the new loan. This could be represented as more onerous in concept than the US deal. That would not be a fair comparison, Eady conceded, but it could be made.

The British recognized that we must be able to justify our loan agreement to Parliament, Eady said. It was clearly much to Canada's advantage, however, for the pound to be sterling convertible and for the United Kingdom to be economically and politically strong. He thought that one should not talk in terms of "being had for a sucker."

Eady then asked Ilsley to put the Canadian proposal briefly in writing, so that the delegation could transmit it to their government. He saw not the slightest prospect that their government would accept it as a basis for agreement. The delegation had not reported what they had been told that morning. Eady was asking Cobbold to fly back to London to see the chancellor of the exchequer and tell him frankly what had happened. He did not want to take the risk of a telegram.

MacDonald then expressed his agreement with Eady's appraisal of the situation. He saw no chance that his government would approve an agreement based on the Canadian proposal, which was harder than the US agreement. When Ilsley asked how it was harder, MacDonald said that it continued the war debt of 1942 and left unsettled the BCATP deficits. Then the argument went back and forth. St Laurent said that the Reconstruction Finance Corporation loan in the United States was harder than the 1942 Canadian loan because interest was payable on the RFC loan right from the beginning. The ministers went on to ask if the delegation thought that Canada should do more than the United States. Eady answered in the affirmative, saying that relations with Canada were better than those with the US. Brand then said that the delegation was asking that Canada take a lead that others would follow, to which Ilsley ruefully responded: "I wish we could be sure that any would follow," meaning the sterling area creditors.[48] Eady quickly observed that full cancellation by Canada would serve as an example, say, to India.

My notes, written at the time, indicate that at this point, King asked Cobbold to explain to the chancellor of the exchequer on his return to London the difficulties of which he as prime minister must beware in getting a loan agreement through Parliament.[49] King said that the reasons for the actions proposed were comprehensible to financial experts like those in the meeting, but much less apparent to members of Parliament. The delegation was asking for a cushion to ease the way of the government of the UK. King said that he needed a cushion, too. In the past, Canadian governments had had some difficulties getting their measures through Parliament. He mentioned Laurier's difficulty with reciprocity, when the difficulties were exaggerated and the government was defeated. He recalled the more recent opposition to Ilsley's proposal about seamless steel tubes, which forced him to withdraw it. The government's majority was now too slim; it could not depend on the Tories to get measures through. King said that all in all, including on federal–provincial relations, he had not had an easy time, and he would like the chancellor and Prime Minister Attlee to be aware of this.

King writes on at length about this meeting in his diary.[50] In particular, he refers to Eady's not wanting to put his ministers in a position where they were having to apologize for bringing on the measure and risking a change of public opinion against Canada. King writes that he "felt incensed at his talking of apology in reference to what Canada was ready to do, on top of all we had done." King also writes: "Malcolm MacDonald unfortunately overplayed his hand today."[51]

Toward the end of this tense discussion, Eady again asked that the Canadian proposal be put briefly in writing so that he could transmit it to London, where Cobbold would be able to fill in the background. Ilsley, who had kept his cool and his determination to get an agreement, said that this was difficult to do immediately; it was only on the previous day that the government had made a proposal, to which the delegation had taken strong exception. He would want to discuss the subject again with cabinet on Monday before it could be put it in writing.[52]

On Saturday, MacDonald came to see the prime minister and

seemed to realize that he had made a bad mistake the previous day. King recounts in his diary the lecture he gave to the very worried high commissioner, who was going back to report to ministers in London. It must have been a great ordeal for MacDonald, and a great release for King's pent-up emotions. Indeed, his account of it indicates that toward the end, he was thinking about concessions.[53] MacDonald, on his side, made clear to King that the real difficulty was being asked to pay the BCATP debts. The high commissioner, however, was not too discouraged to act the host that night for a long, private talk with his British colleagues and senior Canadian officials, including Clark, Heeney, Robertson, Mackenzie, and Rasminsky. Eady reported to London later: "No two of them agreed on what were the crucial issues and who were decisive influences."[54]

During the weekend, Ilsley wrote a memorandum for himself about the climactic meeting on Friday, the problem facing him and the government, and the pros and cons of various courses of action. He believed that the British government would turn down what they had been offered on Friday. He believed that if that happened, the Canadian government would decide to make them a better offer. He thought that it was far better to modify the offer now than later. It might be that the British would reject the proposal that he had proposed to cabinet on Thursday, which included the cancellation of the BCATP debts, though he doubted so. The government should revert to that now, in his view. He was convinced that the British were not just bargaining hard but were deeply disturbed by the proposals and would feel a deep sense of injury if those were pressed. The proposal that he made to the government on Thursday could be defended before Parliament and the public for the reasons given in the memorandum of 21 February.

His judgment was good. His proposal was accepted, as the cabinet conclusion for 25 February tersely records. King's account in his diary of the meeting, as recounted by Pickersgill, indicates that it took three hours to settle the matter, with the course of the discussion diverted and delayed by consideration of an alternative plan for a shorter-term, non–interest bearing loan, worked out on Sunday by St Laurent and Clark.[55] Ilsley and Clark (who was present for the cabinet discussion) thought there was some validity to the British argument that the offer discussed with them on Friday was a harder bargain for them than the American agreement. King's entry recounts further argument and indicates that he proposed writing off the BCATP debt, while retaining the other terms put forward to the British following the last cabinet. This was Ilsley's plan.

Immediately after the cabinet meeting, Clark informed Eady of the decision, which he promptly cabled to London. He advised the Treasury that they probably could not get either an interest-free or a one per cent loan, and that it was better to strike while the iron was hot. This, however, was not enough to end the matter. Just as they were wanting to make one last try with Bridges in Washington, the British ministers, after hearing from Cobbold and MacDonald, instructed Eady to make one last effort to get a new credit of $1.75 billion at one per cent, which would be used in part to pay off the 1942 loan. Eady did this immediately, but cabled back to London that the reactions of Ilsley and Clark were "exceeding unfavourable." On the 28th, the chancellor of the exchequer agreed to the Canadian proposal and authorized Eady to settle it. He did so by giving an *aide-mémoire* to Ilsley.[56]

A few details remained to be drafted to complete the loan agreement. It had been understood from the beginning that there would be a simple reciprocal clause relating to trade and exchange arrangements. We quickly accepted a good draft prepared by the British delegation for an Article 5 in which, in respect of (a) the operation of exchange controls and arrangements and (b) the quantitative import restrictions that each government would grant to the residents and products of the other, treatment not less favourable than that provided for in any instrument of agreement with the government of any other country signed prior to the date of this agreement. This provided Canada with the benefits in these trade and exchange fields equivalent to those provided in the Anglo–American agreement, whether or not it was approved by Congress.

Agreement was also reached on an exchange of letters at the time of signing the agreement, which dealt with the situation that would arise if Congress did not approve the Anglo–American agreement. It was decided that this would constitute, in the wording of Article 8 of our Canadian agreement, "a major change in the international financial situation which materially alters the prospective benefits and obligations flowing from our agreement." The letter stated that the two governments then would consider what changes should be made in our agreement, subject to such legislative approval as might be necessary. Articles 5, 6, and 7 of our agreement would not be implemented until it was known whether Congress had approved the American agreement.

At this meeting on 4 March, when the texts of these letters were worked out, there was also, according to my pencilled notes, an inconclusive discussion on the rate of drawing on the loan. There was no trouble with Parliament. Ilsley spoke at length on the agreement and its background, in moving the resolution to precede the bill to implement it on 11 April. His whole explanation of and argument for the agreement was in terms of economics: trade and international payments, past and future. There was no appeal to sentiment, to justice in sharing the burden, or to Imperial ties. There did not need to be. First, the economic arguments were conclusive, and second, the pro-British feeling of many members, and of many Canadians, was a fact of life that did not need to be spelled out at some risk of offending others. The agreement and the legislation to implement it were properly debated, and many questions were asked and answered, but the resolution and then the bill were passed without a vote until the final stage, when it passed by a vote of 167 to 6. Voting against were only a handful of Quebec nationalists, plus Pouliot, a maverick Liberal who was a perennial critic of the Department of Finance. St Laurent did not speak on the legislation, nor did he need to. He supported the proposal behind the scenes, where it mattered most. He, as well as Ilsley, had made the loan possible and deserved the credit.

It was a very different story in Washington. The Anglo–American agreement ran into serious opposition in both the House of Representatives and the Senate. It passed the crucial decision in the Senate – defeat of a "spoiling" amendment to require the British to transfer bases in the Western Hemisphere to the United States, which the British would not accept – by a vote of only 45 to 40, after the very influential Republican senator Arthur Vandenberg had announced in the Senate that he had decided to switch his position and support the loan. Vandenberg told his fellow senators: "If we do not lead, some other great and powerful nation will capitalize on our failure and we shall pay the price of our default."[57] It was the Russian menace, just becoming apparent, and not the justice of the British need or the broad economic arguments, that persuaded Congress to approve the loan. This enabled the Canadian agreement to come into full effect on 15 July 1946.

THE SETTLEMENT OF WAR CLAIMS

The UK Treasury Mission, sent out to negotiate the loan, had been instructed also to make a comprehensive settlement with the Canadian government of war claims and counterclaims arising on or after 3 September 1939 and prior to 1 March 1946, with regard to supplies, services, facilities, and accommodation delivered or furnished during that period. These claims involved an enormous amount of detailed records, information, and estimates, much of which had not been assembled and systematically appraised. For this reason, I had suggested that we should: assemble and discuss what we could during the weeks in which the Eady mission was to be in Ottawa; settle the principles on which we should make the settlement; but leave the working out of the amounts to be completed "during the ensuing months."[58] Others on our side, including Ilsley, felt that we should make a determined effort to reach a settlement, and we did. I was the Canadian official most familiar with the nature and wide variety of these claims and counter-claims, and I knew whose judgment I could trust and where to get the available information quickly.

The UK claims were mainly large and diverse claims on the Canadian army and air force, arising out of supplies and services provided to them in the UK and in operations in Europe. The UK also had large but ill-defined claims on the Department of Munitions and Supply, arising out of contracts that the UK had placed with that department up to mid-1943 before the Mutual Aid Board took over the contracts. Scores of accountants were working on these Munitions and Supply accounts, but their results would not be in finished form for many months. The main Canadian claim on the UK was for food and other items supplied to or being produced for the UK after the official end of hostilities (and Mutual Aid) on 1 September 1945.

The British claims with regard to the Canadian army and air force were complicated by the changes we had introduced in August 1944 in order to take account of training and other services that our forces had been receiving gratis before that, and also to revise substantially the "capitation rates" that the Canadian Department of National Defence paid to the British War Office regarding supplies, arms, munitions, and services received by the Canadian army, both in the United Kingdom and on the battlefields in Europe. Such capitation rates had to be based on estimates of what would be required in various types of operations. The Canadian deputy minister responsible, a canny Scot, had not been able to reach agreement with the War Office during 1944 or 1945 and, in the end, this major item had to be settled by the minister of finance himself.

Two other large transactions illustrate the conceptual or policy problems involved. One was the transfer to the British army of a large number of Ram tanks, produced in Canada and shipped to the UK for use by the Canadian army. It was decided, however, that the Canadians should be equipped with the best US Sherman tanks, which the American and British forces would be using in France. The Rams, therefore, were turned over to the British army, which used them for training. Some were recovered for a time by the Canadians and the turrets were removed so that they could be used as armoured troop carriers in battle in Normandy. These tanks, with spares, had cost Canada about $58 million. What, if anything, should we include in our claims settlement for them? Ilsley and St Laurent were willing to drop this claim. In the end, we set this very dubious claim off against another rather dubious claim by the UK that we had been unable to define and estimate.

A second example was very different in nature. It had to do with a large order of railway rolling stock being produced in Canada for the Indian state railway, which needed it urgently to replace equipment worn out by excessive use in war. The Mutual Aid Board had refused to approve this order for Mutual Aid during the war, or to have the British pay for it during the war from their Cash Receipts Account, as that would mean something else would have to be given to the UK as aid. Temporarily, we were financing it after the end of the war on short-term credits. The British insisted on its being included specifically in the settlement agreement, with the UK free to sell it to India.

At our first meeting of officials on 4 February, before Eady's arrival, we drew up lists of the main categories of claims that we would have to discuss: sixteen for the army; eight for the air force; and twelve for Munitions and Supply, and the Mutual Aid Board and its administration.[59] In addition, we arranged to get an up-to-date forecast of the interim credits to the UK outstanding as at 28 February, which was the terminal date for claims to be included. Some of these items were discussed at meetings each day of that week, in order to determine how far we agreed on items and what further information or estimates we needed to get. For a number of these items, we also had to take into account, as best we could, what arms or war supplies provided to us by the UK had a US Lend-Lease content, which we should deduct from the UK claims but settle with the US authorities. We had anticipated some of these US obligations and already made payments on account in earlier years.

During the two weeks 11–25 February, while the main loan negotiations were in process, I was unable to devote much time to the settlement account, but others who had attended our earlier meetings were carrying on with the collection of materials on which we would base our decisions and were discussing these items with members of the British delegation. We had to pick up the settlement problems again urgently as soon as the main decision on the loan was taken by cabinet on the 25th. During that meeting, King referred to the settlement discussions immediately after the main decision was agreed on. He records in his diary: "I said I hoped they would clear up at the same time all outstanding obligations to the British, so that there was no further excessively hard driving on their part. This proposal must be linked up with decent treatment in other outstanding amounts. It was evident that we must act quickly to be ready for a settlement."[60]

The specific offer came from London, along with final approval of the terms of the loan. In the *aide-mémoire* submitted by Eady to Ilsley on 28 February, formally accepting the terms of the loan, Eady added that the UK ministers were most anxious to arrive at a comprehensive settlement of all the outstanding war claims between the British and Canadian governments and the post-war purchases on short-term credits. The *aide-mémoire* stated specifically that the United Kingdom would be prepared to pay a sum not exceeding $150 million in cash, if all claims as of 28 February – including those for the Indian rolling stock – were cancelled.

This put it squarely up to us to decide whether this was a fair deal, at least fair to Canada. Ilsley wanted to decide the question in cabinet on Saturday, 2 March. He and Clark asked me to advise them by that time whether this was a deal that they should accept. I secured the latest information that was then available on the size of the claims and counterclaims, and listed them in a memorandum entitled "Effect of U.K. Proposal for Settlement of All Outstanding War Claims for $150,000,000." The long table attached to this memorandum shows the estimated claims under various headings. The simplest was Canada's claim for supplies furnished after September and financed by interim credits amounting to $330 million. From this was deducted the payment of $150 million in cash by the UK, leaving $180 million to be met by transfers from Canadian accounts where there was a net surplus of UK claims over Canadian claims.[61]

The list of categories of claims and their estimated amounts showed a substantial net claim by the UK on the air force account, a small net claim by Canada on the UK in the accounts of the navy, and a large UK claim on balance in the army items, which would be much larger if the very dubious claim for the faulty Ram tanks was omitted. The numerous items relating to the Department of Munitions and Supply showed a mixture of specific claims by Canada amounting to $53 million, while the general claims of the UK on Canada, mainly arising from British contracts placed with that department before mid-1943, were quite large. But estimating even round-sum amounts was almost impossible. All in all, my collection of estimates showed that there was a rough balance between the British and Canadian claims when the $150 million cash payment was taken into account.

I made no recommendation to Ilsley and Clark in this paper, but we discussed the subject on the morning of 2 March before Ilsley went to cabinet. My recollection is that I was in favour of accepting the British proposal. I thought that the British officials were underestimating the value of their equity in the complex Department of Munitions and Supply reserve accounts, revolving funds, and recovery of "excess profits."

That day, cabinet accepted the British proposal and instructed us to draw up a formal agreement. We did this during the next few days with the help of legal and accounting experts. The agreement was very sweeping in its general terms, covering all claims of the categories described, "whether such claims are known or unknown." This agreement was approved and signed on 6 March, along with the Loan Agreement.[62]

We did not need to get legislation from Parliament to implement this settlement agreement; we had sufficient authority under our existing legislation, including the War Appropriation Act. On 6 May, however, Ilsley made a fairly detailed statement on this agreement to the House of Commons, with some examples of particular items and a small summary table of figures indicating that Canada gained a small balance in its favour out of the settlement. Nearly all of the transactions were carried out in the fiscal year 1945–46, and may be found in the Public Accounts for that year as credits and debits to a general account for the settlement.[63]

DRAWING ON THE LOAN

When the 1946 loan was negotiated and approved, there was no agreement or understanding on when drawings on the loan would be made within the six-year period that it would be available. The minister of finance told Parliament that "by consultation, we shall be able to work out such things as the manner and time at which the United Kingdom will draw upon this credit." In the same statement, Ilsley said: "I would expect this credit will be fully drawn upon by the end of 1948."[64] He said this after he made some forecasts of Britain's balance of payments deficits in 1947 and 1948 that turned out to be underestimates.

The British made substantial drawings on the loan each month after it was authorized by Parliament in 1946. In total, these drawings amounted to $540 million, forty-three per cent of the total provided by the agreement.[65] The Canadian authorities did not take any action to restrain the drawings in 1946, perhaps because Canada did not need to sell for cash that year since its reserves of gold and US dollars, although declining, were still high by previous standards.

In October, the United Kingdom authorities began to be concerned about the rapid rate at which the Canadian credit was being drawn down in comparison with the credit under the Anglo–American agreement. Two visiting British officials expressed this concern to Rasminsky at the Bank of Canada, indicating that they foresaw a potential criticism in Washington if the US credit was being drawn after the Canadian credit was fully drawn. To provide some means of stretching out the Canadian credit without making payments directly in US dollars, they worked out a procedure in which the UK would buy Canadian dollars from the Bank of Canada in exchange for a form of convertible sterling, which the bank could sell in the foreign exchange market. This proposal was first put into effect in January 1947, after the Canadian deputy minister of finance had requested the UK High Commission in Ottawa to have the UK begin these payments at a rate of £5 million per month.

During the year 1946, the British balance of international payments had been much as was expected during the negotiation of the 1946 loan in February. British government overseas expenditures were higher than expected, but their overseas exports were also higher. Their imports were limited by world shortages of food and raw materials. Before 1946 ended, however, it was becoming evident that Britain's dollar deficit was more than its overall deficit – and more important, too. This was because the proceeds of British exports to the sterling area and some exports to Europe were not convertible into dollars, while the vital large imports from North and South America required payment in dollars. It was this dollar deficit that required financing from the US and Canadian loans in order to maintain the UK's gold and dollar reserves.

The year 1947 was a very different and difficult one. It began with a very severe winter in Europe, including Great Britain, where it was said to be the worst in recorded history. Fuel and food were both scarce and had to be rationed, and these scarcities limited sorely needed production and construction. The resulting misery led to political troubles, including support for the Communist parties in France and Italy. Britain's scarcities and severe balance of payments deficits forced the British government to inform the US administration in February that Britain could no longer provide troops, supplies, and money to maintain the defence of Greece and Turkey against the communist forces then arrayed against them. President Truman and Secretary of State Marshall quickly persuaded the US Congress to provide the money and the authority needed for the US to assume this burden. This dramatic change, and a careful study of the whole European situation, led to the formulation of the Marshall Plan, announced in June, under which the US would (later) provide money and supplies to enable Europe to achieve economic recovery and reconstruction of its industries. This assistance was offered to Russia and its allies, but after a single, critical meeting, the Russians decided that they would not accept it, and its allies and satellites were led to do the same.[66]

During the first half of 1947, there were recurring troubles and disappointments in Britain's balance of international payments, arising in part out of efforts to make the pound sterling convertible into other currencies for the monetary authorities of countries with which Britain had monetary agreements. In principle, this convertibility was intended to apply only to holdings of sterling that was accruing from trade or other current account transactions and needed to acquire other currency needed for such transactions. This important limitation was usually administered by the monetary authorities of countries that stood to gain from the conversion. While this sort of arrangement had worked for the sterling area during the war, it was being seriously abused in 1947. In addition, the volume of United Kingdom exports stopped rising in the second quarter of the year, and prices of imports were rising more rapidly than those of exports – an unforeseen disaster. Moreover, the Labour government was following an expansionist "full employment" policy that increased imports. This was understandable after long years of wartime austerity for the British people, but unaffordable in 1947.

During the first and second quarters of 1947, the UK drew on the Canadian loan for lesser amounts than in 1946. In March, Canada asked for an increase in the payments of convertible sterling, which was made in April. In May, Towers and other Canadians informed senior British officials that Canada's gold and exchange reserves were falling and that some regular receipt of convertible payments from the UK was needed, despite Britain's difficulties. In June, agreement was reached in London that the British deficit with Canada would be settled on a fifty-fifty basis – one-half in convertible currency, and one-half from drawing on the Canadian loan.[67] This gave rise to a number of British statements that summer that this was an arrangement by which Britain was helping Canada. Although hese statements were annoying, they were not serious.

The British had their most severe foreign exchange crisis in July and August 1947. The troubles in May and June required some kind of action as in part a remedy and in part a demonstration of the seriousness with which the financial authorities confronted their troubles. Unfortunately, the actions taken – for example, the restrictions on imports – were regarded by those in the foreign exchange markets as quite inadequate and as doing more harm than good. The control over capital or anticipatory transactions was not strong enough to safeguard the gold reserves. Moreover, the date on which sterling had to be made generally convertible under the US loan agreement, 15 July, was public knowledge. So, too, were the heavy drawings on the US loan: $500 million in the first quarter and $950 million in the second. When the fateful day arrived, there was a pause and some false confidence. In the week beginning 20 July, the drain on the reserves was $106 million; the next week, it was $126 million; the third week, it was $127 million; and in the week ending 16 August, it was $183 million. By that date, only $850 million of the US loan was left. At this rate of use, it would last barely another month. The British government decided that it could not maintain convertibility but must seek the agreement of the American government to release Britain from its commitment under the Loan Agreement. This led quickly to the "suspension" of convertibility on 20 August. (It was not re-established until December 1958.)

A long meeting took place in Ottawa on 20 August when British officials met with the minister of finance, D. C. Abbott, and senior officials to bring them up-to-date on the sterling crisis and the latest UK–US financial arrangements.[68] At this meeting, the UK received no concessions on their arrangements with Canada. A few weeks later, in London, Abbott met with Dalton, the chancellor of the exchequer, and held to this same position. The fifty-fifty use of the Canadian loan remained in force until the end of 1947 and resulted in total drawings on the 1946 loan of $423 million that year, on top of the $540 million in 1946. This left only $287 million available for later years.

THE CANADIAN DOLLAR CRISIS

By mid-November 1947, Canada's gold and US dollar reserves had declined to a little more than $500 million, compared with almost $1.245 billion at the beginning of the year.[69] A level of $500 million was clearly too low, particularly as Canada was running a huge current account deficit with the United States, a rate of over $1.1 billion during 1947. Consequently, the minister of finance, and the government, decided that it was necessary to launch a temporary program of severe restraint on imports and transfer payments, including restraint on personal expenditures for travel or residence outside Canada. There were also special measures to encourage greater exports, and special concessions were made by the United States to permit greater imports from Canada. In addition, the Canadian government quickly negotiated a standby loan of $300 million from the US government's Export-Import Bank. There is no need to go into further details of this here. Suffice it to say that Abbott's measures were comprehensive and severe, but it was quickly evident that they were effective. The drawings on the Export-Import Bank loan during 1948 were only $140 million, and this was quickly repaid during the year from the proceeds of a sale by Canada of long-term US dollar bonds to three insurance companies. The restraints on imports and foreign expenditures were reduced gradually during 1949, and then wholly withdrawn during 1950 when Canada experienced a great influx of American capital.[70]

The severe Canadian shortage of US dollars in 1947 and 1948 was important in causing the minister of finance to be very reluctant, in 1948, to approve further drawing by the British on the 1946 loan.

One group of drawings early in 1948 was arranged in December 1947. The British government, facing the need to reduce all dollar expenditure not urgently required, decided to reduce its expenditures on food from North America. The government sent a mission to Ottawa, headed by a top-level trade official, to negotiate new arrangements for food purchases. The British wished to retain their very favourable contract for wheat but to end most of their contracts for animal products, notably beef, bacon, cheese, and eggs. (By that time, they hoped to be able to buy these elsewhere for sterling; some of these exports Canada would be able to sell in the United States.) The Canadian minister of agriculture dug in his heels and said that it was "all or nothing." Here the negotiators were deadlocked in mid-December, until the Canadian high commissioner in London met with the chancellor of the exchequer and reported to Ottawa that a compromise was possible, one that King quickly worked out.[71] In this compromise, Canada undertook to release $45 million of the 1946 loan to finance food purchases in the first quarter of 1948, while the UK agreed to pay $100 million in convertible currency for these food supplies in that period.

By the time this brief arrangement expired, a new tension was evident in Europe. The Communist takeover of Czechoslovakia in February 1948 signalled the completion of the division of Europe into two opposed political and economic blocs. The takeover was followed soon by the Brussels Pact for the defence of Western Europe. In the US, President Truman requested Congress to reintroduce conscription for military service and universal military training. The Russians replied in June by imposing a blockade on surface traffic to the Western sectors of Berlin. This remained in effect until May 1949. The Western response to this blockade was an airlift by US and British planes of food, fuel, and other essentials from air bases in Britain. This was backed up by the stationing of many US bombers on these British bases. At this time, the US was known to have nuclear bombs, while the Russians did not.[72]

In this tense situation, the US was bringing into effect the Marshall Plan for economic assistance to Europe, a plan that had been announced the previous year. It took the form of a European Recovery Program, through which the US would provide money and supplies to the Organization for European Economic Cooperation, in which the participating European nations (including Britain) would share providing this assistance in accordance with a recovery program that they would work out jointly. In the United States, Congress established and provided funds to the Economic Cooperation Administration. The EAC was authorized to finance exports to Europe from countries outside the US in appropriate circumstances. This included some exports to Europe from Canada, which were an important source of US dollars to Canada during 1948 and 1949 and in addition saved the Canadian government the cost of financing these exports.[73]

In April 1948, there was a short gap between the end of Canada's special financing of UK food supplies and the effective beginning of the ECA contracts. Abbott agreed to a small release of $7 million from the 1946 loan to cover this gap in the financing of UK imports from Canada. After this small instalment, he resisted all efforts to persuade Canada to release more drawings from the 1946 loan during 1948.[74] These efforts at persuasion in 1948 came from the Americans, not the British. The purpose was really to make it easier for the ECA to get appropriations from Congress by showing that Canada was also providing aid to Europe. Abbott responded to some of these proposals by emphasizing that he had to give priority to rebuilding Canada's exchange reserves, which had been depleted in 1947. When that was accomplished, however, he would resume providing dollars to the UK under the loan agreement.

By December 1948, Abbott agreed that his officials could inform the Americans that in January 1949, Canada would resume the regular release of $10 million a month to the British. This was done, and these monthly drawings continued until mid-1950. The British raised the possibility of accelerating the drawings on two occasions during 1949. The first was in July in London. Once again, the British were facing a rapid decline in their foreign exchange reserves, despite the fact that they were receiving large-scale assistance from the United States and some from Canada.[75] Attlee, the British prime minister, had sent a secret message to St Laurent in Ottawa, noting the run on their reserves and attributing it to the business recession in the United States that was reducing the demand for British exports. He suggested a meeting of Commonwealth finance ministers to consider possible remedies. St Laurent responded quickly, noting that he was in the midst of an election campaign but saying that he would send over his most senior official immediately.

A group of senior Canadian officials went to London in July to discuss the situation. At the key meeting, the senior British official said that at that stage, he was inclined not to press for permission to increase the drawings on the Canadian loan. He thought, however, that the question might be renewed in September. Clark, the Canadian deputy minister of finance, said that an increase was not justified. The whole remaining balance of the Canadian loan was not large enough to make much difference in the desperate situation that was building up. At the conclusion of the meeting, Clark emphasized the disparity between anything Canada could do and actions the UK might take to reduce costs and generally to provide evidence that there was some hope that the UK would return to multilateral trading.[76] This was very tough talk and showed how exasperated the Canadians were over the British inability to get its economy in order, despite all the help it had received. Canadian officials went on to say that the British problem at that time would not be met by more loans or grants. The sterling area by then was insulated from competition, and their costs and prices were too high. Such Canadian talk could have been interpreted as a belief that sterling would have to be devalued.

In late August and September, there were further tripartite discussions in Washington between the Americans, British, and Canadians, preceding the annual meeting of the International Monetary Fund. Senior Canadian officials took part in many of these, and Abbott took part in the meetings of ministers, occasionally accompanied by Pearson. In these meetings, the British situation and the general sterling area situation were examined in depth, and various measures to remove obstacles to British exports were devised. There were no discussions of the devaluation of sterling; while a few of the senior ministers were informed that this was under consideration, there was no leak of the information. The detailed work on other measures would help to make the most constructive use of devaluation should it occur. Decisions on these matters were announced on the same day that a severe devaluation of sterling by thirty per cent was announced after a hectic weekend of meetings of the International Monetary Fund. The devaluation of the Canadian dollar by 9.1 per cent was announced the following day, a devaluation that lasted only twelve months, until 30 September 1950, when the Canadian dollar was allowed to "float" upwards, carried by a large inflow of American capital into Canada.

The balance of payments of the UK and sterling area improved quite substantially following the devaluation of sterling, and the other devaluations that quickly followed it. There was no need for many years for further bilateral discussions between Canada and the UK on currency or balance of payments matters. Assistance from the United States under the European Recovery Program continued until 1952 and then was replaced by burden sharing and mutual aid through the North Atlantic Treaty Organization. Canada contributed substantially to this from 1951 to 1957.

THE "HAVE REGARD TO" CLAUSE

After the events of 1949, the drawings of $10 million per month under the 1946 loan continued for five months in 1950 and then ceased, although there was still $65 million left undrawn. The reason for this did not appear until 1951. It arose from a very Canadian source of dissatisfaction with Great Britain: the price of wheat. In 1946, the Canadian government entered into a four-year contract to sell wheat to the British during the crop years 1946–47, 1947–48, 1948–49, and 1949–50. The contract provided for a specified base price of $1.55 a bushel for the first two years. The prices in the third and fourth years were to be negotiated in advance and were to "have regard to any differences between the price in the first two years and world prices for deliveries ... in those years."[77] The price of $1.55 a bushel in the first two years had been below the market price during most of the time in those years. The price determined in advance for the crop years 1948–49 and 1949–50 was $2 a bushel. This appeared to be a good price at that time because it was above the ceiling price of $1.80 stipulated in the new world wheat agreement that came into effect in 1948. In 1950, after market prices had risen during 1948 and 1949, instead of falling as many knowledgeable people expected, Canadian farmers felt that the price of $2 a bushel they had received in the third and fourth years of their contract did not take into account adequately the clause in the agreement that it should "have regard to" the shortfall in the price that they received in the first two years being below the market price at that time. The British government asserted that the price of $2 a bushel fulfilled their obligation under the contract. When Howe, the minister responsible for selling the wheat, received this answer, he accepted it, and so did cabinet.

When the British decision was made public, however, there was an outcry in Western Canada. St Laurent, the prime minister, considered the British legally correct but believed that Gardiner, the minister of agriculture, and the British minister of food, had, in 1946, given the Western farmers some reason to believe that under the "have regard to" clause, they would receive an additional payment. He presented this argument to British ministers when he was in London in January 1951 but did not succeed in changing their position. When St Laurent returned to Ottawa, Gardiner argued that the Canadian government should make a contribution to the Wheat Board to compensate the Western farmers for the loss that they felt they had incurred.[78] Howe would not support this proposal. These two most senior of St Laurent's ministers were at loggerheads. The prime minister felt that unless the government paid them some compensation, the Western farmers would feel that they had been cheated. He decided himself that Parliament should be asked to appropriate a contribution to be paid into the Wheat Board, to be added to the pool of proceeds from exports that were to be distributed on final settlement for deliveries in the years covered by the British contract. St Laurent made an outstanding speech in the House of Commons in favour of this proposal in which he explained the divergences of view among ministers that had to be resolved by cabinet solidarity.[79]

There was no way of calculating a suitable amount for this contribution to the farmers. By chance, however, there was a balance of $65 million still undrawn in the loan to Britain of 1946. The British had announced (and not by chance!) in February that they would not draw this amount, an amount that was enough to look appropriate as compensation to the Western farmers.

This unusual action in February and March 1951 meant that the full amount of the 1946 loan was never drawn. In fact, Britain did not need it. In 1950, Britain had a small current account surplus with Canada, while the rest of the sterling area had a small deficit. In the next year, Britain had a substantial surplus. The country's post-war balance of payments problem with Canada had gone.

AFTERWORD

The Finance Department and the War at Home

As Robert Bryce's book has made clear, the Department of Finance that fought World War II was a tiny department. The key officials who shaped policy were an even smaller group, a handful or two. Clifford Clark, the deputy; W.A. Mackintosh, brought in from Queen's University; and Bob Bryce himself were the stars. Around them were a second group of generalists, including Mitchell Sharp and A.F.W. Plumptre; a number of academic and private sector experts brought in from outside the civil service; as well as departmental specialists in tax and trade policy, such men as Kenneth Eaton, Harvey Perry, and Hector McKinnon.

Small as it was, the economic constellation of wartime Ottawa was broader than merely the Department of Finance. The Economic Advisory Committee sat at the top of the food chain, an irregular gathering place for the key officials from the departments of Finance, External Affairs, Trade and Commerce, and the cabinet secretariat, and from such agencies as the Bank of Canada and the Wartime Prices and Trade Board. This was where policy was sometimes hammered out but more often smoothed and aligned by the most senior officials. The wartime role of the Bank of Canada and its key officials, such as Graham Towers, Donald Gordon, Louis Rasminsky, Bob Beattie, and others, loomed large. The bank worked closely on foreign and domestic financial matters with Clark's department. The Foreign Exchange Control Board, under the Bank's control, similarly co-operated. The War Finance Committee, charged with managing the Victory Bond campaigns, again was under the bank. The WPTB, controlling wages and prices and rationing, initially came under the Department of Labour and only went to the Finance Department in August 1941. Donald Gordon, its chairman when it became the critical player in late 1941, had come from the bank, and the board fit very much into the Finance ambit.

The extraordinary fact was that all the major financial policy-makers in wartime Ottawa could have crowded around a table in a medium-sized conference room, with only a few sitting on chairs against the wall. Even more extraordinarily, there were few major disputes, few turf wars, few personality clashes. The war was too important for such disputes, for one thing. But strikingly, the Ottawa men shared a broad general agreement on what needed to be done. There were differences in detail, of course, but their education, training, and the deep ties of affection and respect that bound them – and their wives and children – together meant that the policy and personal fights were few. Moreover, what united these men was their capacity to work hard (for low salaries!), to put in fourteen-hour days seven days a week, to master complex issues quickly, and to argue complicated positions to each other and to explain them to their political masters. It was a situation tailor-made for those able to rise and to shine.

If the bureaucrats formed a harmonious and hard-working whole, the Liberal politicians under whom they laboured were only slightly less in agreement and just as industrious. The prime minister, William Lyon Mackenzie King, was almost sixty-five at the beginning of the war, a wily old professional whose caution was well known and whose personal manner and the idiosyncrasies of his style of governing infuriated many. Despite what our mythologists tell us, however, King was no fool, no man in thrall to his dog and his crystal ball. King could lead, and he was strong and confident enough to give his key ministers their heads. Bryce's book makes clear that Colonel J.L. Ralston and J.L. Ilsley, the two finance ministers during the war, were able leaders with a firm grasp of policy and practice. C.D. Howe, the minister of munitions and supply, then minister of reconstruction, and later the "minister of everything," was a hugely powerful figure with matchless ties to the industrial powers in the land. Other ministers hove into view on specific issues, some more happily than others. Louis St Laurent, the successor to Ernest Lapointe as justice minister and Quebec lieutenant, became greatly admired by all who dealt with him. Saskatchewan's Jimmy Gardiner, the agriculture minister, was less esteemed. Brooke Claxton from Montreal could speak the same language as the bureaucrats, and his work on social welfare questions, especially family allowances, brought him into direct – and usually harmonious – contact with Clifford Clark's crew. There were some with leadership ambitions in that group, most notably Saskatchewan's Gardiner, but none who were prepared to challenge the prime minister. Issues such as conscription would force Ralston, then defence minister, out of cabinet, but even that crisis in 1944 did not ultimately shake King's control of his Liberal party, cabinet, or caucus. That King won the election of June 1945 suggests that his grasp of his country was and remained sure. That was a political reality the mandarins in Finance had to live with, and most appear to have done so without any difficulty.

Bryce's study examines the array of difficult international questions that Finance had to deal with during the war. Domestically, the issues were no less complex, touching as they did on raising the monies necessary to fight the war, finding arrangements with the provincial governments in light of the Report of the Royal Commission on Dominion–Provincial Relations, fighting inflation through wage and price controls, and planning for the post-war world. This was a heavy agenda at any time, one made more difficult still because it had to be handled while fighting and financing a vast overseas war. That, by and large, it was brilliantly managed means that it ranks among the greatest governmental feats in Canada's history.

The first point that must be noted is that Canada was a small, weak nation in 1939. The population was only 11.2 million, the Gross Domestic Product only $5.6 billion, and the total of all federal expenditures in 1939 only $680 million. Federal income taxes totalled only $112 million in 1939, and corporation taxes just $115 million. When King took Canada into the war on 10 September 1939, he pronounced Canada's role as one of limited liability. Canadians were not a great power with far-flung interests to protect. They were in the war because Britain was in, and their primary effort at the beginning was to be one of strictly limited economic assistance: no great armies, no efforts to the last man and last dollar, no conscription for overseas service. The constrained fiscal picture perhaps justified that very political approach. The war would change matters dramatically, but nothing occurred by chance.

Taxation policy and the relations of the federal and provincial governments first had to be decided. The Great Depression had hammered the nation and its people for a decade, its effect sharpest on the provinces, which had the responsibilities for dealing with social policies and none of the financial resources to meet them. The King government created the Rowell-Sirois Royal Commission in August 1937 to re-examine "the economic and financial basis of Confederation and of the distribution of legislative powers" and to determine measures that would "best effect a balanced relationship between the financial powers and obligations and functions of each governing body."[1] After exhaustive cross-country hearings, the commission reported in February 1940, early in the war. Its preferred recommendations called for Ottawa to assume the debts of the provinces, for Ottawa to cover the full burden of relief of the "employable unemployed," and for the provinces and municipalities to vacate the fields of corporate and income taxes and succession duties. The report also called for the existing system of federal subsidies to the provinces to end, and for the federal government to pay the provinces a sum equal to ten per cent of their natural resource revenues and a national adjustment grant to allow provinces to maintain the Canadian social and educational average while not levying taxation higher than the country's average level of taxation. Finally, Ottawa would give emergency grants to meet emergency situations. This was a giant step toward what later would be called equalization, but the provinces that would not receive national adjustment grants – Ontario, Alberta, and British Columbia – were not pleased.

The terrible events of May and June 1940 in the Low Countries and France drove the Rowell-Sirois report out of the government's and the public's minds, but the war's increasingly great demands for money made Ottawa anxious to reach a decision on the recommendations as a war measure. Certainly this was the view in Finance and the Bank of Canada, and in November 1940, the government agreed to convene a Dominion–Provincial Conference in January 1941. At the opening session, Prime Minister King delivered the speech that had been drafted and redrafted for him by his key economic advisers: "It is our considered view that the adoption of the commission's recommendations is necessary to put our country in a position to pursue a policy which will achieve the maximum war effort, and at the same time lay a foundation for post-war reconstruction."[2] In essence, Ottawa needed the taxation powers in its hands to fight the war.

The provinces, the opposition led by Premier Mitch Hepburn of Ontario, saw the federal proposals as a tax grab and an attack on provincial autonomy. That led Finance Minister J.L. Ilsley to say that the war situation made it all but certain that Ottawa would "undoubtedly have to invade provincial tax fields such as succession duties" and "increase its rates in such fields of progressive taxation as the income tax."[3] Everyone knew this to be true, but Ilsley failed to move the opponents, and the conference ended without agreement and in much rancour.

Now what? Rowell-Sirois had been put on the shelf, but Ottawa still needed the money. The answer to how to get it was provided by the accountant Walter Gordon, a wartime special assistant to Clifford Clark. Ottawa should impose the taxes it needed to pay for the war and should pay to every province that agreed to surrender its income, corporate, and succession taxes an annual payment equal to its previous revenues from these fields. This was to be a voluntary agreement, Gordon shrewdly said, but any province that failed to agree could face the burden of saddling its citizens with double taxation.[4] This was blackmail, of course, but neither Clark and his colleagues nor cabinet could see any alternative. The government's plan was presented in the budget of 29 April 1941 and, although there were bitter complaints, all the provinces recognized *force majeur* and caved in. The Dominion–Provincial Taxation Agreement Act, 1942, formalized the deal. The government now had the taxation room it needed to fight the war.

Freed to act, Ottawa began to levy the taxes it needed. Excise, sales, and retail purchase taxes were increased or imposed. Raw tobacco faced a ten cents a pound levy; cigarette taxes increased from $5 to $6 a thousand; cameras, photographs, and radio tubes had a ten per cent tax added to their cost; and a luxury tax on virtually all entertainment added twenty per cent to the cost of movies and sporting events. A War Exchange Tax, ordinarily ten per cent, raised revenue and deterred unnecessary imports, thus preserving scarce US dollars. The rates of corporation and income taxes were increased dramatically. At the beginning of the war, a married man with two children paid no income tax at all unless he was in the upper brackets; if he earned $3,000, his income tax was $10. Four years later, after tax increases that squeezed the lemon hard, the $3,000-a-year man was paying $334 in income tax and an additional amount of $1,200 in "compulsory savings," a surcharge in the form of a loan to be repaid at the end of the war. The ingenuity of Ilsley and Clark's team was almost as unlimited as the nation's need for money.[5]

Corporation taxes also increased from eighteen to forty per cent, generating $636 million – or nearly half of all corporate profits – in 1943. Excess profits taxes produced more revenue. All profits in excess of 116 ⅔ per cent of standard profits (the average of profit from the not so buoyant years from 1936 to 1939) were taxed at one hundred per cent. Corporations, however, were to receive a twenty per cent rebate after the war. "No great fortunes," the finance minister said, perhaps with more optimism than was justified, "can be accumulated out of wartime profits."[6]

But taxation could not finance all war costs, though much more was squeezed from the taxpayers than had been the case in World War I. Then, the printing presses had pumped out currency, and some at least of the war's cost had been carried by deliberate inflation. This time, a different tack would be tried, and borrowing was stepped up to cover the huge increases in spending and thus in the federal deficit. In 1939, the deficit (on a national accounts basis) was a mere $2 million; in 1944 and 1945, it was $1.9 billion, and the government raised almost $16 billion from the sale of securities, while seeing net debt rise to just under $18 billion. Almost all of this debt was held in Canada by Canadians – Ottawa did not borrow abroad in World War II as it had done during the Great War. Banks and insurance companies bought some $3.5 billion in government securities, the public taking the rest. In a succession of brilliantly managed War Loan and Victory Bond campaigns, the government raised approximately $12.5 billion, in the process borrowing from its citizens at costs ranging from one and one-half to three per cent, again figures much lower than the five per cent interest cost of the 1914 war. Purchasing Victory Bonds was made as easy as possible with payroll deductions readily available, while citizens could also buy War Savings Certificates and schoolchildren could purchase War Savings Stamps at twenty-five cents each. A children's savings card with sixteen stamps would, after seven years, return $5 tax free. It was a total war.[7]

Despite the burden of taxation and the pressures to buy Victory Bonds, there was still too much money chasing too few goods. Canadians had jobs and all the overtime they wanted; for the first time since the 1920s, people had money in their pockets and they wanted to spend it. Ottawa had created the Wartime Prices and Trade Board at the beginning of the war to oversee the inflationary pressures that were sure to come. In the Great War, huge price increases had wracked the economy and fuelled post-war unrest. No one wanted that to recur.

The difficulty was that inflation was taking hold. In 1940, the cost of living increased by just four per cent, but in the first nine months of 1941, it rose by seven per cent. Support for tighter controls in financial and government circles began to increase, and cabinet made its first gesture in this direction by moving the WPTB to Finance from the Department of Labour. Finance Minister Ilsley and, gradually, his most senior officials came to the conclusion that half measures could not work. Only a total freeze on wages and prices could check the coming inflationary spiral. No one believed that this would be easy to manage. As Ilsley assured a business group in September 1941, however, "things will not be allowed to drift."[8]

Cabinet initially was dubious about a freeze, with the prime minister and agriculture minister Gardiner leading the opposition. This was too much too fast, King argued, and it was better to proceed piecemeal.[9] At a cabinet meeting on 10 October, however, the opposition crumbled in the face of Finance's case, and with the WPTB given a new chair in the person of Donald Gordon, the Bank of Canada's deputy governor, the policy was announced on 18 October 1941. After 1 December, the prime minister stated in his national broadcast announcing the freeze: "No person may sell any goods or supply any services at a price or rate higher than that charged by him for such goods or services during the four weeks from September 15 to October 11 [1941] ..." Prices could fall below the ceiling but could not rise above it. Wages, too, were frozen: "It is obvious that the prices of finished goods cannot be controlled successfully unless the cost of production is also controlled," King said.[10] No employer could increase his present basic wage rates without permission. To ensure that wages kept pace with prices, however, a cost of living bonus, determined by the WPTB, would come into force. Some special arrangements were put in place for agriculture, but essentially the freeze was a total one.

This is not the place to examine in any detail wage and price controls and the way they operated. Many interest groups in manufacturing, commerce, and agriculture were upset by the sweeping nature of the controls; many unions were unhappy that their members would not make gains in a period of full employment. Surprisingly, perhaps, the public was sanguine about the measures, and the mood of confidence in the WPTB's fairness was reinforced by the tough-talking Donald Gordon, who soon made the board into a household word. The confidence was justified. The cost of living, which had increased by 17.8 per cent between 1 August 1939 and 1 October 1941, rose only 2.8 per cent between that latter date and 1 April 1945. The cost of fuel and light actually dropped, the cost of clothing was stable, and the cost of food – much of which was rationed – was the sole major sector to increase.

Strikingly, Canadians generally were better fed and likely better clothed during the war years than they had been in the preceding decade of unemployment and privation. The freeze seemed to be and was fair, and rationing exerted its effect on rich and poor alike. There was a black market, of course, there were employers who cheated, and there was a decline in the quality of goods as industry tried to keep its profit margins in the face of the controls. Overall, however, Canadians approved of what was done in their name to speed victory in the war. In April 1943, in fact, public support for the WPTB stood at an incredible eighty per cent.[11] Canada's successful record of controlling inflation set the pace for the Allies.

What worried Canadians – and the politicians and officials in the Finance Department – was what would happen when the war ended. Would the Depression return with high unemployment? Would inflation take off when the controls were removed? Would there be jobs for the boys who had fought and won the war? What would the federal government do to alter relations with the provinces to sustain into the peace the governmental efficiencies created by the war? All of these concerns were subsumed under a broad, all-encompassing term: "reconstruction."

The first building block in reconstruction came in 1940 when the federal government secured provincial consent to amend the constitution to permit Ottawa to operate an unemployment insurance scheme. This was an insurance plan, one that required the employed to pay into it so that in the event that they lost their jobs, they could draw on the accumulated funds. UI, in other words, could be started only in good times, and the war years were a time of full employment. The UI fund, therefore, was in good shape to meet any post-war downturn.[12]

But the key to planning in Finance and its constellation was to have an array of programs that would put money into the hands of those who would spend it and those who would create jobs. Planning for the reintegration of veterans, for example, was in the hands of the Cabinet Committee on Demobilization and Re-establishment, under Ian Mackenzie, the minister of pensions and health. The Veterans Charter, which eventually emerged from this committee's work, was hugely important in providing an array of services for veterans that were second to none in their generosity and comprehensiveness. Returning men and women received care, training, and cash grants for their services, and the officials in Finance knew that the money would be spent on new houses, furniture and appliances, clothing, and foodstuffs, helping cushion the transition to peace.[13]

That, however, was not enough. Originally devised as a measure to put some extra money into the hands of families hurt by the wage freeze, the idea of family allowances quickly became a massive effort to put spendable cash in the hands of young mothers. Would the national interest not be served by having this money spent to create jobs? Clifford Clark, one reporter in Ottawa confidentially informed his editor in Winnipeg, "is completely sold on family allowances ... the only effective way to deal with slum clearance. You have to give the boys the money to buy the houses you intend to build for them. That is a little crude, but it has the idea."[14] And so it did, as did a memo to King's key political adviser on social welfare, which argued that "the economic problem after the war will not be to produce what we need, but to find markets for what we must produce if we are to avoid unemployment. The provision of family allowances almost certainly would result in a considerable net addition to the home market ..."[15] In effect, the Department of Finance, the Finance constellation, and indeed all of official Ottawa had become converted to Keynesian economics. In the Depression years, governments had dealt with hard times by slashing spending to the bone. Now, the wartime government was preparing plans to spend large sums in order to head off the possible return of economic troubles. That children might be better fed and housed as a result of the "baby bonus" was an equal, if coincident, benefit.

Family allowances passed through Parliament in 1944, encountering some tough opposition. The scale of the measure was huge, its cost approximating $256 million for the first year of operation. That figure was almost half of the total federal pre-war budget, and it was to be spent for a single program, one that was only a part of a coordinated federal effort that encompassed a range of measures. The Veterans Charter cost billions, there was money to promote exports, to convert industry to peacetime, to build houses and offer cheap mortgages. There was a shelf of public works projects that could be dusted off and implemented if the economy was struggling. For a government and bureaucracy that had almost prided itself on thinking small in the 1930s, this was an extraordinary *volte-face*. The days of $600 million budgets were gone – and why not, when the government's spending in 1945 was $5.14 billion and the GDP had more than doubled during the war to $11.8 billion? The elaborate plans for post-war reconstruction, along with Canada's extraordinary war effort, won the 1945 federal election for King's Liberals.

All that remained was to get the provinces to buy into a new domestic order. The Finance constellation of bureaucrats had prepared for the August 1945 Dominion–Provincial Conference on Reconstruction for months, drafting an extensive Green Book of proposals. Essentially, Ottawa proposed a comprehensive plan to restructure Canadian federalism so that the central government would have the essential financial and legislative powers to guide the country forward. In essence, Ottawa was saying that it had demonstrated it could run a great world war successfully; now it ought to have equivalent powers to direct the country in peacetime.

The politicians and bureaucrats may have been correct, but it was not to be. The provinces might have been prepared to tolerate the federal government's grabbing of power and money in wartime; they would not, could not accept it in peacetime. Ontario's George Drew and Quebec's Maurice Duplessis flatly refused to buy into the vision created by what some sneeringly called the "brains trust" in Finance. The Reconstruction Conference ground to an end in April 1946, nothing achieved. The best chance to rationalize Confederation had disappeared.

It would be a gross error to end any account of the Department of Finance's role in directing the domestic war effort on a note of failure. The achievements in raising money and planning its spending, in controlling inflation, and in preparing successfully for reconstruction were so great that the economic mandarins might be forgiven for having believed that they could resolve the age-old conundrums of Canadian federalism. They failed in this, but in this only. Their wartime record, the record of Clifford Clark, Robert Bryce, W.A. Mackintosh, Graham Towers, Donald Gordon, and many others, was simply extraordinary. They had won the economic war at home, and they had properly positioned Canada for the new post-war world.

J.L. Granatstein

Notes

INTRODUCTION

1 For an outline of Clark's career, see two articles written by colleagues soon after his death in December 1952: W.A. Mackintosh, "William Clifford Clark: A Personal Memoir," *Queen's Quarterly* 60 (Spring 1953) and R.B. Bryce, "William Clifford Clark, 1889–1952," *Canadian Journal of Economics and Political Science* 19 (August 1953). J.L. Granatstein has described Clark's career and influence in Ottawa in the context of his study of the civil service from 1935 to 1957. See *The Ottawa Men* (Toronto: Oxford University Press, 1982), especially 44–52. Clark's role as the deputy minister of finance during the Depression is examined in more detail in R.B. Bryce, *Maturing in Hard Times* (Montreal: McGill-Queen's University Press, 1986).

2 David Mansur's career with the Bank of Canada was relatively short. He had come to Ottawa in 1939 to assist in the organization of the Central Mortgage Bank after fifteen years with Sun Life. With the advent of war, the Central Mortgage Bank never became operational, and Mansur's talents were diverted to the Foreign Exchange Control Board, of which he was assistant chairman from 1939 to 1941. He then was appointed assistant chairman of the National War Finance Committee, a position he held until 1945. At the end of the war, Mansur became the first president of the Central Mortgage and Housing Corporation.

3 Louis Rasminsky joined the Bank of Canada in 1940 after ten years of working in Geneva on the professional staff of the Economic and Financial Section of the League of Nations. In 1941, he became assistant to the chairman of the Foreign Exchange Control and, in 1942, its chairman (alternate). The following year, he became executive assistant to the governor of the bank. Rasminsky played a vital role in the long negotiations preceding the Bretton Woods Agreement of 1944 that

established the International Monetary Fund and the International Bank for Reconstruction and Development. His part in those discussions has been described ably in an article by J.L. Granatstein, "The Road to Bretton Woods: International Monetary Policy and the Public Servant," *Journal of Canadian Studies* 16 (Fall–Winter, 1981). Rasminsky went on to become deputy governor of the Bank of Canada from 1955 to 1961, and then governor from 1961 to 1973.

4 James Layton Ralston was pressed into service as minister of finance just before Canada's declaration of war. He had been minister of national defence from 1926 to 1930 and was a leading member of the Opposition from 1930 to 1935. He had not been a candidate in the 1935 election, so after being sworn into cabinet, on 6 September 1939, a seat had to be found for him. He did not stay long in the Finance portfolio, because he was appointed minister of national defence, on 5 July 1940, a position he held until 1 November 1944 when he broke with King during the conscription controversy.

5 James Lorimer Ilsley was to prove a capable and popular minister of finance throughout the war despite King's reluctance to appoint him in July 1940. First elected to the House of Commons in the general election of September 1926, he was appointed minister of national revenue in 1935. Ilsley was to remain in the Finance portfolio until December 1946, when he was appointed minister of justice and attorney general. Two years later, he resigned to resume his law practice and became a judge of the Supreme Court of Nova Scotia the following year.

6 Clarence Decatur Howe, the powerful and able minister of munitions and supply from April 1940 to December 1945, first entered cabinet after the 1935 election as minister of marine and minister of railways and canals. (These ministries were reorganized as the Department of Transport the following year.) In 1944, the government turned its attention to post-war problems, and Howe became the minister of reconstruction. In 1948, he became minister of trade and commerce, a portfolio he retained until the fall of the Liberal government in 1957.

7 The death late in 1941 of Ernest Lapointe, King's trusted lieutenant from Quebec, prompted Louis St Laurent's entry into politics. Chosen by King to be Lapointe's successor as the voice of Quebec in cabinet, he was sworn in as minister of justice on 10 December 1941 and elected in Lapointe's old constituency on 9 February 1942. In 1946, St Laurent was sworn in as secretary of state for external affairs; two years later he succeeded King as prime minister.

8 For an account of this cabinet meeting, see King Diary, MG 26 J 13, 13 January 1944. The memorandum on family allowances prepared by Clark for submission to Council in which the arguments are outlined can be found in "Children's Allowances," Records of the Department

of Finance, RG 19, vol. 304, file 101-53-114. A revised and shortened version of this memo is in Mackenzie King Papers, MG 26, J 4, vol. 273, C137337-97.

9 Walter Gordon's career encompassed business, the civil service, and politics. A chartered accountant and management consultant, he had worked during the 1930s on the Royal Commission on Price Spreads and assisted at the investigations of the Tariff Board. Before his appointment to the Department of Finance as a special assistant to the deputy minister, late in 1940, Gordon had been at the Bank of Canada, working on special assignments. He returned to Toronto and his professional practice in 1942. In 1955, he chaired the Royal Commission on Canada's Economic Prospects. He was elected as a Liberal MP in the general elections of 1962, 1963, and 1965 and returned to the Finance Department as its minister in April 1963.

10 A.F.W. Plumptre joined the Canadian public service in 1941 after ten years of teaching and writing at the University of Toronto. His first appointment was in Washington as the financial attaché at the Canadian Legation and as the Washington representative of the Wartime Prices and Trade Board. After a two-year break from the public service as an editorial writer, he returned to Ottawa to join the Department of External Affairs (1949–54) but returned to Finance in 1954, taking charge of most of the international work. In 1965, he returned to academe to become a professor once more at the University of Toronto.

11 Sir Frederick Phillips's career in the British Treasury spanned thirty-five years. After placing first in the civil service examination in 1908, he entered the Treasury; at his death in 1943, he was joint second secretary, a position roughly equivalent to an associate deputy minister in Ottawa. During the 1930s, he had been secretary of the financial committee of the League of Nations. As head of the Treasury Mission in Washington from 1940 to 1943, he had been responsible for the important financial negotiations between Britain and the United States.

12 Sir Wilfrid Eady was appointed second secretary in the Treasury in charge of overseas finance in July 1942. He had entered the civil service in 1943, and after short stints in the India Office, Home Office, and the Department of Foreign Trade, he was transferred in 1917 to the Ministry of Labour, where he was to remain for the next twenty-one years. Before his appointment to the Treasury, he had been chairman of the Board of Customs and Excise. Eady was deeply involved alongside Lord Keynes in the Bretton Woods discussions and the loan negotiations of 1945–46, when the skills he developed in the Ministry of Labour as a negotiator were required.

13 Henry Morgenthau, Jr, the son of a famous and wealthy ambassador, was the American secretary of the Treasury from January 1934 to July 1945.

A neighbour of Roosevelt at Hyde Park, he had been the publisher of the *American Agriculturalist* and served on several New York State commissions when Roosevelt was governor. He came to Washington in 1933 as the chairman of the Federal Farm Board. Before his appointment as secretary to the Treasury, he was governor of the Farm Credit Administration.

CHAPTER ONE

1 J.L. Granatstein, *Canada's War: The Politics of the Mackenzie King Government, 1939–45* (Toronto: Oxford University Press, 1975), 19. O.D. Skelton, the undersecretary of state for external affairs, expressed this idea more forcefully in March 1939 in a letter to Hume Wrong, then stationed in Geneva. "The plain fact is that if we go into any European War it will be simply and solely on the grounds of racial sympathy with the United Kingdom. Why obscure this fact or try to dress it up with talk about saving democracy or our League obligations? The sooner we face the actual reality the better." Records of the Department of External Affairs, RG 25, vol. 767, file 319, vols 1 and 2.
2 James Eayrs, *In Defence of Canada, Volume II: Appeasement and Rearmament* (Toronto: University of Toronto Press, 1965), 52.
3 Ibid., 63–72. See also John W. Holmes, "Shadow and Substance: Diplomatic Relations Between Britain and Canada," in Peter Lyon (ed.), *Britain and Canada: Survey of a Changing Relationship* (London: Frank Cass, 1976), 108–9.
4 A.J.P. Taylor, *English History 1914–1945* (Oxford: Clarendon Press, 1965), 422.
5 "Gist of Memoranda by O.D.S. to P.M. from Munich to September 1939," RG 25, vol. 767, file 319, vol. 2.
6 It has been said that the modern Canadian civil service was created by O.D. Skelton. Appointed in 1925 as the undersecretary of state for external affairs, he had great influence on public policy until his death in January 1941. He was the trusted adviser of both Mackenzie King and R.B. Bennett and was instrumental in the creation of a modern and professional civil service in Canada. Before coming to Ottawa, Skelton had been a scholar of established reputation, a professor of politics and economics and the dean of the faculty of arts at Queen's. Skelton's career and influence in Ottawa has been described in Granatstein, *The Ottawa Men*. His views on foreign policy have been discussed in an article by Norman Hillmer, "The Anglo-Canadian Neurosis: The Case of O.D. Skelton" in *Britain and Canada: Survey of a Changing Relationship* (London: Frank Cass, 1976). Loring Christie joined External Affairs in 1913 and was legal adviser to the department under Borden, Meighen,

and King until 1923. King, in Granatstein's words, considered Christie to be "too much of a Tory imperialist centralizer," and Christie resigned in frustration in 1923. He retained his interest in international affairs and returned to External as counsellor in 1935, apparently with the concurrence of both Bennett and King. In 1939, he was appointed Canadian minister to the United States, but his duties were interrupted by illness, and he died in April 1941.

7 C.P. Stacey, *Arms, Men and Governments* (Ottawa: National Defence, 1970), 81–9; Eayrs, 91–103.
8 The report of 28 May 1935 titled "The Defence of Canada" by Major-General A.G.L. McNaughton is cited in Stacey, 3.
9 Canada, House of Commons, *Debates* (19 February 1937), 1051. Ernest Lapointe was King's closest political colleague and trusted spokesman for French Canada. First elected to the House of Commons in 1904, he was appointed to cabinet as minister of marine and fisheries in the first King government. In 1924, he became minister of justice, holding that portfolio until his death in 1941, except for the five years that the Liberals were in Opposition.
10 King Diary, MG 26 J 13, 26 August 1936.
11 Joint Staff Committee, Department of National Defence, "An Appreciation of the Defence Problems Confronting Canada with Recommendations for the Development of the Armed Forces," as found in Eayrs, 213–22.
12 Stacey, 3.
13 H.B. Neatby, *William Lyon Mackenzie King, Volume III: The Prism of Unity* (Toronto: University of Toronto Press, 1976).
14 The term "militia" had been used before the war to mean the army and included both a volunteer citizen force and the regular army.
15 Eayrs, 153.
16 Neatby, 190–4, 304.
17 Stacey, 6.
18 This section on Industrial Preparedness has been drawn from Stacey, 100–7 and H. Duncan Hall, *North American Supply* (London: HMSO, 1955), chaps 1 and 2.
19 Mackenzie King Papers, MG 26, reel C4245, C110254ff.
20 Joseph Schull, *The Great Scot* (Montreal: McGill-Queen's University Press, 1979), 34–5.
21 Bryce, "Memorandum for the Minister re: the German Financial Situation," NA, Records of the Department of Finance, RG 19, vol. 3979, file 6-2-10, 31 March 1939. This six-page memorandum discussed, in general terms, the recovery of the German economy in the 1930s. It argued that the recovery was based largely on high levels of government expenditure funded by increased taxes, the expansion of the money

supply, and large government loans. Vigorous control of prices, wages, and profits to keep inflation in check was critical to the program's success. About a year later, another study was made of Germany's finances in greater detail. See Bryce, "Germany – How She Financed It," RG 19, vol. 3449, 25 July 1940.
22 Dunning had offered to resign in August 1938 due both to his failing health and his declining influence in the government, but King persuaded him to stay. In July 1939, Dunning formally submitted his resignation, but King convinced him to stay until after the expected election. With the outbreak of war, King reorganized his cabinet and accepted Dunning's resignation. See Neatby, 322–3.
23 Winston S. Churchill, *The Second World War, Volume I* (Boston: Houghton Mifflin, 1948–53), 311.
24 J.W. Pickersgill, *The Mackenzie King Record, Volume I* (Toronto: University of Toronto Press, 1960), 15.
25 "WWII – Canada's Participation," Mackenzie King Papers, vol. 228, 24 August 1939.
26 "Considerations Relating to War Financial Policy," RG 19, vol. 777, file 400-16, 1 September 1939.
27 Canada, House of Commons, *Debates* (12 September 1939), 135–45.
28 "Canada's National Effort (Armed Forces) in the Early Stages of the War," Records of the Privy Council Office, RG 2, reel C-4653A, 5 September 1939.
29 Telegram from King to the British PM, "Military Cooperation with U.K. 1939–41," Mackenzie King Papers, vol. 395, 3 September 1939.
30 Stacey, 12.
31 Ibid.
32 The Royal Commission to Investigate the Bren Gun Contract was established under order-in-council PC 2251, 7 September 1938. The report, dated 29 December 1938, the Proceedings, and Exhibits can be found in Records of Royal Commissions, RG 33/66, vols I–XI.
33 Canada, *The Defence Purchases, Profits Control and Financing Act, 1939*, 3 George VI, chap. 42 (assented to 3 June 1939).
34 Canada, House of Commons, *Debates* (12 September 1939), 179. Throughout the war, public concern over profits on defence contracts was limited. The tax on excess profits as well as the scope and intensity of war production deterred criticism. Agricultural products and their subsidies, however, did receive some public attention later in the war.
35 Pickersgill, 27.
36 Ibid., 39.
37 Stacey, 486.
38 Hugh Scully brought a wide knowledge of Canadian business to the FECB, the result of twenty-five years in private business, augmented by

his experience as the commissioner of excise (October 1932 to December 1933) and subsequently the commissioner of customs (December 1933–40). In 1940, he became the chairman of the Wartime Industrial Control Board and controller of Steel. In 1943, he was appointed Canada's consul general in New York. Dana Wilgress joined the public service as a junior trade commissioner in 1914. He was stationed in Russia during the tumultuous years of the Revolution and World War I, and throughout the 1920s he promoted Canadian trade in Europe. He returned to Ottawa in 1932 to become the director of the Commercial Intelligence Service of the Department of Trade and Commerce. He assisted in trade negotiations with Britain and the United States during the 1930s, and in 1940 became the deputy minister of trade and commerce. In 1942, he returned to the USSR as Canada's first minister. Norman Robertson was also actively involved in the trade negotiations of the 1930s. He was the External Affairs representative on economic issues, and, as Granatstein has noted, his views were respected by Clark and Towers. Robertston's career is described in detail in Granatstein, *A Man of Influence* (Ottawa: Deneau Publishers, 1981).

39 David Mansur, interviewed by the author on 26 July 1980.
40 Ken Taylor, the child of Chinese missionaries, received his education in economics at the University of Chicago and the Brookings Institute in Washington. He was a member of the department of political economy at McMaster University from 1925 to 1939. At the beginning of the war, he came to Ottawa to be the secretary of the Wartime Prices and Trade Board. He remained with the board throughout the war, serving in several capacities, including chairman from 1947 to 1951. He was appointed assistant deputy minister of finance in 1947. Following the death of Clark in 1953, he was appointed deputy minister of finance.
41 K.W. Taylor, "The War-time Control of Prices" in J.F. Parkinson (ed.), *Canadian War Economics* (Toronto: University of Toronto Press, 1941), 52.
42 R.S. Sayers, *Financial Policy 1939–45* (London: HMSO, 1956), 325–7.
43 Ibid.
44 Sayers, 326–7.

CHAPTER TWO

1 Records of the Privy Council, RG 2, series 1, order-in-council 2698, 14 September 1929.
2 The genesis of the EAC was in discussions between O.D. Skelton, N.A. Robertson, and probably W.C. Clark, in the last days before war was declared. An economic advisory committee was suggested to the prime minister by Skelton on 9 September 1939. In his diary, King states that the order-in-council was prepared by Skelton and Clark. See Robertson

to Skelton, Records of External Affairs, RG 25, D 1, vol. 824, file 705, 1 September 1939; King Diary, MG 26, J 13, 12 September 1939.
3 Skelton's memorandum of 9 September 1939 to the prime minister suggests that the committee members included "Towers, Clark, Wilgress, Robertson, and one or two others." Listed as members on P.C. 2698 are W.C. Clark, G.F. Towers, H.D. Scully, H.B. McKinnon, G.S.H. Barton, C. Camsell, L.D. Wilgress, R.H. Coats, Lt-Col H. Desrosiers, N.A. Robertson, and a representative of the Department of Munitions and Supply.
4 The reports and minutes of the Economic Advisory Committee are in Records of the Department of Finance, RG 19, vols 4660–64. The first volume of the series contains the minutes and reports. Vols 4661–64 contain files of correspondence, memorandums, and draft reports relating to subjects relevant to the EAC discussions. The following discussion of the committee's activities is drawn from these volumes.
5 Minutes, RG 19, vol. 4660, file 187-EAC-4.
6 L.B. Pearson to Skelton, RG 19, vol. 4664, file 187-EAC-64, 9 June 1939; Skelton to Clark, ibid., 7 September 1939.
7 Ibid., vol. 4660, files 187-EAC-3 and 187-EAC-4. See also vol. 4664, file 186-EAC-64, which relates to wheat.
8 C.F. Wilson, *A Century of Canadian Grain* (Saskatoon: Western Producer Books, 1978), 645–6.
9 Minutes, RG 19, vol. 4660, file 187-EAC-4.
10 "Pork," ibid., vol. 4662, file 187-EAC-41. For "Sugar" see ibid., vol. 4663, file 187-EAC-54.
11 Robert H. Coats, Canada's first Dominion statistician, came to Ottawa in 1902 to be the associate editor of the *Labour Gazette*, apparently at the urging of the then deputy minister of labour, Mackenzie King. He subsequently became the Department of Labour's chief statistical officer and in 1915 was appointed Dominion statistician. Under his direction, the collection of statistics became centralized in one government agency. He was one of the pioneers of the modern professional civil service. See O. Mary Hill, *Canada's Salesman to the World* (Montreal: McGill-Queen's University Press, 1977).
12 "Automobile Industry," RG 19, vol. 4661, file 187-EAC-10.
13 A copy of the letter dated 8 March 1940 from Wallace Campbell, president of Ford Motor Company of Canada, to the prime minister can be found in RG 19, vol. 4660, file 187-EAC-4, part 1. This incident occurred just before Wallace Campbell left the War Supply Board. His appointment had not been a success. Campbell was described by King as an "old-fashioned, hard industrialist ... While good as an executive that type is in the industrial world what dictators are in the political world." See Pickersgill, 27 and Robert Bothwell and William Kilbourn, *C.D. Howe* (Toronto: McClelland and Stewart, 1970), 123–4, 129.

14 "Report of EAC on Automobile Export Situation," RG 19, vol. 4660, file 187-EAC-4-part 1, 3 April 1940.
15 Ibid.
16 Ibid., vol. 4661, file 187-EAC-10.
17 "Tourist Trade," ibid., vol. 4663, file 187-EAC-57.
18 Ibid., vol. 4660, file 187-EAC-4.
19 "Report of Sub-Committee on Exchange Conservation," ibid., 19 October 1940.

CHAPTER THREE

1 Dominions secretary to secretary of state for external affairs (DS to SSEA), 26 September 1939. *Documents on Canadian External Relations* (*DCER*), vol. 7 (Ottawa, 1974), 688.
2 Massey's role was stated publicly initially in his memoir *What's Past Is Prologue* (Toronto: Macmillan 1963). Some of this is corroborated by Air Ministry Records cited by Granatstein in *Canada's War: The Politics of the Mackenzie King Government, 1939–45* (Toronto: Oxford University Press, 1975), 67 n11, but as Granatstein notes (45), Massey's leading role was denied by Bruce, the Australian high commissioner at the time, and by the then undersecretary of state for air, Harold Balfour, in his book *Wings over Westminster* (London, 1973). The most recent and detailed account is found in F.J. Hatch's monograph *The Aerodrome of Democracy* (Ottawa, 1983), 13–14. Hatch concludes that the lack of documentation prevents any detailed account of Massey's role, though there is no doubt that it was important.
3 Between the wars there was a series of RAF proposals for air training involving the Dominions. Negotiations between the British Air Ministry and the Canadian government from 1935 to 1939 to establish a training school for British airmen were protracted and were complicated by King's reluctance to avoid any appearance of a military commitment. See chapter 1 of this book, "The Unprepared Beginnings," and F.J. Hatch, 2–12.
4 Minutes of Emergency Council, 28 September 1939, *DCER*, vol. 7, doc. 689.
5 Ibid., SSEA to DS, 28 September 1939, doc. 690.
6 "Air Training Plan 31 October–26 November 1939," Ian Mackenzie Papers, MG 27-III-B-5, vol. 31, file X41.
7 R.S. Sayers, *Financial Policy 1939–45* (London, 1956), 329.
8 Riverdale to PM, 13 October 1939, *DCER*, vol. 7, doc. 712.
9 PAC, Mackenzie King Papers, vol. 31, file X41.
10 "Notes on Canada's War Potential," Records of the Finance Department, RG 19, vol. 777, file 400-16, 31 October 1939.

11 SSEA to DS, 27 November 1939 and Air Mission of New Zealand to Air Mission Great Britain, 28 November 1939, *DCER*, vol. 7, docs 736 and 737.
12 Minutes of Emergency Council, 27 November 1939, *DCER*, vol. 7, doc. 735.
13 DS to SSEA, 27 November 1939, *DCER*, vol. 7, doc. 734.
14 C.P. Stacey, *Arms, Men and Governments* (Ottawa: Department of National Defence, 1970), 19.
15 The text of the agreement is to be found as app. D to Stace.
16 Minutes of Emergency Council, 39 October 1939, paras 3, 4, 10, 14, *DCER*, vol. 7, doc. 715. See also Mackenzie King Papers, vol. 3, file X41, minutes of second meeting of ministers with Air Mission on 3 November 1939.
17 Riverdale to Rogers, 8 December 1939, *DCER*, vol. 7, doc. 747.
18 "Minutes of Cabinet War Committee," *DCER*, 14 December 1939, doc. 756.
19 SSEA to DS, 16 December 1939, *DCER*, para. 6, doc.761.
20 Stacey, 26.
21 Skelton to King, 29 September 1939, penultimate paragraph, *DCER*, doc. 691; Skelton to King regarding conversation with Riverdale, 30 October 1939, *DCER*, doc. 714; ibid., Skelton to King regarding conversation with UK high commissioner, 1 November 1939, doc. 716; ibid., Skelton to King regarding "Paying the Piper," 13 December 1939, doc. 754.
22 J.W. Pickersgill, *The Mackenzie King Record* (Toronto, 1960), 50–9.
23 J.L. Granatstein, *Canada's War: The Politics of the Mackenzie King Government, 1939–45* (Toronto: Oxford University Press, 1975), 56.
24 Stacey, 287.
25 Ibid., 53.
26 Hatch, *Aerodrome of Democracy*, 104; see also chapter 8 of this book, "Financing Britain Further and Keynes's Visits."
27 Hatch, 194 and Stacey, 53. See also chapter 11 of this book, "The 1946 British Loan and Settlement."

CHAPTER FOUR

1 Imre de Vegh, *The Pound Sterling* (Boston: Scudder, Stevens & Clark, 1939), app.; H.C. Urquhart and K.A.H. Buckley, *Historical Statistics of Canada* (Toronto: Macmillan, 1965), series F57-71, F91-103, F104-145.
2 R.S. Sayers, *Financial Policy 1939–45* (London: HMSO and Longmans, Green and Co., 1956), 324. See also Clark to Dunning, PAC, Records of the Department of Finance, RG 19, vol. 3990, file U-3-2, 12 May 1939. This memorandum noted that British requirements in war were likely to amount to "as much as £80 million and might rise to £120 million" per year.
3 Sayers, 325.

4 Towers to Catterns, Bank of Canada Archives (BCA), Graham Towers Papers, 29 March 1939.
5 See chapter 1 of this book, "The Unprepared Beginnings."
6 See the discussion in chapter 2 of this book, "The EAC and Trade Problems."
7 Memorandum, RG 19, vol. 3990, file U-3-2, 2 October 1939.
8 Osborne to Phillips, RG 19, vol. 3990, file U-3-2, 4 October 1939, and Phillips to Osborne, RG 19, vol. 3990, file U-3-2, 13 October 1939.
9 Phillips to Osborne, RG 19, vol. 3990, file U-3-2, 19 October 1939.
10 Bank of Canada, *Bank of Canada Statistical Summary, 1946 Supplement* (Ottawa, 1946), 64.
11 "Notes on Canada's War Potential," RG 19, vol. 777, file 400-16, 31 October 1939.
12 It has not been possible to find a copy of the "secret financial memorandum" given to Crerar as he left for England. A copy of the memorandum revised in view of new figures from Finance sent by telegram November 1939 in the British Treasury files is cited by H.M. Mackenzie in "Mutual Assistance: The Finance of British Requirements in Canada During the Second World War" (Ph.D. thesis, Oxford University, 1981), 115. The telegram is more accessible. See *Documents on Canadian External Relations* (DCER), vol. 7 (Ottawa: External Affairs, 1974), 382–3.
13 Colin Clark was a British statistician who contributed much to the development of national income and related statistics in the 1930s.
14 Clark to Osborne, RG 19, vol. 3992, file U-3-3, 29 January 1940.
15 Sayers, 331. The last sentence of the quotation refers to the burden-sharing exercise in NATO, which I believe Canada opposed.
16 Memorandum, RG 19, vol. 3440, file "Statistics 1940–1942."
17 J.L. Granatstein, *Canada's War: The Politics of the Mackenzie King Government, 1939–45* (Toronto: Oxford University Press, 1975), 63, 70, and n90.
18 "Considerations Relating to War Financial Policy," RG 19, vol. 777, file 400-16, 1 September 1939; "Memorandum on Financial Policy Concerning Additional Defence Projects," ibid., vol. 3984, file N-2-6-1, 15 December 1940.
19 BCA, Graham Towers Papers, 23 January 1940.
20 The second repatriation operation of the war was initiated by the Bank of Canada. They proposed to Clark in late May that they proceed with the British to arrange to requisition in Britain the Dominion of Canada four per cent issue due in 1960, of which it was believed some £16.9 million was held in the UK, equivalent to about $75 million, which then would be paid off by Canada.
21 Mackenzie, 128–30.
22 H. Duncan Hall, *North American Supply* (London: HMSO and Longmans,

Green and Co., 1955), 13–18; A.F.W. Plumptre, *Mobilizing Canada's Resources for War* (Toronto: Macmillan, 1941), 19–20, 69–70.
23 King Diary, MG 26 J 13, 17 May 1940.
24 Cabinet War Committee Minutes, RG 2/7C, reel C4653A, 17 May 1940.
25 Secretary of state for external affairs to high commissioner in Great Britain, *DCER*, vol. 7, 24 May 1940, 846; ibid., 21 May 1940, 874; ibid., 23 May 1940, 769.
26 King Diary, MG 26 J 13, 27 May 1940.
27 Sayers, 366–7.
28 Memorandum of conversation, RG 19, vol. 3987, file R-6-2, 26 July 1940. See also L. Rasminsky to Clark, RG 19, vol. 3987, file R-6-2, 18 February 1941.
29 R.B. Bryce, "Memorandum for Record," RG 19, vol. 3987, file R-6-2, 21 January 1942; Clark to Gardiner, ibid., 30 September 1940.
30 Towers to King, BCA, Graham Towers Papers, memorandum 345, 15 August 1940.
31 Ibid., memorandum 355.
32 J.W. Pickersgill, *The Mackenzie King Record* (Toronto: University of Toronto Press, 1960), 180–5.
33 Sayers, app. IV, 557–9.
34 Memorandum, Records of the Department of External Affairs, RG 25, vol. 775, file 361 (IV-231), 7 December 1940; Clark to Ilsley, RG 19, vol. 3987, file R-6-2, 5 December 1940. The suggestion was badly timed, because King was anxious to adjourn the House of Commons. See King Diary, MG 26 J 13, 6 December 1940.
35 Pickersgill, 185.
36 Robert E. Sherwood, *Roosevelt and Hopkins* (New York: Harper & Brothers, 1948), 223–5. For the text of the letter, see Winston S. Churchill, *The Second World War, Volume II: Their Finest Hour* (Boston: Houghton Mifflin, 1949), 558–67.
37 "Report on Visit to Washington, March 17–21," RG 19, vol. 3991, file U-3-2-4/C, 21 March 1941.
38 Canada, House of Commons, *Debates* (20 March 1941), 1713.
39 *DCER*, vol. 7, telegram 46, 27 March 1941, 496–99.
40 Ibid., telegram 79, 10 May, 1941, 499–501.
41 Malcolm Macdonald to J.L. Ilsley, RG 19, vol. 3990, file U-3-1-2, 6 September 1941.
42 Ilsley to Heeney, minutes of Cabinet War Committee, RG 2/7C, reel C4653A, 19 June 1941.
43 Ibid., 20 June 1941.
44 "Report of the Economic Advisory Committee on Means of Utilizing Canada's Accumulating Sterling Balances," RG 19, vol. 4663, file 187-EAC-53, 8 July 1941.

45 Sayers, 342; Mackenzie, 198–202. For Canadian sources, see "Report of the Economic Advisory Committee," RG 19, vol. 4663, file 187-EAC-53, 8 July 1941, especially 5–6. The negotiations are described in UK high commissioner to secretary of state for dominion affairs, RG 19, vol. 3990, file U-3-1-2, 11 July 1941; from Clark to Coates, ibid., 18 August 1941; Malcolm Macdonald to Ilsley, ibid., 6 September 1941.
46 Howe to Ilsley, C.D. Howe Papers, MG 27 III B20, vol. 4, file S-5, 21 July 1941.
47 BCA, Graham Towers Papers, memorandum 402, 6 August 1940.
48 Memo by Coyne, RG 19, vol. 3446, file R.B.B.-1941, 16 September 1941.
49 BCA, Graham Towers Papers, memorandum 410, 24 October 1941.
50 King Diary, 30 and 31 October 1941. Ernest Lapointe died on 26 November 1941.
51 "Proposal for Reducing Canada's Accumulating Sterling Balance," RG 2/7C, reel C4654, November–December 1941, doc. no. 41, 3 December 1941.
52 Ibid., meetings of 15 and 16 December 1941.
53 King Diary, 18 December 1941.
54 Ibid., 22 and 23 December 1941.
55 Mackenzie, 218.
56 Canada, House of Commons, *Debates* (26 January 1942), 42.
57 Arthur Porter to Turnbull, MG 26 J 1, vol. 331, 8 June 1942. In this file can be found a series of letters between Porter and Turnbull. The issue of most concern was the differences of opinion in Quebec compared with the rest of Canada on the conduct of the war. See also J. Laflamme to Ilsley, RG 19, vol. 777, file 400-16, 24 August 1942.
58 Canada, House of Commons, *Debates* (18 March 1942), 1429.
59 PC 2607, 1 April 1942.
60 Secretary of state for external affairs to acting high commissioner in Australia, *DCER*, vol. 9, 24 October 1942; acting high commissioner in Australia to SSEA, 26 October 1942, 377–9.
61 See RG 19, vol. 399k, file U-3-2-4. This file contains a series of letters dating from June to October 1942 between Clark and other department officials and Gordon Munro on administrative problems.
62 Knox to Clark, RG 19, vol. 3992, file U-3-8-2/2, 30 July 1942.
63 C.P. Stacey, *Arms, Men and Governments* (Ottawa: National Defence, 1970), 277–83 and 564–78 (text of Agreement). See also F.J. Hatch, *The Aerodrome of Democracy* (Ottawa: National Defence, 1983), 101–14.
64 Stacey, 279.
65 "Report of the Conference Committee to Final Plenary Session of the Ottawa Air Training Conference," *DCER*, vol. 9, 22 May 1942, 288–93.
66 Stacey, 281–2.
67 Hatch, 106.

68 C.G. Power, *A Party Politician* (Toronto: Macmillan, 1966), 217.
69 "Ottawa Air Training Conference, Minutes and Agreements, May–June 1942," Ottawa: Department of National Defence Historical Section, DHist 80/255. The following paragraphs are drawn from these records of the conference.
70 Ibid.
71 Clark to Robertson, RG 19, vol. 3992, file U-3-2/2, 1 September 1942; Wrong to Clark, ibid., 9 September 1942. In his letter to Robertson, Clark said that he thought a gift to all the United Nations would be easier to justify "from the public point of view."
72 Mackenzie, 229–39.

CHAPTER FIVE

1 George Watts, interviewed by author.
2 Ibid.
3 The government of Canada issued bonds in New York in January 1937 in an amount of $85 million US, most of them for thirty years at a yield to the buyer of 3.1 per cent. It made another thirty-year public issue in November 1938 (after the Munich crisis) in an amount of $40 million at a yield to the buyer of 3.14 per cent, all of which was used to redeem a maturing issue of short-term notes issued in 1936. The 1937 loan had been issued in order to redeem a maturing 5 per cent tax-free bond issued during the 1914–18 war, payable optionally in US or Canadian dollars.
4 Towers to Catterns, BCA, Graham Towers Papers, memorandum 122, 20 April 1938. See also Catterns to Towers, ibid., 29 March 1939.
5 Memorandum, Records of the Privy Council, RG 2, series 1, PC 2716, 15 September 1939. See also Joseph Schull, *The Great Scot* (Montreal: McGill-Queen's University Press, 1979), 34–9.
6 The Wartime Prices and Trade Board was the first of the economic organizations to be created in September of 1939. Unlike the Foreign Exchange Control Board, which began with a complete set of controls and regulations ready to be implemented, the WPTB did not immediately impose controls on the Canadian economy. Initially, the WPTB used its powers carefully and selectively, and it was not until the fall of 1941 that the government decided to impose a general ceiling on Canadian prices.
7 Alan O. Gibbons, "Foreign Exchange Control in Canada, 1939–51," *Canadian Journal of Economics and Political Science* 19, no. 1 (February 1953), 35. See also Louis Rasminsky, "Foreign Exchange Control: Purposes and Methods," in J.F. Parkinson (ed.), *Canadian War Economics* (Toronto: University of Toronto Press, 1941), 80–127. These two articles, both written by active participants, are useful summaries of the operations of the Foreign Exchange Control Board.

8 See, for example, "Orchids for Exchange Control," *Financial Post*, 15 February 1940. The article comments that a common feature of presidential addresses at the annual meetings of many companies early in 1940 was a tribute to the efficiency of the FECB.
9 Gibbons, 52; see also Rasminsky, 93. The latter article comments that the board's approach to problems was functional rather than legalistic.
10 W.C. Clark, "Suggestions as to a Reasonable Reserve of U.S. Dollar Exchange to be Maintained by Canada," in J.F. Hilliker (ed.), *Documents on Canadian External Relations* (DCER), vol. 9 (Ottawa: Department of External Affairs, 1980), 1404–8.
11 BCA, Graham Towers Papers, 23 January 1940.
12 Rasminsky, 123; H.C. Urquhart and K.A.H. Buckley, *Historical Statistics of Canada* (Toronto: Macmillan, 1965), 147, 161.
13 Memorandum 333, BCA, Graham Towers Papers, 2 April 1940.
14 Press release, ibid., file LR 76-148-2, 30 April 1940.
15 Towers to Ralston, RG 19, vol. 3970, file B-2-8-7 (2-2), 4 June 1940.
16 Canada, House of Commons, *Debates* (24 June 1940), 1016–17.
17 Ibid., 1020–2.
18 J.E. Coyne, memorandum, BCA, file LR 76-150, 5 June 1940.
19 RG 19, vol. 660, file 184. The memorandum of 28 June 1940 recommending the restriction of US dollar sales stated that according to the FECB statistics, travel expenditures in the US by Canadians were estimated to be in excess of $6 million for the month of May 1940. The Dominion Bureau of Statistics estimated that Canadians spent more than $100 million per year travelling in the United States.
20 See the discussion on "Measures to Conserve Exchange" in chapter 2 of this book, "The EAC and Trade Problems." The reports can be found in RG 19, vol. 4660, file 187-EAC-4.
21 Canada, House of Commons, *Debates* (2 December 1940), 551–59.
22 "Conservation of Foreign Exchange," BCA, vol. 87, file LR 76-150-73 and FECB.
23 *DCER*, vol. 9, 1407, 1874–5.
24 W.S. Churchill, *The Second World War, Volume II: Their Finest Hour* (Boston: Houghton Mifflin, 1949), 25. Churchill became the British prime minister on 10 May 1940.
25 H. Duncan Hall, *North American Supply* (London: HMS and Longmans, Green and Co., 1955), 146–9.
26 Wayne Cole, *Roosevelt and the Isolationists* (Lincoln, Nebraska and London: University of Nebraska Press, 1983), 395–404.
27 Warren Kimball, "Lend-Lease and the Open Door: The Temptation of British Opulence, 1937–1942," *Political Science Quarterly* 136, no. 2 (June 1971). The American secretary of state, Cordell Hull, guided US economic foreign policy from the late 1930s through the negotiation of

the Lend-Lease Master Agreement. Hull believed that the only sure way to peace was through economic interdependence between nations, advocating equal commercial opportunity and the elimination of discriminatory trade practices. He condemned Britain's system of imperial preferences while casting an appreciative eye at the "opulent" British Empire. Kimball argues that in the Lend-Lease agreement negotiations, the Americans, led by Hull, were guided by their vision of the wealth of the British Empire, their belief in equal economic opportunity, and the desire to drive a good bargain. They used Britain's dependence on the US as leverage

to "barter Empire preference in exchange for money and goods."

28 Towers, memorandum 370, BCA, Graham Towers Papers, December 1940.
29 R.S. Sayers, *Financial Policy 1939–45* (London: HMSO and Longmans, Green and Co., 1956), 378–81. Sayers has an enlightening few pages on British attitudes on this question of statistics and disclosure.
30 RG 19, vol. 3971, file B-2-8-9-0.
31 J.W. Pickersgill, *The Mackenzie King Record* (Toronto: University of Toronto Press, 1960), 184.
32 Bryce to Clark, RG 19, vol. 3991, file U-3-2-4/C, 20 January 1941.
33 King Diary, MG 26 J 13, 26 February 1941.
34 Minutes of the Cabinet War Committee, RG 2/7C, vol. 3, reel C4653A, 13 March 1941.
35 King Diary, MG 26 J 13, 13 March 1941.
36 RG 19, vol. 3991, file U-3-2-4-1. Many of Coyne's letters dating from early in April to the end of August 1941 can be found in this file. He wrote informal but illuminating letters to Clark once a week or more, describing meetings and giving his impressions of the financial negotiations.
37 "Report on Visit to Washington," RG 19, vol. 399k, file U-3-2-4, 21 March 1941.
38 Minutes, Cabinet War Committee, RG 2/7C, vol. 3, reel C4653A, 21 March 1941.
39 Howe to King, DCER, vol. 8, 307–9.
40 Clark to King, ibid, 9 April 1941.
41 J.M. Little, "Canada Discovered: Continentalist Perceptions of the Roosevelt Administration, 1939–1945" (Ph.D. thesis, University of Toronto, 1975), 455–8. This thesis is largely based on the extensive Morgenthau Diaries. For a Canadian perspective, see Coyne's "Memorandum of Meeting with Morgenthau," RG 19, vol. 3971, file B-2-8-9-1, 18 April 1941.
42 Ibid.
43 Pickersgill, 194–200.
44 DCER, vol. 8, 324–5.

45 Pickersgill, 197.
46 Robertson was the much beloved professor of economics at Cambridge who began each chapter of his books on economics with an apt quotation from *Alice in Wonderland*. His bit of verse was passed on from the British Treasury to the Department of Finance through the high commissioner's office in Ottawa on 23 January 1943.
47 Coyne, "Memorandum of Telephone Conversation with Mr. Hopkins," RG 19, vol. 3991, file U-3-2-4-1, 16 May 1941.
48 Memoranda re: Washington meetings 11–16 May 1941, RG 19, vol. 3971, file B-2-8-9-1, 16 May 1941.
49 "Consolidation of Forecast of Supplies as of 3 December, 1941," ibid., file B-2-9-9C.
50 Ibid., file B-2-8-9, "Canada's U.S. Dollar Exchange Position," 29 December 1941. The $61 million figure comes from subsequent US sources cited in Little, "Canada Discovered," n126. Of this total, $50 million was made up of capital advances to build an aluminum plant.
51 Coyne to Clark RG 19, vol. 3971, file B-2-8-9/A, 20 August 1941.
52 Gordon to Clark, ibid., file B-2-8-9-1, 26 November 1941.
53 Philip Young to J.B. Carswell, ibid., file B-2-8-9-2, 21 November 1941.
54 Howe to Morgenthau, ibid., file B-2-8-9-2, 24 November 1941.
55 Carswell to G.K. Shiels, ibid., file B-2-8-9-3, 18 October 1941; Coyne to Clark, RG 19, vol. 3991, file U-3-2-4-1, 26 August 1941. Coyne's letter had also been shown to Ilsley.
56 "Canada's U.S. Dollar Exchange Position," RG 19, vol. 3971, file B-2-8-9, 29 December 1941.
57 Urquhart and Buckley, *Historical Statistics of Canada*, 130, 134.
58 King Diary, 9 January 1941.
59 Pickersgill, 184. Morgenthau told King that he liked Clark's attitude and that he had been of very great help. See also Little, 441.
60 J.L. Granatstein, *Canada's War: The Politics of the Mackenzie King Government, 1939–45* (Toronto: Oxford University Press, 1975), 145.
61 "Wartime Production – Relations with United States," *DCER*, vol. 8, 277–9.
62 Ibid., 286–9.
63 Ibid., 343–4.
64 "Resolution of the Joint Economic Committees of Canada and the United States Recommending the Establishment of a Joint Committee on Defence Production," *DCER*, 347–51. See also Canada, House of Commons, *Debates* (5 November 1941), 4098.
65 Warren James, *Wartime Economic Cooperation* (Toronto: Ryerson Press, 1949), 327.
66 Resolution no. 6, RG 19, vol. 3977, file E-3-2.
67 W.A. Mackintosh to King, RG 19, vol. 3977, 17 December 1941. See also the minutes of the meeting of 7–9 November 1941 of the Joint

Economic Committees in the same file, where there is discussion of a previous draft of the resolution.

68 "Joint Economic Committees of Canada and the United States," RG 19, vol. 3977, file E-3-2, 2 September 1943.

69 The resolution was discussed at a meeting of the Cabinet War Committee on 19 December 1941. Copies of the resolution, the report, and Mackintosh's letter to the prime minister were circulated to members of the War Committee with "a view to further consideration at a subsequent meeting." Minutes of meeting, PAC, Records of the Privy Council Office, RG 2, 7C, vol. 6, reel of C4654, 19 December 1941.

70 "Memorandum on the Joint Economic Committees of Canada and the United States," RG 19, vol. 3977, file E-3-2, 8 October 1943.

71 James, *Wartime Economic Cooperation*, and P.C. 2586, 11 April 1944.

CHAPTER SIX

1 Winston S. Churchill, *The Second World War, Volume III: The Grand Alliance* (Boston: Houghton Mifflin, 1950), 662–771.

2 Ibid., 641; A.J.P. Taylor, *The Second World War* (London: Penguin Books, 1976), 105, 127.

3 J.W. Pickersgill, *The Mackenzie King Record* (Toronto: University of Toronto Press, 1960), 319, 325–8.

4 Churchill, 689–90.

5 C.P. Stacey, *Arms, Men and Governments: The War Policies of Canada 1939–1945* (Ottawa: Department of National Defence, 1970), 162.

6 *Documents on Canadian External Relations* (*DCER*), vol. 9 (Ottawa: Department of External Affairs, 1980), 118–24.

7 Stacey, 175.

8 Ibid.

9 Warren James, *Wartime Economic Cooperation* (Toronto: Ryerson Press, 1949), 241, 333.

10 Stacey, 176.

11 Ibid., 554–6.

12 *DCER*, vol. 9, 106–9.

13 This letter by Wrong was the first articulation of the Canadian version of functionalism, an approach to international relations that shaped Canadian policy on international institutions such as the UNRRA and the UN during the war. It was defined as a determinant of when "effective international authority in a given matter ought to be concentrated in bodies in which the countries mainly concerned were represented." See John W. Holmes, *The Shaping of Peace: Canada and the Search for World Order 1943–1957, Volume I* (Toronto: University of Toronto Press, 1979), 72–3.

14 *DCER*, vol. 9, 116–18.
15 Ibid., 135–9; Stacey, 163–5.
16 *DCER*, vol. 9, 151–3.
17 Ibid., 169–70.
18 Pickersgill, 410.
19 *DCER*, vol. 9, 180–1.
20 Ibid., 197–8.
21 Ibid., 214–15.
22 Ibid., 187–9, 231–2, 237.
23 James, 24–5, 43.
24 M.J. Bellamy, *Profiting the Crown: Canada's Polymer Corporation* (Montreal: McGill-Queen's University Press, 2005).
25 James, 27–9. The establishment of the Joint War Production Committee had been recommended by the Joint Economic Committees. See the discussion in chapter 5 of this book, "Scarce US Dollars and the Hyde Park Declaration."
26 S.D. Pierce and A.F.W. Plumptre, "Canada's Relations with War-time Agencies in Washington," *Canadian Journal of Economics and Political Science* 11 (August 1945), 404–5; James, 225–6.
27 Ibid., 410.
28 James, 91.
29 Ibid., 97.
30 Pierce and Plumptre, 410–11.
31 Minutes of fourth session of joint meeting of Joint Economic Committees, PAC, Records of the Department of Finance, RG 19, vol. 3977, file E-3-2, 8 November 1941.
32 James, 112.
33 Bryce to Clark, RG 19, vol. 3979, file G-1-1, 8 October 1942. The effects of suspending gold production on exchange, post-war production, the mining communities, and the stock market are outlined in this memo, which concludes that none of the problems was serious enough to justify keeping the gold mines operating. The author first acknowledges his personal interest in the problem (his father was a leading figure in the gold-mining industry) before undertaking the analysis, which then covers several pages.
34 James, 133. James cites "Historical Reports on War Administration, War Production Board, Special Study No. 9" in *The Closing of the Gold Mines, August 1941 to March 1944* (Washington, US Government Printing Office, 1946).
35 J.M. Little, "Canada Discovered: Continentalist Perceptions of the Roosevelt Administration, 1939–45" (Ph.D. thesis, University of Toronto, 1975), 496.
36 Ibid., 497 and n34.

37 L. Rasminsky, "Notes on Visit to Washington and New York, Apr. 5–11, 1942," BCA, LR 76-187, box 187, 11 April 1942.
38 Trade and other balance of payments figures are from Bank of Canada, *Bank of Canada Statistical Summary, 1946 Supplement* (Ottawa, 1946), 122–5. The reserve figures are from DCER, vol. 9, 1404–8, and app. 1874–5.
39 Little, 509–11.
40 Ibid., 528–9.
41 Plumptre to Clark, RG 19, vol. 3972, file B-2-8-9-6, 28 December 1942.
42 DCER, vol. 9, 1404–8.
43 "Discussions with the United States Treasury," RG 19, vol. 3972, file B-2-8-9-6, 11 January 1943.
44 Plumptre to Clark, ibid., 20 January 1943; White to Clark, ibid., 26 January 1943.
45 White to Clark, ibid., 6 March 1943.
46 DCER, vol. 9, 1417–8.
47 Memorandum, RG 19, vol. 3972, file B-2-8-9-7, 13 March 1944.
48 "Memorandum re: Trip to Washington April 6–7, 1943," ibid., file B-2-8-9-6, 8 April 1943.
49 White to Clark, ibid., 9 July 1943; Plumptre to Clark, ibid., 13 August 1943.
50 Clark to Pettigrew, ibid., 17 September 1943; Howe to Clark, ibid., 27 September 1943; Clark to Howe, ibid., 30 September 1943.
51 White to Clark, ibid., 17 November 1943; Clark to White, ibid., 23 November 1943; "Memorandum for Dr. Clark, by R.B. Bryce," ibid., 29 November 1943; "Memo re U.S. Exchange Problem by R.B. Bryce," ibid., 29 November 1943.
52 DCER, vol. 9, 1420–2.
53 DCER, vol. 9, 1175, 1180–1 and 1182–5.
54 R.J. Diubaldo, "The Canol Project in Canadian-American Relations," Canadian Historical Association, *Papers* 1977, 179–95.
55 DCER, vol. 9, 1228–33.
56 Ibid., 1289–90.
57 Ibid., 1290–2, 58, minutes of Cabinet War Committee, Records of the Privy Council, RG 2/7C, reel C-4875, 1 and 3 December 1943.
59 Memorandum re: Visit to Washington, RG 19, vol. 3972, B-2-8-9-6, 7 and 8 December 1943; "Canada's U.S. Dollar Reserves During 1943," ibid., 4 December 1943.
60 Ibid.
61 White to Clark, ibid., 23 February 1944.
62 Memorandum, ibid., 13 March 1944.
63 Pickersgill, 649–50. King was concerned about Ilsley's health in the early months of 1944, but Ilsley was persuaded only with difficulty to take some rest. King noted that Ilsley was "absolutely indispensable,"

but he suspected that without some rest, he would break down completely.
64 Little, 573. For White's memo to Morgenthau, see "Current Status of Negotiations to Reduce Canada's Dollar Balance," RG 19, vol. 3972, B-2-8-9-7, 14 March 1944.
65 Little, 477; Pickersgill, 644.
66 Minutes of the Cabinet War Committee, RG 2/7C, reel C-4876, 1, 8, 15, 22, March 1944.
67 Ilsley to Morgenthau, RG 19, vol. 3972, B-2-8-9-7, 24 March 1944; Morgenthau to Ilsley, ibid., 29 March 1944.
68 Canada, House of Commons, *Debates* (21 April 1944), 2226–8. This expenditure of $66.6 million on airfields soon was given in the summary of public expenditures in the appendix to the 1944 budget, and all the expenses ultimately appeared somewhere in the public accounts, although most of them were unidentifiable items in the huge war expenditures of the National Defence Department and the Mutual Aid Board.
69 Canada, House of Commons, *Debates* (18 May 1944), 2994–5; Towers to Ilsley, RG 19, vol. 660, file 184, 21 February 1944.
70 Canada, House of Commons, *Debates* (26 June 1944), 4185.
71 M.C. Urquhart and K.A.H. Buckley, *Historical Statistics of Canada* (Toronto: Macmillan, 1965), 152, 165, 181, 182.
72 J.L. Granatstein, *The Ottawa Men: The Civil Service Mandarins 1935–57* (Toronto: Oxford University Press, 1982).

CHAPTER SEVEN

1 "Preliminary Notes re: Sterling Problem, Etc." PAC, RG 19, vol. 3449, file "Sterling Problem," 9 December 1942.
2 *Documents on Canadian External Relations* (DCER), vol. 9, 380–94.
3 Ibid., 395–6.
4 Ibid., 396–9.
5 Ibid., 400–1.
6 Canada, House of Commons, *Debates* (2 March 1943), 846.
7 Memorandum, RG 2/18, vol. 40, file D-13-5 (2), 1 February 1943; Canada, House of Commons, *Debates* (6 May 1942), 2436.
8 *Statutes of Canada*, 1943–44, chap. 17, sect. 4, sub-section 2.
9 "Memorandum for the Prime Minister from A.D.P. Heeney," RG 2/18, vol. 40, D-13-5, vol. 2, 1943–44, 23 February 1943; minutes, Records of the Cabinet War Committee, RG 2/7C, reel C4875, 3 March 1943.
10 Wrong to Heeney, RG 2/18, vol. 40, file D-13-5, 26 February 1944.
11 Canada, House of Commons, *Debates* (8 February 1943), 215; ibid. (6 May 1943), 2437.
12 Bryce, "Illustration of How Distribution of Mutual Aid to Sterling Area

Might Be Based on Particular Circumstances of Each Part of Area," RG 19, vol. 416, file 101-106-2E, 6 April 43.
13 "Operation of Mutual Aid," RG 19, vol. 408, file 101-106-2, 21 May 1943.
14 "Memorandum for W.C. Clark by R.B. Bryce," RG 19, vol. 418, file 101-106-1, 19 June 1943; "Mutual Aid Procedures by K. Palmer," RG 2/18, vol. 41, file D-13-5-5, 24 June 1943. Palmer was a senior legal officer of the Department of Munitions and Supply whose legal drafting showed not only competence but also elegance. See also CMAB decision of 12 July 1943 in minutes, RG 19, vol. 418, file 101-106-3, 12 July 1943, and PC 5560 of 13 July 1943. All subsequent references to the Mutual Aid Board minutes in this chapter will be to that file.
15 B.G. McIntyre to Clark, RG 19, vol. 408, file 101-106-2, 21 May 1943.
16 Memorandum, ibid., file 101-106-216, August 1943.
17 Memorandum of Agreement, RG 2/18, vol. 41, file D-13-5-5, 1 December 1943.
18 Canada, *Public Accounts 1943–44*, zz–8
19 "Mutual Aid Legislation," RG 19, vol. 418, 17 January 1944.
20 *DCER*, vol. 9, 442–4.
21 Ibid., 451–2.
22 Canadian Mutual Aid Board, *Final Report* (Ottawa, 1946), 38–9.
23 Ibid.
24 One satisfactory credit transaction was entered into by the Department of Finance and the Russians during the summer of 1945 under part II of the Export Credits Insurance Act of 1944. It was described as follows some years later in a long memorandum by C.L. Read: "In the absence of general credit arrangements, the U.S.S.R. in June 1945 began exploring the possibilities of financing the cost of certain hydro-electric equipment which V.O. Machinoinport had ordered in Canada for Plant 'X' ... On August 20, 1945 the U.S.S.R. requested that a credit amounting to $3 million be extended to finance the cost of this equipment, – the advances made under the credit to be repaid in full on August 31, 1950 with interest payable semi-annually ... at the rate of 2% on the amount of credit outstanding. The credit was made available on August 21, 1945. Semi annual interest payments were made promptly by the U.S.S.R. government on each payment date and the principal amount was paid off in full on August 31, 1950." The memorandum from which this information is quoted is a very comprehensive one of eleven pages with twenty-five annexes, entitled "Notes Relating to Canada's Claim in Respect of Industrial Equipment Supplied to the U.S.S.R. After the Termination of Mutual Aid," 27 August 1951. It was prepared for the Department of External Affairs to give to R.A.D. Ford, their new chargé d' affaires to the U.S.S.R., to enable him to present these claims as instructed by cabinet. The negotiations resulted in a settlement agree-

ment on 28 August 1953 under which the USSR paid Canada $2,807,064 (Department of External Affairs file 4929-V-40). The notes, prepared by Read with an important covering memorandum to John Deutsch, are to be found in RG 19, vol. 405, file 101-106-2.
25 Barbara W. Tuchman, *Stilwell and the American Experience in China 1911–1945* (Toronto, New York, London, Sydney, Auckland: Bantam Books, 1972), 479.
26 Ibid., 387.
27 See the discussion in ibid. and Churchill, *The Second World War, Volume VI: Triumph and Tragedy* (Boston: Houghton Mifflin, 1953), chap. 11.
28 Canada, House of Commons, *Debates* (8 February 1943), 215. See also Kim Richard Nossal, "Business as Usual: Canadian Relations with China in the 1940s," Canadian Historical Association, *Historical Papers* 1978, 137–8.
29 Mutual Aid Board minutes, 7 May 1943 and 27 July 1943.
30 *DCER*, vol. 9, 406–9.
31 Wrong to Bryce, RG 19, vol. 407, file 101-106-2, 28 September 1943. Attached is a letter of 27 September 1943 from N.A. Robertson to L.B. Pearson.
32 King to T.V. Soong, RG 36/21, vol. 30, file "China – General correspondence, vol. I," 20 August 1943.
33 Wrong to Clark, RG 19, vol. 407, file 101-106-2, 9 September 1943.
34 Wrong to Bryce, ibid., file 101-106-228, September 1943; Wrong to Pearson, ibid., 14 October 1943.
35 Mutual Aid Board minutes, 13 December 1943, 30 December 1943, 14 January 1944.
36 "Report of General Pope to Chiefs of Staff with Views of British Joint Staff Mission in Washington, Directed to Canadian Joint Staff in Washington," RG 19, vol. 407, file 101-106-2, 24 February 1944. It is worth recording here that Fraser's files, RG 36/21, vol. 30, show some success on his part in marshalling evidence that the Canadian production and stocks of motor transport were ample at that time to meet known UK requirements, plus the shipment to China, with some to spare. Canada was seeking business in this field, and some of the British apprehension of scarcity may have been based on the limitations of finance and shipping.
37 "Mutual Aid for China," RG 19, vol. 407, file 101-106-229, 8 February 1944.
38 Robertson to King, RG 25, vol. 2, file 4929-F-40, 2 March 1944.
39 The Americans were not pleased about the shipment. At the meeting of the joint war aid committee, William Batt, a member of the War Production Board and the Canada–U.S. materials coordinating committee, hit the ceiling and described the Canadian action as complete

foolishness. As John Hickerson of the State Department and another participant put it: "It was a hot day, the air conditioning in the Chiefs of Staff building was working badly and altogether it was a bad meeting." US State Department, *Foreign Relations of the United States, Diplomatic Papers, 1944, Volume VI, China* (Washington: US Government Printing Office, 1967), 173–5. See also Nossal, 139–40.

40 Mutual Aid Board minutes, 5 June 1944.
41 Canadian ambassador to China to secretary of state for external affairs, RG 2/18, vol. 44, file D-13-5-C, 29 July 1944 and 3 August 1944.
42 This paragraph draws on the conclusions of Tuchman, chap. 17, Churchill, chap. 11, and John Ehrman, *Grand Strategy* (London: HMSO, 1956), vol. V, 415–18 and vol. VI, 174–7.
43 Mutual Aid Board minutes, 30 March 1945.
44 Nossal, 140.
45 Mutual Aid Board minutes, 13 August 1945 and 17 January 1946.
46 Ibid., 13 September 1945.
47 Repayment was to be made in thirty annual installments, beginning in 1948 at an interest rate of three per cent per annum. Ilsley noted that the Canadian government was not willing to agree to a longer period for repayment and also was not prepared at that stage to agree to any larger credit for general post-war purposes despite the strong desire of the Chinese government. J.L. Ilsley to Major General P. Kiang, RG 2/18, vol. 104, file T-50-C, 28 December 1945.
48 Robertson to Howe, RG 2/18, vol. 69, file D-13-5-C, 7 February 1946.
49 The export credit was approved by P.C. 378, 5 February 1946. The agreement between the governments of China and Canada was made on 7 February 1946. A supplementary agreement was signed on 28 May 1947. By 31 December 1948, the termination date of the agreements, $35 million had been advanced for reconstruction and $16 million of the $25 million that had been limited to purchases of goods originally requested by China under Mutual Aid and other surplus war supplies had been advanced. See *Report on Operations Under Part II of the Export Credits Insurance Act During the Fiscal Year 1948–49* submitted by D.C. Abbott, Minister of Finance, 18 October 1949. For the further history of the loan to China and its repayment, see subsequent *Reports* submitted annually to Parliament by the minister of finance.
50 The rebirth of the Ming Sung Shipping Co. Ltd. is described in an article by Allen Abel, "Profit Motive to Propel Chinese Line," *Globe and Mail*, 4 February 1985, B13. The guaranteed loan to the original company was given in November 1946, as described in *Report on Operations Under Part II of the Export Credits Insurance Act During the Fiscal Year 1946–47*.
51 Tuchman, 678.

52 Telegram, RG 2/18, vol. 40, file D-13-5(2), 23 February 1943.
53 Canadian Mutual Aid Board, *Report*, 20 May 1943 to 31 March 1944 (Ottawa: King's Printer, 1944), 28–9.
54 The figures in the 1944–45 Public Accounts are only $47,672,519.12. The higher figure quoted in the text is from the *Final Report* of the Mutual Aid Board and includes the items in shipment. These were relatively high in the case of Australia, and mainly involved automotive equipment.
55 Mutual Aid Board minutes, 30 December 1944 and 19 January 1945.
56 DCER, vol. 9, 624–5. For the text of the Mutual Aid Agreement, see Canadian Mutual Aid Board, *Final Report* (Ottawa, 1946), app. III, 52–4.
57 DCER, vol. 9, 419–20.
58 Mutual Aid Board minutes, 30 December 1943 and 4 February 1944.
59 Canadian Mutual Aid Board, *Final Report* (Ottawa, 1946), 30.
60 Late in 1942, the Americans took Giraud, an elderly French general who had escaped from a German prison, to North Africa. He was not accepted by the French officials there and in addition proved tiresome, demanding that he be made Allied Supreme Commander in North Africa. The Americans had also been negotiating with Admiral Darlan, Pétain's right-hand man, who turned up in Algiers. His order to the French troops to cease resisting the Allies was obeyed. When Eisenhower then recognized him as high commissioner, there was an outcry over the elevation to power of a former Nazi collaborator. The deal was defended by Roosevelt as a temporary expedient, justified by the exigencies of war. The immediate problem was solved, however, when Darlan was assassinated; Giraud was put in as the least objectionable substitute. See A.J.P. Taylor, *The Second World War: An Illustrated History* (London: Penguin Books, 1976), 159–60, 169–72. See also J.W. Pickersgill, *The Mackenzie King Record, Volume I, 1939–1944* (Toronto: University of Toronto Press, 1960), 535, 536–54; DCER, vol. 9, 1728–9.
61 DCER, vol. 9, 402–3.
62 Canadian Mutual Aid Board, *Final Report*, 28–9.
63 Mutual Aid Board minutes, 13 December 1943 and 17 April 1944.
64 Minutes of the mutual aid committee meeting, RG 19, vol. 418, 21 June 1944.
65 Ibid., meeting of 29 November 1944.
66 Mutual Aid Board minutes, 13 August 1945; Canadian Mutual Aid Board, *Final Report*, 28–9.
67 See the discussion of Military Relief in chapter 9 of this book, "Working up to Bretton Woods."
68 Minutes of the mutual aid committee meeting, RG 19, vol. 418, 20 December 1944.
69 Mutual Aid Board minutes, 12 February 1945. See also RG 2, PC 8964,

27 November 1944; PC 8965, 27 November 1944; Department of Supplies and Services, and Records of the Office of the Custodian of Enemy Property, files 7 and 8.
70 Mutual Aid Board minutes, 16 November 1944.
71 Ibid., 18 June 1945.
72 *Report on Operations Under Part II of the Export Credits Insurance Act for the Fiscal Year 1945–46*, submitted by J.L. Ilsley, minister of finance, 28 May 1946.
73 Eric Adams to Bryce, RG 19, vol. 416, file 101-106-2E, 10 March 1943.
74 "Memorandum re: Conversation with Sir David Whaley, Mr. Munro and Mr. Williams, August 16th 1943," RG 19, vol. 408, file 101-106-2, 19 August 1943.
75 "Special Problems in Allocating Mutual Aid to Parts of the Sterling Area," RG 19, vol. 416, file 101-196-2E, 28 June 1943.
76 DCER, vol. 9, 1091–8. See also A.J.P. Taylor, *English History 1914–1945* (Oxford: Clarendon Press, 1965), 563. Taylor notes that the diversion of shipping to sustain the Mediterranean campaign had disastrous consequences when the harvest failed in Bengal: "A million and a half Indians died of starvation for the sake of a white man's quarrel in North Africa."
77 Canadian Mutual Aid Board, *Final Report*, 30.
78 Ibid., 26. See also DCER, vol. 9, 415–19.
79 See the discussion in chapter 9 of this book, "Working up to Bretton Woods."
80 Canadian Mutual Aid Board, *Final Report*, 15.
81 Ibid., 44.
82 PC 14/6767, 17 August 1944.
83 Secretary of state for external affairs to the Canadian ambassador to the United States, RG 19, vol. 3405, 29 May 1944.
84 Minutes of the Cabinet War Committee, RG 2/7C, reel C-4876, 28 February 1945.
85 Robertson to Gordon Munro, RG 2/7C, reel C-4876, 18 September 1945.
86 Canadian Mutual Aid Board, *Final Report*, 12.
87 *Statutes of Canada* 1943–44, War Appropriation (United Nations Mutual Aid) Act, 1943, chap. 17. Under the act, war supplies were to be made available to any of the United Nations, to be used in the joint and effective prosecution of the war but only under the terms and conditions approved by the governor-in-council.
88 Canada, House of Commons, *Debates* (11 February 1944), 404.
89 Pickersgill, 650.
90 Mutual Aid Board minutes, 20 March 1944.
91 Heeney's record of the meeting speaks only of "the total net deficit of the sterling area" being estimated at $1.774 billion, but the context and

the CMAB doc. no. 63 and the memorandum given to Ralston that day make clear that this figure applied to the total as described here in the text. For the Cabinet Conclusions, see RG 2/16, vol. I, reel T2364, 27 March 1944. The CMAB doc. no. 63 is in RG 19, vol. 419, file Canadian Mutual Aid Board Agenda. The memorandum apparently given to Ralston by Clark is in ibid., file "Mutual Aid – Index of Correspondence," titled "Mutual Aid and Relief Appropriation 1944–45," 27 March 1944. An earlier draft of the memorandum by Bryce, dated 24 March 1944, is in the same file.

92 Bryce to Clark, RG 19, vol. 418, file "Mutual Aid Legislation," 28 March 1944.
93 Cabinet War Committee minutes, RG 2/7C, reel C4875, 8 September 1943.
94 King Diary, MG 26 J 13, 21 October 1943; Cabinet War Committee minutes, RG 2/7C, reel C4875, 21 October 1943.
95 Canada, *Public Accounts* 1943–44, xxix; for expenditures for allotments from the war appropriation 1944–45, see Canada, House of Commons, *Debates* (11 February 1944) 392–400.
96 "W.W. II, Mutual Aid, Memorandum for the Prime Minister," Mackenzie King Papers, MG 26 J 4, 31 December 1943. Unsigned copies of this memorandum in the Finance files could be misleading, because in the upper right corner the initials HW/AH appear, leading to speculation that the author was Hume Wrong and/or Arnold Heeney. The authorship of the memorandum is quite clear, however, on the original in King's files. The Finance copy is in RG 19, vol. 418, file "Mutual Aid Legislation."
97 Memorandum, RG 19, vol. 418, file "Mutual Aid Legislation," 6 November 1943.
98 King Diary, MG 26 J 13, 4 January 1944.
99 "Memorandum for Dr. Clark re: Mutual Aid Requirements, 1943–44 and 1944–45," RG 19, vol. 418, file "Mutual Aid Legislation," 17 January 1944.
100 King Diary, MG 26 J 13, 24 and 25 January 1944.
101 Bryce to Clark, RG 19, vol. 419, file "Mutual Aid Legislation, 1943–44," 10 January 1944.
102 Bryce to Clark, RG 19, vol. 409, file 101-106-1, 15 February 1944.
103 Pickersgill, 649–50.
104 Ibid. See also the discussion in chapter 6 of this book, "US Economic Arrangements and Dollars Galore," regarding the Washington negotiations.
105 "Canadian Mutual Aid Board Agenda," RG 19, vol. 419, doc. no. 63.
106 "Mutual Aid and Relief Appropriation 1944–45," ibid., 24 March 1944.
107 The British apparently were given some warning by Fraser, the Mutual Aid administrator, who passed on to them the financial details of my

draft memorandum of 24 March 1944. See H.M. Mackenzie, "Mutual Assistance: The Finance of British Requirements in Canada During the Second World War" (Ph.D. dissertation, Oxford University, 1981), 277, n1. Mackenzie makes extensive use of British sources in his detailed account of these events.

108 C.P. Stacey, *Arms, Men and Governments: The War Policies of Canada, 1939–45* (Ottawa: National Defence, 1970), 61, 483–4.
109 John Ehrman, chap. 8.
110 Cabinet War Committee minutes, RG 2/7C, reel C4877, 14 February 1945.
111 Canada, House of Commons, *Debates* (3 April 1945), 365–6.
112 Canadian Mutual Aid Board, *Final Report*, 33–5.
113 Ibid., 33–4.
114 Mutual Aid Board minutes, 12 July 1945.
115 Ibid., 20 July 1945; "CMAB Document No. 139," RG 2/18, vol. 46, file D-13-5-9.
116 Ehrman, vol. 5, 476–7, vol. 6, 222.
117 Mutual Aid Board minutes, 20 July 1945.
118 Taylor, 225–6.
119 Ehrman, vol. 6, 311–13.
120 Secretary of state for external affairs to secretary of state for dominion affairs (SSEA to SSDA) MG 26 J 1, vol. 391, 23 February 1945.
121 Canadian Mutual Aid Board minutes, *Final Report*, app. III, 52–4.
122 Cabinet Conclusions, RG 2/16, reel T2364, 10 August 1945.
123 Mutual Aid Board minutes, 13 August 1945.
124 SSEA to SSDA, RG 2/18, vol. 45, file D-13-5-u, 15 August 1945.
125 Ibid., memo for the undersecretary from Hume Wrong.
126 R.S. Sayers, *Financial Policy 1939–45* (London: HMSO and Longmans, Green and Co., 1956), 479; H. Duncan Hall, *North American Supply* (London: HMSO and Longmans, Green and Co., 1955), 461.
127 Sayers, 482.
128 Mutual Aid Board minutes, 27 August 1945 and Cabinet Conclusion, RG 2/16, reel T2364, 31 August 1945.
129 Cabinet Conclusions, RG 2/16, reel T2364, 5 September 1945; Canada, House of Commons, *Debates* (7 September 1945), 11.
130 Ilsley memorandum, RG 19, vol. 4369, file 4-3-11, 13 September 1945.

CHAPTER EIGHT

1 Mutual Aid Board minutes, PAC, Records of the Department of Finance, RG 19, vol. 418, file 101-106-3, 31 March 1944. Further references to the Mutual Aid Board minutes are to the complete set of minutes in this file and will be identified simply by the date of the meeting.

2 Ibid., 17 April 1944. The Canadians felt that they should have been given more warning of this major increase in requirements.
3 Hector M. Mackenzie, "Mutual Assistance: The Finance of British Requirements in Canada During the Second World War" (Ph.D. thesis, Oxford University, 1981), 279–83.
4 Eady to Robertson, RG 19, vol. 4369, file U-3-8-4, 19 May 1944.
5 "Mutual Aid Appropriations," RG 19, vol. 4369, file U-3-8-4, 13 June 1944. It apparently was used in discussions at the Cabinet War Committee but was not circulated as a committee document.
6 Minutes of the Cabinet War Committee, RG 2/7C, microfilm reel C4876, 14 June 1944.
7 Ibid., 21 June 1944.
8 During the summer of 1944, the department was busy preparing legislation anticipating post-war conditions, including veterans' programs and, most notably, family allowances.
9 This incident has been recounted from memory with the assistance of Louis Rasminsky.
10 My detailed account of this meeting, with Keynes's corrections marked on it in pencil, is in "Mr. Bryce's Working Papers," RG 19, vol. 45, file 101-106-2E. Keynes's letter commenting on the minutes is dated 7 August 1944.
11 Mutual Aid Board minutes, 1 August 1944.
12 "Outline of Discussions Towards a Financial Settlement," RG 19, vol. 4369, file U-3-8-4, 1 August 1944.
13 Donald Moggridge (ed.), *The Collected Writings of John Maynard Keynes, Volume XXIV, Activities 1944–46, The Transition to Peace* (Cambridge: Macmillan and Cambridge University Press for the Royal Economic Society, 1979), 76–97. See also Keynes to Clark, RG 19, vol. 4369, file U-3-8-4, 7 August 1944 and attached paper "Statistics Bearing on the Dimensions of the United Kingdom's Problem of External Finance in the Transition."
14 "Financial Arrangements Between Canada and the United Kingdom," RG 19, vol. 4369, file U-3-8-4, 10 August 1944; "Memorandum of Comment on the United Kingdom Proposals for Adjustments in Financial Arrangements for the Fiscal Year 1944–45," ibid., 6 August 1944.
15 Copies of Heeney's letter to Ilsley setting forth cabinet decisions of 14 August 1944 relating to the proposals for improving the UK balance of payments with Canada during the fiscal year 1944–45 are found in RG 19, vol. 415, file 101-06-E and RG 19, vol. 4369, file U-8-4.
16 Careful estimates of the quantitative effects of the measures approved by cabinet on 14 August 1944 are found in a letter from R.B. Bryce to G.F. Towers, RG 19, vol. 415, file 101-106-2E, 1 September 1944.
17 R.B. Bryce to J.L. Ilsley, RG 19, vol. 4369, file U-3-8-4, 29 August 1944.

18 C.P. Stacey, *Arms, Men and Governments: The War Policies of Canada 1939–1945* (Ottawa: National Defence, 1970), 54–6.
19 J.W. Pickersgill, *The Mackenzie King Record, Volume I: 1939–1944* (Toronto: University of Toronto Press, 1960), 685.
20 Stacey, 56–7.
21 J.W. Pickersgill and D.F. Forster, *The Mackenzie King Record, Volume II: 1944–1945* (Toronto: University of Toronto Press, 1968), 62–3.
22 Ibid., 63.
23 Minutes of the Cabinet War Committee, RG 2/7C, reel C4876, 31 August 1944.
24 King to C.D. Howe, Mackenzie King Papers, MG 26 J1, vol. 362, 30 August 1944, 313224-6; King to J.L. Ralston, 30 August 1944, 313227-30.
25 Pickersgill and Forster, 64; Stacey, 61–2.
26 Stacey, 59.
27 Pickersgill and Forster, 74–7.
28 Ibid., 76.
29 Stacey, *Arms, Men and Governments*, 59–62. An interim appropriation was requested in the resolution of 19 March 1945, and the bill was passed 13 April 1945.
30 Canada, House of Commons, *Debates* (4 April 1945), 433–5.
31 Stacey, 61–2.
32 Robertson to Ilsley, RG 19, vol. 474, file "U.K.–U.S. Discussions," 9 September 1944.
33 Ibid.
34 Minutes of Meeting, RG 2/18, vol. 42, file D-13-5-6(4), 13 October 1944. The minutes of this meeting, which arose out of a regular CMAB meeting the previous day, are not included in the regular series of the Mutual Aid Board minutes.
35 "The Place of Mutual Aid in Stage 2 of the War," RG 2/18, vol. 46, file D-13-5-9, 6 October 1944.
36 "Probable Sterling Area Requirements for Mutual Aid 1945–46," RG 2/18, vol. 46, file D-13-5-9.
37 Minutes of Meeting, RG 2/18, vol. 42, file D-13-5-6(4), 13 October 1944.
38 Robertson to MacDonald, MG 26 J 1, vol. 364, 20 October 1944.
39 "British Requirements for the First Year of Stage II," RG 19, vol. 474, file "U.S.–U.K. Discussions," 27 October 1944.
40 Plumptre to Clark, ibid., 23 November 1944.
41 Donald Moggridge (ed.), *The Collected Writings of John Maynard Keynes, Volume XXIV*, 188.
42 Memorandum, RG 19, vol. 474, file "U.K.–Canada Discussions." The Canadian officials present were Robertson and Wrong from External Affairs; Heeney, the secretary of cabinet; Towers of the Bank of Canada; Shiels, the deputy minister of munitions and supply; Fraser of the

Mutual Aid Administration; and Clark and Bryce from Finance, with McLeod as secretary.
43 "Arrangements for Supplies from Canada in the first year of Stage II," ibid., 27 November 1944.
44 "Notes on Meeting Thursday November 30, 1944 re: Miscellaneous Problems Relating to Mutual Aid and u.k. Financing," ibid., 27 November 1944.
45 "Notes on Meeting in Mr. Ilsley's Office, regarding Mutual Aid for 1945–46," ibid., 29 November 1944.
46 I received this information from J.L. Granatstein, who showed me his copy, obtained from the Public Record Office, of a UK Treasury memorandum, T160/1377-4680, dated 1 December 1944.
47 "Notes of Meeting in Office of Minister of Finance to Consider Stage 2 Mutual Aid Program," RG 19, vol. 474, file "u.k.–Canada Discussions," 1 December 1944.
48 "Notes on Discussion of Air Force Matters with u.k. Treasury Delegation," RG 19, vol. 3672, file N2-8-1-7, 2 December 1944.
49 "Mutual Aid and Related Problems with the United Kingdom: Alternative Courses of Action," RG 19, vol. 474, file "u.k.–Canada Discussions," 4 December 1944.
50 "Post-war Commercial Policy Prospects: A Proposal for Averting a Breakdown in International Trade Relationships," RG 19, vol. 4369, file U-3-11, 12 January 1945.
51 "Notes on Meeting of Ministers and Officials in the Office of Minister of Finance to Discuss Immediate Post-war Commercial Policy Outlook," RG 19, vol. 4369, file U-3-11, 18 January 1945.
52 King Diary, MG 26, J 13, 13 February 1945.
53 Cabinet War Committee minutes, RG 2/7C, C4876, 14 February 1945.
54 King Diary, MG 26 J 13, 16 February 1945.
55 Telegrams 45, 46, and 47, RG 19, vol. 4369, file U-3-11, 23 February 1945.
56 Hudd to Robertson, ibid., file U-3-11, 28 February 1945.
57 Secretary of state for dominion affairs to secretary of state for external affairs, RG 19, vol. 4369, file U-3-11, 21 March 1945.
58 Ibid.
59 Douglas LePan, *Bright Glass of Memory* (Toronto: McGraw-Hill Ryerson, 1979), 53–110.
60 Ibid., 100–1.
61 Canada, House of Commons, *Debates* (28 September 1945), 549. The final figures for expenditure on Mutual Aid that year, including expenditures on "Materials Declared Surplus," were $7.669 billion. The amount of this for the support of the sterling area (apart from the materials declared surplus), comparable with our November 1944 forecasts, was $635 million for about half a year.

CHAPTER NINE

1 Charles P. Kindleberger, *The World in Depression 1929–39* (London: Allen Lane, Penguin Press, 1973), 157–70, 199–231, 257–61.
2 Louis Rasminsky, "Plans for Post-war Currency Stabilization," *The Canadian Banker* 51 (1944), 32–6.
3 The persons named in this paragraph have been identified in notes to earlier chapters. See Index. Harry White's title in the US Treasury Department changed during the years covered in this book. In this chapter, I have used the title he had during 1944.
4 There were several versions of the Clearing Union paper produced during the year 1942. The one received by Clark appears to have been a lengthy, undated one containing much explanatory material. The most accessible and authoritative version is one that was circulated to the UK cabinet in April, which is reprinted in vol. 3 of J.K. Horsefield, *The International Monetary Fund 1945–65* (Washington: International Monetary Fund, 1969). The outline given in this chapter is based on that version. The Commonwealth Conference of October 1942 reviewed a later version distributed by the Dominions Office on 23 October, which may be found in the Bank of Canada archives (BCA) file IS. 76-188-32-1. A revised draft, dated 9 November 1942, was printed after the conference. It is in BCA in the same file.
5 In the Commonwealth Conference of October, Keynes made clear that, as a condition of being able to use the resources of the Union after they had already incurred and maintained certain levels of debit balances of bancor, member countries would be expected to follow "certain internal policies."
6 The conference took place in London between 23 October and 9 November 1942. A "draft" report of it is in PAC, RG 19, vol. 3989, file T-2-9-2 (v).
7 Copy of letter from Rasminsky in London to Towers at the Bank of Canada, dated 4 November 1942, reporting on the Clearing Union plan and on other discussions he had in London, ibid., file T-29. In ending this very enthusiastic letter, Rasminsky states: "On the whole, I feel in duty bound to say I am having a very good time and enjoying the discussions, though I say in self defence it is quite hard work."
8 This version of the White Plan is to be found in PAC, RG 19, vol. 3981, file M-1-7-2. It is the source of the summary description in the following paragraphs.
9 Plumptre to Clark, ibid., 16 January 1943.
10 This UK Treasury comparison of the plans is found in PAC, RG 19, vol. 3447, file "International Clearing Union," 20 February 1943.
11 Rasminsky to Macintosh, PAC, RG 19, vol. 3447, file "International

Clearing Union," 23 March 1943. The four other officials besides me were S. Turk of the Foreign Exchange Control, Prof. Knox, who was working on balance of payments figures for Mackintosh, John Deutsch of External Affairs, and Jean Chapdelaine of the Privy Council Office.
12 Meeting minutes, RG 19, vol. 3447, folder entitled "International Stabilization Fund."
13 A typed copy of this comparison is in BCA, file LR-76, 203-9.
14 See printed file copy in PAC, RG 19, vol. 3391, file 4747-P-13. This large file contains several printed copies of this paper.
15 Memorandum for the Minister, PAC, RG 19, vol. 3447, file "International Clearing Union," file 04747-P-13, 2 June 1943.
16 Mackintosh to Plumptre, PAC, RG 19, vol. 3981, file M-1-7-2, 3 June 1943.
17 Canada, House of Commons *Debates* (12 July 1943), 4628–30.
18 "Memorandum of Conversation with Keynes Lunch – House of Lords," RG 19, vol. 3447, file "International Exchange Union," 22 June 1943. See also Donald Moggridge (ed.), *The Collected Writings of John Maynard Keynes, Volume XXV, Shaping the Post-war World: The Clearing Union* (Cambridge: Macmillan and Cambridge University Press for the Royal Economic Society, 1979).
19 Deutsch to Clark, RG 19, vol. 3981, file M-1-7-2, 15–17 June 1943.
20 Plumptre to Clark, ibid., file M-1-7-2, 7 July 1943.
21 Clark to White, ibid., 29 July 1943.
22 White to Clark, ibid., 1 September 1943.
23 H. Morgenthau, Jr, secretary of the treasury in Washington, to J.L Ilsley, ibid., 14 September 1943.
24 PAC, RG 19, vol. 3391, file M-1-7-5. This file contains as its first item a carbon typed copy of a three-page note by Lord Keynes to the War Cabinet of the UK dated 13 October 1943 and entitled "The Conclusion of the Currency Talks," and related documents including two letters from Keynes to White, a seven-page draft statement by experts on the establishment of an international stabilization fund, and joint minutes of a meeting of US and UK experts on 9 October 1943.
25 "Circular telegram D-7 from the Secretary of State for Dominion Affairs" (SSDA), ibid., 3 January 1944.
26 L. Rasminsky to W.C. Clark, ibid., 15 January 1944.
27 Moggridge, 395.
28 Ibid., 396–407.
29 Ibid., 410–13.
30 Ibid., 412.
31 BCA, Rasminsky Papers, folder 76-210.
32 Moggridge, 428.
33 PAC, RG 19, vol. 3391, file M-1-7-5.

34 Horsefield, vol. II, chap. 12.
35 Moggridge, 44.
36 The Joint Statement was published by Canada by arrangement with both the us and uk. See Plumptre to Clark, RG 19, vol. 3391, file M-1-7-5, 19 April 1944.
37 See uk printed version of Joint Statement in RG 19, vol. 3391, file M-1-7-5.
38 Ibid.
39 Horsefield, vol. I, 84.
40 Moggridge, XXVI, 57.
41 Ibid., 93.
42 Horsefield, vol. I, chap. 5.
43 *Proceedings and Documents of the United Nations Monetary and Financial Conference, Bretton Woods, New Hampshire, July 1–22, 1944*, issued by the Department of State, us Government Printing Office, Washington, 1948.
44 Deutsch to Robertson, P RG 25, vol. 3259, file 6000-F-40 (I), 5 July 1944.
45 Memorandum, RG 19, vol. 3391, file M-1-7-5.
46 Horsefield,, vol. I, p. 92.
47 D. Fullerton, *Graham Towers and His Times* (Toronto: McClelland and Stewart, 1986).
48 PAC, RG 25, vol. 3259, file 6000-D-40, part 3.
49 Ibid.
50 Edward S. Mason and Robert E. Ascher, *The World Bank Since Bretton Woods* (Washington: Brookings Institution, 1973), 17.
51 Henry J. Bitterman, *The International Lawyer*, vol. 5, 59–86.
52 PAC, RG 19, vol. 3447, pamphlet loose in box.
53 The main relevant External Affairs file is that cited in n48 above. The main Rasminsky papers in the Bank of Canada archives relating to the ibrd are cited in notes below.
54 "Article VII Discussions with Representatives of Dominions and India," BCA, LR 76-210-I8; uk Document ASD (Bank) 44, Draft Minutes of the First Meeting, Thursday, 14 March 1944. (Cited below as Minutes.)
55 Moggridge, 419–27.
56 Minutes, para. 2.
57 Minutes, paras 3, 7.
58 Minutes, para. 2.
59 Minutes, para. 22.
60 Moggridge, 48. See also Mason and Asher, 12–13.
61 Telegram, RG 19, vol. 3391, file M-1-7-5, 26 May 1944.
62 Mason and Asher, 13, para. 2.
63 Moggridge, 48.
64 Ibid., 49–54.
65 Ibid., 55.

66 Quoted in R.F. Harrod, *The Life of John Maynard Keynes* (London: Macmillan, 1951), 576.
67 *Proceedings and Documents*, as cited in n43 above, vol. I, 192–214.
68 Mason and Asher, 129–33, 106–7.
69 Ibid., 144–47.
70 Ibid.

CHAPTER TEN

1 John Holmes, *The Shaping of the Peace* (Toronto: University of Toronto Press, 1979), 27.
2 A. Acheson, J. Chant, and M. Prachowny, *Bretton Woods Revisited* (Toronto: University of Toronto Press, 1972), 44–5.
3 Brooke Claxton, "The Place of Canada in Post-war Organization," *Canadian Journal of Economics and Political Science* (November 1944), 412.
4 George Woodbridge, UNRRA: *The History of the United Nations Relief and Rehabilitation Administration*, 3 vols (New York: Columbia University Press, 1950), vol. I, 7–8.
5 Grace Fox, "The Origins of UNRRA," *Political Science Quarterly* (December 1950), 562–3.
6 *Documents on Canadian External Relations* (*DCER*), vol. 9 (Ottawa: External Affairs, 1980), 769. See also L.B. Pearson, *Mike: The Memoirs of the Rt. Hon. Lester B. Pearson, Volume I* (Toronto: University of Toronto Press, 1972), 250–1.
7 See the discussion of the question of Canadian representation on the Combined Boards in chapter 6 of this book, "US Economic Arrangements and Dollars Galore."
8 Canada, House of Commons, *Debates* (9 July 1943), 1089.
9 J.L. Granatstein, *Canada's War* (Toronto: Oxford University Press, 1972), 301–3.
10 *DCER*, vol. 9, 783–4.
11 Pearson, vol. I, 253.
12 Minutes of the Cabinet War Committee, Mackenzie King Papers, MG 26 J 4, vol. 425, 7 April 1943; King Diary, MG 26, J 13, 7 April 1943.
13 Woodbridge, 4.
14 Ibid., 21.
15 Ibid., 81.
16 Ibid., 81–3.
17 Rive to Wrong, RG 19, vol. 3396, file WA5451, 16 October 1943.
18 Plumptre to Clark, ibid., 2 November 1943.
19 Clark to Plumptre, ibid., 26 October 1943.
20 Plumptre to Clark, ibid., 2 November 1943.
21 *DCER*, vol. 9, 835–36.

22 See the discussion of Canada's use of national income statistics in chapter 4 of this book, "Financing Britain."
23 Woodbridge, vol. III, app. 4, sect. II, resolution 14: Financial Plan for the Administration, 57–60; ibid., vol. I, 89–91.
24 Canada, *Public Accounts of the Dominion of Canada for the Fiscal Year Ended March 31, 1944* (Ottawa, 1945), 166; Woodbridge, vol. I, 98–102.
25 Woodbridge, vol. I, 98–102.
26 Ibid., 20.
27 Ibid., 108, 143.
28 Ibid., vol. I, 252 and vol. II, 200–29.
29 The Berlin Declaration of July 1945 stated the intention of the USSR, the UK, and the US to prepare a peace treaty with Italy, arguing that it was the first of the Axis to break with Germany and had then joined the fight against Japan. The conclusion of such a peace treaty with a recognized and democratic Italian government would make it possible for Italy to become a member of the United Nations. Against this background, it was decided at UNRRA's third council session that their program of relief and rehabilitation assistance in Italy should be of the same standard as that applied to liberated areas of the United Nations. Ibid., vol. II, 257–67.
30 F.S.V. Donnison, *Civil Affairs and Military Government North-West Europe 1944–1946* (London: HMSO, 1961), 202.
31 Woodbridge, vol. II, 295–7.
32 *DCER*, vol. 9, 834–5.
33 Ibid., 838; Pearson to Robertson RG 19, vol. 3406, file "International Relief," 27 January 1944; Pearson to Robertson, ibid., 27 January 1944.
34 Pearson to Robertson, RG 19, vol. 3406, file "International Relief," 27 January 1944; Robertson to Clark, ibid., 3 February 1944.
35 External Affairs, meeting of 4 March 1944.
36 RG 19, vol. 3406, "International Relief," Bryce to Clark, 3 March 1944.
37 *DCER*, vol. 10, 65.
38 Secretary of state for external affairs to Canadian ambassador to the United States, RG 19, vol. 3405, "Financing Relief 1944," 29 May 1944.
39 Minutes, Records of the Treasury Board, RG 55, file Treasury Board Minute 6467, 17 August 1944.
40 Lt-Col G.W.L. Nicholson, *Official History of the Canadian Army in the Second World War, Volume II – The Canadians in Italy 1943–1945* (Ottawa: National Defence, 1956), 485.
41 Woodbridge, vol. II, 81–2, 203.
42 Donnison, 29–31.
43 C.P. Stacey, *Official History of the Canadian Army in the Second World War, Volume III, The Victory Campaign: The Operations in North-West Europe 1944–1945* (Ottawa: National Defence, 1960), 337, 351; Nicholson, 661.

44 External Affairs, minute of meeting of Treasury Board approved 6 December 1944.
45 Plumptre to Pearson, RG 19, vol. 3405, file "Financing Relief (Canada) 1944," 1 December 1944.
46 Clark to Robertson, ibid., 4 December 1944.
47 Plumptre to the ambassador, ibid., 26 January 1945.
48 "Reasons for Suspension by Canada of Financing Supplies for Military Relief," Records of the Mutual Aid Board, RG 36/21, vol. 15, file 1-7-31, 22 February 1945.
49 Minutes of the Canadian Mutual Aid Board, RG 36/21, vol. 46, file 1-7-31, 30 March 1945; minutes of the Cabinet War Committee, RG 2/7C, reel C-4876, 28 February 1945. See also the discussion in chapter 7 of this book, "Mutual Aid to Allies."
50 Pearson to Robertson, External Affairs, *DCER* (draft), vol. 10, 5 April 1945.
51 Clark to Robertson, ibid., 5 April 1945.
52 External Affairs, H.F. Angus to W.A. Mackintosh with UK *aide-mémoire* enclosed, 7 July 1945.
53 Ritchie to Pierce, External Affairs, *DCER*, vol. 10 (draft), 10 August 1945.
54 Pierce to Washington, ibid., 15 September 1945; minutes of the Canadian Mutual Aid Board, RG 36/21, vol. 46, 13 September 1945.
55 Memorandum, RG 19, vol. 405, file 101-06-2(2), 22 May 1947.
56 Michiel Horn and David Kaufman, *A Liberation Album: Canadians in the Netherlands 1944–45* (Toronto: McGraw-Hill Ryerson, 1980), 91.
57 War Diary, Civil Affairs Headquarters, First Canadian Army, Weekly Report No. 23, Records of the Department of National Defence, RG 24, vol. 16, 632, 15–21 April 1945.
58 Horn and Kaufman, 133–5. The authors describe in pictures and text how the Canadians kept themselves busy during the summer of 1945 in Holland as they waited to return to Canada.
59 Canada, House of Commons, *Debates* (29 June 1950), 4381 and James Sinclair Papers, Diary of 1950 Trip, University of British Columbia, Special Collections Division, 1.
60 Sinclair wrote a diary of this trip to Europe in 1950, recounting not only the negotiations in each country but also his impressions of the cities and the people. It forms part of the James Sinclair Papers held at the University of British Columbia Library, Special Collections Division.
61 Canada, House of Commons, *Debates* (29 June 1950), 4381.
62 This payment in 1950 was only an interim payment since the British had requested that Canada delay making a settlement because they were waiting for the sterling position of France to improve in hopes of getting a better settlement and wished to settle their outstanding loan first. Canada made their final settlement in a formal exchange of notes on 26 June and 4 July 1951. See Canada, House of Commons, *Debates*

(29 June 1950), 4379 and "Journal Voucher," RG 19, vol. 3407, file: "Military Relief – Payments," 15 September 1951.
63 Sinclair Diary, 48–51.
64 Ibid., 68.
65 Canada, House of Commons, *Debates* (29 June 1950), 4380.
66 Dean Acheson of the US State Department stated in his memoirs that the source of the idea of a food and agriculture conference was, and remained, obscure. Pearson speculated that a contributing reason (in addition to motives based on international goodwill) was the fact that such a conference would keep the United Nations busy on a relatively non-controversial matter, allowing Roosevelt, Churchill, and Stalin to run the war with less interference. See Dean Acheson, *Present at the Creation* (New York: Norton, 1969), 73; Pearson, vol. I, 245–6.
67 DCER, "Impressions of the United Nations Food Conference at Hot Springs Virginia," vol. 9, 850–3.
68 "The Food and Agriculture Organization of the United Nations," RG 19, vol. 828, file 800-1-4-1, 9 October 1945.
69 The subcommittee consisted of H.F. Angus, External Affairs; D.B. Finn, Fisheries; C.F. Wilson, Trade and Commerce; Mitchell Sharp, Finance; G.F.H. Barton, Agriculture; D.B. Pett, Pensions and National Health. T.L. Avison of Finance was the secretary.
70 "Report of the Economic Advisory Committee on First and Second Draft Reports of the Interim Commission on Food and Agriculture," RG 19, vol. 828, file 800-1-4-1, 10 April 1944.
71 Ibid.
72 Pearson to Robertson, RG 19, vol. 828, file 800-1-4-1, 23 May 1944; Clark to Angus, ibid., 31 May 1944.
73 "Report of the Economic Advisory Committee," ibid., 10 April 1944; "Comparison Between Draft Second Report," ibid., 26 January 1944; "First Report to the Governments of the United Nations by the Interim Commission on Food and Agriculture," ibid., 1 August 1944.
74 "The Food and Agriculture Organization," ibid., 5 May 1944.
75 Pearson, vol. I, 249–50.
76 Richard N. Gardner, *Sterling-Dollar Diplomacy in Current Perspective* (New York: Columbia University Press, 1980), 62.
77 Ibid., 71.
78 J.L. Granatstein, *A Man of Influence: Norman A. Robertson and Canadian Statecraft, 1929–68* (Ottawa: Deneau, 1981), 118–20.
79 Secretary of state for dominion affairs to secretary of state for external affairs, RG 19, vol. 3989, file T-2-0-2, 22 May 1942; Clark to Robertson, ibid., 27 May 1942. Clark suggested quoting the resolution of the Joint Economic Committee on the importance of economic collaboration as part of the reasoned argument for including Canadians in the talks.

See the discussion of this resolution in chapter 5 of this book, "Scarce US Dollars and the Hyde Park Declaration."
80 "Report of the Canadian Representatives at the 'Post-war Economic Talks' Held in London Between October 23rd and November 9th, 1942," RG 19, vol. 3989, file T-2-9-2, 10 November 1942.
81 *DCER*, vol. 9, 618–25.
82 Clark to Wrong, RG 19, vol. 3989, file T-2-9-2, 8 May 1943; "Report of the Advisory Committee on Economic Policy on Trade Policy," ibid., 14 May 1943.
83 "Report of the Canadian Representatives at the 'Post-war Commercial Policy Discussions' Held in London Between June 15 and June 30, 1943," RG 19, vol. 3989, file T-2-9-2, 16 July 1943. W.A. Mackintosh represented Finance at these talks.
84 Clark to Robertson, RG 19, vol. 3989, file T-2-9-2, 2 August 1943.
85 Gardner, 103–5.
86 *DCER*, vol. 9, 693–4.
87 Granatstein, 125.
88 "Informal Exploratory Conversations Between Officials of the United States and Canada," RG 19, vol. 3989, file T-2-9-2, 12 April 1944.
89 Robertson to Clark, ibid., 10 March 1944.
90 Wrong to Robertson, ibid., 8 May 1944.
91 Granatstein, 128–9.
92 Gardner, 146–7.
93 Ibid.
94 Ibid., 150–1.
95 Frank Stone, *Canada, the GATT and the International Trade System* (Montreal: Institute for Research on Public Policy, 1984), 18–19.
96 Holmes, 285.

CHAPTER ELEVEN

1 In writing this chapter, I have relied almost entirely on Canadian rather than British sources. It was the Canadian information that determined our policies and actions at the time. Those who wish to take the British sources into account can do so conveniently by referring to the long and informative article by Hector Mackenzie entitled "The Path to Temptation: The Negotiation of Canada's Reconstruction Loan to Britain in 1946" in *Historical Papers* 1982 of the Canadian Historical Association. I believe the additional information does not materially change the narrative.
2 The detailed minutes of the morning meeting of the officials on 1 August 1944 (which were circulated), with Keynes's corrections of a few details marked on it, are in PAC RG 19, vol. 415, file 101-106-2E.

The formal minutes of the Mutual Aid Board meeting in the evening are in RG 19, vol. 418, file 101-106-3, tab no. 25. These are very much in summary form. My detailed handwritten notes on this meeting are in file 101-106-2E cited above.

3 "A Proposal for Maintaining Canada's Exports to the Sterling Area During the Post-war Transitional Period, by G. Towers," RG 19, vol. 4369, file U-3-11, 25 November 1944. This was sent to Clark on 1 December 1944. (This memorandum of 25 November should not be confused with one that Towers wrote shortly after, on 29 November, his number 475, which records a conversation he had with Lord Keynes.)
4 Ibid.
5 Minutes of meeting, ibid., 18 January 1945. (This important meeting is also described in chapter 8 of this book, "Financing Britain Further and Keynes's Visits.")
6 Secretary of state for external affairs, Ottawa, to the secretary of state for dominion affairs (SSEA to SSDA), London: RG 19, vol. 4369, file U-3-11, 23 February 1945.
7 SSDA London to SSEA Ottawa, ibid., 21 March 1945.
8 Donald Moggridge (ed.), *The Collected Writings of John Maynard Keynes, Volume XXIV, Activities 1944–46: The Transition to Peace* (Cambridge: Macmillan and Cambridge University Press for the Royal Economic Society, 1979), 256–95.
9 Minutes of Conversation, RG 19, vol. 4369, file U-3-11. The *mémoire* "Introduction to Economics: Lord Keynes and the Audit Room Meetings" is in Douglas LePan, *Bright Glass of Memory* (Toronto, New York, London: McGraw-Hill Ryerson, 1979), 55–110.
10 JMK, XXIV, 257, 275.
11 Minutes of conversations, 2, para. 6.
12 LePan, 87.
13 Moggridge, 280.
14 Minutes of Conversations, 10.
15 Ibid., 11.
16 LePan, 90.
17 Ibid., 92.
18 Ibid., 93.
19 Ibid., 95.
20 Ibid., 94.
21 Moggridge, 260.
22 Ibid., 457; Towers memo 491, 5 September 1945.
23 Ibid., 563; Towers memo 495, 5 November 1945, Bank of Canada Archives (BCA).
24 Ibid., 411; R.F. Harrod, *The Life of John Maynard Keynes* (London: Macmillan, 1951), 593–6.

25 Richard N. Gardner, *Sterling-Dollar Diplomacy in Current Perspective* (New York: McGraw-Hill, 1980), 188.
26 Moggridge, 420–4.
27 Ibid., 492–5.
28 Ibid., 537.
29 Ibid., 600–3.
30 Ibid., 604.
31 Ibid., 604.
32 The text of the US–UK loan agreement is printed as an appendix to Gardner, *Sterling-Dollar Diplomacy*, 387–92.
33 "Talks with UK Officials," RG 19, vol. 3437, file R.B.B, 6–20 December 1945.
34 M.W. Mackenzie, deputy minister for trade and commerce, negotiated a "token import" agreement with British officials in London in January 1946, but it was vetoed by Hugh Dalton, the chancellor of the exchequer. This information is recorded by Hector Mackenzie on 210 of the article referred to in n1 of this chapter.
35 Memorandum to the High Commission (in London) from D.V. LePan, RG 19, vol. 4369, file U-3-11, 23 January 1946.
36 Minutes of meeting, RG 19, vol. 414, R.B.B. working file.
37 J.W. Pickersgill, *The Mackenzie King Record, Volume III* (Toronto: University of Toronto Press, 1970), 160.
38 *Documents on Canadian External Relations* (*DCER*), vol. 12, section entitled "Commonwealth Relations": minutes of meetings on Anglo-Canadian Loan Negotiations, Monday, 11 February 1946. These minutes were prepared by Arnold Smith of the Department of External Affairs. I made my own notes on the discussions. Smith reported as well on later meetings. My notes are in RG 19, vol. 414, file 101-106-2E. They cover meetings on 11–13 February as carbon copies of typescript. Further to these, there are detailed handwritten notes of meetings on 20 February and 22 February, the climactic meeting. In addition, King wrote in his diary about most of these meetings and these are in Pickersgill, 160–75. King's records are particularly useful in covering cabinet discussions, of which no minutes or "conclusions" were made in those days.
39 This is from my own notes of that meeting, located as stated in n38 above. I have now added the words in square brackets to clarify what he undoubtedly meant.
40 *DCER*, vol. 12, 1404–7.
41 Pickersgill, vol. III, 163.
42 Clark to minister, RG 19, vol. 763, file 304-6, 14 February 1945.
43 *DCER*, vol. 12, 1409–11, letter and *aide-mémoire* by delegation of Great Britain, 16 February 1946.
44 Pickersgill, vol. III, 165.

45 Ibid., 166.
46 "Notes of Meeting with Five Senior Members of u.k. Delegation and Ilsley, St Laurent, W.C. Clark, Towers, Robertson and Bryce," RG 19, vol. 414, file 101-106E, 20 February 1946.
47 Memorandum, RG 19, vol. 763, file 304-6, 21 February 1946.
48 Pickersgill, 168–70; "Notes," RG 19, vol. 414, file 101-106-2E, 22 February 1946.
49 Handwritten notes of meeting, ibid., 22 February 1946.
50 Pickersgill, vol. III, 169–70.
51 Ibid., 168.
52 "Notes of Meeting," RG 19, vol. 414, file 101-106-2E, 22 February 1946.
53 Pickersgill, vol. III, 171–2.
54 "Memo: Present Stage of Negotiations with British and Suggestions as to Course Which Should Be Taken," RG 19, vol. 763, file 304-6, 1 March 1946.
55 Pickersgill, vol. III, 172–74.
56 Memorandum, RG 19, vol. 763, file 304-6.
57 Gardner, 250.
58 *DCER*, vol. 12, 139.
59 Minutes of meeting, RG 19, vol. 414, file 101-106-2E, 4 February 1946.
60 Pickersgill, vol. III, 174.
61 Memorandum, RG 19, vol. 414, file "u.k. Financial Discussions," 101-106-2E.
62 The quotation is from the text of the agreement: "Agreement Between the Government of Canada and the Government of the United Kingdom on the Settlement of War Claims," Treaty Series 1946, no. 10. The Loan Agreement of 1946 is no. 9 in that series.
63 Public Accounts of Canada for the fiscal year ending 31 March 1946, part II, F64, Sundry Suspense Accounts, line M, United Kingdom – General Settlement Account. (Receipts: $410,862,105.94; disbursements: $406,676,586.25; credit balance, 31 March 1946: $4,185,519.69.)
64 Canada, House of Commons, *Debates* (11 April 1946), 766–71.
65 William R. Keylor, *The Twentieth Century World* (New York and Oxford: Oxford University Press, 1984), 270–86. This provides a background for the economic events affecting the uk balance of payments from 1947 to 1950.
66 Gardner, chap. 16.
67 Telegram, RG 19, vol. 3437, file "Deputy Minister on uk finances," 5 June 1946. He reports that Eady of Treasury had suggested a short-term agreement to finance the uk deficit with Canada on a fifty-fifty basis – half by drawing on Canadian credit, half by payment of convertible currency. Later in June there was an exchange of messages, eventually agreeing to this arrangement.
68 Memorandum, RG 19, vol. 3437, file "Deputy Minister on uk finances," 21 August 1946. Cobbold of the Bank of England and Clutterbuck, the

UK high commissioner, met with Abbott, Clark, and others. After a long and very serious discussion, the UK got no concessions on its current arrangements with Canada. A press release published by Abbott the next day is also in the file.

69 Canada's deficit in US dollars during 1947 and the decline in its reserves have been described in detail in R.D. Cuff and J.L. Granatstein, *American Dollars – Canadian Prosperity* (Toronto and Sarasota, Samuel-Stevens, 1978), chap. 2. It is also described well, but in less detail, in A.F.W. Plumptre, *Three Decades of Decision: Canada and the World Monetary Situation, 1944–75* (Toronto: McClelland and Stewart, 1977), 97–103. The decline in reserves began in mid-1946 and accelerated in early 1947. By February 1947, the Department of Finance expected that measures to reduce the deficit, including restrictions on imports, would be necessary by the end of the year. By May, the prospective problem had been thoroughly analysed and key American officials had been secretly briefed. The Marshall Plan in Europe had been announced in June, and some hope was expressed that it would help finance Canadian exports. During the summer, there were several consultations with American officials. In August, the sterling crisis added to Canada's problem. In September, there were several high-level discussions with the Americans, but no substantial assistance was provided or promised. Immediate action by Canada to reduce imports was delayed by the need to wait until key negotiations in Geneva were concluded. Necessary emergency measures were prepared in Ottawa under Abbott's direction and were announced by him on 17 November, immediately after the announcement from London by Prime Minister King of the successful conclusion of the trade negotiations.
70 See budget papers, 22 March 1949, 69.
71 See Pickersgill, vol. IV, 127–9; see also J.L. Granatstein, *A Man of Influence*, 222–4.
72 Keylor, 278–86.
73 Cuff and Granatstein, 98–109.
74 Ibid., 123.
75 Ibid., 125.
76 "Note on Discussion Under the Aegis of the U.K.–Canada Continuing Committee on Trade and Economic Affairs," RG 2 (Privy Council Office), vol. 108, file U-10-15, 11 July 1949.
77 See Plumptre, *Three Decades of Decision*, 103–8.
78 C.F. Wilson, *A Century of Canadian Grain* (Saskatoon, 1978), chap. 47, 1017–43. See also Plumptre, 79–81.
79 This attitude and action of St Laurent is described in J.W. Pickersgill, *My Years with Louis St. Laurent: A Political Memoir* (Toronto and Buffalo: University of Toronto Press, 1975), 150.

AFTERWORD

1. P.C. 1908, 14 August 1937.
2. *Dominion–Provincial Conference Tuesday January 14, 1941 and Wednesday January 15, 1941* (Ottawa, 1941), 1–10.
3. Ibid., 71–5.
4. J.L. Granatstein, *Canada's War: The Politics of the Mackenzie King Government 1939–45* (Toronto, 1975), 172–3.
5. A fine account is Jeffrey Keshen, *Saints, Sinners, and Soldiers: Canada's Second World War* (Vancouver, 2004), 53ff.
6. J.L. Ilsley, "Speaking of Money and War: Extracts from a Series of Addresses by Hon. J.L. Ilsley" (Ottawa, 1941), address of 3 September 1941.
7. Keshen, 53ff.; Robert Bothwell et al., *Canada 1900–1945* (Toronto, 1987), 361ff.
8. Ilsley, address of 18 September 1941.
9. Queen's University Archives, Grant Dexter Papers, memorandum, 9 October 1941.
10. W.L.M. King, *Canada and the Fight for Freedom* (Toronto, 1944), 30ff.
11. The best account is Christopher Waddell, "The Wartime Prices and Trade Board" (Ph.D. thesis, York University, 1981). See also Keshen, chap. 3.
12. Granatstein, 252–4.
13. See Peter Neary and J.L. Granatstein, *The Veterans Charter and Post–World War II Canada* (Montreal, 1998).
14. Dexter Papers, memorandum, 23 December 1943.
15. J.W. Pickersgill to Claxton, LAC, Brooke Claxton Papers, vol. 62, 12 January 1944.

Bibliography

PRIMARY SOURCES

Manuscript Collections

National Archives of Canada:
   Gordon Churchill Papers
   Walter Gordon Papers
   C.D. Howe Papers
   W.L.M. King Papers

Bank of Canada:
   Graham Towers Papers

Public Records

National Archives of Canada:

RG 2	Privy Council Office
RG 17	Department of Agriculture
RG 19	Department of Finance
RG 20	Department of Industry, Trade and Commerce
RG 24	Department of National Defence
RG 25	Department of External Affairs
RG 27	Department of Labour
RG 28	Department of Munitions and Supply
RG 55	Treasury Board
RG 58	Auditor General
RG 77	National Research Council
RG 98	Department of Supply and Services
RG 117	Office of Custodian of Enemy Property

National Archives of the United States:

RG 234   Reconstruction Finance Corporation

Government Documents

Canada. House of Commons. Special Committee on War Expenditures: *Report* (Ottawa: Queen's Printer, August 1944).
Canada. *White Paper on Employment and Income,* Department of Reconstruction (Ottawa 1945).
Canada. *Public Accounts of the Dominion of Canada for the Fiscal Year Ended March 31, 1944* (Ottawa, 1945).
Canada. Department of Reconstruction. *Reconstruction* (Ottawa, 1945).
Canada. Department of Reconstruction and Supply. *Research and Scientific Activity: Canadian Federal Expenditures 1938–1946* (Ottawa: King's Printer, 1947).
Canada. Canadian Mutual Aid Board. *Final Report* (Ottawa, 1946).
Canada. Royal Commission on Canada's Economic Prospects. *Final Report* (Ottawa, November 1957).
Canada. House of Commons Standing Committee on Public Accounts. *Proceedings* (Ottawa, 1958).
Canada. House of Commons. Standing Committee on Public Accounts. *Minutes* of Proceedings and Evidence 11 (9 May 1961).
Canada. Dominion Bureau of Statistics. *Consumption, Production and Inventories of Rubber*, vol. 20, no. 1 (January 1966).
Canada. Privy Council Office. Task Force on the Structure of Canadian Industry. *Report* (Ottawa: Queen's Printer, 1968).
Canada. Privy Council Office. Foreign Direct Investment in Canada. *Report* (Ottawa: Queen's Printer, 1972).
Canada. *Documents on Canadian External Relations (DCER)*, vol. 7, 1939–41 (Ottawa: 1974).
Canada. Privy Council Office. *Crown Corporations: Direction, Control, Accountability* (Ottawa: Minister of Supply and Services, 1977).
Canada. House of Commons. Standing Committee on Public Accounts. *Minutes* of Proceedings and Evidence 39 (5 July 1977).
Canada. House of Commons. *Minutes* of Proceedings and Evidence of the Standing Committee on Public Accounts. Issues 19, 20 (1–3 March 1977).
Canada. Supply and Services Canada. Petrochemical Industry Task Force. *Report* (Ottawa, February 1984).
United States. *The Closing of the Gold Mines, August 1941 to March 1944* (Washington: US Government Printing Office, 1946).
United States. State Department, *Foreign Relations of the United States, Diplomatic Papers, 1944,* vol. VI. China (Washington: US Government Printing Office, 1967).

Interviews

George Watts
David Mansur

Newspapers and Periodicals
   Financial Post
   Globe and Mail
   Labour Gazette
   Saturday Night

SECONDARY SOURCES

Unpublished Theses and Manuscripts

J. M. Little, "Canada Discovered: Continentalist Perceptions of the Roosevelt Administration, 1939–1945" (Ph.D. thesis, University of Toronto, 1975).
H.M. Mackenzie, "Mutual Assistance: The Finance of British Requirements in Canada During the Second World War" (Ph.D. thesis, Oxford University, 1981).
C. R. Waddell, "The Wartime Price and Trade Board: Price Control in Canada in World War II" (Ph.D. thesis, York University, 1981).

Articles

H.G.J. Aitken, "Defensive Expansionism: The State and Economic Growth in Canada," in W.T. Easterbrook and M.H. Watkins (eds.), *Approaches of Canadian Economic History*, 183–221.
S. Azzi, "Intuitive Nationalist: Walter Gordon as Thinker," *Journal of Canadian Studies* 34, no. 1 (Winter 2000), 121–35.
M. Bliss, "'Rich by Nature, Poor by Policy': The State and Economic Life in Canada," in K.R. Carty and P.W. Ward (eds.), *Entering the Eighties: Canada in Crisis* (Toronto: Oxford University Press, 1980), 78–90.
R.B. Bryce, "William Clifford Clark, 1889–1952," *Canadian Journal of Economics and Political Science* 19 (August 1953).
B. Claxton, "The Place of Canada in Post-war Organization," *Canadian Journal of Economics and Political Science* (November 1944).
R.J. Diubaldo, "The Canol Project in Canadian–American Relations," Canadian Historical Association, *Papers* 1977, 179–95.
G. Fox, "The Origins of UNRRA," *Political Science Quarterly* (December 1950), 562–3.
A.O. Gibbons, "Foreign Exchange Control in Canada, 1939–51," *Canadian Journal of Economics and Political Science* 9, no. 1 (February 1953).

J.L. Granatstein, "The Road to Bretton Woods: International Monetary Policy and the Public Servant," *Journal of Canadian Studies* 16, nos 3, 4 (Fall–Winter, 1981).

N. Hillmer, "The Anglo-Canadian Neurosis: The Case of O.D. Skelton," in *Britain and Canada: Survey of a Changing Relationship* (London: Frank Cass, 1976).

J.W. Holmes, "Shadow and Substance: Diplomatic Relations Between Britain and Canada," in P. Lyon (ed.), *Britain and Canada: Survey of a Changing Relationship* (London: Frank Cass, 1976).

W. Kimball, "Lend-Lease and the Open Door: The Temptation of British Opulence, 1937–1942," *Political Science Quarterly* 86, no. 2 (June 1971).

H. Mackenzie, "The Path to Temptation: The Negotiation of Canada's Reconstruction Loan to Britain in 1946," *Canadian Historical Papers* (1982).

W.A. Mackintosh, "William Clifford Clark: A Personal Memoir," *Queen's Quarterly* 60 (Spring 1953).

J.A. Munro, "Loring Christie and Canadian External Relations, 1935–1939," *Journal of Canadian Studies* (1972).

S.D. Pierce and A.F.W. Plumptre, "Canada's Relations with War-time Agencies in Washington," *Canadian Journal of Economics and Political Science* 9 (August 1945).

L. Rasminsky, "Foreign Exchange Control: Purposes and Methods," in J.F. Parkinson (ed.), *Canadian War Economics* (Toronto: University of Toronto Press, 1941), 80–127.

K.W. Taylor, "The War-time Control of Prices" in J.F. Parkinson (ed.), *Canadian War Economics* (Toronto: University of Toronto Press, 1941).

Books

D. Acheson, *Present at the Creation: My Years at the State Department* (New York: Norton, 1969).

A. Acheson, J. Chant, and M. Prachowny, *Bretton Woods Revisited* (Toronto: University of Toronto Press, 1972).

H. Balfour, *Wings over Westminster* (London, 1973).

Bank of Canada, *Bank of Canada Statistical Summary, 1946 Supplement* (Ottawa, 1946).

E. Barnett, *The Keynesian Arithmetic in War-time Canada: Development of the National Accounts, 1939–1945* (Kingston: Harbinger House Press, 1998).

M.J. Bellamy, *Profiting the Crown: Canada's Polymer Corporation, 1942–1990* (Montreal: McGill-Queen's University Press, 2005).

M. Bliss, *Northern Enterprise: Five Centuries of Canadian Business* (Toronto: McClelland and Stewart, 1987).

M. Bliss, *Right Honourable Men: The Descent of Canadian Politics from Macdonald to Mulroney* (Toronto: HarperCollins, 1994).

Bibliography

R. Bothwell, *Canada and the United States: The Politics of Partnership* (Toronto: University of Toronto Press, 1992).

R. Bothwell and W. Kilbourn, *C.D. Howe: A Biography* (Toronto: McClelland and Stewart, 1979).

R.B. Bryce, *Maturing in Hard Times: Canada's Department of Finance Through the Great Depression* (Montreal and Kingston: McGill-Queen's University Press, 1986).

K.A.H. Buckley and H.C. Urquhart, *Historical Statistics of Canada* (Toronto: Macmillan, 1965).

A. Cairncross, *The Price of War* (Oxford: Basil Blackwell, 1986).

A. Cairncross, *Economic Ideas and Government Policy* (New York: Routledge, 1996).

R.M. Campbell, *Grand Illusions: The Politics of the Keynesian Experience in Canada, 1945–1975* (Peterborough: Broadview Press, 1987).

W.S. Churchill, *The Second World War*, 6 vols (Boston: Houghton Mifflin, 1948–53).

W. Cole, *Roosevelt and the Isolationists* (Lincoln, Nebraska and London: University of Nebraska Press, 1983).

D. Creighton, *Canada's First Century* (Toronto: Macmillan, 1970).

R. Cuff and J.L. Granatstein, *American Dollars – Canadian Prosperity: Canadian-American Economic Relations, 1945–1950* (Toronto: Samuel-Stevens, 1978).

I. de Vegh, *The Pound Sterling* (Boston: Scudder, Stevens & Clark, 1939).

F.S.V. Donnison, *Civil Affairs and Military Government: North-West Europe, 1944–1946* (London: HMSO, 1961).

J. Eayrs, *In Defence of Canada, Volume II: Appeasement and Rearmament* (Toronto: University of Toronto Press, 1965).

J. Ehrman, *Grand Strategy* (London: HMSO, 1956).

R.F. Harrod, *The Life of John Maynard Keynes* (London: Macmillan, 1951).

R.N. Gardner, *Sterling-Dollar Diplomacy in Current Perspective* (New York: Columbia University Press, 1980).

J.L. Granatstein, *Canada's War: The Politics of the Mackenzie King Government, 1939–45* (Toronto: Oxford University Press, 1975).

J.L. Granatstein, *A Man of Influence: Norman A. Robertson and Canadian Statecraft, 1929–68* (Ottawa: Deneau Publishers, 1981).

J.L Granatstein, *The Ottawa Men: The Civil Service Mandarins 1935–1957* (Toronto: Oxford University Press, 1982).

H.D. Hall, *North American Supply* (London: HMSO, 1955).

F.J. Hatch, *The Aerodrome of Democracy* (Ottawa, 1983).

O.M. Hill, *Canada's Salesman to the World* (Montreal: McGill-Queen's University Press, 1977).

M. Hogan, *The Marshall Plan: America, Britain, and the Reconstruction of Western Europe, 1947–1952* (Cambridge: Cambridge University Press, 1987).

J.W. Holmes, *The Shaping of Peace: Canada and the Search for World Order 1943–1957, Volume I* (Toronto: University of Toronto Press, 1979).

M. Horn and D. Kaufman, *A Liberation Album: Canadians in the Netherlands 1944–45* (Toronto: McGraw-Hill Ryerson, 1980).
C.D. Howe et al., *Canada: Nation on the March* (Toronto: Clarke, Irwin, 1953).
W. James, *Wartime Economic Cooperation* (Toronto: Ryerson Press, 1949).
J. Kennedy, *History of the Department of Munitions and Supply*, 2 vols (Ottawa, 1950).
W.R. Keylor, *The Twentieth Century World* (New York and Oxford: Oxford University Press, 1984).
J.M. Keynes, *The General Theory of Employment, Interest and Money* (Cambridge: Cambridge University Press, 1936).
C. Kindleberger, *The Marshall Plan Days* (Boston: Allen, 1987).
P. Lyon (ed.), *Britain and Canada: Survey of a Changing Relationship* (London: Frank Cass, 1976).
H. Marshal et al., *Canadian-American Industry: A Study in International Investment* (Toronto: McClelland and Stewart, 1976).
A. Milward, *The Reconstruction of Western Europe, 1945–1951* (London: Methuen 1984).
H.B. Neatby, *William Lyon Mackenzie King: The Prism of Unity, Volume III* (Toronto: University of Toronto Press, 1976).
R. F. Neill, *A History of Canadian Economic Thought* (London: Routledge, 1991).
G.W.L. Nicholson, *Official History of the Canadian Army in the Second World War: The Canadians in Italy 1943–1945* (Ottawa: National Defence, 1956).
J.F. Parkinson (ed.), *Canadian War Economics* (Toronto: University of Toronto Press, 1941).
L.B. "Mike" Pearson, *The Memoirs of the Rt. Hon. Lester B. Pearson, Volume I* (Toronto: University of Toronto Press, 1972).
J.W. Pickersgill, *The Mackenzie King Record, Volumes I, II, and III* (Toronto: University of Toronto Press, 1960).
J.W. Pickersgill, *My Years with Louis St. Laurent: A Political Memoir* (Toronto and Buffalo: University of Toronto Press, 1975).
A.F.W. Plumptre, *Mobilizing Canada's Resources for War* (Toronto: Macmillan, 1941).
C.G. Power, *A Party Politician* (Toronto: Macmillan, 1966).
R. S. Sayers, *Financial Policy 1939–45* (London: HMSO, 1956).
J. Schull, *The Great Scot* (Montreal: McGill-Queen's University Press, 1979).
J. Schumpeter, *History of Economic Analysis* (New York: Oxford University Press, 1954).
J. Schumpeter, *The Theory of Economic Development* (Cambridge: Harvard University Press, 1934).
R.E. Sherwood, *Roosevelt and Hopkins* (New York: Harper & Brothers, 1948).
C.P. Stacey, *Arms, Men and Governments* (Ottawa: National Defence, 1970).
F. Stone, *Canada, the GATT and the International Trade System* (Montreal: Institute for Research on Public Policy, 1984).

A.P.J. Taylor, *English History 1914–1945* (Oxford: Clarendon Press, 1965).

A.P.J. Taylor *The Second World War: An Illustrated History* (London: Penguin Books, 1976)

G.D. Taylor and P.A. Baskerville, *A Concise History of Business in Canada* (Toronto: Oxford University Press, 1994).

J.H. Thompson, *The Harvests of War: The Prairie West, 1914–1918* (Toronto: McCelland and Stewart, 1978).

B.W. Tuchman, *Stilwell and the American Experience in China, 1911–1945* (Toronto, New York, London, Sydney, Auckland: Bantam Books, 1972).

H.C. Urquhart and K.A.H. Buckley, *Historical Statistics of Canada* (Toronto: Macmillan, 1965).

I. Wexler, *The Marshall Plan Revisited: The European Recovery Program in Economic Perspective* (Westport: Greenwood, 1983).

C.F. Wilson, *A Century of Canadian Grain* (Saskatoon: Western Producer Books, 1978).

G. Woodbridge, *UNRRA: The History of the United Nations Relief and Rehabilitation Administration*, 3 vols (New York: Columbia University Press, 1950).

Index

Abbott, D.C., 316, 318
agricultural exports, 33–5, 69, 70, 72
aircraft production, pre-war years, 17–18
air training
  Allied co-operation, 79–83
  British Commonwealth Air Training Plan. *see* British Commonwealth Air Training Plan
  Combined Committee on Air Training in North America, 80
Aitken, Max, 118
Alaska Highway, 138
Angus, Henry F., photo, xxiii
appeasement, 13
Atlantic Charter, 274–5
Australia, Mutual Aid to, 163–6, 357n54
auto industry, 36, 94, 97

balance of payments
  with United Kingdom, 60, 78
  with United States, 85, 109–10, 113, 131, 144, 192
bancor, 226–7
Bank of Canada, 18–19, 323
Batt, William, 355n39
Beaverbrook, Lord, 118
Berkinshaw, R.C., photo, xix
Berlin Declaration, 368n29
Big Four, 257, 279
blocked payments, 271
bonds, 53–4, 346n3
Bouchard, Dr., photo, xix
Bren gun, 17, 24
Bretton Woods Conference, xxiii, 242–4, 333n3

Britain, 52–84. *see* financing Britain
  agricultural exports to, 33, 34
  air training, 18, 41–51
  munitions procurement, 17–18, 26, 69
  post-war economy, 283–321
  trade with, 17–18, 26, 33, 34, 37
British Commonwealth Air Training Plan
  "aerodrome of democracy," 41
  Australian pilots, 164
  committee members, 43
  establishment of, 18, 41–2
  financing of, 29, 49–51, 55
  negotiations, 41–51, 79–83, 341n3
  photo, xx
  post-war debt settlement, 301, 303–5 passim, 307
  RCAF squadrons, 47–79
British post-war economy
  Anglo-American negotiations, 289–95
  Cambridge talks, 286–9
  Canadian loan, 284, 285, 293–309, 313–16, 374n67, 374n68
  Canadian proposal, 284–6
  Eady delegation, 295–6
  "have regard to" clause, 320–1
  Keynes, John Maynard, 286–9
  US loan, 285, 291–4
Brussels Pact, 317
Bryce, Robert
  background, vii–xi, xiii–xiv
  photos, xvii–xix, xxiii–xxiv

Cambridge meetings, 222–4, 286–9
Campbell, Wallace, 340n13
Canadian Associated Aircraft, 18

Canadian Defence Committee,
  establishment of, 14
Canadian dollar crisis, 316–19, 375n69
Canadian–US co-operation, 125–8
cancellation of contracts, 213–14
CANEX, 107–8, 112, 135
Canol oil project, 138, 142
CANPAY, 107, 135
CANSHIP, 107–8, 112
Carswell, J.B., 106
Casselman, Cora, photo, xxiv
Chaput, R., photo, xxiv
China, Mutual Aid to, 157–63, 355n36, 355n39, 356n47, 356n49
Chipman, W.F., photo, xxiv
Churchill, Winston
  appointment as prime minister, 347n24
  on declaration of war, 20
  meetings with Roosevelt, 117–18
  on Mutual Aid, 185, 221
  on US dollar shortage, 98
  visit to Ottawa, 118
Clark, Colin, 58, 343n13
Clark, William Clifford
  appointment to FECB, 27
  on Article VII talks, 370n79
  background, 1, 333n1
  in Canadian loan negotiations, 300–1
  on Canadian reserve levels, 133–7, 139–42
  on combined boards, 123–4
  on family allowances, 5
  on financing Britain, 53, 66–7, 68, 71, 73, 75, 100, 147–9
  on financing stage II, 191–2
  on military relief, 266, 268
  photos, xix, xxiv
  on UNRRA, 258
Coats, Robert H., 31, 36, 340n11
Cobbold, C.F., 298–300 passim
Coldwell, M.J., photo, xxiv
combined boards, 119–25
Combined Committee on Air Training in North America, 80
Combined Food Board, 120, 123, 124
Combined Munitions Assignment Boards, 119, 121, 124, 125
Combined Production and Resources Board, 119, 120, 125
Combined Raw Materials Board, 119, 121
Combined Shipping Adjustment Board, 119, 121

competitive tenders, 24
compulsory savings, 327
convertibility, 287, 292, 316
Coyne, James E., 6, 74, 90, 105
Crerar, T.A., 57, 59–61
Crimson Route, 139, 141, 143

Davis, Henry H.
Defence of Canada Regulations, 18
Defence Purchasing Board, 24–7
Department of Finance, personnel, 2–3, 6–7, 323
Department of Munitions and Supply, 25
Desy, Jean, photo, xxiv
devaluation of Canadian dollar, 87, 316–19
Diefenbaker, viii
dollar area, 91
Dominion–Provincial Conference of 1941, 326, viii
Dominion–Provincial Taxation Agreement Act, 1942, 327
Dominion Training Scheme. *see* British Commonwealth Air Training Plan
Dunning, Charles, 19, 53, 338n22

EAC. *see* Economic Advisory Committee
Eady, Sir Wilfrid
  background, 335n12
  in Canadian loan negotiations, 298–301 passim, 303–8 passim
  photo, xxiv
  on RCAF training, 191, 193–6
Economic Advisory Committee (EAC)
  establishment of, 30–3, 339n2, 340n3
  export policies, 33–5
  and Food and Agriculture Organization, 272–3
  import controls, 95
  purpose of, 30–1
  role of, 323
  sugar, 36
  trade issues, 36–8
  wheat exports, 34–5
Economic Cooperation Administration, 318
European Recovery Program, 317, 319
excess profits tax, 19, 21, 338n34
Exchange Conservation Bill, 95. *see also* foreign exchange
Exchange Control Order, 89. *see also* foreign exchange
export policies, 33–5

Index   387

family allowances, 330–1
financial preparedness, 19
financing Britain, 29, 52–84
  alternative measures, 72–4
  Canada's capacity, 56–9
  Canadian gift, 72–9
  Canadian loan 1946, 283–321, 374n67, 374n68
  Canadian proposal, 69–70
  Clark memo, 147–9. *see also* Clark, William Clifford, on financing Britain
  contingency planning, 64–5
  effects of US action, 68–9
  fall of France, 63–4
  French gold, 65, 100
  gold, 101
  January to June 1940, 61–3
  Lend-Lease program, 67–9, 79, 81–2, 99–105
  Mutual Aid, 146–88, 189–90, 204–5, 208–9, 211, 215–24
  pre-war years, 53–4
  purchase of munitions plants, 83
  RCAF, 83, 191, 192
  repatriation of Canadian securities, 54–5, 69, 343n20
  in stage II, 189–224
  sterling balances, 71–2
  stockpiles, 191–2
  United States, 63, 66–9
financing Canada's war, 326–29
Food and Agriculture Organization, 271–4, 370n66, 370n69
foodstuffs. *see* agricultural exports
Ford Motor Company, 37, 340n13
foreign exchange
  centralizing reserves, 92–3
  conserving, 93–4
  control of, 18–19, 27, 86–7, 88–98
  dollar area, 91
  establishment of FECB, 27, 88
  Exchange Conservation Bill, 95
  Exchange Control Order, 89
  gold standard, 225
  import controls, 95–6
  International Clearing Union, 228
  measures of last resort, 97
  measures to conserve, 39–40
  reserves, 87–88, 91–93, 98, 131–7, 192, 316, 375n69
  rules, 89

  sterling area, 91
  and tourism, 38, 92, 94–5, 144, 347n19
  UK situation, 98
  US dollar shortage, 85–6, 91–2, 97, 98, 130–7
  war exchange tax, 94
Foreign Exchange Control Board (FECB), establishment of, 27, 88
France
  fall of, 63–4, 98
  General Giraud, 357n60
  gold, 65, 100, 168
  Mutual Aid to, 166–70
  payment for military relief, 271, 369n62

General Agreement on Tariffs and Trade (GATT), 282
German finances, 337n21
the gift to Britain, 72–9
Giraud, General, 357n60
Glassco Commission, ix
gold
  British, 63, 66, 70, 98, 101
  devaluation, 225
  and foreign exchange, 94
  French, 65, 100, 168
  production policy, 129–30, 351n33
Gold, Norman Leon, photo, xxiii
Gordon, Donald
  appointment to FECB, 90
  photo, xix
  role of, 3
  on US dollar shortage, 97
Gordon, Walter, 71, 335n9
Granatstein, J.L. (Jack), xiii, 4, 12, 50
Grand Trunk Perpetual Stock, 64
Graydon, Gordon, photo, xxiv
Green Book, viii

Havana Charter, 282
Hickerson, John, 355n39
Hiroshima, 184
Holland, 269–70
Hopkins, Harry, 67, 107–8, 110, 112, 123, 125
Hot Springs conference, 272
Howe, Clarence Decatur
  background, 5, 324, 334n6
  on combined boards, 123
  on financing Britain, 72–3

on Lend-Lease, 103
on limitation of profits, 25–6
as minister of munitions and supply, 26
and Mutual Aid, 152
on US–Canadian co-operation, 126
Hull, Cordell, 347n27
Hyde Park Declaration, 68, 105–13, 130

Ilsley, James Lorimer, 112
background, 4–5, 324, 334n5
in Canadian loan negotiations, 297–8 passim, 300, 303, 306–9 passim
health of, 352n63
on Mutual Aid to China, 158
photo, xxiv
on taxation, 326
Imperial Conference, 1937, 17
import controls, 95–6
India
Mutual Aid to, 170–2, 358n76
railway rolling stock, 212, 311
initial war expenditures, 21–3
International Bank for Reconstruction and Development, 244–53
"boat draft," 250–3
Commonwealth conferences, 248–50
composite proposal, 252
Keynes, John Maynard, 248–9
US proposal, 245–8
International Clearing Union, 226–30, 233, 242, 364n4, 364n7
international institutions, Canadian influence, 254–6
International Monetary Fund
Canadian concern, 240–1
Commonwealth discussion, 240–1
establishment of, 238, 243–4
joint statement, 241–3
transitional arrangements, 241
International Trade Organization, 281–2
Italy, and UNRRA, 262–3, 368n29

James, Warren, 127–8
Japan
attack on Pearl Harbor, 117
Canadian participation in war against, 199–203
collapse of, 184–5
stage II, 189
John Inglis Company, 17, 24
Joint Defence Production Committee, 126
Joint Economic Committees, 113–16, 129

Joint Resolution No. 6, 115
Joint Statement by Experts on the Establishment of an International Monetary Fund, 229, 238, 241–3
Joint War Aid Committee, 152
Joint War Production Committee, 126

Keynes, John Maynard, 291–2
background, 8
on financing Britain, 194–6
influence on Canadian policy, ix, 205–6, 330
on international bank, 248–9, 251
International Clearing Union, 226–7, 233, 364n4, 364n5
on International Monetary Fund, 239–40
on Mutual Aid termination, 187–8
on post-war economy, 286–9, 290–2 passim
on RCAF training, 191
visits to Ottawa, 193–6, 206
King, William Lyon Mackenzie
and appeasement, 13
background, 5, 324
on British Commonwealth Air Training Plan, 42, 45, 47, 48, 50
on Canada's alliance with Britain, 20
on Canadian loan negotiations, 303, 306–7
on financing Britain, 66, 69, 76, 85, 344n34
Hyde Park Declaration, 105–6
on Ilsley, 113
on Lend-Lease, 102
on Mutual Aid appropriations, 176–7, 179
photos, xix, xx, xxi, xxiv
on Rowell-Sirois Commission, 326
on UNRRA, 257, 258
on war against Japan, 202
on war expenditures, 22–3

Lamontagne, Yves, photo, xix
Lapointe, Ernest, 337n9, 345n50
Law, Richard, 238–9
Lee, Frank, 207–12
Lehman, Herbert, 259
Lend-Lease
Article VII, 274–82 passim
British Commonwealth Air Training Plan, 81–2

Index 389

Canadian input, 79, 99–108
of Canadian manufacturing, 140–1
components of, 107
establishment of, 67–8
Hull, Cordell, 347n27
post-war economic collaboration, 274–5
post-war settlement, 287, 291–2
termination of, 186–7
LePan, Douglas, 286, 289, 295
limitation of profits, 25–6
London conference (1942), 226–30

MacCallum, Elizabeth, photo, xxiv
MacDonald, Malcolm, xxiv, 305–7 passim
Mackenzie, Hector, 371n1
Mackintosh, W.A. (Bill)
  background, 6
  on international bank, 249–50
  on monetary reform, 234
  photo, xix
Mansur, David, 90, 333n2
Marshall Plan, 314, 317, 375n69
Massey, Vincent, 42, 341n2
Materials Co-ordinating Committee (US–Canada), 126, 128
McGregor, F.A., xix
McKinnon, Hector, xix, 28
McNaughton, A.G.L., 14
McTavish, Duncan, 151
memorandums
  Arrangements for Supplies from Canada in Stage II, 205
  Canada's National Effort (Armed Forces) in the Early Stages of a Major War, 22
  on Canadian reserve levels, 133–4
  Effect of U.K. Proposal for Settlement of All Outstanding War Claims for $150,000,000, 312
  Financial Arrangements with the United Kingdom (and Other Countries), 147–9
  on joint economic committees, 116
  on Lend-Lease, 103
  Mutual Aid and Related Problems with the United Kingdom, 215
  on Mutual Aid to Russia, 354n24
  Notes on Canada's War Potential, 56–7
  re: financing Britain, 342n2
  re: the German Financial Situation, 19, 337n21

Should Canada Be Forced to Liquidate Her Holdings of U.S. Securities?, 104
W.W.II, Mutual Aid, 177–8, 359n96
What Proportion of the National Income Can Be Taken for Defence, 58–9
military relief, 263–71
militia, 15, 337n14
monetary reform, 225–53. *see also* International Monetary Fund
  British dissension, 238–40
  Canadian input, 232–36, 254–5
  International Clearing Union, 226–30, 233, 364n4, 364n7
  multilateral discussions, 236–7
  US–UK negotiations, 237–8
  White Plan, 230–2, 233
Moraud, Lucien, photo, xxiv
Morgenthau, Henry Jr
  background, 335n13
  financing Britain, 8, 66, 100
  on international bank, 246
Munich crisis, 15
munitions
  British procurement, 17–18, 26, 69
  in early war, 26
  pre-war years, 16–18
  in stage II, 207–8
Munro, Gordon, photo, xxiv
Mutual Aid
  accounting arrangements, 154–6
  administration of, 152
  agreements, form of, 165–6
  appropriations, 174–85, 358n87, 358n91, 359n107
  to Australia, 163–6, 357n54
  to China, 157–63, 355n36, 355n39, 356n47, 356n49
  to France, 166–70
  to India, 170–2, 311, 358n76
  legislation, 150–1
  military relief, 173–4, 265, 267
  to New Zealand, 166
  post-war, 285
  role of board, 151–2
  to Russia, 156–7, 354n24
  and stage II, 189–90, 204–5, 208–9, 211, 215–24
  sterling area, 153–6, 363n61
  termination of, 185–8
  and UNRRA, 172–3, 261
  to West Indies, 172

Nagasaki, 184
New Zealand, Mutual Aid to, 166
Norman, Montagne, photo, xxi
North Atlantic Treaty Organization, 319

Osborne, J.A.C., 7, 29, 53

Palmer, K., 354n14
parliamentary system, vii
Pearl Harbor attack, 117
Pearson, Lester B.
  photos, xxiii, xxiv
  on UNRRA, 258, 259
Phillips, Sir Frederick, 60–1, 335n11
phoney war, 41, 91
Pickersgill, J.W., 65
Pierce, S.D., 128
Plumptre, A.F.W., 88, 133, 335n10
pooling of resources, 122–4, 126, 147, 148, 203
Pope, M.A., 121, xxiv
pork, 37–8
post-war, 373n34
  British economy, 283–321
  Canadian dollar crisis, 316–19, 375n69
  economic policy, 274–5
  Food and Agriculture Organization, 271–4
  loan to Britain, 284, 285, 295, 295–309, 313–16
  Marshall Plan, 314, 317
  military relief, 263–71
  reconstruction, 330–1
  trade policy, 275–82
  UNRRA, 256–71
  war claims settlement, 309–13
Post-War Commercial Policy Prospects, 284–5
Power, Chubby, 75, 81
pre-war years
  defence programs, 14–16
  diplomatic background, 12–14
  financial preparedness, 19
  financing Britain, 53–4
  industrial preparedness, 16–18
  non-military preparedness, 18–19
profits
  limitation of, 25–6
  tax on excess, 19, 21, 338n34
Provisional Government War Book, 18
public service, role of, vii

Quebec conference, 176, 201, 211

railway rolling stock, 212, 311
Ralston, James Layton
  background, 4, 324, 334n4
  on British Commonwealth Air Training Plan, 43, 44, 45–6
  photo, xx
  swearing in as minister, 20
Rasminsky, Louis
  background, 333n3
  International Clearing Union, 228, 364n7
  on International Monetary Fund, 243–4
  on monetary reform, 232–4
  photo, xxiv
rationing, 96
Rawlinson, H. Graham, xiii
Read, C.L., 354n24
reconstruction, 330–1
Reid, Escott, photo, xxiv
Renaud, P.E., photo, xxiv
repatriation of Canadian securities, 54–5, 69, 343n20
Richie, C.S., photo, xxiv
Riverdale, Lord, 43–5, 48–9
Robbins, Professor, 252
Robertson, D.H., 107, 348n46
Robertson, Norman
  appointment to FECB, 27, 90
  background, 338–9n38
  on Lend-Lease, 103
  on Mutual Aid appropriations, 177–8, 359n96
  photo, xxiv
  on trade policy, 280
Rogers, Norman
  on British Commonwealth Air Training Plan, 43, 48
  death of, 4
  mission to London, 62
Roosevelt, Franklin D.
  on financing Britain, 63
  Hyde Park Declaration, 106
  meetings with Churchill, 117–18
  photo, xxi
Roosevelt, Eleanor photo, xxi
Royal Canadian Air Force (RCAF)
  Canadianization of, 199
  financing of, 71–2, 83
  organization of, 47–51

Index

training in Britain, 191, 192, 197
Royal Commissions, 326
　Bren Gun Contract, 24
　Dominion–Provincial Relations, vii–viii
　Financial Management and Accountability, ix–x
　Rowell-Sirois, 325
Russia, Mutual Aid to, 156–7, 354n24

St Laurent, Louis
　background, 5, 324, 334n7
　in Canadian loan negotiations, 297–300 passim, 303–4 passim
　"have regard to" clause, 320
　photo, xxiv
Sayers, Richard, 54, 58
Scully, Hugh, 27, 90, 338n38
Shaw, Dean, photo, xix
Sinclair, James, 270, 271, 369n60
Skelton, O.D., 336n6, xx
Soong, T.V., 158–9
SS *Toronga Park*, photo, xxii
St. Pierre and Miquelon, 118
Stabilization Fund, 230–2, 236–7
Stacey, C.P., 15, 16, 26, 119, 120
stage II, 189, 203–12, 215–22
sterling area, 91, 153–6, 363n61
Study of Parliament Group, ix
sugar, 36

taxes
　compulsory savings, 327
　corporation tax, 327
　Dominion–Provincial Taxation Agreement Act, 1942, 327
　excess profits tax, 19, 21
　on passenger automobiles, 94
　war exchange tax, 94, 327
　war surtax, 21, 327
tax rental agreements, viii
Taylor, E.P., 106
Taylor, Kenneth
　background, 339n40
　photo, xix
　on Wartime Prices and Trade Board, 28
Tentative Draft Proposals of Canadian Experts, 234–6
tourist trade, 38–9, 92, 94–5, 144, 347n19
Towers, Graham F.
　appointment to FECB, 27, 90
　in Canadian loan negotiations, 303
　on financing Britain, 99
　mission to London, 59–61
　photo, xxi
　on post-war economy, 284–5, 288–9
　role of, 3
trade issues
　agricultural, 33–5, 36, 69, 72
　auto industry, 37–8
　with Britain, 17–18, 26, 33, 34, 37
　with France, 39
　with Poland, 39
　post-war policy, 275–82, 370n79
　tourism, 38–9
　with United States, 38
　wheat, 34–5
truck production, 37, 160, 164, 355n36
Tuchman, Barbara, 158, 163
Turk, Sydney, 86, 87, 90

unitas, 231, 240, 242
United and Associated Nations' Stabilization Fund, 230–2, 236–7
United Kingdom. *see* Britain
United Kingdom Loan Agreement, photo, xxiv
United Nations
　Canadian involvement in, 282
　Conference on International Organization, photo, xxiv
　first multilateral meeting, 80
United Nations Relief and Rehabilitation Administration (UNRRA), 172–3
　Canadian involvement in, 255, 257–8, 261–2
　establishment of, 256–9
　financing of, 259–63
　military relief, 263–71
United States
　entry into war, 117–18
　financing Britain, 63, 66–9
　Lend-Lease program. *see* Lend-Lease
　military projects in Canada, 137–45
　US–Canadian co-operation, 125–8
　US dollar shortage, 85–6, 91–2, 97, 98, 108–10, 130–7, 375n69
　US Neutrality Act, 87
　US Supply Priorities and Allocations Board, 129

Vandenberg, Arthur, 309
Victory Bonds, 328

wage and price controls, 328–9
war claims settlement, 309–13
War Exchange Conservation Act, 39, 97
war exchange tax, 94
War Loans campaigns, 328
War Savings Certificates, 328
War Savings Stamps, 328
War Supplies Limited, 106
War Supply Board, 25
war surtax, 21
Wartime Prices and Trade Board, 27–8, 346n6, xix
wheat, 34–5, 72, 320–1
White, Harry
  on Canadian reserve levels, 133–7, 139–42
  International Bank for Reconstruction and Development, 245
  on UNRRA, 260
  White Plan, 230–2, 236–7
White Plan, 230–2, 233, 236–7

Wilgress, Dana, 27, 90, 338–9n38
  photo, xxiv
wood issues, 115
world bank. *see* International Bank for Reconstruction and Development
World War II
  Canada's reasons for entering, 12, 336n1
  declaration of, 19–20
  diplomatic background, 12–14
  early weeks, 23–7
Wrong, Hume
  on combined boards, 121, 124, 350n13
  on Mutual Aid to China, 160
  photo, xxiv

X-Dominion locomotive, photo, xxii

Young, Phillip, 110
Young rulings, 110–13, 130